ALSO BY DAVID L. FAIGMAN

Legal Alchemy

LABORATORY OF JUSTICE

LABORATORY OF
JUSTICE

THE SUPREME COURT'S
200-YEAR STRUGGLE TO
INTEGRATE SCIENCE
AND THE LAW

DAVID L. FAIGMAN

TIMES BOOKS
HENRY HOLT AND COMPANY ■ NEW YORK

To Lisa

My Love, My Muse, My Editor,
My Best Friend

Times Books
Henry Holt and Company, LLC
Publishers since 1866
115 West 18th Street
New York, New York 10011

Henry Holt® is a registered trademark of
Henry Holt and Company, LLC.

Library of Congress Cataloging-in-Publication Data is available.
ISBN: 0-8050-7274-8

Henry Holt books are available for special promotions and
premiums. For details contact: Director, Special Markets.

First Edition 2004

Designed by Kelly S. Too

Printed in the United States of America
1 3 5 7 9 10 8 6 4 2

CONTENTS

Preface   ix

1. The Lesson of Leeches   1

2. If Men Were Angels: A Constitution by and for
   "Corruptible Human Hands"   11

3. A Covenant with Death: *Dred Scott* and the
   Biology of Slavery   45

4. The Roots of Modernity: Holmes, Brandeis,
   and the New Legal Science   70

5. "Let Us Not Become Legal Monks": Legal Realism
   and the Realistic Jurisprudence of the Supreme Court   107

6. "Attainder of Blood": Race and Eugenics
   in the 1940s   130

7. Autocracy of Caste: *Brown v. Board of Education*
   and the Golden Age of Social Science   161

8. The Right to Be Let Alone: Privacy and the Problem
   of Defining Life and Death   205

9. Lifter or Leveler?: Equal Protection in
   the Land of Rugged Individualism   251

10. In the Supreme Court We Trust:
    Science and Supposition in the Religion Clauses   295

11. Shouting Fire: The Moral and
    Empirical Consequences of Free Speech   324

12. The House That the Court Built:
    The Future of Science at the Supreme Court   342

Notes   365
Bibliography   387
Acknowledgments   399
Index   401

PREFACE

Laboratory of Justice is a consequence of my interest in two convention-
ally unrelated subjects—science and constitutional law. In the law, those
having an interest in science mainly focus on subjects like DNA profiling
and psychological syndromes or, alternatively, patents and intellectual
property. Constitutional lawyers focus on history, legal analysis, and moral
and social philosophy. They are lawyers of different breeds.

I began my scholarly career primarily in the science camp, though I had
a great interest in constitutional law, about which I taught and wrote from
the start. At first, I, too, thought of the two subjects as virtually unrelated.
When I attended conferences in one subject I never met colleagues from
the other. Nor did I ever expect to. However, as I continued to teach and
study constitutional law and its origins and history, I could not help but
notice how much science imbued the subject. Science, or what the drafters
and nineteenth-century justices called "natural philosophy," pervades constitutional decision-making, sometimes in subtle ways, but often in surprisingly robust and explicit ways.

At the start, I should be clear what I mean by "science," for the term is
used in a great many ways. In this book, I use it broadly to refer to any
factual subject or statement that is amenable to test and that falls generally
into the purview of natural philosophers or scientists. Today, this group
would include the natural and social sciences. Practitioners of "science"
range from economists and political scientists to psychologists and neuro-
scientists. Important to note is the fact that science does not exist as an
ethereal category into which some kinds of knowledge can be dumped.
Science is a method—really methods—of studying the factual or empirical
world. The statement, for instance, that six-person juries are less likely to
be representative of the community than panels of twelve is a hypothesis
that can be tested. Social scientists and possibly statisticians might bring
their methods to bear on this question. The *relevance* of the answer, it

should be emphasized, depends on an interpretation of the Constitution. Specifically, is the Constitution offended by the use of six-person juries if such panels are less representative than (and possibly not as deliberative as) twelve-person panels? Constitutional law is rife with such empirical propositions. Underlying the right to abortion is the medical fact of "viability," a statistical prediction of when the fetus can survive outside the womb. The constitutionality of segregated schools, the subject of *Brown v. Board of Education* and, more recently, *United States v. Virginia,* involving the Virginia Military Institute, centered on the question of the effects of segregation. In litigation challenging the constitutionality of the death penalty, empirical questions abound, including whether particular schemes discriminate and how the mental competence of children or the mentally retarded should be treated.

The linchpin of science is testing. Not all factual matters having constitutional relevance are testable or are equally amenable to test. This was especially true historically. We live in an age of science in which many of the questions scientists study were once the subject of religion or philosophy. For instance, not long ago, scientists did not consider consciousness to be a ripe area for scientific investigation. It was an area more fit for philosophical speculation. Today, it is one of the hottest areas of brain research. Similarly, the idea that human behavior might be partly a function of genes continues to be a hugely controversial proposition. Nonetheless, behavioral genetics is increasingly a subject of serious scientific research. The history of science, in fact, has largely been a study of subjects that have moved from philosophy and religion to science. The object or hypothesis did not typically change—though sometimes it did—but its amenability to the scientific method did. Whether the earth or the sun lay at the center of our galaxy was a question that preoccupied Aristotle, Pope Urban VIII, and Galileo. The respective answers they gave came from philosophy, religion, and science. In this case, science got it right. Constitutional decision-makers do not always explicitly state the scientific bases for their factual suppositions, but their views of the nature of the world are usually an explicit part of their argument for a certain result.

Although science may be a relatively recent phenomenon, grounding policy decisions in factual assumptions is nothing new. The framers of the Constitution understood this lesson better than most modern policy makers, judges, and scholars. As James Madison put it, "But what is government itself, but the greatest reflection on human nature." At the constitutional convention, he insisted that, in framing the government, "we must not shut our eyes to the nature of man, nor to the light of experience."[1] Indeed, many of the framers were the leading scientists of their time. Thomas Jefferson, James Madison, Alexander Hamilton, Benjamin Franklin, George Washington, and many others actively pursued and were generally recognized for their scientific or engineering proficiency. They were men of the Enlightenment and were deeply influenced by the science of their times. They studied Newton's physics and Galton's medicine. More important, they were also students of the natural philosophy of human nature and political systems. Natural philosophers, like David Hume and his *Treatise on Human Nature,* deeply influenced James Madison and the other framers. Hume employed Newton's empiricist methods in an effort to create an experimental science of human nature. More influential still was the work of Montesquieu, who brought a sociological approach to politics and law. It was Montesquieu's hypothesis that a government of separated powers that balanced and checked one another was the best guarantee of individual freedom.

Contemporary constitutional scholars readily accept that science is a component of modern constitutional law, since its pervading presence can hardly be ignored. Indeed, these days, it is hard to find a constitutional subject that does not incorporate sundry empirical assumptions that either have been or could be tested scientifically. Yet most constitutional scholars display little interest or aptitude in studying the factual propositions and hypotheses that inform constitutional law. The subject is about as welcome as a sales pitch by a zipper salesman to a group of button manufacturers. Scholars thrill in the normative and substantive aspects of the Constitution. However practical and valuable zippers might be, buttons connote prestige, artistry, and imagination, whereas zippers are mundane, dull, and obvious. This is due at least partly to lawyers' general lack of training in math and science. Scholars ignore what they can't readily understand. But there is more to it. Constitutional interpretation has developed in a nonempirical way mainly because the Constitution was intended to endure forever. Scholars seem to fear the possibility that explicitly recognizing the ways contemporary worldly facts inform the Constitution's meaning will make the document pedestrian, rather than transcendent.

Most interpreters of the Constitution do not separate their empirical assumptions from their beliefs about how the Constitution should be read. Facts, whether about human nature or political institutions, become the premises of constitutional arguments. The meaning of the Constitution thus comes to reflect—and to impose on society through constitutional rules—facts known or supposed by the interpreters. Yet this creates a paradox of sorts. Constitutional law is built largely on the tenet of stare decisis, the legal principle that prior cases should be followed where possible, because people arrange their affairs and behave in accordance with settled precedent. Although the Court regularly disregards prior case law, it expresses reluctance in doing so, and sometimes suffers criticism for having done so. Yet science operates in almost the opposite fashion. Science progresses, and while precedent is certainly relevant as a starting point, good research is *expected* to make change.

The Constitution, therefore, is a strange admixture of ancient and abiding fundamental values and archaic and obsolete natural philosophy. The science of the eighteenth and nineteenth centuries helped shape the doctrine of the twentieth and twenty-first centuries. The meaning of the Constitution thus oftentimes reflects scientific beliefs that we haven't believed for a century or more. Not unlike the Church of Galileo's time, which denied empirical reality for the sake of ecclesiastical doctrine, the Supreme Court adheres to constitutional doctrine sometimes in the face of overwhelming evidence to the contrary. Yet, somehow, this ancient document, born in a preindustrial age, has survived and prospered in our posttechnological society. The reason for its success is its flexibility. Through the generations of justices charged with giving it life, it has evolved to take into account and to account for scientific and technological advances, from a natural philosophy of racial differences to scientific proof of genetic similarities, and from the telegraph to the computer.

This book is the story of that evolution and the successive generations of justices who read into the Constitution their beliefs about the empirical world. The people who brought the Constitution into being, nurtured it, and gave it life were people of their times. Their understanding of the mechanics of their world affected the rules they crafted and applied to their affairs. It would be impossible for me to describe how the Supreme Court used science without describing the times in which the Constitution took shape and the people who shaped it. The story of the science behind the Constitution is thus part biography, part intellectual history, and part constitutional law. But it also has great contemporary relevance, for it highlights the pressing need to be clear about the factual premises of constitutional rules, bases that are often subject to empirical test. The grandeur of the Constitution comes from its complexity as well as its simplicity. It mandates, for instance, that no law shall infringe free speech, but leaves silent the myriad practical problems of enforcing this prescription.

Does this injunction include violent pornography that some social scientists believe increases violence in society? The Constitution must be interpreted in light of past practice, in consideration of current knowledge, and in anticipation of future events. At its most basic, the Constitution is a document of aspiration. But it is eminently practical, too. It regulates society and guides adjudications of concrete disagreements. It is a document conceptualized in the eighteenth century, yet cast for the ages. To accomplish its limited goals, and its unlimited aspirations, it must account for the nature of what is, anticipate what might be, and embody what we hope to become.

1

THE LESSON OF LEECHES

To the memory of the MAN, first in war, first in peace, and first in the hearts of his countrymen.

Thursday, December 12, 1799, George Washington awoke to an overcast and cold dawn. At ten that morning, he donned his greatcoat and set out to inspect his property. Snow, sleet, and, finally, a cold steady rain fell atop the great man's shoulders. In his last diary entry, Washington wrote, "Morning snowing and about 3 inches deep. Wind at northeast and mercury at 30. Continuous snowing till 1 o'clock and about 4 it became perfectly clear." By evening, his throat, which had begun bothering him earlier in the day, worsened considerably. His voice grew hoarse. A cold, it seemed, had settled into his throat. Before going to bed, his secretary, Tobias Lear, urged him to take something for it. "You know I never take anything for a cold," he answered. "Let it go as it came."[1]

Washington slept a fitful sleep, waking after two with fever and trouble breathing. He refused to allow Martha to leave the warm bed to call for help, because she had just recently overcome a serious illness of her own. She held him close through the remaining terrible hours of darkness. With the rising sun, Martha summoned Lear, who came into the room to find his friend able to speak only in a cracked whisper and struggling to breathe. His condition would later be described in a variety of ways. It was classified as "an inflammatory affection of the upper part of the wind pipe called in technical language cynanche trachealis." A leading practitioner explained this as "an inflammation of the glottis, larynx or upper part of the trachea . . . known by a peculiar croaking sound of the voice" and "associated with difficulty breathing, sometimes leading to suffocation."[2] Although the ailment was something of a mystery, the treatment was straightforward and well known. In fact, Washington prescribed it for himself before any doctors arrived. The time-tested remedy of bloodletting was clearly indicated.

Washington sent for an overseer, George Rawlins, and asked him to bleed him. Rawlins, fretting this great responsibility, had to be steadied by his patient. "Don't be afraid," Washington told him as he held out his arm to the waiting knife. But the overseer made too small an incision. "The orifice is not large enough," Washington said. He instructed him to extend the cut. At around eleven, medical help finally arrived. Dr. James Craik, of Alexandria, immediately recognized the gravity of the situation. Craik called for the assistance of Dr. Elisha Cullen Dick, someone who could share the responsibility for treating the quickly deteriorating condition of the former president. Before Dick arrived, Craik tried an assortment of measures. Principal among them was bleeding Washington twice. The therapy seemed only to weaken the patient more. Dick arrived at three, and the doctors bled Washington a fourth time, still with no salutary effect. As John Marshall described in *The Life of George Washington,* "The utmost exertions of medical skill were applied in vain."[3] Washington was slipping away and the best modern medicine available could do nothing for him.

Bloodletting was a centuries-old therapeutic practice that had the virtue of both conforming to medicine's knowledge of human anatomy at the time of its invention and having passed the test of clinical observation and experience. It thus worked in theory and practice. Bloodletting was based on theories promulgated in the *Hippocratic Corpus,* written by several authors between 420 and 370 BC. The *Corpus* advised doctors to closely observe symptoms, be open to ideas from all sides, and be willing to identify the causes of disease. A typical passage advised as follows:

> Declare the past, diagnose the present, foretell the future: practice these things. In diseases make a habit of two things—help, or at least do no harm. The art involves three things—disease, the diseased, and the doctor.

The doctor is the servant of the art. The diseases must join with the doctor in combating the diseased.[4]

Disease was associated with an imbalance stemming from one of several sources. The four possibilities were the elements (the building blocks of the body and the whole universe), the fluids (known as "humours"), the powers (hot and cold and sweet and sour), or fluxes that might have settled in the wrong place.

With any illness, then, the probable cause might be found in an imbalance existing in one of the four humours. The main two were bile and phlegm, with the first considered the cause of summer diseases, such as diarrhea, and the second the cause of winter colds. A third humour was black bile or melancholy, a deadly substance in pure form. The fourth fluid was blood, and it was the foundation of the theory of plethora, which provided that certain illnesses were caused by an excessive buildup of blood. Bloodletting offered a certain cure for imbalances of the blood. The therapy was compelled by the theory. If the disease was caused by excessive blood, bleeding would relieve the condition by attacking the roots of the ailment. Curiously, by the time of Washington's mortal illness, the medical community had long discarded the theory of humours. As is not unusual, in medicine as in law, the treatment far outlived its original rationale.

The gentler form of bloodletting was to put leeches on the affected area. Leeches, because they were imported from Russia, were a rich man's remedy. Savannah doctor Richard Arnold, for instance, wrote in 1838 to a friend in Philadelphia to "beg a favor." Arnold could not find affordable leeches. He complained that "leeches sell here at the very high price of 50 cents each and there is not a regular leecher here to apply them." He explained that the local medical society had arranged to supply leeches at not more than 25 cents each, but the supplier "sold out" before complying with his contract. "If leeches were not so dear many more would be used. At present they are only in the reach of the rich."[5]

Although Washington could well afford leeches, they were not always readily available, and not routinely kept in most medicine cabinets. Using a knife to open his veins, Washington's attendants employed the more dramatic and painful form of bloodletting. Isabella Beeton, in her *Book of Household Management* (1861), explained the bloodletting procedure, also known as venesection or phlebotomy. "Place a handkerchief or piece of tape rather but not too tightly round the arm, about three or four inches above the elbow." When the veins swell, she wrote, one should "take the lancet in his right hand, between the thumb and first finger . . . then gently thrust the tip of the lancet into the vein." She then explained how to bandage the wound and what to do if the patient fainted. It was generally advised, in fact, that a patient should be bled "until syncope," or fainting.[6]

As the futility of Washington's doctors' efforts became palpable, he asked in a vanishing voice to be allowed to die without further interruption. "I thank you for your attentions, but I pray you to take no more trouble about me."[7] He told his doctor, "My breath cannot last long." He added, "Doctor, I die hard, but I am not afraid to go. I believed from my first attack that I should not survive it." His secretary, Lear, vainly tried to comfort him. Washington thanked him for his efforts, saying, "It is a debt we must pay to each other, and I hope when you want aid of this kind you will find it."

Evening trod heavily into night. The only sounds heard in the enveloping darkness were Washington's labored breathing and the ticking of a clock. His breathing became shallower with each passing moment. Several times through the night he attempted to speak to the anguished souls nearby, mainly without success. Martha sat in a chair at the foot of the bed, awaiting the tolling of the fateful hour.

Shortly after ten o'clock, he told Lear, "I am just going." He whispered one final order. "Have me decently buried, and do not let my body be put into the vault in less than three days after I am dead." Given the technology of the time, he astutely feared being buried alive. Minutes later, Washington took his own pulse, and found it fading away. At twenty minutes past the hour, his hand fell from his wrist and he breathed his last.

Martha, interrupting the clock's forward march, asked, "Is he gone?" Lear could only confirm the fact with the sorrow on his face and a weak gesture of his hand. " 'Tis well," she said. "All is now over. I shall soon follow him. I have no more trials to pass through."

Washington was buried four days later without, at his request, any funeral oration. But no shortage of testaments to his greatness marked his passing. "Our Washington is no more," exclaimed John Marshall. "The Hero, the Sage, and the Patriot of America—the man on whom in times of danger every eye was turned, and all hopes were placed—lives now only in his own great actions and in the hearts of an affectionate and afflicted people." In Congress, Marshall introduced resolutions drafted by Henry Lee, one of Washington's officers, which concluded famously, "to the memory of the MAN, first in war, first in peace, and first in the hearts of his countrymen."[8]

In an age before antibiotics, Washington's doctors' failure to save him can hardly be condemned. Medicine would not enter the scientific age for more than a century after Washington's death. Even today, clinical medicine is as much art as it is science. Although bloodletting was based on theories considered obsolete even then, experience seemed to demonstrate its value. Certainly, many of those receiving the treatment improved. But as we know today, the same number, and probably more, would have improved without the treatment or with a placebo substitute. The human body has great restorative powers, resources that seem buttressed by psychological expectations regarding a prescribed "cure." Only in the future would fidelity to the scientific method require doctors to demonstrate the efficacy of their treatments. At the close of the eighteenth century, bare assertion premised on naked authority was enough.

The American Constitution was born in this prescientific age. Yet it remains viable in the age of science. The Constitution has survived from the days of the horse and carriage to the jet age, from quill pens to microprocessors, and from celestial mechanics to quantum mechanics. How is this possible? Does the Constitution transcend the knowledge of a particular time and the generations that live by it? Or is it a document malleable enough to mean what each new generation sees in it? Is the Constitution like the child's game of identifying objects in the passing clouds, in which everyone sees the image he or she wishes to see?

The Constitution's secret of success is that its provisions mainly express aspirations. Free speech, due process, equal protection, and sundry other grand phrases articulate ideals. Even the main textual articles that organize the framework of the national government and set the boundaries between it and the states are written in broad strokes. For the most part, the Constitution provides an architectural blueprint for the good society. The engineers who followed the framers have shaped that plan to fit the peculiar circumstances of the day.

The Constitution has always been interpreted through the lens of contemporary knowledge. The pool of contemporary knowledge has grown and changed fundamentally in the more than two centuries since the

Constitution was ratified. It is not only our view of the medicinal value of bloodletting or leeches that has been transformed. Our knowledge of the physical and social worlds has changed dramatically in an assortment of important ways. In particular, science has affected our sense of reality in three ways. First, our conception of the nature of humanity has undergone basic and fundamental changes. Despite the founders' stated belief in equality among men, we are a profoundly more egalitarian society than they could have believed possible. Second, and most obviously, technology has changed to an extent that we live in a completely alien world compared to the one experienced by the founding generation. News of the Constitution's ratification took weeks to reach the four corners of the relatively compact thirteen states. Today, reporters read and parse Supreme Court opinions on television only minutes after they have become public. Lastly, the tools of science, especially statistics, by which we describe and understand the world are almost completely new. The power of measurement is many orders of magnitude greater than what the framers knew.

In 1776, Thomas Jefferson penned the immortal words that "all men are created equal." This was a radical leap of faith regarding the perceived nature of man and one far from universally accepted. Not until 1870 were all men formally included, since only then did the Thirteenth, Fourteenth, and Fifteenth Amendments guarantee basic equal rights to blacks. Much more time would pass before this formal equality would become realized in fact. It would take fifty more years before women would be accorded a portion of equal protection when the Nineteenth Amendment gave them the right to vote. Not until the 1970s did the Supreme Court include women in the Fourteenth Amendment's guarantee of equal protection. Even today, the Court struggles to resolve what is meant by equality and how it is to be guaranteed. In the context of gender equality, for instance, the Court must attempt to delineate what it refers to as the biological and cultural differences that distinguish men and women. The challenge, as the Court has described it, is to ensure that no laws prevent men and women from fully and equally realizing their potential, but to allow laws to distinguish between the sexes—that is, discriminate—when the relevant differences are a product of biology. The Court increasingly turns to the biological and social sciences in making these determinations.

Easily the most dramatic development that has occurred since the eighteenth century is the transformation of society in the wake of technological innovation. From jets to the Internet, we live in a technological world that the framers would not recognize and could never have imagined. Benjamin Franklin devised and implemented the Pony Express, an institution that immediately fell within the prescriptions of the Fourth Amendment's injunction against unreasonable searches and seizures by government officials. The First Amendment was born in the world of newspapers and pamphlets. The Second Amendment, to the extent that it concerns the private right to possess guns (a hotly debated interpretation), was conceived in a time of the top-loading musket. Today, television, the Internet, and semiautomatic weapons all fall within the parameters of these ancient provisions. And as technology advances, allowing manipulation of DNA and the creation of life outside the womb, courts will increasingly face challenges in the legal area of reproductive privacy, dealing with technologies ranging from in vitro fertilization and frozen embryos to gene therapy and cloning.

The final area of dramatic change since 1787 is in the area of statistical assessment and evaluation. The field of statistics burgeoned in the nineteenth century and truly came of age in the twentieth. In the area of applied science—the only kind of science the law cares about—statistics are the hammers and nails in the scientist's toolbox. Physics, biology, ecology, psychology, sociology, and many other disciplines are entirely dependent on statistical methods. For instance, the constitutionality of an environmental regulation designed to save an endangered species might depend upon the scientific basis for the intervention. If the regulation restricts land development but is not reasonably tailored to accomplish its objectives, the regulation might violate the Constitution. Statistics are necessary to make this determination. Statistical evaluations can be found throughout constitutional law, covering such topics as the existence of discrimination, the validity of predictions of violence in capital cases, and the pervasiveness and effects of Internet pornography on children.

While science and technology have advanced profoundly over the last two centuries, the Constitution has been amended only seventeen times since the Bill of Rights was ratified in 1791. The responsibility for daily application of the Constitution's ancient words falls mainly upon the judiciary, led by the United States Supreme Court. The duty to align constitutional law with the modern world thus rests with the judges. Yet a basic principle of law, precedent, or, in Latin, stare decisis, mandates that judges not depart from past practice without good reason. Unlike the scientist who sees virtue in progress and change, the judge finds virtue in the status quo. In the case of ordinary law, both statutory and common law, this deference to precedent makes good sense. People come to rely on existing rules and often fashion their behavior to conform to or take advantage of them. Also, ordinary laws can be changed by simple legislative action and are thus amenable to regular democratic processes.

Constitutional law is quite different and the usual reasons for requiring consistency with past practice do not apply. Constitutional law is primarily the product of past decisions of the Supreme Court. There is no obvious reason why the justices of today should follow uncritically justices who have long since passed from the scene. To be sure, in some constitutional contexts, adherence to past practice may be well advised, because societal practices have developed around particular constitutional rulings. Property rights and rules surrounding police discretion may be areas in which maintaining consistency—just for the sake of consistency—makes sense. In most constitutional contexts, however, the decision whether to maintain the status quo, a status quo possibly premised on obsolete views of the empirical world, will be considerably more complicated.

Constitutional law is different also in the very limited ways it can be altered. Other than by the extraordinarily cumbersome process of amendment, precedent can only be changed by judicial decision. Justice Felix Frankfurter described the Court's continuing obligations as follows:

> We recognize that *stare decisis* embodies an important social policy. It represents an element of continuity in law, and is rooted in the psychologic need to satisfy reasonable expectations. But *stare decisis* is a principle of policy and not a mechanical formula of adherence to the latest decision, however recent and questionable, when such adherence involves collision with a prior doctrine more embracing in its scope, intrinsically sounder, and verified by experience. . . . This Court, unlike the House of Lords, has from the beginning rejected a doctrine of disability at self-correction.[9]

Despite this recognized need for justices on the Supreme Court to adjust constitutional principles to accord to the modern world, there remains a strong tendency toward inertia. Shouts of judicial activism inevitably accompany judge-initiated doctrinal reform. Yet, very often, these reforms merely overturn past judicial decisions that have no greater claim to sanctity other than their advanced age. As Oliver Wendell Holmes Jr. put it, "It is revolting to have no better reason for a rule of law than that so it was laid down in the time of Henry IV."[10] Still, many doctrines today were crafted decades or centuries ago and enforce in the present the vulgar scientific beliefs of those earlier times.

While bloodletting, long a subject of scientific derision, is no longer practiced today as it was in Washington's time, leeches have reemerged in a dramatic way. But it is not their effectiveness in relieving excess blood that is so valuable. Instead, doctors employ them as therapeutic tools to assist advanced medical procedures. In order to carry out their "bloodsucking," leeches, as is true for mosquitoes and ticks, had to somehow overcome the clotting processes of their victims. The potential value of this anticlotting property is vast.

In modern plastic and reconstructive surgery, leeches are used directly to impede the patient's natural clotting mechanisms. When surgeons reattach body parts, such as fingers, they usually have little difficulty reconnecting the ends of arteries. Arteries have thick walls that can be readily sutured. Thin-walled veins, however, present greater challenges. Very often, surgeons can reestablish circulation in arteries but not in veins. With the circulation compromised, the blood going to the reattached finger becomes congested and eventually blocked, threatening the success of the procedure. Leeches interrupt the clotting that leads to this congestion. Leech saliva anaesthetizes the wound area, dilates blood vessels to increase blood flow, and prevents the blood from clotting.

Leeches have also become the subject of twenty-first-century recombinant DNA technology. In the nineteenth century, John B. Haycraft, a physiologist at the University of Wales, discovered that blood did not coagulate in the gut of the leech. In the 1950s, a German scientist, Fritz Marquardt, isolated a protein from leeches called hirudin, which contains sixty-five amino acids that operate to inhibit blood-clot formation. Scientists are studying hirudin, seeking to develop drugs that will act as clot-busters ("fibrinolytics"), anticoagulants (sometimes erroneously referred to as blood thinners), and antiplatelets (to prevent platelet aggregation). Genetic technology is central to the success of these efforts.

Just as in the somewhat sportive example of leeches, the Constitution was framed on factual bases that no longer pertain today. Its basic factual premises—knowledge of human nature, contemporary technology, and

the methods by which the social and biological worlds are measured—
have undergone constant and drastic change since the day the Constitution came into being. Yet we continue to rely on those ancient words.
This reliance, however, is not necessarily misplaced. It may be that the
forms and structure continue to be valid, but for different reasons.
Leeches were employed in 1799 to reduce excess blood, a derisive use,
but have a function today as an anticoagulant. Similarly, in 1799, the
notion of federalism and states' rights depended largely on the prevalent
agrarian lifestyle and a confidence in Montesquieu's theories regarding
the virtues of small republics. In a sprawling modern urban society, many
of the premises supporting states' rights are no longer believed. This does
not necessarily mean that state sovereignty has no place in modern America. It does mean, however, that we should interpret and use the idea of
states' rights in accordance with our contemporary understanding of the
facts.

Blind adherence to the past and ignorance of the factual premises upon
which our Constitution was framed and by which it has been interpreted
through history are a prescription for disaster. We are beholden to past
generations for the ideals they espoused, but we should not be prisoners
of their beliefs about human nature or the nature of the world. States,
like leeches, may have their uses in modern society, but we ought to
understand and make explicit the reasons for thinking so. Otherwise,
unthinking advocacy of states' rights, because that is what has "always
been done," is tantamount to employing leeches for purposes of bloodletting rather than as a modern medical tool with specific salutary uses.
As the story of Washington's last days teaches, this is no way to treat a
great nation.

2

IF MEN WERE ANGELS:

A Constitution by and for
"Corruptible Human Hands"

But what is government itself, but the greatest reflection on human nature? If men were angels, no government would be necessary. If angels were to govern men, neither external nor internal controls on government would be necessary. In framing a government which is to be administered by men over men, the great difficulty lies in this: you must first enable the government to control the governed; and in the next place oblige it to control itself.

JAMES MADISON, *THE FEDERALIST,* NO. 51

The times in which we live never reach the romantic sublimity that posterity bestows upon them. From our romantic vantage point, the generation living in the fledgling United States at the end of the eighteenth century and the first part of the nineteenth century occupied a moment in time with few parallels. Theirs was a new nation, flush with victory over the greatest military power of the time, a society with the extraordinary opportunity to redefine itself almost completely. Before them lay great promise, but also profound peril. The Articles of Confederation, the governing scheme since the war, was an abject failure. The choices they made would not simply affect their own fortunes, but those of generations to come. Yet, although they could hardly appreciate just how great their task was, more than in most eras, they understood that their actions would deeply affect both themselves and posterity.

Writing in the *New York Journal* in October 1787, in opposition to the newly proposed Constitution, "Brutus"—who was probably Robert Yates, a New York judge, Anti-Federalist, and close ally of New York governor George Clinton—assured the public that if the Constitution "be a wise one, calculated to preserve the invaluable blessings of liberty, to secure the inestimable rights of mankind, and promote human happiness, then, if you accept it, you will lay a lasting foundation of happiness for millions yet unborn; generations to come will rise up and call you blessed."[1] But errors committed at the outset, he warned, would have dire consequences for future generations. As Patrick Henry would put it, "if a wrong step be now made, the republic may be lost forever."[2] If the Constitution embodies principles that will "lead to the subversion of liberty—if it tends to establish a despotism, or, what is worse, a tyrannic aristocracy," Brutus advised, "then, if you adopt it, this only remaining asylum for liberty will be shut up, and posterity will execrate your memory."[3] Future Americans, he warned, would condemn the founders if they chose the wrong path.

Few government systems were construed so self-consciously as the United States, or with such a deep sense of destiny. They lived in the age of reason, but sought to construct a government that would control irrationality, the hunger for power of the leaders, and the passionate vicissitudes of those led. In *The Federalist,* no. 1, Alexander Hamilton observed "that it seems to have been reserved to the people of this country, by their conduct and example, to decide the important question, whether societies of men are really capable or not of establishing good government from reflection and choice, or whether they are forever destined to depend for their political constitutions on accident and force."[4] But it was not simply a chosen few who would impose their sense of political enlightenment on the whole. The debate over the new Constitution was a public one, engaging the broad expanse of people. As one writer implored, "in principles of politics, as well as in religious faith, every man ought to think for himself."[5]

In contemplating the form of government to be created, the founding generation reflected on the nature of man and the nature of the society this government would serve. They sought a government that would ensure liberty and the pursuit of happiness, but that would be strong enough to guarantee security, from both monstrous governmental tyranny and the grand and petty tyrannies of their neighbors. The task, never considered to be a simple one, was to know enough about the nature of man to create a government that would permit him to pursue the heights of his ambitions, but stop him from descending into the depths of his impulses. Its constitution had to be tailored to the practicalities of society and well grounded in empirical reality. At the New York Constitutional Convention, Hamilton said that he had found that

"Constitutions are more or less excellent as they are more or less agreeable to the natural operation of things." The Constitution, he explained, would "adopt a system, whose principles have been sanctioned by experience," one that was designed for "the real state of the country."[6] Still, they were not unrealistic in their expectations, for they knew that a perfect government was not within their power to create. As Noah Webster put it, in one of his eloquently concise responses to critics of the Constitution, "Perfection is not the lot of humanity."[7] The best that could be hoped for was that the new Constitution would effectively—even if imperfectly—govern deficient humanity.

Occupying much of the debate over the new Constitution was the founders' disagreement concerning basic facts regarding the nature of man, the nature of government, and the dynamics between the two. Those in favor of the Constitution, the Federalists, believed man to be treacherous and guided by passion and self-interest. They believed that men corrupted government, and that government was a necessary evil that had to be controlled through internal checks achieved by dividing power among the various parts. Men's ambitions would make government energetic, but only by dividing power could every man's ambition be made to check every other man's ambition. This theory of human behavior underlies the checks and balances that make up the essence of American constitutional democracy. The Federalists also believed that the public good was best served by legislators who were one step removed from the teeming masses, rather than by direct participation of the people. They reasoned that this separation would permit deliberation and reflection and temper the passions of popular will.

In contrast, those who urged defeat of the Constitution, the Anti-Federalists, considered man to be basically good and guided by reason and civic virtue. It was their belief that government corrupted man. Although government must exist, it must be severely curtailed. Tyranny increased in proportion to the size of government. The bigger the government, the greater the threat to liberty. They also believed that a small republic, one in which the people had as much direct influence as possible, would best achieve the public good. Whereas the Federalists sought to check the natural tendencies of the people to abuse the powers of government, the Anti-Federalists sought to empower the people to check the abuses that government power naturally led those who governed to commit.

The Federalist roster reads like a who's who from the founding generation: George Washington, Samuel Adams, John Adams, Benjamin

Franklin, John Hancock, and many others strongly supported the Federalist cause. The roster of Anti-Federalists, in contrast, is better suited today as a subject for parlor games. But on the philosophical and scientific questions underlying the debate, certain personalities stand out, and on both sides the names are familiar. More important, their strongly held beliefs resonate to this day. By far the two strongest proponents of Federalism, and its most articulate and gifted spokesmen, were James Madison and Alexander Hamilton. For the Anti-Federalists, Patrick Henry, Elbridge Gerry, Luther Martin, and George Mason were particularly influential in leading the drive against the Constitution. Joining them philosophically, though in the end a friend of the Constitution, was Thomas Jefferson.

Jefferson ardently believed in the premises underlying the Anti-Federalist opposition to the Constitution and he initially found much to dislike in that document. He was perhaps spared the historical opprobrium of being an Anti-Federalist only by being in Paris during the hot summer of 1787. His writings during the ratification debates and his lifelong political philosophy reflect a strong kinship with the beliefs of the Anti-Federalists. Indeed, when he first received a draft of the new Constitution from Madison, he was stunned by the power invested in the national government. He found "things in it which stagger all my dispositions." Jefferson had assumed that the convention had been called merely to fix the errors of the Articles of Confederation, not to write a new governing document. He wrote to Madison that he had expected only "three or four new articles to be added to the good, old, and venerable fabrick . . . which should have been preserved even as a religious relique."[8]

Jefferson's views are particularly important historically. Unlike Patrick Henry, who battled against the Constitution with formidable oratory, Jefferson's weapon of choice was the pen. The written word has greater influence through the ages. Although historians are divided regarding just how strongly Anti-Federalists influenced later Jeffersonian Republicans, the two groups clearly shared many operating premises about human behavior and the processes of political communities.[9] Moreover, Jefferson's philosophy and operating presumptions became a part of the American tradition. While the Anti-Federalist label became an albatross, Jefferson, less tainted, would regularly employ many of their arguments to advocate a limited role for the national government. Indeed, in a brash rhetorical move, Jeffersonians and their intellectual heirs made the claim that the Constitution, in fact, reflected and created *their* worldview. Whereas the original constitutional debate concerned the wisdom of adopting a strong national government, the Jeffersonians claimed that the American Constitution actually enacted the weak national government that the Anti-Federalists advocated. And these arguments continue today, with the misnamed Federalist Society—it should be the Anti-Federalist Society—taking up the Jeffersonian banner. Today's polemics over states' rights, federal power, and judicial review are directly traceable to the political, sociological, and psychological debates between Madison, Hamilton, and the Federalists on the one hand, and Jefferson and the Anti-Federalists on the other.

In laying down the intellectual foundations for the American republic, three great personalities loom large on the historical horizon: Jefferson, Madison, and Hamilton. Jefferson and Madison had one of the warmest and most intimate political friendships in American history. John Quincy Adams observed that "Mr. Madison was the intimate, confidential, and devoted friend of Mr. Jefferson, and the mutual influence of these two mighty minds upon each other is a phenomenon, like the invisible and mysterious movements of the magnet in the physical world, and in which the sagacity of the future historian may discover the solution of much of our national history not otherwise easily accountable."[10] Jefferson and Hamilton, in contrast, vie for the mantle of having the greatest enmity for each other among all American statesmen. In time, Madison, too, joined this blood feud against Hamilton, as Madison became more closely aligned politically with Jefferson.

Jefferson and Madison met for the first time in October 1776. They would be friends for fifty years. Jefferson was considerably older and more accomplished in the fall of '76, having already gained fame as the author of the Declaration of Independence and for being a veteran state legislator at thirty-three. The twenty-five-year-old Madison was a freshman legislator, not long out of Princeton, then known as the College of New Jersey. Madison was duly impressed by Jefferson, considering him a prodigy with whom "the Genius of Philosophy ever walked hand in hand."[11] Madison, later in life, described his friend: "The law itself he studied to the bottom, and in its greatest breadth." And Jefferson's skills were as varied as they were deep. "For all the fine arts, he had a more than common taste; and in that of architecture, in which he studied in

both its useful, and its ornamental characters, he made himself an adept."
Jefferson gushed similarly about Madison. He considered him the embod-
iment of Enlightenment thought and the substantiation of republican
principle. "I can say conscientiously that I do not know in the world a
man of purer integrity, more dispassionate, disinterested and devoted to
republicanism; nor could I, in the whole scope of America and Europe,
point out an abler head."[12]

Although Jefferson and Madison would become political allies, both
sharing an enthusiasm for republican idealism and a strong skepticism
of national power, especially power that served northern commercial
interests, their philosophical differences at the time of the constitutional
convention were profound. In 1789, during the ratification debates, Madison was a highly articulate, energetic proponent of national power. Jefferson never wavered, at least in his writings, from the conviction that a
strong national government posed a dire threat to liberty. Yet, however
deep their disagreement at that time, they never permitted it to interfere
with their friendship. In fact, in their regular correspondence, especially
around the fall of 1787, they both assiduously avoided raising issues at
which the other might take umbrage.

As warm and insistently cordial as Jefferson's relationship with Madison was, his relations with Hamilton were cold and vehemently mean-
spirited. Each man was the other's devil incarnate, personally, culturally,
and philosophically. Jefferson was a patrician. His mother was a Randolph, who, Jefferson said in his autobiography, "trace their pedigree far
back in England and Scotland." William and Isham Randolph, Jefferson's great-grandparents, have been referred to as "the Adam and Eve
of Virginia." In addition to Thomas, they included among their descendants Peyton Randolph, "Light Horse Harry" Lee, John Marshall, and
Robert E. Lee. Jefferson was first and foremost a Virginian. He believed
earnestly in the agrarian lifestyle, wished to live it himself, and thought
it necessary for the strength of the nation. He trusted democracy, the
purer the better, and distrusted the commercial concentrations of power
and the urban northeast. Hamilton was an immigrant from humble roots,
but who had excelled in school and in the military and later married into
elite New York society, the Schuyler family. Hamilton was a New
Yorker, but identified foremost with being an American. He believed in
the power and value of business and reveled in the urban lifestyle. He
accepted democracy, but thought the nation's future depended on a
strong central government.

Jefferson despised Hamilton and Hamilton loathed Jefferson. In a letter to George Washington reiterating his long-standing desire to resign and return to private life, Jefferson's opinion of Hamilton, Washington's secretary of the Treasury, comes through sharply: "I will not suffer my retirement to be clouded by the slanders of a man whose history, from the moment at which history can stoop to notice him, is a tissue of machinations against the liberty of the country which has not only received [him] and given him bread, but heaped honors on his head."[13] Hamilton, never reticent to make his opinion clear regarding Jefferson, called him "the intriguing incendiary, the aspiring, turbulent competitor," who, like Caesar, "coyly refus[es] the proffered diadem" while "grasping the substance of imperial domination."[14]

If Madison had never met Jefferson, or perhaps had been born five hundred miles north, he likely would have been steadfast friends with Hamilton. (In fact, when Hamilton's troubles with Jefferson came to a head during the first Washington administration, and Madison allied himself with Jefferson, Hamilton considered the loss of Madison's friendship to be tragic and incomprehensible.) They were philosophical allies, having together contributed the lion's share to *The Federalist*. At the time of the Constitution, Madison's views were closely aligned to Hamilton's. Although Hamilton was always a bit more monarchical and imperialistic than Madison, they shared the belief, during the ratification debates, that a strong national government was necessary to ensure liberty, and both distrusted man's inherent goodness and capacity for virtue. It was Madison who shifted to Jeffersonian republicanism in the decades after 1789. There were sundry reasons for his changing views, though he would never be as convinced as Jefferson that the states could be the repository of liberty that Jefferson hoped or that civic virtue would be sufficient to check man's baser impulses. On the personal level, however, Madison veered strongly to Jefferson's side, becoming in time one of his chief defenders, together with James Monroe, against Hamilton's defamatory charges.

All this, however, would be many years later. In the 1780s, as the Constitution was being formed, Madison and Jefferson saw society and the government that could oversee that society very differently. Jefferson, though, was in Paris as ambassador to France, and thus could only observe events from a distance. Because he was away, we have a good record of his views through his correspondence, especially in his letters to Madison. It is safe to say that Jefferson wanted to be in Philadelphia with his friend. Writing in regard to the making of the Virginia Constitution in 1775, which he also missed due to his obligations in Europe, Jefferson wrote, "[Constitution making] is a work of the most interesting nature and such as every individual would wish to have his voice in."[15] He added, sagaciously, "In truth it is the whole object of the present controversy; for should a bad government be instituted for us in future it had been as well to have accepted at first the bad one offered to us from beyond the water without the risk and expence of contest."[16]

In *The Federalist*, no. 15, Hamilton had asked, "Why has government been instituted at all?" His response is instructive: "Because the passions of men will not conform to the dictates of reason and justice." It was not that Hamilton supposed that every man was uniformly corrupt or that people could not sometimes act for noble and just purposes. Rather, he shared the Federalist view that government needed to be organized *as if* this were true. Drawing on the philosophy of David Hume, Hamilton wrote, "Political writers have established it as a maxim, that, in contriving any system of government, and fixing the several checks and controls of the constitution, every man ought to be supposed a knave; and to have no other end in all his actions, but private interest. By this interest, we must govern him, and by means of it, make him co-operate to public good, notwithstanding his insatiable avarice and ambition."[17] While Hamilton believed that individual men could act with honor and with virtue, it was when in large groups, especially, that "man must be supposed a knave."[18]

Madison shared this view of the corrupting influence of the group or mob, observing that the character flaws of individuals were stoked by the multitude. "A prudent regard to the maxim that honesty is the best policy is found by experience to be as little regarded by bodies of men as by individuals. Respect for character is always diminished in proportion to the number among whom the blame or praise is to be divided. Conscience, the only remaining tie, is known to be inadequate in individuals: In large numbers little is to be expected from it."[19]

Although they lived in the "age of reason," the Federalists did not suppose man to be reasonable. Noah Webster observed that "every person, moderately acquainted with human nature, knows that public bodies, as well as individuals, are liable to the influence of sudden and violent passions, under the operation of which, the voice of reason is silenced."[20] Although this irrationality can be found in adequate abundance in individuals, "its effects are extensive," Webster theorized, "in proportion to the members that compose the public body."[21] Man is governed by passion, by a "desire for pleasure and an aversion to pain."[22] Ambition and avarice drove most men's actions. The rules of government, then, had to recognize and harness this fact, for man could be made to work for government if its interests were parallel to his own. Hume, on whom Madison and Hamilton strongly relied, considered the "love of fame" to be particularly commendable, since it amounted to the "love of laudable actions for their own sake." Man's behavioral predisposition was self-interest, and any governing scheme that relied only on his altruism and civic virtue would fail. The key to successful government was to align men's passion for self with the interests of society.

The psychology underlying the Federalists' political theory fully informed the structure of government they sought to institute. They believed that man was a selfish and irrational being, and that these characteristics largely existed before the environment or situation in which he found himself. The Anti-Federalists, by contrast, believed that man was primarily affected by the environment, and thus blamed the trappings of government for leading virtuous men astray. Therefore, while Anti-Federalists believed that the situation largely influenced behavior, Federalists believed man brought certain characteristics to the situation. The distinction was important, for if evil was to be checked, the source of it had to be identified. Benjamin Rush, for instance, argued the Federalist perspective when he asked, "Are we to consider men entrusted with power as the receptacles of *all* the depravity of human nature?" He answered, "By no means." He explained that history is "as full of the vices of the people, as it is the crimes of the kings." He queried, "What is the *moral* character of the citizens of the United States?" For him, and for all to see, the answer was plain. Americans, he said, "are as much disposed to vice as their rulers, and . . . nothing but a vigorous and efficient government can prevent their degenerating into savages, or devouring each other like beasts of prey."[23]

For Jefferson and the Anti-Federalists, the notion that government should be founded on the conviction of man's inherent selfishness was anathema. Jefferson questioned the wisdom of any "system rigged to substitute the countervailing forces of self-interest for the defect of public virtue and the supposed danger of majority rule."[24] He did not doubt the corruptibility of man, but he doubted the value of establishing a government structured on this premise. He earnestly believed that man himself was not evil, though he ardently believed that power could make him so. The Federalists, Jefferson thought, had it exactly backward: people need not be restrained, for it was government that posed the danger. Only the people could restrain government's tendency toward corruption. Certainly, governing leaders did not always act without probity. But virtue in government would come from the vigilance of general citizens who would actively participate in public affairs and, by this vigilance, check the excesses of the governing body. Samuel Bryan, an Anti-Federalist writing under the pseudonym "Centinel," asked, "If the administrators of every government are actuated by views of private interest and ambition, how is the welfare and happiness of the community to be the result of such jarring adverse interests?"[25]

The Federalists and Anti-Federalists shared a basic doubt about the perfectability of man, but the view of how this original sin manifested itself differed profoundly between the two camps. For the Federalists, man had resource to reason, but this reason was readily overborne by passion and prejudice. Man had a wellspring of virtue upon which to draw, but it was too often contaminated by vice. Government was merely a reflection of man's character and was as little to be trusted as the men who controlled it and the people whose wishes it represented. Hamilton considered it "a great source of error" to presume that people act according to certain "abstract calculations." He insisted that people are "beings governed more by passion and prejudice than by an enlightened sense of their interests."[26] But government itself was not the danger to a person's pursuit of happiness; the people behind a government were most to be feared.

Jefferson shared the predominant view among Anti-Federalists that it was government that should be feared, for therein lay the power of oppression. The people must be vigilant against such abuse, and in their virtue liberty would find refuge. Only the shared values of the community and the fulsome responsibility of political citizenship could provide sufficient checks on government excess. Although man was corruptible, this vice was most to be feared when coupled with the power of government. Democratic checks, the power wielded by the enlightened sentiment of the populace, would best restrain abuses of liberty.

The Federalists specifically rejected this benign view of human nature. Government had to be organized in a manner that would check man's tendency toward self-interest. John Stevens criticized the Anti-Federalists' "talk of virtue as the spring of action." He considered such a basis for government "too feeble." He implored his fellow Americans to consider the truth of human nature. "Can any man, who has a tolerable acquaintance of human nature, imagine that men would so eagerly engage in public affairs, from whence they can hope to derive no personal emolument, merely from the impulse of so exalted, so pure, so disinterested a passion as patriotism, or political-virtue?" In answer, he declared, "No! It is ambition that constitutes the very life and soul of Republican Government. As fear and attachment insure obedience to Government, so does ambition set its wheels in motion."[27]

The late eighteenth century's starting point for thinking about the establishment of government came largely from the prevailing picture of man in the state of nature. Philosophers engaged in a sort of thought experiment of what the world would be like "without a common power to keep them all in awe." Thomas Hobbes envisioned this world to exist in a perpetual condition of war; "and such a war as is of every man, against every man." Hobbes famously described the state of nature as having "no arts; no letters, no society; and which is worst of all, continual fear and danger of violent death; and the life of man, solitary, poor, nasty, brutish, and short."[28] This fate could be avoided only by entering civil society. For Hobbes, this meant monarchy, in which citizens trade their liberty and autonomy, in some measure, for the protection afforded by authoritarian government. This version of government stems directly from Hobbes's inferences about human nature. Man's inherently selfish and violent nature could only be subdued by a strong despot.

People entered civil society in order to obtain protection and to permit them to pursue their desires. Civil society, then, worked a compromise of sorts, requiring individuals to give up some of their brute liberty in order to be guaranteed a measure of protection against the brute liberties exercised by others. Blackstone explained that in order to enter organized society, man gives up "part of his natural liberty, as the price of so valuable a purchase." This obliges him "to conform to those laws, which the community has thought proper to establish. And this species of legal obedience and conformity is infinitely more desirable than that wild and savage liberty which is sacrificed to obtain it."[29]

Toward the end of his life, Madison reflected on the starting premises of government in light of the nature of man. "Some gentlemen," he observed, "consulting the purity and generosity of their own minds, without averting to the lessons of experience, would find a security against [tyranny and malice] in our social feelings; in a respect for character; in the dictates of

the monitor within." Experience, however, suggested that it would be better to assume the worst. "But man is known to be a selfish, as well as a
social being. Respect for character, though often a salutary restraint, is but
too often overruled by other motives. . . . We all know that conscience
itself may be deluded; may be misled . . . into acts which an enlightened
conscience would forbid."[30] It was better to frame a government in anticipation that men would do wrong, rather than in the hope that they would
do right. How this should be accomplished has proved to be one of the
most enduring debates of American constitutional law.

There was little question from the start that the United States would be
"democratic." The problem is that *democracy* is a word with widely
varying meanings. The Athenians, who invented it, would have been
astonished to hear Americans proclaim the American republic to be democratic. Athenians established the first democratic constitution in the
decade prior to 500 BC. Although Athens had anything but a fully participating populace, since women, slaves, children, and resident-aliens
could not participate or vote, those within the political community fully
participated in all of the nontrivial matters confronting the city-state.
This meant that citizens met, deliberated, and voted directly on all substantial laws and policies enacted and pursued by the Athenian state. The
citizenry was the legislature. Madison called this "pure democracy," by
which he meant "a society consisting of a small number of citizens, who
assemble and administer the government in person."[31]
    Greek democracy was a direct or pure democracy in this sense, and
it must be contrasted to the representative democracy practiced by most
modern states. In Athens, every citizen participated in the affairs of state.
In a representative democracy, the legislators are at least one step
removed from the populace or, perhaps more accurately, the populace is
at least one step removed from lawmaking.
    Underlying the practice of democracy, no matter what form it takes,
some notion of equality operates. Defining equality, however, requires
some philosophy of the nature of man, for only those who can claim a
functional equivalence can claim a right to equal treatment. Children are
accorded fewer rights in most, if not all, societies because they are not
considered biologically or psychologically equivalent to adults who constitute the political core of the community. Historically, slaves and
women were similarly excluded from political life and for supposedly

similar biological reasons. Differential treatment or discrimination requires some real or perceived difference between the *us* of the political community and the *them* excluded from it. In the Virginia Declaration of Rights, for instance, Madison wrote, "all men by nature are equally free and independent, and have certain inherent rights, of which *when they enter into a state of society* they cannot by any compact deprive or divest their posterity."[32] Madison added the italicized words to exclude slaves, for, according to the prevailing view of the day, they had yet to enter into a state of society. Their biological and cultural inferiority, it was widely believed, rendered them incapable of fully participating in political society.

The concept of the state of nature combines with principles of equality to provide one of the primary rationales underlying the democratic state. Each person is a sovereign unto himself, and thus freely contracts to join the community. As equals, community members expect to be treated no more or no less generously than those with whom they contract. No person has the inherent right to exercise dominion over another, absent consent. Madison explained: "If 'all men are by nature equally free and independent,' all men are to be considered as entering into Society on equal conditions; as relinquishing no more, and therefore retaining no less, one than another, of their natural rights."[33] In a democracy, each person is presumed to have an equal contribution to make to the political direction of the community. Majority rule is premised on this basic principle, with individuals' desires being essentially additive, and the side with the most votes prevailing.

This operating principle motivated Greek democracy as it did the founders. Protagoras explained about the Greeks that "when the subject of their deliberation involves political wisdom . . . they listen to every man, for they think that everyone must share in the virtue; otherwise, there could be no poleis."[34] Donald Kagan, in his excellent study of Pericles and the birth of democracy, described the great power of majority rule in Athens's direct democracy: "Almost no constitutional barrier prevented a majority of the citizens assembled on the Pnyx on a particular day from doing anything they liked."[35] Plato, one of the most eloquent and ardent critics of democracy, unfavorably compared Athenians' critical assessment of expertise in nonpolitical matters and their blind acceptance of it in the political domain. A citizen ignorant about constructing ships would be resoundingly ignored when it came time to build a ship, but that same citizen ignorant about politics would be heard when it came time to make a political decision.

Yet, although in theory all Athenian citizens had equal power to make proposals, offer ideas, and make speeches, the practical realities were somewhat different. When the citizens would climb up to the Pnyx, a natural amphitheater on a hill, they would go to set basic policy for the city. As a practical matter, Athenian democracy was not as pure, or participatory, as theory might contemplate. Forty times a year, thousands of Athenians would climb the hill to the Pnyx. There, they could not all participate equally, even if they had the inclination to do so. The average Athenian did not have the knowledge, wealth, or time to devote to the polis. A small political elite controlled most of the debate and directed the assembly to particular outcomes. It was this group that Thucydides referred to when, after a Sicilian military campaign turned to disaster, the people "turned against the public speakers (rhetores) who had favoured the expedition, as though they themselves had not voted for it."[36]

A democracy, by its nature, involves conflict, because sovereign individuals do not share an identity of interests in all matters. These differences inevitably result in the development of what Madison referred to as "factions." He defined faction as some number of citizens "whether amounting to a majority or minority of the whole, who are united and actuated by some common impulse of passion, or of interest, adverse to the rights of other citizens, or to the permanent and aggregate interests of the community."[37] Any political system that gives voice to people's natural disagreements will produce conflict. With tyranny, no dissent is tolerated, and thus factions present few political annoyances. Liberty, on the other hand, brings faction and, indeed, invites discord. Madison observed, "Liberty is to faction what air is to fire, an ailment without which it instantly expires."[38] For a democracy to survive, this conflict cannot burn so far out of control that it destroys itself. At the same time, to extinguish dissent would extinguish liberty. One group cannot so dominate others that it threatens to end their liberty to dissent. To a large degree, the success of a democratic society thus depends on its ability to maneuver between these two poles, anarchy and dictatorship. For the founders, the choice between tyranny and liberty was plain. To abolish liberty "because it nourishes faction," Madison wrote, "could not be less folly . . . than it would be to wish the annihilation of air, which is essential to animal life, because it imparts to fire its destructive agency."[39] The framers were determined to design a system of governance that would strike the perfect balance.

Disagreement was "sown in the nature of man." The question thus presented was how to control it, not whether to extirpate it. Madison found the causes of this inherent tendency to be both natural and a product of societal circumstances. It was natural, since "as long as the reason of man continues fallible, and he is at liberty to exercise it, different opinions will be formed." Compounding this defect of reason were the inevitable disparities in wealth that resulted from a free-market economy. In eighteenth-century America, wealth was equated with property ownership. "Those who hold and those who are without property have ever formed distinct interests in society."[40] These natural and social circumstances would lead to division and could threaten the whole. The survival of the union, therefore, depended on solving the problem of faction.

The main thrust of the debate resolved down to a choice between a large and powerful national government and small states that retained authority over most areas of life. Aristotle believed that there was a natural size for a polis. "A state composed of too many . . . will not be a true polis because it can hardly have a true constitution."[41] He asked, "Who can be the general of a mass so excessively large?" He thought that the "optimum size of a polis occurs when the numbers are the greatest possible for self-sufficiency, while living within sight of one another."[42] The Anti-Federalists adopted this principle as their first operating premise.

Anti-Federalist Luther Martin argued that the war of independence had thrown the colonies into a state of nature. From this, Martin insisted, the colonies had emerged as sovereign entities that, through the Articles of Confederation, had joined to create the Union. The proposed Constitution, therefore, undermined this sovereignty by bypassing state governments and enlisting the people as the sovereigns to consent to the new government. The framers of the Constitution had exceeded their mandate by bypassing the states. They had been dispatched to Philadelphia as representatives of the states, and had returned with a document that would destroy those states. To Martin's dismay, the government created by the Constitution was not at all *federal* in nature, but was a *national* government with power over the people and over the states. Patrick Henry similarly found it to be "demonstrably clear" that the Constitution created a "consolidated Government." "The danger of such a Government," he maintained, was "very striking." He queried, "What right had they to say, *We, the people*?" Henry exclaimed, "My political curiosity, exclusive of my anxious solicitude for the public welfare, leads me to ask, who authorized them to speak the language of *We, the people,* instead of *We, the States?*"[43]

The Federalists did not specifically rebut Henry's charge, since it was largely true. For them, it was a moot point if now the people were to ratify their work. The people had the sovereign authority to enact the kind of government that would suit their needs, whether or not they had authorized the framers to start from square one in Philadelphia. Therefore, the Federalists joined the issue at the level of philosophical or empirical expedience. Having appropriated the Federalist label, of course, they did not concede that the Union would be one consolidated mass. Although Hamilton and others might have preferred exactly this, it was not a position that had a chance for political success. Instead, the Federalists advocated a strong national government, but not one that was fundamentally inconsistent with state sovereignty. The national government would be superior to the states in all matters in which it was empowered to act, but those powers were enumerated and thus limited. Matters of general import would lie with the national government, and those of local concern would remain with the states. Their principal arguments in favor of this scheme were that it would work, that it would better secure liberty and maintain peace than a collection of intermediate-sized sovereign states.

An easily anticipated problem associated with a multitude of state sovereigns was the likelihood of conflicts between them. Hamilton wrote that a "man must be far gone in Utopian speculations who can seriously doubt that, if these States should either be wholly disunited, or only united in partial confederacies, the subdivisions into which they might be thrown would have frequent and violent contests with each other." The experience of history, he cautioned, made clear that man's nature will lead to constant confrontations between the states. Man's nature would provide motive enough for war. "To presume want of motives for such contests as an argument against their existence would be to forget that men are ambitious, vindictive and rapacious." For Hamilton, history bore out this lesson: "To look for a continuation of harmony between a number of independent, unconnected sovereignties in the same neighborhood, would be to disregard the uniform course of human events and to set at defiance accumulated experience of ages."[44]

The Anti-Federalists considered the issue to be somewhat more basic, since they feared that a vast national government would itself become tyrannical. Warring states might be preferred to a colossal national government that waged war on its people. Hamilton's attempt to maintain peace between the states by creating a national overseer did little good if that overseer trampled the liberties of the people. The cure would be worse than the disease. The size of government, Anti-Federalists asserted, was tied inextricably to the nature and diversity of the society for which it was formed. Anti-Federalists, such as George Mason, had difficulty understanding how a government could adequately encompass so many diverse peoples, climates, and cultures.

George Mason was a boyhood friend of George Washington and a descendant of a well-respected family in the Northern Neck of Virginia. He was extremely influential in Virginia, having drafted both the Virginia Declaration of Rights and the Virginia Constitution. He was not well known outside Virginia, however, since, for reasons ranging from temperament to gout, he preferred not to travel. Mason asked, "Is it to be supposed that one National Government will suit so extensive a country, embracing so many climates, and containing inhabitants so very different in manners, habits, and customs?" He could not imagine it, and could find no historical precedent to support it. Such a government, he said, would inevitably threaten the people's liberty. "It is ascertained by history, that there never was a Government, over a very extensive country, without destroying the liberties of the people."[45] The Anti-Federalists believed that in a large and diverse republic the government would not have the loyalty and natural allegiance of the people. In order to govern, therefore, the rulers would need to rely on coercion to compel obedience.

James Winthrop, in an article addressed to the Massachusetts Constitutional Convention, reached a similar conclusion. Winthrop was a descendant of a prominent New England family. A librarian of Harvard College, but twice passed over for his father's professorship in mathematics, he was a part of the Anti-Federalist elite. Historical experience, he claimed, proved the folly of creating a large and diverse republic. "The idea of an uncompounded republick, on an average, one thousand miles in length, and eight hundred in breadth, and containing six millions of white inhabitants all reduced to the same standards of morals, or habits, and of laws, is itself an absurdity, and contrary to the whole experience of mankind."[46]

Mason, the Virginian, however, would have taken extreme umbrage at the next step of Winthrop's reasoning. Winthrop argued that "it is much easier to adapt the laws to the manners of the people, than to make manners conform to laws." He asserted that a general government should not rule at the expense of local state control, because "the idle and dissolute inhabitants of the south, require a different regimen from the sober and active people of the north." He found numerous differences between the people of the northern and southern states. In the South, he observed, "the unequal distribution of property, the toleration of slavery, the ignorance and poverty of the lower classes, the softness of the climate, and dissoluteness of manners, mark their character."[47]

Anti-Federalists invoked Montesquieu's name to lend authority and weight to their argument for giving substantial power to the states at the expense of the Constitution's plan for a strong national government. Montesquieu had written:

> It is natural to a republic to have only a small territory, otherwise it cannot long subsist. . . . In a large republic, the public good is sacrificed to a thousand views, it is subordinate to exceptions, and depends on accidents. In a small one, the interest of the public is easier perceived, better understood, and more within the reach of every citizen; abuses are less extent, and of course are less protected.[48]

Jefferson strongly embraced Montesquieu's political philosophy, firmly believing that power inevitably threatened liberty. Jefferson wrote to Madison, "I am not a friend to a very energetic government. It is always oppressive."[49] Still, being in Paris, Jefferson well appreciated that a disunited America led to disrespect and disrepute among European nations. But he could not countenance a united domestic sphere, for this would threaten liberty and frustrate majoritarian control. The perfect solution, he suggested, was a united front on international matters, but a weak national sovereign on domestic concerns. He counseled Madison accordingly: "To make us one nation as to foreign concerns, and keep us distinct in Domestic ones, gives the outline of the proper division of powers between the general and particular governments."[50]

For Jefferson, the danger lay in the government itself, and the concentrations of power that led men to abuse the trust given them. Government needed to be organized so as to be responsive to the people who could put pressure directly on it. Only a small republic could accomplish this. An Athenian-styled republic was necessary to ensure the proximity between government and citizen, a nearness that was necessary to allow the people to exert control over those who governed. The vigilance of the citizenry would restrain government.

Madison held a directly contrary view, believing the people themselves to be the source of tyranny. He wrote to Jefferson that "the real power lies in the majority of the Community, and the invasion of private rights is *chiefly* to be apprehended, not from acts of Government contrary to the sense of its constituents, but from acts in which the Government is the mere instrument of the major number of constituents."[51] The people could not be trusted to be vigilant on behalf of liberty or minority rights. It was the majority's vigilance, Madison feared, that would manifest itself in a tyranny brought about by its abuse of the instruments of government.

The Federalists, in advocating the new Constitution, disputed the claim that Montesquieu's philosophy could answer the American question. They argued that Montesquieu's glorification of small republics did not support the Anti-Federalists' desire to vest the lion's share of power in the states. The states violated every important premise upon which Montesquieu had based his argument. John Stevens Jr. of New Jersey complained that Anti-Federalist writers try to "impress us with this idea, that the axioms of Montesquieu, Locke, etc. in the science of politics, are as irrefragable as any in Euclid."[52] Stevens came to politics only briefly; writing as "Americanus," he published a series of essays in New York newspapers urging ratification of the Constitution. He would later invest his energies in trying to develop steam power, and he built the first American steam railroad, which ran at the "excessive" speed of six miles per hour through Hoboken.[53] For Stevens, the "wretched attempts" in the past to establish a republic on principles embraced by Montesquieu were no proof. The American experience, he declared, was as different from the failures of antiquity "as light is from darkness."[54] He explained that the "political institutions we have construed and adopted in this new world differ as widely from the republics of old . . . as does a well-constructed edifice, where elegance and utility unite and harmonize, differ from a huge misshapen pile reared by Gothic ignorance and barbarity."[55]

Hamilton agreed, arguing that Montesquieu's political theory was inapposite, since, in his exhortation, he did not contemplate republics as large as the states then in existence in America. Therefore, to advocate a weak national government in favor of the powerful state sovereigns on the basis of Montesquieu was fallacious, since the states already were far larger than the size Montesquieu thought necessary to prosper democratically. In Virginia, in 1789, traveling just from Lexington to Charlottesville, a distance of sixty-five miles through the Blue Ridge Mountains, could take days, and going on to Williamsburg might require more than a week. Hamilton wrote, "When Montesquieu recommends a small extent for republics, the standards he had in view were of dimensions far short of the limits of almost every one of these States."[56] Stevens buttressed Hamilton's argument, noting that while Montesquieu made direct participation the linchpin of his theory, "none of the states are so organized even now." Precedent, therefore, was silent on the question of the prospects for a vigorous national sovereign. That being so, Stevens pointed out, "the principles and consequences" of a large republic based on representation "must be sought after and discovered from our own experience and from deductions from the peculiar nature of these institutions."[57]

Moreover, there was little reason to believe that a vastly proportioned state would be more protective of liberty and better informed by consent than a vastly proportioned national government. Once the basic antiquarian model was violated, the truth of its basic premise does not necessarily apply in a linear way to successively larger entities. There was no reason to believe, for instance, that New York would be substantially less protective of liberty than North Carolina simply because it was greater in size. Both states violated the basic model of small republics. It is like adding air to a balloon: once too much air is added, more air will not affect the result. The balloon has already burst.

In a letter to Thomas Jefferson, Madison complained that "[t]hose who contend for a simple Democracy, or a pure republic, actuated by the sense of the majority, and operating within narrow limits, assume or suppose a case which is altogether fictitious."[58] He observed that they base "their reasoning on the idea, that the people composing the Society, enjoy not only an equality of political rights; but that they have all precisely the same interests, and the same feelings in every respect."[59] This perspective ignored reality. "No Society ever did or can consist of so homogeneous a mass of Citizens."[60]

The Federalists, however, did not simply declare that Montesquieu's model did not fit or merely challenge the claim that the states would be better protectors of liberty than a strong national government. They doubted the very presumption that pure democracy was friendly to liberty. The Federalists attacked head-on the romantic notion that pure democracy was "the most perfect government." At a level difficult to imagine occurring today, the founders questioned whether true popular democracy was a wise form of government. Even if, they argued, societies could be organized to permit all members to exert direct control over the affairs of state, such a government should not be desired. Hamilton was perhaps the most vehement opponent of the idea "that a pure democracy, if it were practicable, would be the most perfect government." He argued that "[e]xperience has proved, that no position in politics is more false than this." He had little patience for those who dwelled on the Athenian experience. "The ancient democracies," Hamilton exclaimed, "never possessed one feature of good government—their very character was tyranny." He likened the Athenian assembly to "an ungovernable mob," a mob that was "incapable of deliberation," and was "prepared for every enormity." The only question for this mob, according to Hamilton, was "whether the people subjected themselves to be led by one tyrant or by another."[61]

Noah Webster, author of *An American Dictionary of the English Language,* first published in 1828, also disputed the notion that, in a perfect world, "all the members of a society should be present, and each giving his suffrage in acts of legislation, by which he is to be bound." Although acknowledging that pure democracy was, in fact, "practiced in the free states of antiquity," he boldly pronounced that this pure democracy "was the cause of innumerable evils." The passions of the moment too often stirred the people's prejudices and whipped the winds of tyranny. Direct democracy allowed insufficient time for reflection. Impulse became action. To avoid these evils, he contended, "the moderns have invented the doctrine of representation, which seems to be the perfection of human government."[62] The doctrine of representation would permit deliberation to defeat precipitate action.

The problem inherent in factions is their tendency to ignore the rights and interests of others. In democratic theory, this is not troublesome so long as the faction does not constitute a majority. "If a faction consists of less than a majority, relief is supplied by the republican principle, which enables the majority to defeat its sinister views by regular vote."[63] The "great inquiry," as Madison defined it, concerned "when a majority is included in a faction." Such a faction has the potential to be tyrannical.

The two potential solutions to this inherent defect in democratic principle were, according to Madison, contrary to pure democratic theory as employed in Athens, described by Montesquieu, and embraced by Jefferson and the Anti-Federalists. The first solution came by way of rejecting pure democracy, and choosing instead a representative form of government. The second was to reject a small republic in favor of a large one that would contain a great many factions. A third solution, and one not originally embraced by Madison and the Federalists, was a Bill of Rights that would guarantee minority factions rights against a tyranny of the majority.

Madison considered the Athenian version of democracy to be the least able to cope with the pernicious effects of faction. "Pure democracy," he wrote, "can admit of no cure for the mischiefs of faction."[64] It also explained the tumultuous experiences of democracies in antiquity. "Hence it is that such democracies have ever been found incompatible with personal security or the rights of property," Madison explained, "and have in general been as short in their lives as they have been violent in their deaths."[65] Fisher Ames, arguing for ratification in the Massachusetts Constitutional Convention, echoed this warning concerning factions. "Faction and enthusiasm are the instruments by which popular governments are destroyed." Ames was a classic New England conservative who defeated Samuel Adams in 1788 for a seat in the first session of the U.S. House of Representatives. He was an ardent supporter of Hamilton and when Jefferson was elected president expected the nation to fall into anarchy and ruin. Ames believed that a "democracy is a volcano, which conceals the fiery materials of its own destruction."[66]

A republic, in which the citizenry elects a representative body to act for them, resolves many of the defects inherent in a pure democracy. In a republic, the public view is channeled through a chosen group who can be expected to bring deliberative judgment to their decisions. In fact, "under such a regulation," Madison wrote, "it may well happen that the public voice, pronounced by the representatives of the people, will be more consonant to the public good than if pronounced by the people themselves, convened for the purpose."[67] Ames explained the logic of representation, suggesting that "the representation of the people, is something more than the people." Elected representatives, contrary to much popular belief, could do more to achieve the "public good" than having the public themselves enact the laws. Pure democracy, Ames asserted, "would be very burdensome, subject to faction and violence." Too often, he warned, decisions would be "made by surprise, in the precipitancy of passion, by men who either understand nothing, or care nothing about the subject; or by interested men, or those who vote for their own indemnity." Such a government, in fact, "would be a government not by laws, but by men. Such were the paltry democracies of

Greece and Asia Minor, so much extolled and so often proposed as a model for our imitation."[68]

Madison understood well that, given the nature of man, legislators too could bring their "sinister designs" and "factious tempers" to their decisions. One way to avoid this possibility was to have a large enough scheme of representation that those elected reflected a broad coalition of opinions. The danger in this was that if the size of the represented group was too large, the representative would be too far removed from the local concerns of his electors. The Constitution, according to Madison, struck a compromise, with "the great and aggregate interests being referred to the national, the local and particular to the State legislatures."[69]

A second advantage of a republic over pure democracy lay, contrary to much democratic theory, in its size. Bigger states, Madison claimed, better protect liberty. The smaller the republic, the greater the danger that a faction would gain majority support. A small society has a smaller variety of interests and a greater likelihood, based on opportunity and chance, for a majority to assert its hegemony. But, Madison observed, "Extend the sphere and you take in a greater variety of parties and interests; you make it less probable that a majority of the whole will have a common motive to invade the rights of other citizens; or if such a common motive exists, it will be more difficult for all who feel it to discover their own strength, and to act in unison together."[70]

Madison predicted that, as between the state governments and the proposed national government, the latter would be less likely to invade the rights of minority groups. "The extent of the Union gives it the most palpable advantage." For example, he stated, "A religious sect may degenerate into a political faction in a part of the Confederacy; but the variety of sects dispersed over the entire face of it must secure the national councils against any danger from that source."[71] Faction would battle faction, and the larger the society, the less able would any faction be to dominate and tyrannize any others.

The national government's tendency toward tyranny thus would be curtailed partly by the multitude of factions that would check one another's ambitions. The Constitution took a brilliant step beyond this, however, by adopting a different idea associated with Montesquieu, the separation of national powers between three coordinate branches of government. Although the Federalists and Anti-Federalists disputed the details, the two sides generally agreed on the need to separate the powers bestowed upon the national government. Dividing the national power among the legislative, executive, and judicial branches would allow ambition to check ambition. The Constitution is replete with mechanisms by which government is "obliged to control itself." Authority is divided between the national and state governments in a large, and ever-growing, republic with a multitude of factions, with a national government divided into three coequal branches with the perceived most powerful, Congress, being divided still further into two houses with different representation schemes. Authority, however, does not automatically constitute power. It would take over a decade after the Constitution was ratified for the outlines to be drawn, and a couple of centuries for those outlines to be filled in. In particular, the judiciary needed life to be breathed into it.

In 1789, George Washington nominated John Jay, a coauthor of *The Federalist,* member of the Continental Congress, and diplomat, to be the first chief justice of the United States. Washington sought to place someone at the head of the Supreme Court who would ensure that "the due administration of justice is the firmest pillar of good government." He considered "the judicial department as essential to the happiness of our country, and to the stability of its political system."[72] Just six years later, Jay resigned from the bench after being elected governor of New York. He explained upon his departure that the Court lacked "energy, weight, and dignity." A New York newspaper described his move to the governor's mansion as "a promotion." After Jay left, Washington nominated John Rutledge, who had earlier resigned from the Court to become chief justice of the South Carolina Court of Common Pleas. Rutledge was a recess appointment during the August 1795 term, but the Senate subsequently voted to defeat the nomination. Among other grounds, John Adams explained that the Senate feared his "accelerated and increased . . . Disorder of the Mind." After another of his choices refused the post, Washington turned to Oliver Ellsworth, a well-respected senator from Connecticut. Ellsworth was seen as "a valuable acquisition to the Court," and "a great Loss" to the Senate. With a longer tenure there he might have had a lasting impact. After just four years, however, he resigned due to his "constant, and at times excruciating pains," sufferings recently exacerbated by his travel to Europe as a special envoy to France. The fourth chief justice would be John Marshall, appointed by Adams toward the end of his term. Near his death, Adams commented that "the proudest act of my life was the gift of John Marshall to the people of the United States."[73]

As one of Marshall's biographers put it, "If George Washington founded the country, John Marshall defined it."[74] Marshall, by force of personality and power of intellect, transformed the Court from a weak and disparaged body to one having energy, weight, and dignity. One writer observed that Marshall "hit the Constitution much as the Lord hit the chaos, at a time when everything needed creating."[75] He was a Federalist who sought to implement the Madisonian/Hamiltonian vision into the practical realities of American government. Not surprisingly, this put him at odds with Thomas Jefferson, a feud that did not quite reach the ugliness of Hamilton's and Jefferson's relations, but came very close.

Unlike Hamilton, Marshall had much in common with Jefferson. They were second cousins on their mothers' side, both descendants of Virginia royalty, the Randolphs. They were also both lawyers. Each had strong and accomplished parents, and neither was particularly religious. They also identified deeply with their native Virginia and would regularly state their desire to return to those roots when they retired from public service. And while they profoundly disagreed about the shape it should take, each was fully devoted to the success of the new nation.

In the end, however, their differences overwhelmed the abundance of similarities. When Marshall became chief justice, he was the leader of the moderate wing of the Federalists. Jefferson was the soul of the Republican Party. Marshall distrusted pure democracy, applauded the checks and balances embedded in the Constitution, and considered a strong national government to be essential to the survival of the nation. Jefferson trumpeted democratic principles, thought that the checks and balances inherent in the Constitution frustrated the public will, and considered the powerful national government the first step to tyranny.

More than their intellectual disagreements, and much like Hamilton's relations with Jefferson, Marshall held a deep personal dislike for the man. He found Jefferson duplicitous and mistrusted him completely. Henry Adams described Marshall's feelings toward Jefferson in a verbal portrait: "This great man nourished one weakness. Pure in life; broad in mind, and the despair of bench and bar for the unswerving certainty of his legal method; almost idolized by those who stood nearest him . . . this excellent and amiable man clung to one rooted prejudice: he detested Thomas Jefferson. . . . No argument or entreaty affected his conviction that Jefferson was not an honest man."[76]

The dislike was mutual. Jefferson thought Marshall a hypocrite and dissembler. Jefferson wrote a friend that Marshall's "inveteracy is profound, and his mind of that gloomy malignity which will never let him forego the opportunity of satiating it on a victim."[77] He respected but distrusted Marshall's legal acumen, finding his arguments to be based on guile. Jefferson wrote to Joseph Story that when Jefferson talked with Marshall, he was careful to never admit anything: "So sure as you admit any position to be good, no matter how remote from the conclusion he seeks to establish, you are gone. So great is his sophistry you must never give him an affirmative answer or you will be forced to grant his conclusion. Why, if he were to ask me if it were daylight or not, I'd reply, 'Sir, I don't know, I can't tell.' "[78] This belief in Marshall's sophistry extended fully to Jefferson's evaluation of his interpretations of the Constitution. Under Marshall, the Court would realize its potential as a fully coordinate branch of government. To Jefferson's chagrin, the Court reached this position during his watch and somewhat at his expense.

In *The Federalist,* no. 78, Alexander Hamilton commented that among the three branches of the federal government, the judiciary is likely to be "the least dangerous to the political rights of the Constitution." The Anti-Federalists had, however, believed that the judiciary, with its life tenure, and duty to decide all cases arising under the Constitution, had the potential to be the most dangerous. Before John Marshall ascended to the bench, though, at least based on the experience of the country's first years, few would have argued with Hamilton's observation. The Court was least dangerous because it was the least effective. Marshall gave the Court the wherewithal to make it effective, and so gave it power enough to pose a greater danger to the political rights guaranteed by the Constitution. For Jefferson, Marshall embodied everything to be feared. In two cases, in particular, Marshall would lay the cornerstones of judicial power: *Marbury v. Madison*[79] and *McCulloch v. Maryland.*[80] Jefferson and the Republicans were intimately involved in the circumstances that would come before the Court. And in both cases they would be deeply disappointed in the Marshall-led outcome.

At the end of the Federalist administration of John Adams, the reins of power were to be handed over to Jefferson and the Republican Party. In many respects, this transfer of power would be a major test of the fledgling nation, since the earlier change of administrations, between Washington and Adams, did not involve a change in parties. The Federalists, however, had no intention of exiting quietly, and sought to leave a lasting legacy. If they could not have the executive branch, then they intended to take the judiciary.

At that time, the president-elect did not assume the duties of the office until the beginning of March. Between the elections of November 1800 and March 1801, Adams and his secretary of state, John Marshall, attempted to pack the judiciary with Federalists. Adams began by appointing Marshall to be the chief justice. He was not Adams's first choice, but Adams came to appreciate that he was his best choice. Marshall, however, would not don his robes until his duties as secretary of state were completed. One of those duties was to assist Adams in filling the many vacant posts created when the Federalist Congress vastly expanded the federal judiciary. Marshall was responsible for signing and delivering the commissions to the new judges. But, in the crush of business as the Federalists prepared to leave office, some of the commissions were never delivered. To William Marbury's great disappointment, but everlasting fame, his commission was left in a stack on the secretary of state's desk.

When Jefferson took office, he found the commissions, but had no intention of delivering them. He considered them to be nullities. Jefferson ordered James Madison, his secretary of state, to do nothing with them. Marbury tried to force Jefferson's hand by bringing suit directly in the Supreme Court against James Madison, asking the Court to order Madison to deliver his commission. The case would become the most celebrated litigation in American constitutional history. To this day, portraits of William Marbury and James Madison grace the wall of the justices' private dining room at the Supreme Court. His misfortune in life led to his immortality in American jurisprudence.

In *Marbury v. Madison,* John Marshall demonstrated his prodigious abilities both as a jurist and in realpolitik. On the merits, Marshall wrote, Marbury was entitled to receive his commission, because it had become valid when signed by the president. Jefferson, therefore, had interfered with Marbury's rights by not delivering the commission to him. Yet this did not necessarily mean that Marbury was entitled to relief. He had brought the case under a congressional statute that permitted a cause of action to be filed directly in the Supreme Court under what is called a writ of mandamus. This law, according to the Marshall Court, was contrary to Article III of the Constitution, which requires such suits to be initiated in the lower federal courts. The law was unconstitutional. Judgment, therefore, was for Madison, and he and Jefferson were not ordered to deliver the commission. Because this was an order that Marshall believed would not be followed in any event, Marshall lost nothing politically, while greatly strengthening the judiciary's power over constitutional matters.

In one fell swoop, and without permitting Jefferson any formal recourse, Marshall had asserted the Court's authority over both the executive and legislative branches. Jefferson, Marshall determined, had violated William Marbury's lawful right to his commission. The executive's conduct, Marshall ruled, could be the subject of judicial inspection. Yet the law that entitled Marbury to seek redress directly in the Supreme Court violated the Constitution and had to be invalidated. Marshall thus brought congressional enactments within the subject of judicial inspection. Judicial review was born. *Marbury v. Madison* gave the Court the final word on what the Constitution means, and acts of both of the other branches could be set aside if they were contrary to that interpretation.

Although *Marbury v. Madison* may be the most famous case in constitutional law, *McCulloch v. Maryland* is the most important. The case sits at the crossroads of the American scheme of government. It involved many of the major personalities and most of the pressing issues of the day. It secured the power of the national government, but set the nation on a path toward future conflict. Although *McCulloch* could hardly be blamed for the war between the North and the South that erupted forty-two years later, it substantially widened the intellectual battleground between the Union and the states that would define that war. The case also cemented the power of the Court to be the ultimate arbiter of the meaning of the Constitution and became the blueprint for the Court's exercise of that power. This blueprint, however, would not be fully realized until the second half of the twentieth century. *McCulloch,* therefore, was not only a notorious case in its time, but one with profound consequences for the times to come.

In 1791, Secretary of the Treasury Alexander Hamilton proposed the establishment of the Bank of the United States, a private corporation chartered by Congress that would be modeled on the Bank of England. According to John Marshall, in his *Life of Washington,* the political battle over the Bank directly led to the formation of political parties and factionalism. Despite President Washington's profound desire to save the new nation from such misfortune—an outcome that was an inevitable product of liberty—he was destined to see this fate befall the country during his watch. Indeed, he unwittingly brought it about.

When the bank bill was before Congress, James Madison was a member of the House of Representatives. Thomas Jefferson was the secretary of state and Edmund Randolph, from Virginia, was the attorney general. At first, the bank proposal did not raise much opposition, and Madison did not oppose it. Instead, his main objective was to limit the bank's charter to ten years, because he feared that a longer period would entrench the bank, and thus the national capital itself, in Philadelphia. At that time, the mutual jealousies and competitions between North and South resulted in a particularly unpleasant battle over the future site of the nation's capital. The bank bill became hopelessly entangled with the fierce struggles over whether the seat of government would be located in the North or in the South. Madison and his fellow Virginians, including Jefferson, Randolph, and the president himself, had preliminarily succeeded in making the capital's future home on the banks of the Potomac. That deal began to unravel as the Pennsylvanians, led by Robert Morris, conspired to retain the capital where it presently resided, Philadelphia. Initially, Madison sought to maneuver around the northerners by limiting the bank's charter. Once it became apparent that he would fail in this, he threatened to attack the constitutionality of the bank if the Pennsylvanians did not yield. When they did not, he made good his threat.

In two long speeches, Madison argued that Congress did not have the constitutional authority to charter the bank. He pointed out that a national bank had been proposed and defeated when the Constitution was drafted. Moreover, the enumerated powers could be stretched to reach this purpose only by multiplying those powers in a way that would eviscerate the limitations placed on the national government. If those enumerated powers could be heaped one upon another to reach any objective, he asserted, then the government would no longer be limited at all. "If implications thus remote and thus multiplied, can be linked together, a chain may be formed that will reach every object of legislation, every object within the whole compass of political economy."[81] In making this argument, however, Madison proved himself inconsistent with his preratification self. In *The Federalist,* no. 44, he made exactly the opposite argument. "No axiom is more clearly established in law, or in reason," he wrote, "than that wherever the end is required, the means are authorized; wherever a general power to do a thing is given, every particular power for doing it is included."[82] The Congress followed the

Madisonian view of two years earlier and passed the bill. Congress then sent it to the president for his signature.

President Washington was deeply troubled by the constitutional arguments. He had tremendous respect for Madison's constitutional acumen and felt himself to be the principal guardian of that sacred instrument. In addition to Madison's doubts, Washington had received the opinion of Attorney General Randolph who, not surprisingly, concurred that the bill suffered constitutional defects. Washington then went to Jefferson for his opinion. Jefferson's response would become one of the classic statements of strict constructionism, with the object of limiting the power of the federal government. Jefferson employed many of the arguments previously made by the opponents of the Constitution—the Anti-Federalists—in his case against the bank.

Jefferson's starting point was the language that would soon become the Tenth Amendment. "The powers not delegated to the United States by the Constitution, nor prohibited by it to the States, are reserved to the States respectively, or to the people." The federal government's power was only as great as that given to it by the Constitution. It had no implied powers to reach beyond those subjects specifically enumerated. The drafters, according to Jefferson, had "intended to lace [the Congress] up straitly within the enumerated powers and those without which, as means, those powers could not be carried into effect."[83] No leeway could be permitted. "To take a single step beyond the boundaries thus especially drawn around the powers of Congress [in the Tenth Amendment]," he stated, "is to take possession of a boundless field of power, no longer susceptible of any definition."[84]

Hamilton's response to the Virginia group of Jefferson, Madison, and Randolph was a tour de force in legal argument and constitutional interpretation. He began by asserting a self-evident proposition, "that every power vested in a Government is in its nature *sovereign,* and includes by *force* of the term, a right to employ all the *means* requisite, and fairly *applicable* to the attainment of the *ends* of such power; and which are not precluded by restrictions & exceptions specified in the constitution; or not immoral, or not contrary to the essential ends of political power."[85] A government not empowered to effectuate the objectives to which it is entrusted would be a government in name only. By its nature, sovereignty bestows upon governments the reasonable means to accomplish legitimate ends.

Hamilton thus turned Jefferson's argument on its head. For Jefferson, the Constitution limited the national government to those powers specifically enumerated. Hamilton refuted this strong limitation, pointing out that no one advocated the complete absence of implied powers. No government would long survive if every delegated power had to be expressly enumerated. The issue was the extent of those powers. Hamilton explained that "it is nothing more than a consequence of this republican maxim, that all government is a delegation of power."[86] For the federal government, as was true for the states, the question concerned the scope of sovereign power in a government of delegated powers. If the federal government did not have implied powers, how could it be said that the states possess this power, since these sovereigns all received their mandates from the people.

Jefferson's mistake, Hamilton maintained, was that he considered the bank to be the end objective of the law. It was not. The bank was a means of accomplishing legitimate national objectives. Therefore, Congress could not establish a corporation to supervise the police of Philadelphia, Hamilton wrote, for it was "not authorised to regulate the police of that city." However, Congress could establish a corporation to collect taxes or regulate interstate commerce, for these ends were well within its enumerated power. Moreover, contrary to Jefferson's argument that only those means that are *strictly* necessary to reach legitimate ends could be employed, Hamilton argued that such a reading would disable the government from effective administration of its duties. Hamilton stated, "If the end be clearly comprehended within any of the specified powers—[and] if the measure have an obvious relation to that end and is not forbidden by any particular provision of the constitution—it may safely be deemed to come within the compass of the national authority."[87]

Despite the overwhelming force of Hamilton's argument, the fate of the bank bill remained uncertain. Although convinced by Hamilton's constitutional arguments, Washington felt compelled to hold the bank bill hostage in order to press Congress to fix the Potomac as the capital's future home. The Senate had postponed consideration of amending the federal district act until February 25, the last day on which Washington had to sign or veto the bank bill. And so the fate of the capital's location and the bank were fully intertwined. The historical record is unclear on the dynamics of what occurred to seal the deal. But a deal was struck. Sometime on the twenty-fifth the president signed the bank bill into law and, at the end of the day, the four senators who previously had opposed putting the capital on the Potomac reversed their positions, guaranteeing its future home in the South.

As is true of many political battles, what was settled by the legislature and executive would eventually be fought again in the courts. It sometimes takes time and changing circumstances, however, to get the issue there. The first national bank was chartered for twenty years and went out of business in 1811. The Republicans, who had fought the bank in 1791, then blocked renewal. However, a variety of factors, including a deepening financial crisis exacerbated by the War of 1812, convinced Republicans that the bank was needed. In 1816, Congress chartered the Second Bank of the United States. President Madison, without hesitation, signed the measure into law.

Initially, the bank proved a great success. Its liberal credit policies contributed to postwar economic prosperity. However, in 1818, when commodity prices fell sharply, the bank abruptly called in its loans, resulting in business failures and bank insolvencies. The "monster" bank was blamed for the ensuing financial panic. Outraged state legislatures imposed various measures designed to curtail the bank's activities. Maryland passed a stamp tax on all banks "not chartered by the [state] legislature." James McCulloch, the cashier of the Baltimore branch of the U.S. bank, however, refused to pay the tax. McCulloch himself was a shady character who would later be charged with misappropriating more than $500,000 of the bank's funds. He was ultimately acquitted of this more egregious offense, because Maryland had no embezzlement statute at the time. He was, however, convicted in Maryland County Court for failure to pay the stamp tax. After the Maryland Court of Appeals affirmed the judgment, the bank sought review by the Supreme Court.

The case was argued in March 1819 and its importance was immediately understood. *McCulloch v. Maryland* concretely presented the old Federalist–Anti-Federalist dispute regarding the proper boundary between state and national authorities. Was the federal government immune from discriminatory state taxation? The answer would depend on the Court's view of whether the Constitution created a Jeffersonian republic in which states were ascendant, or a Hamiltonian republic in which the national government reigned supreme. The argument before the Court involved some of the greatest names of the day. Maryland was represented by the seventy-five-year-old Luther Martin. This would be his last appearance at the bar. He was joined by two celebrated appellate attorneys, Joseph Hopkinson and Walter Jones. The bank was represented by Daniel Webster, an orator with no equal at that time or arguably any time since, William Wirt, the attorney general of the United States, and William Pinkney, an attorney with an esteemed reputation at the bar.

The argument lasted nine days, three times longer than was ordinary. It closely tracked the dueling memoranda submitted to Washington in 1791 by Jefferson and Hamilton. Counsel for Maryland argued that the national authority's power does not exceed what was expressly given to it by the sovereign states: "The Constitution was formed and adopted, not by the people of the United States at large, but by the people of the respective states. . . . It is therefore a compact between the states, and all the powers which are not expressly relinquished by it, are reserved to the states."[88] Counsel for the bank argued Hamilton's claim for implied powers. Pinkney, who concluded the bank's argument on March 1, 1819, spoke for three days. Justice Joseph Story later commented that "[n]ever, in my whole life, have I heard a greater speech." On the merits, he said, "All the cobwebs of sophistry and metaphysics about States' rights and State sovereignty he brushed away with a mighty besom."[89]

The Court took just three days to deliver its opinion. Chief Justice John Marshall began his opinion by noting the profound weight of the case. Reiterating the power he had secured for the Court in *Marbury*, he began, "On the Supreme Court of the United States has the constitution of our country devolved this important duty." Marshall then considered the matter that "counsel for the State of Maryland have deemed . . . of some importance." Are the powers of the federal government delegated to it by the states, or do they emanate from the people? He found it "difficult to sustain" the proposition that the federal government owed its power to the states. "The Convention which framed the constitution was indeed elected by the state legislatures. But the instrument, when it came from their hands, was a mere proposal, without obligation, or pretensions to it."[90] He admitted that, when considering the Constitution, the people assembled in their respective states. "Where else," he asked, "should they have assembled?" "No political dreamer was ever wild enough to think of breaking down the lines which separate the states, and of compounding the American people into one common mass. Of consequence, when they act, they act in their states. But the measures they adopt do not, on that account, cease to be the measures of the people themselves, or become the measures of the state governments."[91] He concluded with the following words, which future American leaders would return to over and over again, "[The] government of the Union, then, . . . is, emphatically, and truly, a government of the people. In form and in substance it emanates from them. Its powers are granted by them, and are to be exercised directly on them, and for their benefit."[92] Patrick Henry, the arch Anti-Federalist, had predicted decades before that the words "we the people" would one day be used to exalt the national power at the expense of the states. The *McCulloch* decision was the realization of his deepest fears.

Marshall next turned to the crux of the case before the Court. Did the Constitution confer onto Congress the power to incorporate a bank? His affirmative response closely tracked Hamilton's of almost thirty years before. He rejected the Tenth Amendment claim, pointing out that it did not limit the federal government to only those powers "*expressly* delegated." Indeed, Marshall reasoned, the Articles of Confederation had employed such language, and the Constitution's framers' failure to use the word *expressly* indicated their desire to avoid the "embarrassments resulting from the insertion of the word" in the earlier document. A constitution required to expressly detail every delegated power was doomed to fail. "A constitution, to contain an accurate detail of all the subdivisions of which its great powers will admit, and of all the means by which they may be carried into execution, would partake of the prolixity of a legal code, and could scarcely be embraced by the human mind." He exclaimed famously, "In considering this question, then, we must never forget that it is a constitution we are expounding."[93]

In *Marbury v. Madison,* John Marshall had defended the power of judicial review partly on the basis that the process of interpreting the Constitution was largely mechanical. In effect, he implied that it was simply a process of placing the law down alongside the Constitution to determine if the former conformed to the latter. In *McCulloch,* we got a very different sort of Constitution. Marshall gave it life. Forever after, the Court claimed primary responsibility to give form to that life. The great authority of the judiciary had begun at the tip of Marshall's pen in *Marbury* and was expanded through that same pen in *McCulloch.* After *Marbury,* however, the Court would not overturn another federal law on constitutional grounds for fifty-four years. Then it would be in the lamentable *Dred Scott* case and, ironically, in service of states' rights.

3

A COVENANT WITH DEATH:

Dred Scott and the Biology of Slavery

Tragedie is to seyn a certeyn storie,
As olde books meken us memorie,
Of Hym that stood in greet prosperitee,
And is yfallen out of heigh degree,
Into myserie, and endeth wrecchedly.

— GEOFFREY CHAUCER,
THE CANTERBURY TALES

In 1836, Roger Brooke Taney succeeded Chief Justice John Marshall as the head of the federal judiciary. To be chief justice had been his one consuming goal, an objective that would allow him to help set the course of the nation and secure his name in its history. Taney (pronounced "Tawney") led a remarkable career, having been born well—onto a "good landed estate"—to a prosperous Maryland family. He was one of the leading lawyers of his time, and served as attorney general to the state of Maryland and the United States. He was a close confidant of President Andrew Jackson, who nominated him to be chief justice. After twenty years on the Court, his reputation was thought by many to rival Marshall's himself, and all agreed that his command of legal doctrine was rivaled by none. His fall from grace came suddenly and, from history's perspective, completely. In 1857, tragedy befell him in the name of Dred Scott. As author of *Scott v. Sandford,* Chief Justice Taney helped to ignite the simmering blaze that would shortly explode into the Civil War.

All the more tragic, Taney's intention, and every expectation, was that *Dred Scott* would preserve the Union. Seldom has such gross miscalculation led to such great misery. From the modern perspective, the Civil War can be understood as a salutary event, by ending slavery, preserving the Union, and ushering in a new era of equality. For Roger B. Taney, however, his name has ever after been associated with blindness, ignorance, and prejudice.

Roger Taney had the sort of appearance that made people comment, and the comments were invariably negative. Even when young he appeared pinched and frail. He had the visage of an old man almost from the start and only late in life did his body truly fit his years. Growing old did nothing except deepen his already sallow features. John Latrobe, a neighbor, fellow lawyer, and sometimes political antagonist, offered this graphic physical description:

> When Mr. Taney rose to speak, you saw a tall, square shouldered man, flat breasted in a degree to be remarked upon, with a stoop that made his shoulders even more prominent, a face without one good feature, a mouth unusually large, in which were discolored and irregular teeth, the gums of which were visible when he smiled, dressed always in black, his clothes sitting ill upon him, his hands spare with projecting veins,—in a word a gaunt, ungainly man. His voice too, was hollow, as the voice of one who was consumptive.[1]

Yet, despite his meager physical appearance and "hollow voice," he was acclaimed as a gifted advocate and a compelling speaker. His manner was quiet and reserved and he was exceedingly kind and generous to all. Even his ideological foes, at least those who knew him personally, liked him and many came to love him deeply. William Pinkney said of him, "I can answer his arguments, I am not afraid of his logic, but that infernal apostolic manner of his, there is no replying to."[2] Taney was deceptively effective before a jury. Latrobe described why this was so:

> He used no gestures. He used even emphasis but sparely. There was an air of so much sincerity in all he said that it was next to impossible to believe he could be wrong. Not a redundant syllable, not a phrase repeated, and, to repeat, so exquisitely simple. I remember once hearing him in a complicated case, and when he sat down, fancying that I, in my first year's practice, could have done as well, so simple had become complications in his hands.[3]

Taney's manner seemed to engender admiration and respect in all those who came to know him. His many successes in life had given him enough confidence and self-assurance to comfortably permit others to preen their egos around him without ruffling his own. He was comfortable with himself, confident of his ideas, and generally avoided imposing either on others. Yet he was adamant about many things, and never shrunk from an ideological battle. With the benefit of more than a century, however, it is clear that his ideas were mostly pedestrian. He did not possess Marshall's soaring vision and his ideas would never be seen as heralding the future course of the nation. No one, then or now, would suggest that Taney was ahead of his time. Indeed, he was as thoroughly a man of his times as could be imagined.

Taney wrote over 250 opinions for the Court, yet few remain landmarks to this day. Only a handful of cases from his pen are studied, and most of these are not specifically associated with Taney's hand. One reason for this is that the Civil War and the constitutional amendments that followed reoriented basic national-state relations and resolved the slavery question, the issue with which Taney has so infamously become associated. Indeed, although his brand of federalism came back into favor with the activist Supreme Court of Chief Justice William Rehnquist, it is part of Taney's tragedy that today's justices only rarely name him as a predecessor who championed their judicial philosophies, and when they do so it is with apologies. Taney lived a prosperous life, but following his opinion in *Dred Scott* he fell into misery and his reputation ended wretchedly.

Taney was born in Calvert County, Maryland, in 1777, a member of the first generation of American independence, and in some respects representative of that age. In his never-completed memoirs, Taney conceded that he shared the vision and myopia of his generation; he had "lived and acted in it and with it."[4] He observed that "the history of my life is necessarily associated with the manners, habits, pursuits, and characters of those with whom I lived and acted."[5] His father owned slaves, which gave to the young Taney the impression that this "peculiar institution" was the natural state of things. "Neither the public nor the private conscience revolted at an institution," he wrote, "which, because of the inferiority of the negro, seemed natural to those familiar with it from their birth."[6] The relationship mutually benefited both parties: "The slaves rocked the cradle and dug the graves of their masters; and the masters, from the birth to the death of the slaves, in sickness and health, sheltered and protected them." In fact, Taney believed, the slave might have benefited more: "For a long period, if not through its whole duration, the relation of master and slave was best for both races, and especially for the negro, as it raised him from pagan barbarism to a phase of Christian civilization."

Taney, however, was not a champion of slavery. Like many of his generation, especially in the border states, he considered slavery to be an evil and "a blot on our national character."[7] He was a Roman Catholic, and slavery sat uncomfortably with his deeply held religious beliefs. He freed his own slaves, except in cases where they were unable to care for themselves. He had always acted kindly toward them, and they appeared to reciprocate those feelings. He knew that slavery must end, but he feared that it might end too abruptly, reaping unknown disaster. Sudden emancipation, Taney said, "would be absolute ruin to the negroes, as well as to the white people."[8] The abolitionist cause he considered to be a direct threat to "these United States," and he hoped and believed that the southern states would eventually see fit to end slavery. Most ardently, however, he maintained that the decision was a local matter. It was a matter to be decided by the states, and a solution could not be imposed from without. In his eyes, the *Dred Scott* case presented an opportunity to avoid a sudden and calamitous end to slavery and a chance to keep the Union together. Taney believed completely that the moral bearing and political capital of the Supreme Court could be employed to accomplish this task.

Not all suffered Taney's myopia. Senator George P. Marsh of Vermont asked, "Is that Court a fit tribunal for the determination of a great political question like this?" Marsh thought not. In assuming this burden, he felt that the Court risked all. "We should hazard not its impartiality and its high moral influence only, but its constitution and even its existence." Marsh warned that the "Court itself would become, with the defeated party, the object of a hostility as deep-rooted, as persevering, as widely diffused, and as rancorous as are at this moment the feelings and prejudices now arrayed against each other upon this great issue."[9] Taney ignored the danger and sought the glory of ending the nation's strife. *Dred Scott v. Sandford* would be the donkey on which he would ride.

The *Dred Scott* case took shape in the first half of the nineteenth century and was inextricably linked with America's expansion west. Scott was a slave of Dr. John Emerson, a surgeon in the United States Army, who took him from Rock Island, Missouri, to the free state of Illinois in

1834. Two years later, Scott traveled with Emerson to a new assignment at Fort Snelling, near present-day St. Paul, Minnesota, then a part of the Wisconsin Territory. In Minnesota, Scott married Harriet, another of Emerson's slaves, and they had a daughter who was born on a steamboat just north of Missouri. In 1838, Emerson and Scott's family returned to Missouri. Scott's travels had brought him north of the line set in 1820 known as the Missouri Compromise.

In 1819, Missouri petitioned Congress to be admitted as the twenty-third state of the Union and as a slave state. At that time, there were an equal number of free and slave states. Missouri's petition brought to the fore a seething tension that had been successfully suppressed when the Constitution was adopted. Missouri would upset the balance, and, more ominously, it was feared, establish a precedent of congressional acquiescence in bringing slavery to the new lands of the expanding Union. This situation led to acrimonious debate between northern and southern states. Northerners, such as Rufus King of New York, argued that Congress had the power to prohibit slavery in new states. Southerners, led by William Pinkney of Maryland, claimed that new states had the same right as the original thirteen and could choose slavery if they so wished.

In time, and following great rancor, a deal was struck. Missouri was admitted together with Maine (formerly part of Massachusetts), with the former admitted as a slave state and the latter a free state. In addition, except for Missouri, slavery would not be allowed north of latitude 36°30'. As is true with many such compromises, both sides despised the result. Northerners objected to the expansion of slavery into the new territories and southerners protested Congress's assumption of power to decide a matter they considered an integral component of state sovereignty. Although the Missouri Compromise kept an uneasy peace for over thirty years, it was little more than a temporary obstruction against the rising floodwaters. Thomas Jefferson said that when he heard news of the Missouri Compromise, it was like the sound of a firebell in the night.[10] It made him tremble for the nation's fate.

Not long after the Scotts returned to Missouri, Emerson died, leaving his property to his wife, Irene, in trust for his child. Since Scott was now bound in a legal trust arrangement, Irene could not emancipate him. This arrangement proved highly inconvenient, since she planned to move to Massachusetts. When she left, she gave Scott and his family to Taylor Blow. Blow was the son of Scott's former owner, but he did not quite know what to do with his new bounty. He sought the advice of the law firm of Field and Hall, and, as lawyers are wont to do, they sued. They filed suit on behalf of Scott claiming his freedom. In their complaint against Irene Emerson, they argued that Scott had become irrevocably free once he was brought to live in the territories where slavery was prohibited. The narrative became more complicated when Irene Emerson married Dr. Calvin C. Chaffee of Massachusetts, a representative in Congress. Chaffee, an outspoken opponent of slavery, suddenly found himself a slave owner. In order to avoid the inconvenience of continuing the suit against Irene and her politically exposed husband, ownership of Scott was transferred to Irene's brother, John H. Sanford, whose name was wrongly spelled "Sandford" by the court reporter. In 1855, *Scott v. Sandford* reached the Supreme Court.

The year 1855 can be seen in retrospect as the juncture at which tragedy began to befall Taney. As is true in Greek tragedy, not just one calamity would visit him. Professional disaster is often accompanied by heavy personal loss, and Taney's tale would play true to this script.

Throughout his life, Taney sought respite from the travails of Washington politics by escaping with his family to a cottage at Old Point Comfort, Virginia. He had married Anne Phebe Charlton Key, the sister of Francis Scott Key, and by all accounts they enjoyed an idyllic nineteenth-century family life. In the summer of 1855, Taney and Anne, together with one of their unmarried daughters, Ellen, boarded the steamer *Louisiana* for the journey down the Chesapeake. Seeing them off were their other unmarried daughter, Alice, and a married daughter, Sophia, and her son Roger. Alice was to travel to Old Point later in the summer. Foreshadowing the coming events, storm clouds gathered as they readied to sail. Taney would later write of his trepidation upon seeing his family engulfed by the deluge as thunder rocked the heavens and the boat receded from the pier.[11]

Within a month at Old Point, Taney received news that Sophia's husband had abandoned Roger and her. Sophia remained in seclusion in Baltimore from the disgrace brought about by her husband, whom Taney described as "a mean miserable hypocrite." Things would grow worse.

In August, an outbreak of yellow fever struck Norfolk and Portsmouth, introduced there by the steamer *Ben Franklin,* which had transported it from St. Thomas in the Virgin Islands. The disease raged through the poorer sections of the towns affected, and authorities evacuated entire areas and burned houses in an attempt to stanch the outbreak. The smoke and heat of the fires exacerbated the misery of the hot and humid Virginia summer. These measures also brought about the opposite of their intended effect by scattering the plague-carrying mosquitoes. Toward the end of August severe storms brought relief from the heat but forced the mosquitoes to spread still further. Panic began to well out to nearby towns. Although Old Point had yet to suffer one case of the fever, the epidemic occupied the residents' every conversation. Under the strain, Anne Taney suffered a mild stroke. The Taneys considered returning north, but they would have had to join the thousands crowding the steamers that traveled the Chesapeake. They considered themselves safer where they were. But Taney's youngest daughter, Alice, soon fell ill. In September, Anne suffered a massive paralytic stroke and on September 29 she died. The *Baltimore Sun* reported that, in addition to the paralysis, Anne apparently also suffered from yellow fever. Although there was uncertainty about the cause of his wife's death, only one day later Taney's daughter Alice died from the dreaded fever.

Taney's world had crashed down around him. Overwhelmed with grief, Taney made arrangements to have mother and daughter buried together. On their stone, he inscribed David's lament for Saul and Jonathan:

> LOVELY AND COMELY IN THEIR LIFE
> EVEN IN DEATH THEY WERE NOT DIVIDED.[12]

He might well have wished to join their repose. Less than three months later the *Dred Scott* case was added to the Supreme Court's docket.

Dred Scott was first argued in the spring of 1856. At that time, the Supreme Court shared space underneath the old Senate chamber. A New York paper described the room as "a triangular, semi-circular, odd-shaped apartment, with three windows [behind the justices] and a profusion of arches in the ceiling, diverging like the radii of a circle from a point over the bench."[13] In 1859, the *New York Tribune* described the chamber less reverently, as "a potato hole of a place . . . a queer room of small dimensions and shaped overhead like a quarter section of a pumpkin shell."

In their initial deliberations, the justices disagreed whether Scott could sue in federal court. They decided to rehear the case the following term, which was not unusual in important cases. After the rehearing, a majority of the Court agreed that Scott did not have a right to sue and, moreover, the fact that Emerson brought Scott north of 36°30' did not free him from his bondage. In a moment of lucidity, the majority also decided to render the case less important by limiting the written opinion to the facts of Scott's case alone, and not attempting to answer the great questions of the day. Justice Nelson would write the decision.

Justices McLean and Curtis, however, informed their colleagues that they each intended to write extensive dissents touching on all of the most controversial issues raised by the case. McLean, in particular, posed concern, for he intended to use his office and this opinion as a springboard to the presidency. He had sought the Republican nomination in 1856 and would do so again in 1860. Today, candidates write books establishing their bona fides to be president—Justice McLean intended his *Dred Scott* dissent to accomplish this result.

The majority now reconsidered its options, fearful that the dissenters' opinions would be taken up by abolitionists bent on imposing their views on the South. They decided to write an opinion that would answer all of the terrible questions raised by the case. Taney believed that such an act of statesmanship would maintain the status quo until slavery could come to a gradual, graceful, and peaceful end. He delegated to himself the important duty of writing the opinion for the Court, though eventually every justice would write his own opinion explaining his vote.

Taney viewed *Dred Scott* as an opportunity to calm the sectional strife dividing the Union. He approached the decision with an arsenal of judicial tools well honed from past practice. While John Marshall had believed the Constitution lived and breathed, and it was the Supreme Court's task to sustain it by adapting it to an ever-changing world, Taney considered the Constitution fixed in the eighteenth-century firmament. The Court did not have the duty or the prerogative to adjust the Constitution to meet contemporary demands. Only the people had the power of constitutional amendment. "If any of its provisions are deemed unjust, there is a mode prescribed in the instrument itself by which it may be amended; but while it remains unaltered, it must be construed now as it was understood at the time of its adoption."[14] The Constitution thus meant what the founding generation intended it to mean. "Any other rule of construction would abrogate the judicial character of this Court, and make it the mere reflex of the popular opinion or passion of the day."

Taney also differed from Marshall in his view of the states and their place in the American federation. Marshall, an original Federalist, advocated a dominant role for the federal government, power that came at the expense of the states. Marshall was aligned with Washington, Adams, and Hamilton on this issue. Taney more nearly followed the Jeffersonian Republicans. State sovereignty was the default rule, and the federal government had its sphere of action, but it had to be strictly curtailed. Taney's approach to *Dred Scott* was thus informed by his strict constructionist view of constitutional interpretation and his ardent belief in state sovereignty. He was a states' rights enthusiast. In a quickly changing world that was being torn asunder, his jurisprudence was exactly the wrong one for the time. Taney's *Dred Scott* decision would be an appeal to the past at a time when the nation could only go forward or fall apart.

In his opinion for the Court, Taney said that two general questions must be answered. First, was Scott a "citizen" of the United States? If not, the Court did not have jurisdiction to hear the case at all. Second, if he was a citizen, was he still a slave after having been taken to the free territories north of the line set by the Missouri Compromise? Because Taney interpreted the Constitution strictly, whether a black man could be a citizen of the United States depended entirely upon whether those who ratified the Constitution intended this result. Resolution of the second question, Scott's status after residing in free territory, involved both the issue of the founding generation's views of blacks and the other great question of the day, states' rights.

In his opinion, Taney observed that, looking back to the time of the Constitution's drafting, "It is difficult at this day to realize the state of public opinion in relation to that unfortunate race, which prevailed in civilized and enlightened portions of the world at the time of the Declaration of Independence, and when the Constitution of the United States was framed and adopted."[15] In strong words, he emphasized that a "stigma, of the deepest degradation, was fixed upon the whole race."[16] He then added these words that heaped more stigma atop the pile: "They had for more than a century before been regarded as beings of an inferior order, and altogether unfit to associate with the white race, either in social or political relations; and so far inferior, that they had no rights which the white man was bound to respect; and that the negro might justly and lawfully be reduced to slavery for his benefit."[17] William Seward, then senator from New York, would say about this line that the

Court forgot that one "foul sentence does more harm than many foul examples; for the last do but corrupt the stream, while the former corrupteth the fountain."[18]

According to Taney's method of constitutional interpretation, he was bound to a meaning fixed to that document by the founders. Because the natural philosophy and social practices of the eighteenth century considered blacks so inferior as to be unqualified to be citizens, subsequent generations were, in Taney's interpretation, bound to this view of the nature of man. For Taney, the Supreme Court could not on its own update the Constitution to meet with the progress of science. To interpret the meaning of the Constitution, Taney insisted, we must look to the science of the times when the Constitution was written.

At the time of the Constitution's founding, in the late eighteenth century, great men had debated the fundamental principles of constitutional democracy such as liberty, equality, and due process, and these same great men had debated the nature of man and, in particular, the science of race. The science of race was inextricably interwoven with the institution of slavery. Unfortunately, the early history of the taking of blacks into slavery in America is documented only enough to provide historians with fodder for debate. After around 1640, however, surviving records make clear that blacks and their progeny were the subject of contract and sale. As repugnant as it sounds today, the question for the people of the seventeenth century was not whether blacks were property, but what sort of property—real or personal (chattel)—they were. As one historian observed, "Chattel slavery required, in common with other manifestations of the commercialization of society, decisions as to how the account books were to be kept."[19] But slavery itself was not unique in the annals of history. Virtually all of the great societies of antiquity practiced it. It was not uncommon for seventeenth-century Americans to think of black slavery as a modern incarnation of the tenure practiced by ancient societies. Slavery in antiquity, however, was a function of conquest or circumstance, not inherent inferiority. An Athenian slave, for instance, was inferior because he was not a "citizen," a status only achieved by accident of birth. Thus, it was not at all that Athenian slaves could not be citizens because they were inferior; rather, they were inferior because they could not be citizens.

Over time, however, perceptions of those enslaved changed, and this change was closely associated with Western society's increasing interest in man's natural place in the grand scheme of things. Although still primitive in its development, the scientific age had arrived. In particular, Isaac Newton's great success at describing the universe sparked natural philosophers' enthusiasm to do the same with the earthly environment. Man himself was becoming a fit subject to study and categorize. The peculiar institution of slavery would become fully entangled with the early musings of scientific investigation.

In 1684, François Bernier propounded one of the first systematic classification schemes when he described four basic stocks of man. The first included most Europeans as well as peoples from southern Asia, North Africa, and America; the second included all other Africans; the third encompassed all other Asians and inhabitants of the islands of the East; and in the fourth he placed those "wretched animals," the Lapps. Bernier's scheme was revolutionary, not just in his attempt to classify mankind, but in his decision to do so largely based on physical characteristics and especially skin color.

The process of classification was placed on a somewhat firmer scientific basis with Linnaeus (Carl von Linné, 1707–1778), who sought to classify all living things into a chart popularly known as the Great Chain of Being, which first appeared in 1735. As Linnaeus originally conceived it, this chain was not hierarchical. All God's creatures had value and the objective was mainly taxonomy, not arranging the social order. Inevitably, however, as the metaphor grew in popularity, the chain became a ladder, with man naturally occupying the uppermost rung. It was clear, too, that men differed among themselves. The intriguing question posed concerned whether hierarchical differences existed between men.

European man was doing the classifying, so not surprisingly the taxonomy of man began with the classifier as the prototype. Oliver Goldsmith, author of She Stoops to Conquer, considered dark skin as "marks of the degeneracy in the human form." "European beauty" provided the benchmark, and degeneracy could be measured "in proportion as he differs more widely, he has made greater deviations from his original form."[20] Johann Friedrich Blumenbach, considered the father of anthropology, believed that white must have been the original skin color, since "it is very easy for [white] to generate into brown, but very much more difficult for brown to become white." Moreover, he observed that the white race displays "the most beautiful form of the skull, from which, as from a mean and primaeval type, the others diverge by most gradations on both sides to the ultimate extremes."[21] The different kinds of men could be traced back to the first man. "That we have sprung from one common parent, we are taught, both by reason and religion, to believe; and we have good reason also to think that the Europeans resemble him more than any of the rest of his children."[22] It was undoubtedly very comforting for the European to discover that Adam, and thus the face of God, was white.

The self-serving narrow-mindedness of these beliefs was pointed out by, of all people, Captain Thomas Phillips, a captain of a slave ship. In 1694, he wrote that he could not "imagine why they should be despis'd for their colour, being what they cannot help, and the effect of the climate it has pleas'd God to appoint them." What's more, he could not "think there is any intrisick value in one colour more than another, nor that white is better than black, only we think it so because we are so, and are prone to judge favourably in our own case, as well as the blacks, who in odium of the colour, say, the devil is white, and so paint him."[23]

The fifteenth and sixteenth centuries were times of great exploration, so only recently had Europeans discovered the wide variety of not just their own species but of all species. In particular, Africa offered up a smorgasbord of natural delights. Two discoveries especially shaped the eighteenth-century perception of the nature of man. Explorers happened upon the black man and apes at about the same time. This coincidence helped to cement, in the popular mind, an appalling interpretation of connection. Georges Cuvier, in his description of the "three races"— Caucasian, Mongolian, and the Negro—asserted that "the projection of the lower parts of the face, and the thick lips [of the Negro], evidently approximate it to the monkey tribe: the hordes of which it consists have always remained in the most complete state of barbarism."[24] It was not that blacks were considered apes or apes men, since blacks had souls and rationality, traits apparently missing from apes. But on the ladder of life, blacks were deemed the lowest order of men and apes the highest order of animal. The races lay along a continuum. Although clear divisions existed between the rungs, each rung might contain a variety of subcategories, with greater and lesser abilities spread among them. The many races appeared to plainly confirm this hypothesis.

The study of race was an essentially comparative enterprise. The African's perceived barbarity was contrasted with the civility of the European. In particular, the late eighteenth century saw a boon in comparative anatomy. Peter Camper initiated much of this work with his research on the "facial angle," an effort to measure skulls in order to quantify the Chain of Being. Dr. John Hunter, a renowned English surgeon, followed in Camper's footsteps with his work on "the gradation of skulls." To the envy of many scientists, Hunter maintained a large collection of animal and human skulls. He assiduously avoided, however, drawing any "conclusion from the difference in them respecting African inferiority."[25] Others would be considerably less reluctant to draw such conclusions.

One scientist envious of Hunter's skull collection was Dr. Charles White, a member of the Royal Society and an accomplished comparative anatomist. Like Hunter, he endeavored with his research to do nothing that would "countenance" that "pernicious practice of enslaving mankind." He sought only "to investigate the truth." Nonetheless, White devoted his studies to comparing blacks and whites, what he considered the "capital varieties" of mankind, with the European variety invariably faring superior. He systematically cataloged the physiological inferiorities of the Africans and placed the order of beings, from the European at the top to the lowest reptile. He found that Africans more nearly resembled the ape in a wide variety of physiological characteristics. White also was interested in documenting the general feeling, well served by the association with apes, "that Negroes were a lewd, lascivious, and wanton people."[26] The civilized English had a certain envy, disguised as disdain, for the natural barbarism, and the unrestrained sexuality that seemingly accompanied it.

To support the proposition that blacks are highly sexual, White looked for physiological evidence to prove it. And he found it. "That the PENIS of an African is larger than that of an European has, I believe, been shewn in every anatomical school in London. Preparations of them are preserved in most anatomical museums; and I have one in mine."[27] Presumably, Dr. Hunter still preferred his skulls.

Lest the physiological endowment with which African males appeared to be blessed might upset the European sense of superiority, White assured his audience that Europeans were the archetype of beauty:

Ascending the line of gradation, we come at last to the white European, who being most removed from the brute creation, may, on that account, be

considered as the most beautiful of the human race. No one will doubt his
superiority in intellectual powers. . . . Where shall we find, unless in the
European, that nobly arched head, containing such a quantity of brain . . . ?
Where that variety of features, and fulness of expression; those long, flowing
graceful ringlets; that majestic beard, those rosy cheeks and coral lips . . . ?
In what other quarter of the globe shall we find the blush that overspreads
the soft features of the beautiful women of Europe, that emblem of mod-
esty, of delicate feelings, and of sense? Where that nice expression of the
amiable and softer passions in the countenance; and that general elegance
of features and complexion? Where, except on the bosom of the European woman, two such plump and snowy white hemispheres, tipt with
vermillion?[28]

European glory remained intact.

As slavery became more deeply entrenched in American society, both
the rule of law and the science of race evolved to account for this reality.
Both the law and the science were shaped to describe and justify the
status quo. Laws prohibiting intermarriage between free blacks and
whites and penalties exacted against runaway slaves and those who aided
them all followed the growing institutionalization of slavery. Slavery,
however, also created a glaring tension for the founding generation: as
Americans began to awaken to liberty, they necessarily had to justify
denying to others that which they cherished for themselves. The question
of the black man's place in the great chain of being became a question
of great import and high-minded debate. The science of race was never
a mere academic exercise; it informed and, more usually, served the political debate. It would become a core premise in the argument over the
organization of American society. It thus became a justification for
oppression.

In the late eighteenth century, the scientific debate about men's natures
contained a surprisingly modern resonance. Were widely observed differences between blacks and whites a product of nature or nurture? Few
disagreed that blacks did not meet white standards of achievement—
though counterexamples were regularly proposed and just as regularly
dismissed—but was this a product of their biology or their experience?
Some early abolitionists claimed that the perceived disparity lay merely
in prejudice, a newly discovered concept. Samuel Hopkins, a New Divin-
ity minister in Newport, reflected on why whites believed blacks were

"fit for nothing but slaves." The blame, he said, lay in white perceptions: "We have been used to look at them in a mean, contemptible light. . . . Our education has filled us with strong prejudices against them," he explained, leading "us to consider them, not as our brethren . . . but as quite another species of animals, made only to serve us and our children; and as happy in bondage, as in any other state."[29] Not until the twentieth century would this view reach ascendance. At the end of the eighteenth century, the argument over nature and nurture usually assumed black inferiority and then asked whether it was a product of experience or it resulted from their very nature.

William Dillwyn, a Quaker, nicely articulated the environmental position when he asked whether black inferiority is "not the natural consequence of a State of Slavery?" He went on to say, "Can we reasonably expect their Morals or Manners will equal those of Freemen, until they are cultivated with the same Degree of Care, in an equally extensive Field of Action, and with the same Encouragement?" He even hinted at a very modern scientific thought experiment, suggesting that "were a number of Whites treated just as they are . . . who will venture to assert that it would not occasion a like Depression of Spirit, and consequent Depravity of Manners?"[30] Clement Clarke Moore, a New York scholar of Hebrew and the author of The Night Before Christmas, asked, "Does justice bid us examine their mental powers, while in a state of servitude, rendered sullen by ignominy, and broken down by labour?"[31] William Pinkney, in 1789, emphatically declared that blacks and whites were "endued with equal faculties of mind and body." Pinkney continued, finding that blacks were "in all respects our equals by nature; and he who thinks otherwise has never reflected, that talents, however great, may perish unnoticed and unknown, unless auspicious circumstances conspire to draw them forth, and animate their exertions in the round of knowledge."[32]

The biological argument was advanced by many, especially in the South, but its most articulate spokesman was, ironically, the author of the Declaration of Independence. Thomas Jefferson, one of the preeminent scientific minds of his day, sought to bring a critical perspective to the question of nature versus nurture. In his well-regarded and popular Notes on Virginia, Jefferson wrote that blacks differed from whites on several intellectual dimensions: "Comparing them by their faculties of memory, reason, and imagination, it appears to me, that in memory they are equal to whites; in reason much inferior, as I think one could scarcely

be found capable of tracing and comprehending the investigations of
Euclid; and that in imagination they are dull, tasteless, and anomalous."[33]
Jefferson's theories of biological determinacy were based on careful
observation and experience. He had approximately two hundred slaves
himself, and came into daily contact with many blacks both free and not.
To objections regarding his methods of investigation, Jefferson said it
"would be unfair to follow them to Africa for this investigation." He
understood that he had "to make great allowances for the difference of
condition, of education, of conversation, of the sphere in which they
move." At the same time, Jefferson maintained, many "might have
availed themselves of the conversation of their masters; many have been
brought up to the handcraft arts," and "some have been liberally educated. . . . But never yet could I find that a black had uttered a thought
above the level of plain narration; never seen even an elementary trait of
painting or sculpture."[34] Based on this evidence, he concluded, "It is not
their condition then, but nature, which has produced the distinction."[35]

Jefferson was too good a scientist not to realize that his "data" failed
to fully prove his conclusion. Immediately upon reaching the precipice,
he stepped back. We should hesitate, he said, in reaching a conclusion
that "would degrade a whole race of men from the rank in the scale of
beings which their Creator may perhaps have given them." In the end,
Jefferson considered his finding to be only a working hypothesis, "that
they are inferior in the faculties of reason and imagination, must be haz-
arded with great diffidence." More scientific scrutiny was needed:

> To justify a general conclusion requires many observations, even where
> the subject may be submitted to the Anatomical knife, to Optical glasses,
> to analysis by fire, or by solvents. How much more then where it is a
> faculty, not a substance, we are examining; where it eludes the research
> of all the senses; where the conditions of its existence are various and
> variously combined; where the effects of those which are present or absent
> bid defiance to calculation.[36]

For Jefferson, and his southern contemporaries, the nature/nurture
debate assumed great social and political importance. It was comforting
indeed to lay black inferiority at the feet of nature, rather than to take
responsibility for it as an accompaniment to their bondage. The righ-
teousness of Americans' cry for liberty stood uncertainly atop the ques-

tion of black equality. Could a southern patriot declare himself for liberty in Philadelphia and return home to deny that self-evident truth to others? A Philadelphia newspaper asked this question in 1768: "How suits it with the glorious cause of Liberty," while keeping "your fellow men in bondage, men equally the work of your great Creator, men formed for freedom as yourselves?"[37] The scientific debate informed the political battle. Those who sought to end slavery stressed environmental influences and condemned an institution that would bind their brethren. Those who maintained the justness of enslaving blacks asserted the race's innate inferiority in order to deny them the freedom that is an inherent attribute of being human.

The nature/nurture debate thus served competing views of social organization. In reality, as is always true but nearly as often forgotten, scientific "truth" need never dictate social practice. Many in the founding generation considered the nature/nurture debate irrelevant to the political controversy of their time. For instance, in 1789 the Maryland Abolition Society rejected the relevance of so-called natural differences where liberty was concerned: "The human race, however varied in color or intellects, are all justly entitled to liberty."[38] The science of race could not determine political entitlement.

Still, if a union was to be forged, some middle ground would have to be found. And, indeed, the focus centered on the status of slaves themselves, since the description of them as people or property dictated how they would be counted for purposes of representation and taxes. Ultimately, the drafters settled on the infamous three-fifths compromise. Given the continuing and intense debate about the nature of blacks, counting each as three-fifths of a white did not shock the conscience of most Americans at the time. For the South, it was a just solution that would maintain their way of life while allowing them to join a strategic alliance with the foreign cultures of the North. For the North, it was a necessary solution if they were to build one nation. The problem of slavery would have to be laid upon future generations to suffer and, it was hoped, solve.

At the start of the constitutional convention, it appeared that the divide separating the states was between the large and the small. And, indeed, the delegates wrangled mightily to solve the perceived inequalities that might develop in a nation composed of different-sized states. The composition of the Senate, in which each state received two representatives, was dictated by the need to appease the small states that feared being overwhelmed in a national legislature composed according to population. However, in the end, the divide that truly threatened the Union was that between the North and the South. Following the Constitution's adoption, James Madison pointed out, "the institution of slavery and its consequences formed the line of discrimination." Appeasement on the slavery issue could not guarantee the peace, but could only delay the hostilities. Slavery would settle in as an institution and become a basic component of southern society. If it was not permanent, it was clear, as one historian put it, that "it was going to be a long siege."[39]

Looking back from his vantage point in 1857, Taney found the evidence compelling that the founding generation deemed blacks to be naturally inferior. "This opinion was, at that time, fixed and universal in the civilized portion of the white race," Taney wrote. He continued, "It was regarded as an axiom in morals, as well as in politics, which no one thought of disputing, or supposed open to dispute."[40] He dwelt not at all on the validity of the empirical bases for the then prevailing view. He was not troubled by the lack of consensus or the division of opinion that existed then, and which had only deepened since, between the North and the South. For Taney, the Constitution's implicit embrace of black inferiority had transformed that scientific theory into positive law to be enforced in perpetuity.

Taney's judicial philosophy required him to rely on the science of the eighteenth century, but the science of his day had not advanced appreciably either. Taney was almost certainly comforted that his historically based premises had the support of some voices in contemporary science. For instance, in the 1840s, Samuel George Morton, a Philadelphia physician and anthropologist, published research purportedly showing that the average cranial capacity of blacks was twelve cubic inches less than that of the average Anglo-Saxon.[41] Louis Agassiz, a Harvard professor and eminent naturalist, asserted that "a peculiar conformation characterizes the brain of an adult Negro. Its development never gets beyond that observable in the Caucasian in boyhood."[42] Perhaps Taney would have hesitated in following the founding generation's science if his own generation's had been more advanced.

On the question of Dred Scott's citizenship, therefore, the answer was clear. Since such persons were not meant to be included under the word *citizen* as it was used in the Constitution, Dred Scott could not be a citizen. Indeed, this declination extended not just to all slaves but to free blacks as well. The stigma "was fixed upon the whole race."[43] Taney rejected the argument that the power to naturalize foreigners belonged to the national government and thus could be extended to blacks. Taney stated that this power did not reach so far. "It is not a power to raise to the rank of a citizen any one born in the United States, who, from birth to parentage, by the laws of the country, belongs to an inferior and subordinate class."[44] In Taney's reading of the Constitution, the states could not give blacks citizenship, since they had surrendered sovereign power when they joined the Union. And the national government's power in this regard extended only to aliens. Only a constitutional amendment could admit blacks into the body politic.

As inflammatory as was Taney's rejection of Scott's claim of citizenship, if he had stopped there the Chief Justice would not have become such a lasting icon of bigotry. Nor did he need to write more. If Scott was not a citizen, he could not bring suit in federal court. A venerable, albeit venerably ignored, tenet of constitutional jurisprudence holds that courts should not reach constitutional issues if a decision can be rendered without doing so. By considering the second issue, the constitutionality of the Missouri Compromise, Taney reached beyond the issues necessary for setting the dispute in the *Dred Scott* case. This strictest of judicial conservatives, in other words, had become a judicial activist. Contrary to popular belief, as Taney would prove, judicial conservatism is not the same as judicial restraint. In an effort to maintain his cherished conservative regime, Taney had to affirmatively act beyond the strict limits of the Court's mandate. Intertwined with his positive desire to end the sectional strife afflicting the nation was his concern that the dissents of Curtis and McLean would deepen the country's division. He forged ahead, bounding heedlessly into the area at the core of the dispute: the extent of the sovereign power of the states.

The constitutional question regarding slavery in the territories and, more specifically, the constitutionality of the Missouri Compromise, had two components. The first was perversely related to the initial question concerning Scott's eligibility for citizenship. If Scott was a slave, did not the Constitution make slaves "property" that could not be "taken" by the government without "just compensation"? In Taney's mind, blacks' natural inferiority, their exclusion from citizenship, and their status as property were all components of a single disability incorporated into the Constitution itself. In a letter written in 1858 attempting to defend his opinion, he insisted that the drafters of the United States Constitution "could not fairly be construed to embrace a description or class of persons, whom they regarded as inferior and subordinate to the white race, and, in the order of nature, made subject to their domination and will, and [whom] they were accustomed to buy and sell like any other property."[45]

The second aspect of the question of the constitutionality of the Missouri Compromise lay at the core of the structural problem that has plagued, and continues to plague, the American Union. Specifically, what is the power of the national government vis-à-vis the states. Or, stated another way, do the states have rights that the Supreme Court is obliged to protect? In the *Dred Scott* case, this second component was presented as the question whether Congress had the power to prohibit slavery in the territories and in the newly created states—or, more succinctly put, was the Missouri Compromise constitutional?

The Fifth Amendment of the Constitution provides that the government shall not "take" private property without just compensation. If Congress takes your house to build a road, or your livestock to feed the poor, it must pay a fair price for those items. But can a person be property such that granting him his freedom constitutes a "taking" of property from his "owner"? Many people argued at the time that slaves, although "owned," were not property in any conventional sense. Taney, however, could find no legal justification for making the distinction. His source, he said, was the Constitution itself. "And if the constitution recognizes the right of property of the master in a slave, and makes no distinction between that description of property and other property owned by a citizen, no tribunal . . . has a right to draw such a distinction, or deny to it the benefit of the provisions and guarantees which have been provided for the protection of private property against the encroachments of the government."[46] Property was property, and in all of its manifestations was protected against government interference by the guarantee of due process of law.

The framers, however, had never used the words *slave* and *slavery* and thus had not explicitly expressed their views on the subject. Indeed, on this subject, the Constitution is a marvel of slanted prose and avoidance. But Taney sliced through the diplomatic double-talk and concluded that the Constitution guaranteed the right of property in a slave. "The right to traffic in it, like an ordinary article of merchandise and property, was guaranteed to the citizens of the United States, in every State that might desire it, for twenty years."[47] Moreover, he wrote, "the government in express terms is pledged to protect it in all future time, if the slave escapes from his owner."[48] Finally, Taney found, what the Constitution did *not* say was possibly as important as what it did say. "And no word can be found in the constitution which gives congress a greater power over slave property, or which entitles property of that kind to less protection than property of any other description."[49]

In the end, the Civil War was about sovereign power and the structural makeup of the country. Would it be *the* United States, or *these* United States? At the start, the Federalists and Anti-Federalists had disagreed strenuously over the question of state sovereignty and national supremacy. This issue had separated the Federalist Party of Washington, Adams, and Hamilton from the Jeffersonian Republicans. John Marshall had weighed in on the issue time and again, most famously in *McCulloch v. Maryland* and the National Bank. The states throughout the first half of the nineteenth century would ground their right to enslave blacks on this principle. In the Missouri Compromise, Congress asserted its power over the slave question, and southerners bitterly opposed it. When the Civil War came, the southern states organized their country in the form they believed the original Constitution had already guaranteed *these* United States. They would become the *Confederacy,* the concrete realization of much of the Anti-Federalist agenda. The North would fight for the *Union,* their vision of the Constitution's meaning. In *Dred Scott,* the Supreme Court threw its weight behind the South's interpretation of the Constitution and thereby did much to trigger a martial settlement of the question, a settlement that began with a cannon shot in South Carolina.

The Missouri Compromise had prohibited slavery above 36°30' north latitude. Dred Scott's attorneys had claimed that the Constitution had expressly provided Congress with the power to "dispose of and make all needful Rules and Regulations respecting the Territory or other Property belonging to the United States." Despite the seeming relevance of this provision, Taney ruled that it did not apply. He said, "That provision has no bearing on the present controversy, and the power there given, whatever it may be, is confined, and was intended to be confined, to the territory which at that time belonged to, or was claimed by the United States, and was within their boundaries as settled by the treaty with Great

Britain, and can have no influence upon a territory afterwards acquired from a foreign government."[50] He concluded summarily, "It was a special provision for a known and particular territory, and to meet a present emergency, and nothing more."

This interpretation of the Constitution makes sense only if we can assume the founders never considered the possibility of acquiring more territory. Although undoubtedly some held this view at the start, it was not the prevailing view. Americans, from the beginning, fully expected to expand across the continent. Even Jefferson, who unilaterally purchased the Louisiana Territory from France, but who similarly believed in strict construction of the Constitution and a restricted national government, never doubted the Congress's power over newly acquired territories. Territorial expansion was too obviously a part of the American mandate to believe otherwise. And the Constitution specifically provided for Congress "to make all needful Rules and Regulations" respecting these lands.

Taney, it should be emphasized, never went so far as to assert that Congress did not have any power to acquire new territories. He admitted that this power was "plainly given" by the Constitution. But Congress's power was merely administrative, until such time that the territory became a state. From that time forward, the state as sovereign could define its own fate. Moreover, Taney relied on his findings that slaves were property and that the Bill of Rights protected the owners' right not to be deprived of property without due process. He wrote that an "Act of Congress which deprives a citizen of the United States of his liberty or property, merely because he came himself or brought his property into a particular Territory of the United States, and who had committed no offence against the laws, could hardly be dignified with the name due process of law."[51]

In his dissent, Justice Curtis made the point that eight times prior to 1848 Congress had excluded slavery from newly acquired territories and on six occasions it had permitted slavery. These actions were carried out by men who had either participated in or lived through the founding of the nation. Using Taney's own method of querying the original understanding, Curtis stated, "If the practical construction of the Constitution contemporaneously with its going into effect, by men intimately acquainted with its history from their personal participation in framing and adopting it, and continued by them through a long series of acts of the gravest importance, be entitled to weight in the judicial mind on a question of construction, it would seem to be difficult to resist the force of the acts above averted to."[52] Curtis boldly hoisted Taney on his own petard. Proponents of a judicial philosophy that relies on the beliefs and practices of the past cannot pick and choose only those traditions to their liking. This is a perverted sort of conservatism, one that truly does not endeavor to preserve the status quo, but instead strives to define and impose new conditions under the guise of honoring posterity.

The immediate aftermath of *Dred Scott* was the proverbial calm before the storm. Scott himself displayed little interest in the case or its outcome and the decision ordering him a slave paradoxically led to his freedom. Congressman Chaffee assigned Scott and his family to Taylor Blow, who emancipated him on May 26, 1857. He was now famous. Then, as is true still, fame allowed him certain dubious comforts. Theron Barnum's Hotel in St. Louis made an exhibition out of him, and supported him for the short remainder of his life. Scott died on September 17, 1858, the seventy-first anniversary of the Constitution.

In general, and not surprisingly, abolitionists led the initial rally cry against the decision. It was, they proclaimed, "a covenant with death and an agreement with hell."[53] The *New York Tribune* announced that "the long trumpeted decision . . . is entitled to just so much moral weight as would be the judgment of a majority of those congregated in any Washington bar-room."[54] A more stylish damnation was provided by the *Independent,* Henry Ward Beecher's abolitionist paper. Reverend Beecher was the silver-tongued orator whose sister Harriet had written *Uncle Tom's Cabin.* His paper called Taney's opinion a "concatenation of corrupt opinions and falsehoods," adding that it "out-Herods Herod himself. . . . If the people obey this decision, they disobey God."[55]

As the election campaigns of 1858 and, especially, 1860 approached, the clamor against the opinion, the Court, and, most vehemently, Taney became deafening. According to Samuel Tyler, Taney's friend and first biographer, "The chief question involved in the presidential election of 1860 was, whether the decision of the Supreme Court in the *Dred Scott* case was to stand or not as the true construction of the Constitution of the United States."[56] Much of the criticism was directed at the infamy of the decision. Charles Sumner said that Taney's opinion "must forever stand forth among the inhumanities of this generation." The Court, he said, had "erred infinitely and wretchedly."[57] Sumner believed, and history would ratify, that the *Dred Scott* decision was "the most thoroughly

perverse and reprehensible in judicial history." It was, he said, "an insult
to conscience, to reason, and to truth."[58] Abraham Lincoln, the newly
elected president, made clear his disdain for the decision and, in his inau-
gural address, his intention to ignore it:

> The candid citizen must confess that if the policy of the Government, upon
> vital questions affecting the whole people, is to be irrevocably fixed by
> decision of the Supreme Court, the instant they are made in ordinary lit-
> igation between parties in personal actions the people will have ceased to
> be their own rulers, having to that extent practically resigned their Gov-
> ernment into the hands of that eminent tribunal.[59]

The most scandalous attack would come from William H. Seward,
the senator from New York. Seward sought the Republican nomination
in the election of 1860 and, after he lost, he campaigned faithfully for
Abraham Lincoln. Lincoln rewarded him by making him secretary of
state. In 1858, however, on the Senate floor, Seward alleged that Taney
had entered into a conspiracy with President James Buchanan, a plod-
ding, unimaginative failure as a president who strongly sympathized with
the South.

Of Buchanan, such a conspiracy was entirely believable. And, indeed,
he had pressured northern justice Robert Grier of Pennsylvania to join
the majority so that the decision would not appear to be a southern-led
insurrection. Seward asserted that Taney, too, had been corrupt, and
made a deal with Buchanan in rushed whispers on the day of the president's inauguration. The people, Seward said, were "unaware of the
import of the whisperings carried on between the President and the
Chief Justice, and imbued with reveration for both, filled the avenues
and gardens as far away as the eye could reach. The President addressed
them in words as bland as those which the worst of all the Roman
Emperors pronounced when he assumed the purple." Buchanan told the
assembled crowd that, as regards the *Dred Scott* case, he "pledged his
submission to it as authoritative and final." On that day, Seward added,
"the judges, without even exchanging their silken robes for courtiers'
gowns paid their salutations to the President in the Executive Palace."
He concluded, "Doubtless the President received them as graciously as
did Charles I the judges who, at his instance, subverted the statutes of
English liberty."[60]

Before the *Dred Scott* decision, the Supreme Court, along with its chief justice, Roger Taney, each enjoyed reputations as the ballast that steadied the ship of state. The storm surrounding the case swamped both their reputations. Taney went from having "one of the most distinguished careers in American annals," to being "most remembered next to Pontius Pilate, perhaps the worst that ever occupied the seat of judgment."[61] He had, said the *Atlantic Monthly* soon after his death, "denied the settled truths of science." His opinion had "slandered the memory of the founders of the government and framers of the Declaration." As for the Court itself, the *Dred Scott* case was announced just a little more than fifty years after John Marshall had steered that eminent tribunal to the center of constitutional democracy in *Marbury v. Madison*. In the decades after *Marbury*, it had gained the deep respect of the nation as a whole. Attorney General Caleb Cushing told the Court on the day of Buchanan's inauguration, "You are the incarnate mind of the political body of our nation." Their exalted tribunal, he told them, was "the pivot, upon which the right of all—government and people alike—turn: or rather, you are the central light of constitutional wisdom, around which they perpetually revolve."[62] The Court, and especially its chief justice, believed it. It was this hubris that led the justices to "thrust themselves forward to sit as umpires in a quarrel of parties and factions."[63] The Court would need nearly half a century to recover from this self-inflicted wound.

Roger Taney would never recover. "There was," said Mrs. John A. Logan, "no sadder figure to be seen in Washington during the years of the Civil War than that of the aged Chief Justice. . . . He had outlived his epoch, and was shunned and hated by the men of the new time of storm and struggle."[64]

4

THE ROOTS OF MODERNITY:
Holmes, Brandeis, and the New Legal Science

For the rational study of the law, the black-letter man may be the man of the present, but the man of the future is the man of statistics and the master of economics.

—OLIVER WENDELL HOLMES

Oliver Wendell Holmes Jr. turned sixteen one day after Roger Taney announced the decision in *Dred Scott v. Sandford.* He would leave for Harvard College that same year. Louis Dembitz Brandeis was just four months old when the fateful ruling was handed down, but his earliest memories would be of one of the consequences of that decision—Union troops encamped near his home in Louisville, Kentucky. Holmes fought three long years in that war. The two men were a generation apart, a separation made deeper by the revolutionary changes in American society wrought by the war. Yet their destinies, and the fate of American law, were inextricably bound. Many years later, when they served together on the Supreme Court, Holmes and Brandeis lived just a block apart. These two fountainheads of modern law regularly walked together to and from the Court. They became nearly inseparable. Each deeply admired the other professionally and intellectually, and they shared great mutual affection. In 1924, Holmes described their walks in a letter to Felix Frankfurter, a close friend of both men and a future justice himself. Holmes wrote that "Brandeis is in good shape." Holmes was eighty-three and Brandeis sixty-eight. Holmes added that Brandeis "insists on coming to my door and I express fears to trust him to get back across the street."[1] Holmes would live another eleven years and Brandeis another seventeen.

And although they arrived by very different paths, each man, and each in his own manner, was devoted to science and empiricism, and they both imbued the law with modern notions of the scientific method. Holmes and Brandeis were the first modern lawyers.

When Holmes was in grade school, his teacher wrote on his report card that he "talks too much." A Holmes biographer reports that in college, he "was tall and very thin, not at all athletic, but cheerful, talkative, and self-confident to the point of arrogance, a young man devoted to words, talking when he was not reading."[2] These traits, and particularly his devotion to words and his arrogance, would endure throughout his lifetime. His father had become famous partly for his facility with words and his conversational repartee. Dr. Oliver Wendell Holmes Sr. had dabbled first in the law and eventually chose medicine. Although he wrote a seminal article on germ theory, joined the Harvard Medical School faculty, and later was the school's dean, he was never entirely comfortable as a physician. Dr. Holmes most fervently loved words, however, especially in conversation, and he gained his greatest fame with his enormously popular *Autocrat of the Breakfast Table* in 1857.

The son's arrogance may have been partly inherited from his father, and partly a defensive reaction to his father's teasing and constant verbal challenges. The doctor was indeed an autocrat at the Holmes's table, and his son was his not always loyal subject. His father regularly commented on Holmes's appearance and, in particular, his long thin neck. "The stately neck is manhood's manliest part," the doctor informed him, "it takes the lifeblood freshest from the heart." Thick necks, the doctor said, were a mark of distinction, especially in lawyers. "You remember what they tell of William Pinkney, the great pleader: how in his eloquent paroxysms the veins of his neck would swell and his face flush and his eyes glitter, until he seemed on the edge of apoplexy."[3] Despite his father's ungenerous statements, it was generally conceded that Holmes was "exceptionally attractive." He had the good fortune to grow ever more so as he aged. He had piercing blue-gray eyes, a prominent mustache, and a countenance that in time reflected the soldier and the jurist, the two roles that formed his life.

Holmes did well academically at the not yet competitive Harvard College, though not extraordinarily so. He was twice elected class poet, served as secretary to the Hasty Pudding Club, and was one of three editors for the *Harvard Magazine*.[4] Coming from a famous family, Holmes was surrounded from the start by the men of genius who resided in the Boston area. This was Brahmin society at its historical height. Dr. Holmes invented the term to describe descendants of colonial governors, "the harmless, inoffensive, untitled aristocracy" of New England. It was a tribe defined not by money—at least not originally—but by intellect. As a group, they were intellectually broad-minded, but culturally narrow-minded. Growing up, Holmes came to know such local luminaries as William Ticknor, James Fields, William Prescott, James Russell Lowell, Henry Wadsworth Longfellow, and Ralph Waldo Emerson, whom he called Uncle Waldo.

Emerson was a particularly influential force in Holmes's life. Holmes was naturally drawn to the literary arts, but his allegiances were torn between poetry and philosophy. He thought he had to choose between them. "Emerson was a poet," Holmes said, "and from my point of view, the poet and philosopher are two opposite poles of the conscious life."[5] Later, he would primarily choose the philosopher's life, as lived through the law. Yet he also endeavored, mostly successfully, to bring the poet's sensibilities to his legal writings. Emerson was instrumental in Holmes's intellectual development, a debt Holmes never forgot. "I saw him on the other side of the street and ran over and said to him: 'If I ever do anything, I shall owe a great deal of it to you,' which was true. He was one of those who set one on fire."[6]

Before he had the opportunity to find his voice in either poetry or philosophy, Holmes was swept up in the swirl and storm of war. His experiences in the Civil War would greatly influence and darken his later beliefs and would supply him with analogies and metaphors to fill a long lifetime's worth of speeches. From the very start, Holmes declared, he and his friends "believed in the principle that the Union is indissoluble." He added that "many of us, at least, also believed the conflict was inevitable, and that slavery had lasted long enough."[7]

During his three-year enlistment, Holmes experienced all of the drudgery, intensity, excitement, honor, brutality, and, ultimately, senseless cruelty of war. He was wounded three times, with the first coming at the Battle of Ball's Bluff. He was hit in the chest. Although serious, the wound was not life-threatening. He returned to Massachusetts to convalesce, where he received a hero's welcome due to the considerable attention the battle had received locally. His father described the scene: "Wendell is a great pet in his character of young hero with wounds in the heart, and receives visits *en grand seigneur*. I envy my white Othello, with a semicircle of young Desdemonas about him listening to the often told story which they will have over again."[8] *Harper's Weekly* proudly noted Holmes's wound:

> In the front of the fearful fire, with no means of retreat, with every chance against them, these young men stood serene, each man a hero. . . . Lieutenant Holmes, said the first dispatch, "wounded in the breast"; not in the back; no, not in the back. In the breast is Massachusetts wounded, if she is struck. Forward she falls, if she falls dead.[9]

Holmes suffered his second wound in the battle at Antietam Creek, this time in the back of the neck. His regiment, the Twentieth, had just entered the battle when the Confederates attacked from the flank, resulting in the order to retreat "double-quick." The bullet traveled clear through, leaving a gaping hole but without hitting any vital parts. Holmes later said that he recalled "that *Harper's Weekly* was flamboyant on my first wound at Ball's Bluff." He thought to himself, though, that "this time I am hit in the back, and bolting as fast as I can—and it's all right—but not so good for the newspapers."[10] Holmes again returned home to recover.

Holmes's third war injury was suffered near Fredericksburg, where he was wounded in the heel of his foot from artillery shells filled with shot that exploded high in the air.[11] This least conspicuous wound turned out to be the most vexatious. It took seven months to mend, though some of this time was devoted to regaining his psychological health. By this time, he had had enough of war, and even registered regret in not losing his foot, which would have exempted him from the remainder of his enlistment. He had suffered terribly, both in his injuries and in the travails of the military campaigns. When he returned to the war, he was able to secure a staff position. Mercifully away from the front lines, it was a slightly more tolerable form of hell, though the battlefield remained a very dangerous place. He wrote his mother shortly after the attack on Richmond that "these nearly two weeks have contained all of fatigue & horror that war can furnish . . . nearly every Regimental officer I knew or cared for is dead or wounded." In July 1864, he announced that his service was over. "I have made up my mind to stay on the staff if possible till the end of the campaign & then if I am still alive, I shall resign."[12] By late July he was home in Boston.

Holmes now faced his future. Although he considered a career in medicine, and still yearned to be a poet or philosopher, he soon decided on the more practical course of law. In October 1864, he joined the entering class at the Harvard Law School. Throughout his time there, the specter of the war loomed about him, and he thought he might yet have to return the next spring. Lincoln was reelected president that November and the war dragged on. Holmes devoted himself to his studies and mainly attended the dry technical lectures that were then the stuff of legal education. Lawyers in the generation before had not even attended school, and instead apprenticed with a learned member of the bar. The law school began as a sort of formalized version of the old practice. The Harvard faculty consisted of only three professors—Joel Parker, Emory Washburne, and Theophilus Parsons—all of whom had active practices outside the academy. They did not give examinations and were, in effect, merely masters who imparted unto their classes of apprentices the basic skills of the law.

The law fitted Holmes perfectly. He found in it a discipline that would permit him to join philosophy and poetry. It was a subject that ignited his passion and tested his intellect. "What a profession the law is!" he exclaimed. "What other gives such scope to realize the spontaneous energy of one's soul? In what other does one plunge so deep in the stream of life—so share its passions, its battles, its despair, its triumphs?"[13]

After law school, Holmes entered practice and simultaneously ventured into the incipient world of legal scholarship. His close friends John Gray and John Ropes founded the *American Law Review* and Holmes contributed essays, book reviews, and case comments, mostly written after long days of handling a variety of legal matters. He would later become the *Review*'s editor. He wrote on a wide variety of subjects. In one of his early pieces, Holmes reviewed Alfred Swain Taylor's *Manual of Medical Jurisprudence*. He criticized the author for attempting to combine law and medicine in one volume, thinking it would be of practical use to neither profession. "We may express a doubt whether doctors would regard a work on 'medical jurisprudence' as a sufficient handbook of science; and we are very confident that few lawyers would feel strongly bound by its opinions on a point of law."[14] Lawyers, Holmes explained, "want to know under what circumstances the courts have admitted [a medical] defense, [such as insanity] in a criminal action." The law should be contained in law books and medicine in medical texts, and the two professions, he believed, need not be troubled with the details of the other. Yet Holmes remained deeply interested in science and at this time believed that law itself might be put on a scientific footing. He also never doubted the value of borrowing scientific concepts to help inform the law, however much he doubted early on that law and science might share space in the same treatise.

Holmes cherished the intellectual milieu of Brahmin society, and increasingly sought ways to bathe in it. Although short-lived, a highly influential meeting of great minds occurred in the formation of The Metaphysical Club, a group that included Holmes, William James, and Charles Sanders Pierce.[15] This interdisciplinary representation of law, psychology, and mathematics met regularly for a brief time to discuss a variety of intellectual subjects. High on their agenda were issues surrounding the emerging new biology of Charles Darwin's *Origin of Species*. Darwin, together with two closely parallel lines of scientific thought, those of Thomas Malthus and Herbert Spencer, would greatly influence Holmes's constitutional views.

Malthus, Spencer, and Darwin all contributed to the single most important idea of the nineteenth century: evolution. Thomas Robert Malthus, writing in the early part of the century, published two major studies of population dynamics. He theorized that human populations naturally expand in a geometrical progression, while food supplies only increase arithmetically. Inevitably, then, human population growth must be, and would be, checked in a variety of possible ways, ranging from war and famine to moral or other restraints on the birthrate. The disparity between population growth and available food to feed the ever-expanding number of mouths would lead to "a struggle for existence"—a term used by Malthus. Both Charles Darwin and his fellow biologist Alfred Russel Wallace explicitly acknowledged their indebtedness to Malthus's description of the inexorable fight for survival in a world of finite resources.

Herbert Spencer similarly anticipated much of the evolutionary framework later to be developed so exquisitely by Darwin. Spencer published his first book, *Social Statics*, in 1851, eight years before *Origin of Species*. Spencer's conception of evolution had strong Lamarckian tendencies. It was Chevalier de Lamarck who first articulated a general theory of evolution, writing at the end of the eighteenth and first part of the nineteenth centuries. Influenced by the theory of the great Chain of Being, Lamarck had sought to explain the crooked lines of the hierarchical flowchart that led from the lowest forms of life to the highest— man. Perfection would demand a smooth and straight ordering, yet nature evidenced a rough, broken tangle of species. Life manifested itself not as a ladder, with each rung distinctly demarcated, but as a tree with branches interlaced and twisted and reaching out in many directions. This seeming disorder, Lamarck thought, could be explained if species adapted to their changing environments. Lamarck's conception differed from Darwin's in that he believed that adaptations developed during an animal's life were handed down to its progeny. Darwin discovered the dynamic of natural selection, whereby subsequent generations manifested adaptive designs because they were descendants of those who had struggled and survived long enough to reproduce in the generations before. For Darwin, natural advantages were inherited by chance and circumstance, with no benevolent hand directing evolution's course. Lamarck's conception was more modest, since animals evolved merely to adapt to environments that changed within a certain range. Where Lamarck believed animals could adapt within certain set parameters, Darwin found that, over generations, animals could evolve, completely breaking the preexisting molds. Nonetheless, Darwin heralded Lamarck's contribution, for he was the first to challenge the received wisdom that organic life was unalterable. Lamarck "first did the eminent service," Darwin said, "by arousing attention to the probability of all change in the organic world being the result of law, and not of miraculous interposition."

When Darwin's work was published in 1859, Spencer was so excited by it that he started work on a series of volumes that would apply the theory of evolution to all the sciences. Spencer thought evolution provided the heroic unification to the science-philosophy dichotomy. Individually, he believed, neither science nor philosophy could solve the complete riddle of life's meaning. Science was limited in that it gathered empirical experience into subject-matter compartments without generating theory that transcended those categories. Philosophy, which offered universal theories, did not systematically incorporate the empirical world into its structure or vision. Evolution offered a unifying principle that would allow Spencer, or so he thought, to work out the first truly scientifically informed universal philosophic theory. He worked on this project for over thirty years and produced volumes on metaphysics, biology, psychology, sociology, and ethics. Although in the end he did not succeed, Spencer was enormously influential as well as wildly popular in his time. His fame has not endured, partly due to subsequent philosophers' criticisms and partly because of the very negative associations that became attached to others' efforts to apply evolutionary theory to human populations in the century that followed him.

Holmes's experience in the war deeply affected his view of the struggle that inhered in the natural order. Darwin, Malthus, and Spencer contributed considerable intellectual content to his experiences. Evolutionary theory painted a gloomy, cynical picture, one that fully accorded with the blood and despair of Holmes's battlefield experience. There was no ultimate end to which the struggle for existence worked. Holmes once said, "My bet is that we have not the kind of cosmic importance that the parsons and philosophers teach. I doubt if a shudder would go through the spheres if the whole ant heap were kerosened."[16] Some scholars, including Spencer, drew ethical lessons for structuring society from the presumed "morals" of nature. In contrast, for Holmes, evolution, and the struggle for existence it embodied, beheld a world bereft of ethical values, and even of moral goodness. Spencer's "evolutionary ethics" would later gain a foothold in constitutional cases, one that Holmes tried repeatedly to dislodge throughout his tenure on the Court. Evolutionary theory left Holmes fatalistic about the state of, and the prospects for, society. He wrote Harold Laski in 1927: "You respect the rights of man—I don't, except those things a given crowd will fight for—which vary from religion to the price of a glass of beer."[17] Holmes was thus modern also in his nihilism.

Holmes's biological determinism unfolded in a judicial opinion many years later when, in a 1927 case, the Court upheld a Virginia law providing for the sterilization of mental defectives. In *Buck v. Bell*,[18] Holmes wrote fervidly for the Court, employing language that would echo with ignominy. The challenge came from Carrie Buck, a resident of a mental health facility in Virginia whose mother was institutionalized and whose daughter was described as "not quite normal." The sterilization law was a capstone of the eugenics movement. In the early part of the twentieth century, eugenic reform—through voluntary birth control and involuntary but humane sterilization programs—was considered an enlightened way to remove the feeble-minded and mentally ill from the population. Years later, after the experience with Hitler's hauntingly similar statutes, eugenic reform came to be seen as repressive or worse. But in 1927 eugenics was part of the political mainstream, and Holmes not only believed that the Court should defer to the legislative will, but supported the statute with enthusiasm. He wrote infamously:

We have seen more than once that the public welfare may call upon the best citizens for their lives. It would be strange if it could not call upon those who already sap the strength of the State for these lesser sacrifices, often not felt to be such by those concerned, in order to prevent our being swamped with incompetence. It is better for all the world, if instead of waiting to execute degenerate offspring for crime, or to let them starve for their imbecility, society can prevent those who are manifestly unfit from continuing their kind. The principle that sustains compulsory vaccination is broad enough to cover cutting the Fallopian tubes. . . . Three generations of imbeciles are enough.

After the decision, Holmes wrote Laski that he felt *Buck v. Bell* "was getting near to the first principle of real reform."[19] It was a widely shared sentiment. Ironically, and tragically, close examination of the evidence indicates that Carrie Buck was not an "imbecile." It was doubtful that her mother was either, and her daughter Vivian, who died at eight, did well enough in her two years of schooling to earn a spot on the "Honor Roll."[20]

Holmes's first major entrée into legal scholarship came at the invitation of one of the partners at his firm, James B. Thayer, just as Holmes started to become restless and disenchanted with law practice. Thayer offered him the opportunity to update the venerable work of James Kent's *Commentaries on American Law*. Kent had approached Thayer, asking him to assume the task. Kent's *Commentaries* were badly in need of revision, but the demands of practice were forbidding, so Thayer needed a "laboring oar." Holmes seized the assignment with enthusiasm. When it was done, in 1873, Holmes displayed a fair degree of arrogance toward Thayer and was greatly reluctant to share credit. The title page and preface bore Holmes's name alone. Only in the acknowledgments did Holmes mention Thayer, "upon whom has rested the whole responsibility for my work to the owners of the copyright," and who has "read all that I have written, and . . . given it the great benefit of his scholarly and intelligent criticism." Holmes failed to mention James Kent entirely. While Holmes had indeed done all of the work, his less than selfless advertising of that fact greatly annoyed Kent and Thayer. Kent had expected Thayer's name to appear on the title page, and Thayer later commented that Holmes's actions were "wanting sadly in the noblest region of human character—selfish, vain, thoughtless of others."[21]

Kent's *Commentaries,* even under Holmes's nimble pen, remained a dry and laborious treatise that interminably cataloged extant case law. The education he received in editing this voluminous compendium of cases, however, proved priceless. He began writing a series of essays exploring a host of subjects, most associated with the common law. In areas such as contracts, property, and the law of "trespass and negligence" (i.e., torts), he began a systematic study of the law. His analysis was based consciously on the methodology of the natural sciences and, in particular, biology. General legal principles were the "genus" of the law, he thought, and their specific applications were tantamount to "classes" and "species" of legal doctrine. His work led to an invitation to give the Lowell Lectures, a series of public lectures sponsored by the eponymous institute founded by the textile magnate John Lowell Jr. in 1836. Holmes described the methodology he was working out over the two decades preceding the lectures in the following way:

> No one will ever have a truly philosophic mastery over the law who does not habitually consider the forces outside of it which have made it what it is. More than that, he must remember that as it embodies the story of a nation's development over centuries, the law finds its philosophy not in self-consistency, which it must always fail in so long as it continues to grow, but in history and the nature of human needs.[22]

Holmes was preparing his assault on the main intellectual theme of the nineteenth century, legal formalism. Formalism privileged logic over experience. Formalism was particularly identified with Christopher Columbus Langdell, the great Harvard Law School dean and the progenitor of the case method of teaching law—the method still used today. In a review of Langdell's *Law of Contracts,* Holmes described him—not meaning to be complimentary—in this way: "He is, perhaps, the greatest living legal theologian . . . so entirely is he interested in the formal connexion of things, or logic, as distinguished from the feelings which make the content of logic, and which have actually shaped the substance of the law."[23] Formalism in Holmes's view, was a theology that gained adherents not through real-world demonstrations, but through the insistent preachings of a believing priesthood to a congregation of the faithful.

Holmes, in contrast, sought to move "history and the nature of human needs" to the forefront. The law could not be discerned through formal logic alone, Holmes maintained, but had to be discovered by examining what judges did and what circumstances led them to those actions. Law

was not self-contained or finite, merely locked in syllogistic chains waiting to be freed by rigid application of the formal logic of the lawyerly
mind. It was the product of evolutionary processes and could not be
understood without appeal to the historical and contemporary circumstances in which it once lived and now breathes.

Holmes's conception of law never fully broke away from the
nineteenth-century view that believed that law, itself, could be a worthy
subject of science. Cases, for Holmes, were like Darwin's finches arrayed
over the Galápagos Islands. To be understood, cases needed to be
observed, dissected, and classified. Langdell also wished to study law as
a science, and this belief underlay his case method of teaching. Holmes
differed from Langdell, however, in that he believed laws, like animals,
are deeply affected by their environments and surrounding circumstances. Langdell studied laws in the laboratory, while Holmes went
into the field to see them behave in their natural habitats. Indeed,
Holmes expected, at least early in his career, that natural laws would
eventually be expounded to explain legal behavior. Like evolution, these
laws would be descriptive; they would not dictate what ought to be,
only what is and has been. But, also like evolution, once man understood the mechanism, he could take control of his own fate and mold
law and man into an ideal form. Eugenic principles could be applied to
both man and law.

Holmes's Lowell Lectures were developed into a book—*The Common
Law*—that would change the course of legal thought. Most immediately,
Holmes was immensely proud that the book arrived five days before his
fortieth birthday. He had long considered it a mark of success—or, perhaps, avoidance of failure—to publish a book before that age. The following weekend he and his wife, Fanny, went to his farm where they
celebrated with a bottle of champagne. He kept the bottle's cork in his
desk drawer for the rest of his life.[24]

In the opening paragraph of *The Common Law*, Holmes explained
that he sought to present a general view of the subject. He then
announced unambiguously his break with legal formalism. In order to
accomplish the task of understanding the common law, he explained,
"other tools are needed besides logic." Logical consistency, he maintained, was only a part of the analysis; it could not be all. He then wrote
the often-quoted line that would become the mantra of modern law:
"The life of the law has not been logic: it has been experience." He
elaborated:

The felt necessities of the time, the prevalent moral and political theories, intuitions of public policy, avowed or unconscious, even the prejudices which judges share with their fellow men, have had a good deal more to do than the syllogism in determining the rules by which men should be governed. . . . The substance of the law at any given time pretty nearly corresponds, so far as it goes, with what is then understood to be convenient; but its form and machine, and the degree to which it is able to work out desired results, depends very much upon its past.[25]

Holmes rejected the geometry model of law, and substituted an anthropological and evolutionary model in its place. Law was not static, he believed, but obeyed particular principles of change.

Where Holmes's great work *The Common Law* stands in the intellectual pantheon of the law is a subject of some debate. A consensus developed late in Holmes's lifetime, one that remains mostly prevalent today, that *The Common Law* stands alone at the top. However, many critics make the point that Holmes's writings still remained deeply embedded in formalism and that his great work and surrounding scholarship did not fully implement or even anticipate the twentieth century's two major intellectual movements in the law: sociological jurisprudence and legal realism. While both of these schools of thought were antiformalistic and strongly empirically based—two of Holmes's main themes—the real revolution, according to critics, was orchestrated and carried to fruition by his successors, men like Louis Brandeis, Roscoe Pound, and Karl Llewellyn.

While these revisionist criticisms are essentially accurate, they are pertinent only to a point. Holmes himself explicitly recognized the role of logic or formalism in legal discourse and rule formation. He never advocated, or thought prudent or necessary, the abandonment of sound logical reasoning. He was the first modernist, not the first postmodernist. Logic was a necessary component of legal reasoning, but empiricism was the principal tool of the law's development. He aimed to free the law from the archaic forms of the past. He complained, "As it is now, we rely upon tradition, or vague sentiment, or the fact that we never thought of any other way of doing things, as our only warrant for rules which we enforce with as much confidence as if they embodied revealed wisdom." Holmes believed that an enduring history alone was not enough to sustain a law. "An ideal system of law," he maintained, "should draw its postulates and its legislative justification from science."[26]

It is also true that *The Common Law* is often quoted but rarely read.

It has been attributed with the qualities of modernist jurisprudence, but, critics contend, did not bring that revolution about. But this might be said of many revolutionary tracts. Charles Darwin, Albert Einstein, and James Joyce might all be accused of having fired the first shot in revolutions that were eventually taken from their hands. Holmes was, as were these others, a bridge between the old regime and the new order. As the bridge between formalism and what would come to be called realism, he had footings on both sides of the divide. Revolutions typically reside in one, or a few, great ideas. In this way, Holmes's *The Common Law* was indeed revolutionary, but few revolutions are the work of one person. They require apostles to spread the word, if the word is to become gospel.

Holmes continued developing his ideas in his subsequent work, including two notable articles, "The Path of the Law" and "Law in Science and Science in Law." In "The Path of the Law," Holmes joined his ideas of evolutionary struggle with the empirical aspects of measuring real law formation. He again criticized Langdell's formalist approach for ignoring the world beyond the ink of the printed page. Law was a practical discipline, in which "People want to know under what circumstances and how far they will run the risk of coming against what is so much stronger than themselves, and hence it becomes a business to find out when this danger is to be feared." The lawyer's job, Holmes argued, "is prediction, the prediction of the incidence of the public force through the instrumentality of the courts."[27] In "Law in Science and Science in Law," he described the methodology of the lawyer who is also "the man of science." He stated, "We must think things not words, or at least we must constantly translate our words into the facts for which they stand, if we are to keep to the real and the true." Only by considering the factual ends or objectives sought, and the means by which they might be accomplished, could a law be fashioned or evaluated. "Inasmuch as the real justification of a rule of law . . . is that it helps to bring about a social end which we desire," Holmes wrote, "it is no less necessary that those who make and develop the law should have those ends articulately in their minds." Still, Holmes did not believe that science would or could subsume traditional legal analysis, or that law would ever fully conform to scientific rigor. "Very likely it may be that with all the help that statistics . . . can bring us," Holmes pointed out, "there will never be a commonwealth in which science is everywhere supreme. But it is an ideal, and without ideals what is life worth?"[28]

As a result of his growing scholarly reputation, and excellent familial connections, Holmes was asked to join the faculty of the Harvard Law School. He was somewhat torn, having a strong predilection for scholarship, but holding out hope that he might yet be made a judge. He decided to accept the offer pending funding of the position and subject to the condition that he was free to leave if offered a judgeship. After funding was secured in the spring of 1882, Holmes formally joined the faculty and began teaching that fall semester.

Before the semester ended, however, Holmes was offered a seat on the highest court in Massachusetts, the state's Supreme Judicial Court. Holmes quickly accepted, but in so doing effected his departure from Harvard ungracefully. The opening on the court had come near the end of Governor John D. Long's term and there was great pressure on Holmes to accept the position immediately. As a result, he did not consult with or even inform officials at Harvard, including its president, Charles William Eliot. They learned about the appointment from the newspapers. Only after many years did Eliot forgive him. For Holmes it was a dream realized. His friends shared his excitement and celebrated his good fortune. Louis Brandeis, who lectured at Harvard at the time, sent Holmes a note of congratulations: "As one of the bar I rejoice. As part of the Law School I mourn. As your friend I congratulate you."[29]

On the Massachusetts Court, Holmes relished the incessant march of common law cases and assumed more than his share of the writing burden, but the work was tedious and not of transcending importance. Holmes described it as "trifling and transitory."[30] During this time, Holmes developed some melancholy over his place in the intellectual milieu of his times. The court offered few challenges, and friends, such as William James, were receiving accolades that Holmes hungered after. He had yet to garner the recognition he thought was due. Around this time he decided to collect his speeches into book form, a decision indicating reflection on a life lived rather than expectations of more to come. The book numbered only fifty pages, and Holmes bought up most copies to send to friends and acquaintances. He sent a copy to Walt Whitman, whom he greatly admired. Whitman replied graciously: "When I came from the country yesterday, dear Judge Holmes, there greeted me that little white book with contents like the Puritan which it describes, . . . full of a high & mystical beauty."[31] Brandeis, too, received a copy, and replied encouragingly: "When the Lawyer's Bible comes to be made up—

the book of Holmes will be its Job, and your hymn of Praise will be the Te Deum of their service."[32]

Holmes believed that he inherited his " 'perverse' tendency to feel melancholy and unfulfilled in the midst of apparent success" from his mother.[33] Alexander Bickel, the great Yale Law School professor, offered a description of Holmes's yearning for public recognition at the time:

> Nearly thirty years after the publication of *The Common Law* and his first judicial appointment, the public hardly knew him. . . . [E]ven among his professional peers, the general acknowledgment of greatness was still to come for Holmes, and he himself felt its absence rather painfully. He was . . . almost all that he would be, lacking only the magnificence of very great age. But no one yet was writing that to know him was "to have had a revelation of the possibilities . . . of human personality." No one was yet regarding him as "a significant figure in the history of civilization and not merely a commanding American figure." And Benjamin Cardozo's later judgment of Holmes as "probably the greatest legal intellect in the history of the English-speaking judiciary" had not yet been rendered.[34]

Holmes's fortunes, however, were changing.

In 1901, Supreme Court Justice Horace Gray, a New Englander, was close to retirement and Holmes coveted his seat. William McKinley had just been reelected president, and the forty-three-year-old Theodore Roosevelt was his vice president. Although the opening on the Court was destined to be filled by someone from New England, McKinley preferred Alfred Hemenway to Holmes. Since Holmes was sixty, an advanced age for consideration to the High Court, his time seemed to have passed. Holmes once said that "a great man represents . . . a strategic point in the campaign of history [and that] part of his greatness consists in being there." Just as his moment seemed past, fate stepped in, in the form of Leon Czolgosz, an anarchist and presidential assassin. McKinley suffered for a week before succumbing. Roosevelt became the twenty-sixth president of the United States.

As is often true, the new president sought to fill the vacancy with a person of like mind on one particularly pressing issue of the day. For Roosevelt, the issue was tariffs and the integrity of the new American colonies of Puerto Rico and the Philippines. The justices were evenly divided on this issue and the new appointment would break the tie. Holmes had earlier made clear in a speech that he shared the president's position. This was enough for Roosevelt, and Holmes received the nomination.

Upon Holmes's appointment to the Court, Brandeis once again wrote to congratulate him. "I trust that years enough may be given you to make the deep impression which you can upon Federal Jurisprudence." Holmes responded with gratitude. "For many years you have, from time to time, at critical moments said things that have given me courage, which probably I remember better than you do. You do it again now, with the same effect and always with the same pleasure to me. I thank you."[35]

On the tariff issue, as well as many other Progressive issues Roosevelt held dear, Holmes would not disappoint. One historian described Progressivism as a broad and diverse "movement aimed at controlling corporations, rationalizing social and economic institutions, ameliorating the harsh consequences of industrialism, utilizing science and expert knowledge for democratic ends, and, in the name of the 'people,' taking control of government from political 'bosses' and 'special interests.' "[36] Although he was no Progressive, Holmes's judicial philosophy well served their program. On the Supreme Judicial Court of Massachusetts and now on the Supreme Court of the United States, Holmes religiously followed the principle we would today call "judicial restraint." Constitutional law, as Holmes described it, meant "the government of the living by the dead."[37] Therefore, too active an enforcement of the law—the dead hand of the past—stifled innovation and deprived the living of self-governance. "The present has a right to govern itself so far as it can."[38] Courts ordinarily should not stand in the way of legislative majorities, Holmes contended, whatever legislatures sought to accomplish.

In their efforts to check growing corporate power and its abuses, Progressives garnered many successes, especially in the state legislatures. The Court increasingly threatened these hard-won reforms. Learned Hand, then a young attorney in New York who would later become a renowned federal trial judge, stated that "Progressivism reflects a suspicion of courts."[39] Holmes shared this suspicion. However, his belief that the Court should defer to legislative majorities did not spring from agreement with the legislators' political objectives. Indeed, he did not share their political values in the least. Rather Holmes believed that as a manifestation of the Darwinian struggle, who should ultimately prevail in the legislature was less important than that the struggle should be allowed to take place. Holmes was cynical about the eventual outcome, but ardently believed that "the crowd" should have its say. "The fact is that legislation," Holmes observed, "is necessarily made a means by which a body having the power, puts burdens which are disagreeable to them on the shoulder of somebody else."

A majority of Holmes's brethren, however, took a more sporting interest in legislative outcomes. They felt that the Court itself should participate, and they sought opportunities to throw their weight behind the class they thought should prevail. The struggle was mainly between capital and labor and the Court had served the moneyed classes since the end of the Civil War. Employing a hackneyed social Darwinism, the Court repeatedly restrained government intervention on behalf of workers. Labor legislation designed to improve the lot of workers infringed individual rights, the Court held, violating the liberty of all parties to contract as they pleased and according to what the marketplace would allow. Therefore, a majority of the Court shared Holmes's belief in social Darwinism. They differed in that Holmes thought legislative reform was a natural consequence of the struggle, whereas a majority of the Court considered it their responsibility to prevent government from intervening in the battles for resources, especially between labor and capital.

Although it was not the first case protecting capital against the democratic masses, *Lochner v. New York*[40] became the most notorious. New York had passed legislation limiting the number of hours bakers were permitted to work to ten hours a day or sixty hours a week. New York justified the law as necessary to protect bakers from the debilitating effects of toiling long hours in a miserable work environment. A secondary benefit accrued to the public, according to supporters of the law, since "a man was more apt to be cleanly when not overworked." Many scientific authorities were advanced in support of the New York enactment. Justice John Marshall Harlan, who voted to uphold the legislation, quoted from Professor Hirt's treatise "Diseases of the Workers." "The labor of the bakers is among the hardest and most laborious imaginable, because it has to be performed under conditions injurious to the health of those engaged in it." Hirt continued, writing that baking "is hard, very hard work, not only because it requires a great deal of physical exertion in an overheated workshop and during unreasonably long hours, but more so because of the erratic demands of the public, compelling the baker to perform the greater part of his work at night."[41]

The Court was dismissive of New York's health claims. Justice Rufus

Wheeler Peckham, writing for the Court, stated, "It's manifest to us that the [New York law] . . . has no such direct relation to and no such substantial effect upon the health of the employee, as to justify us in regarding the section as really a health law."[42] All labor, the Court pointed out, is potentially detrimental to the laborer's health. "To the common understanding," the Court stated, "the trade of a baker has never been regarded as an unhealthy one," or, at least, no more dangerous than any other.[43] As regards the claim that overworked bakers might produce unhealthy bread, the Court did not believe it was even "possible in fact to discover the connection between the number of hours a baker may work in the bakery and the healthful quality of the bread made by the workman." Drawing a line at ten, rather than, say, ten and a half or eleven, was "unreasonable and entirely arbitrary." New York's health arguments, Peckham asserted, were "too shadowy and thin to build any argument for the interference of the legislature."[44]

The Court thus thought the health arguments a complete sham and a cover for a sinister ulterior motive. "[T]he real object and purpose," Peckham accused, "were simply to regulate the hours of labor between the master and his employees."[45] This was an assault on liberty. New York's actions were "an illegal interference with the rights of individuals, both employers and employees, to make contracts regarding labor upon such terms as they may think best."[46] Spencer had written that "no one may force another to part with his goods; no one may force another to take a specified price; for no one can do so without assuming more liberty of action than the man whom he thus treats."[47] The Court echoed these sentiments, concluding that such statutes, "limiting the hours in which grown and intelligent men may labor to earn their living, are mere meddlesome interferences with the rights of the individual."[48]

In one of his most famous dissents, in a career of famous dissents, Holmes criticized the *Lochner* majority for elevating their social philosophy into constitutional principle. He wrote:

> This case is decided upon an economic theory which a large part of the country does not entertain. If it were a question whether I agreed with that theory, I should desire to study it further and long before making up my mind. But I do not conceive that to be my duty, because I strongly believe that my agreement or disagreement has nothing to do with the right of a majority to embody their opinions in law. . . . The Fourteenth Amendment does not enact Mr. Herbert Spencer's *Social Statics*.[49]

Just as Holmes predicted, future generations would find *Lochner* to be anachronistic. Yet it embodied the seeds of modernity, as well as its own destruction. Holmes correctly described the decision as premised on a social theory that was principally fact-based. As such, if the facts could be demonstrated to be otherwise, the outcome presumably would have to change. Indeed, there were two factual premises informing, and thus threatening, *Lochner,* one general and one specific. The general premise was the Spencerian assertion that labor laws were unreasonable attempts to equalize bargaining power, contravening natural differences in the marketplace. The second, more specific, premise was that limiting working hours had no relation to workers', or the public's, health.

The belief that labor laws were unreasonable depended on a simple truth: the sociological fact that capital and labor could freely contract. To be sure, the *Lochner* majority was under no illusion that capital and labor had equal bargaining power, for social circumstances plainly proved the contrary. But, as Louis Brandeis pointed out many years later, the *Lochner*-era Court was guided by "nineteenth-century half-truths, like 'The survival of the fittest,' which, translated into practice, meant 'The devil take the hindmost.' "[50] Inequalities, the Court had ruled, were a function of the competition between free individuals for scarce resources where the competitors came to the field with varying skills and thus varied results should be expected. Spencer had declared, "Some will compete more, and more successfully than others; the economically fit will prosper to the cost of the economically weak."[51] Brandeis complained, "Where statutes giving expression to the new social spirit were clearly constitutional, judges, imbued with the relentless spirit of individualism, often construed them away."[52] Individualism, believed to be integral to the natural order, had become part of the constitutional order. For the *Lochner* Court, it was as if the legislature had sought to make dogs better predators of mice than cats by legislating sharper claws for the former or slower reflexes for the latter. By violating the natural order, such legislation contravened the Constitution.

Possibly the most egregious example in which the Court pressed its Spencerian philosophy was in the case of *Coppage v. Kansas.*[53] Kansas had outlawed "yellow dog" contracts, which required employees to agree as a condition of employment not to join any labor organization. The Court ruled that the Kansas law violated the liberty guaranteed by the Fourteenth Amendment. The state had urged the fact that employees, "as a rule, are not financially able to be as independent in making contracts for the sale of their labor as are employers" who purchase this labor.[54] Justice Mahlon Pitney, writing for the Court, agreed that "wherever the right of private property exists, there must be and will be inequalities of fortune; and thus it naturally happens that parties negotiating about a contract are not equally unhampered by circumstances."[55] The state was powerless to remove these inequalities, since they resulted from the exercise of the very rights of liberty and property protected by the Constitution.

Holmes, who believed that the Darwinian struggle occurred not only between worker and owner but also among the electorate in the legislative process, dissented. "In present conditions," he declared, "a workman not unnaturally may believe that only by belonging to a union can he secure a contract that shall be fair to him."[56] Legislatures have the power to enable the workman to organize in order to compete effectively. If the perceived need to organize, Holmes stated, "may be held by a reasonable man, it seems to me that it may be enforced by law in order to establish the equality of position between the parties in which liberty of contract begins." He concluded, saying, "Whether in the long run it is wise for the workingman to enact legislation of this sort is not my concern, but I am strongly of opinion that there is nothing in the [Constitution] to prevent it."[57]

It would not be until after the Great Depression, in the 1930s, that the Court—increasingly populated by justices educated in Progressivism and Holmes's realism—would fully eschew *Lochner*'s assumptions about the natural order. But the more specific premise of *Lochner* came under fire almost immediately. Justice Peckham had concluded that New York failed to demonstrate that bakers were in need of legislative protection for their health. "In looking through statistics regarding all trades and occupation," he explained, "it may be true that the trade of a baker does not appear to be as healthy as some other trades, and is vastly more healthy than still others."[58] Accordingly, even under Peckham's reasoning, the Fourteenth Amendment did not entirely bar state remedial measures, so long as the state could establish the justification for these measures. New York simply failed to make this proof.

Lochner, therefore, sets forth the means by which a state legislature could enact Progressive statutes and protect them against constitutional attack: just amass proof of the relationship between the means chosen, such as maximum hours or minimum wages, and the legitimate ends you wish to achieve, such as workers' health and welfare. The empirical gauntlet had been thrown down, and all that was needed was a young knight to pick it up.

In February 1903, the Oregon legislature passed a law that prohibited the employment of any female "in any mechanical establishment, or factory, or laundry in this state more than ten hours during any one day." Punishment was "a fine of not less than $10 nor more than $25." In September 1905, Joe Haselbrock, the supervisor of Grand Laundry in Portland, required Mrs. Elmer Gotcher to work beyond the ten-hour legal requirement. Curt Muller, the owner of the establishment, was charged under the law. Following a trial, Muller was convicted and ordered to pay a $10 fine. The case of *Muller v. Oregon*[59] arrived at the Supreme Court in 1907, to be argued and decided in early 1908.

The National Consumers' League had long worked for better working conditions for women, including maximum-hour laws and minimum-wage guarantees. Florence Kelley, the secretary-general of the League, and Josephine Goldmark, a key associate, were therefore keenly interested in the case of *Muller v. Oregon*. Kelley wanted to attack the weak underbelly of *Lochner* by demonstrating Oregon's valid factual reasons for limiting women laundry workers to ten hours a day. League officials arranged, to Kelley's chagrin, an appointment with Joseph H. Choate, a leading member of the New York bar, to enlist his assistance and ask him to participate in the case. To her relief, Choate declined the opportunity, telling Kelley that "a big husky Irishwoman should . . . work more than ten hours a day in a laundry if she and her employer so desired."[60] Kelley was delighted, for now she could ask her first choice, the man known widely as the "people's attorney," Louis Dembitz Brandeis.

When Brandeis was born in Louisville, Kentucky, in 1856, his given middle name was David. As a teenager, Brandeis adopted his revered Uncle Dembitz's name, though he had already received his uncle's first name at birth. Lewis Naphtali Dembitz was a great influence in Brandeis's life, and always stood as a role model worthy of emulation. Dembitz was a broadly gifted man, being accomplished in law, mathematics, astronomy, linguistics, and politics. His accomplishments covered a wide spectrum, from serving as a delegate to the 1860 Republican Convention, where he cast his vote for Abraham Lincoln, to forecasting the 1869 solar eclipse within one minute. He was an abolitionist and, before Lincoln emerged on the scene, an ardent supporter of Henry Clay. He named his first son after Clay and his second after Lincoln. Brandeis described life with his uncle as an "unending intellectual ferment." Brandeis gave his uncle the ultimate compliment in comparing him to his historical ideal: "In the diversity of his intellectual interests, in his longing to discover truths, in his pleasure in argumentation and the process of thinking, he reminded one of the Athenians."[61] Brandeis always kept his uncle and the Athenian citizen he embodied as lodestars for his own life.

Brandeis was born into a Jewish home that was thoroughly assimilated American. Growing up, his family was comfortable, if not wealthy. Anticipating a major recession in 1872, his father, Adolph Brandeis, sold his business and the family sojourned to Europe for a brief visit that extended to three years. Brandeis continued his formal education in the Vienna Gymnasium, and received a bounty of informal education from his travels throughout Europe. There appeared no question about his future course of studies, however, since his adored uncle was a lawyer. "I wanted to go back to America and I wanted to study law," Brandeis said. "My uncle, the abolitionist, was a lawyer; and to me nothing else seemed really worth while."[62] About the law, he said, it "seems so interesting to me in all its aspects, it is difficult for me to understand that any of the initiated should not burn with enthusiasm."[63]

After the family returned to Louisville, Brandeis migrated to Boston for his legal studies, where he attended the Harvard Law School. His brilliance was immediately evident and his classmates soon sought him out for ideas and for comfort. He would graduate number one in his class, and to this day his performance has not been surpassed. After law school, Brandeis faced the question that bedevils many graduates: where to set up shop. His family wished him to return west. Although unsure of his prospects if he returned home, Brandeis finally agreed to leave Boston, where he had spent "the wonderful years" at Harvard. He did not make it all the way back to Louisville, and instead settled upon St. Louis as a compromise choice. His stay in St. Louis did not last long. He soon moved back to Boston, where he would live until he moved to Washington, D.C., to join the Court.

In Boston, he formed a partnership with his classmate Samuel Warren, who had finished second in their class. Just after returning to Boston he wrote his mother about his decision and about himself. "Of course one man can live anywhere, but there is also ambition to be satisfied," he wrote. "Man is strange, at least this one is; he does not enjoy what he has—and he always wants what he does not yet have. That," he told her, "probably is called ambition." He concluded, "And so I think that I shall be happier here, in spite of being alone, and if I can write you of successes, I shall be compensated for all I am missing. I think you will be too."[64]

Brandeis loved Boston. His friendship with Warren permitted him entry into the most exclusive strata of Brahmin society, and into its social groups, such as the Dedham Polo Club. Brahmin prejudice did not fully extend to Jews at the time, especially intellectually gifted Harvard Jews. In fact, Brahmins identified with the Jewish people, feeling themselves similarly to be "chosen ones." Over time, Brandeis slowly separated from most segments of Brahmin society, due partly to a growing anti-Semitism and more fully to a lack of identity between his and their social ideals. However, he never tired of all things New England, and was fully enamored by the region's landscapes and Boston's intellectual vibrancy. He also, as did Holmes, revered Emerson. "I have been indulging in 'Emerson,'" he wrote, "and can conscientiously say, that my admiration for him is on the increase. I have read a few sentences of his which are alone enough to make a man immortal."[65]

Writing about his first trial, Brandeis considered it a case that "we . . . fully expect to lose, in fact, our only chance of winning rests in the possibility of total mental aberration of the judge."[66] Very quickly, however, he gained a reputation as an industrious and talented lawyer and his practice flourished. It also proved enormously lucrative, and together with his frugal lifestyle, the practice of law allowed him to amass a sizable fortune. But Brandeis's ambition did not extend to riches, nor did he covet possessions. He lived prudently. If he tended toward the Athenian ideal intellectually, he lived his personal life according to the Spartan code. Dinner guests at the Brandeis home would comment afterward on the sparse furnishings and even, on occasion, the meager portions served. One friend joked that he and his wife would make sure that they ate well before, and a hearty dessert after, one of the Brandeis dinner parties.

Brandeis's practice was a rare combination of corporate representation and public interest litigation. His business clients were mainly small manufacturing plants and retail stores. Much of his public interest work was in opposition to large trusts and transportation conglomerates. He distrusted large companies, and consistently espoused the principle that small was beautiful. In his personal relationships, he continued to share the traditional Brahmin's love of ideas, independence, and innovation, but he found disagreeable their lust for power and possessions. He preferred the blue-collared man. "I am experiencing a growing conviction that the labormen are the most congenial company," he wrote his brother. "The intense materialism and luxuriousness of most of our other people makes their company quite irksome."[67]

In 1892, Brandeis was teaching business law at the Massachusetts Institute of Technology. Meanwhile, events were unfolding in Homestead, Pennsylvania, that would deeply affect his attitude about the subject he taught and would color much of his thinking on labor and capital thereafter. In Homestead, the powerful Carnegie Steel Company sought to crush one of the strongest craft unions in the country, the Amalgamated Association of Iron and Steel Workers. The union had called a strike in 1889 and had won a favorable three-year contract. In 1890, however, the steel industry stumbled along with the national economy, with rolled-steel products declining from $35 a gross ton to $22 by 1892. Andrew Carnegie wanted to cut wages, and his plant manager at Homestead, Henry Clay Frick, saw an opportunity to break the union. Frick began by increasing production demands and, when the contract expired, slashed wages. The union refused to comply with the new demands, so Frick locked the workers out of the plant. Although the union was limited to tradesmen, comprising only one-fifth of the nearly four thousand employees, three thousand of the rest voted to join the strike. Carnegie had a reputation as a benevolent employer and a supporter of the workers' right to organize, but he made an assortment of fateful errors in dealing with the strike. Most egregiously, he gave carte blanche to Frick. In addition, he was largely inaccessible as events escalated, because he was on an extended vacation at a remote Scottish castle on Loch Rannoch. In a telegram he would regret sending, he told Frick, "We . . . approve of anything you do. We are with you to the end."

Frick responded to the strike by immediately building a fence three miles long and twelve feet high around the plant, with built-in apertures from which private militiamen could fire. The workers dubbed the plant "Fort Frick." Frick called upon the Pinkerton Detective Agency to supply the militia. Shortly after midnight on July 6, three hundred Pinkertons boarded barges and sailed up the Monongahela River armed with Winchester rifles. They were spotted, and a latter-day Paul Revere rode "at breakneck speed into the streets of Homestead giving the alarm as he sped along." The roused strikers rushed to the riverbank and ordered the Pinkertons not to disembark. When the Pinkertons disobeyed the order and stepped off, gunfire erupted, though who fired the first shot will never be known. The Pinkertons retreated to the barges, seeking cover. The battle raged for fourteen hours. The strikers attempted to sink the barges by tossing dynamite at them, rolling a burning freight train car down a slope on top of them, and lighting oil that they had pumped into the river all around them. When the Pinkertons finally surrendered, nine strikers and three detectives were dead, and many more on both sides were seriously injured. Pennsylvania's governor ordered the state militia into Homestead and workers were arrested and the strike leaders were charged with murder. Members of the Strike Committee, which had directed the strike, were charged with treason. Sympathetic juries, however, refused to convict any of the strikers.

The events in Homestead deeply impressed the young Brandeis. In his business law class, he said, "[I] threw away my notes and approached my theme from new angles."[68] He had learned a lesson: "I saw at once that the common law, built up under simpler conditions of living, gave an inadequate basis for the adjustment of the complex relations of the modern factory system." Homestead had made him seriously rethink "the labor problem." "It took the shock of that battle, where organized capital hired a private army to shoot at organized labor for resisting an arbitrary cut in wages, to turn my mind definitely toward a searching study of the relations of labor to industry."[69] After the events of July 1892, Brandeis increasingly turned his attention toward what was morally right and away from what was legally deigned.

When Florence Kelley approached Brandeis to ask him to participate in the case of *Muller v. Oregon,* he was eager and ready for the challenge. Before he would agree, however, he insisted that Oregon permit him to be lead counsel so that he might write the brief and orally argue the case before the Court. Around this time, a Louisville newspaper noted that Brandeis was "in his fifties, but doesn't look it." The story continued, "His smooth face is square and strong, but irregular, and expresses a lively sense of humor. His eyes twinkle behind his nose glasses." It concluded, "His voice is soft and drawling, but it can snap like a whip lash on occasion."[70] By 1908, Brandeis had ascended to the top rung of his profession. Oregon welcomed him to the case.

Most of the principals agreed on the basic task before them, the need to marshal the facts to support Oregon's basis of limiting laundresses' working hours to ten per day. They aimed at the weak underbelly of

Lochner. Yet how was this to be done? In turning to Brandeis, supporters of the Oregon law had found someone who brought an empiricist's mind-set to the problem at hand. Brandeis once told a Boston reporter that he enjoyed detective stories, and that Sherlock Holmes was his favorite. In fact, though he did not aspire to be a detective himself, he likened his approach to that employed by Sherlock Holmes: "I use practically the same method. . . . It's a matter of having special knowledge and being able to draw the only possible conclusion."[71] Sherlock Holmes once explained, "It is a capital mistake to theorize before one has data."[72] Brandeis similarly believed that "the logic of words should yield to the logic of realities."[73] But Brandeis was not just a detective; he was also a scientist. Oliver Wendell Holmes had written famously that "the black-letter man may be the man of the present, but the man of the future is the man of statistics and the master of economics." By that definition, Brandeis was the man of the future. It was said of "the composition of his intellect," that "one of the most important elements is his compre-hension of figures."[74] His greatness as a lawyer was due, in part, to his greatness as a mathematician.

Brandeis believed it was the lawyer's job first to know the facts and then apprise judges of them. "Nobody can form a judgment that is worth having," Brandeis said, "without a fairly detailed and intimate knowl-edge of the facts." In *Lochner,* Brandeis said, the lawyers were to blame for the judges' ignorance. "The judge came to the bench unequipped with the necessary knowledge of economic and social science, and his judg-ment suffered likewise through lack of equipment in the lawyers who presented the cases to him."[75] The judge relied on the competence of the counsel before him, which was woefully inadequate in *Lochner.* Quoting Charles Henderson, a political psychology professor at the University of Chicago, Brandeis warned, "One can hardly escape from the conclusion that a lawyer who has not studied economics and sociology is very apt to become a public enemy."[76]

Brandeis thus saw *Muller* as an opportunity to educate the justices regarding the effects of long working hours on women and their conse-quences for society. The usual brief submitted to the Court at that time was long on argument and legal theory. It relied on formal logic and aged doctrine, rather than the light of experience. Brandeis, in contrast, devoted a meager two pages to the law, and actually trumpeted *Lochner*'s holding, inviting subsequent parties to prove the bases for challenged legislation. He used ninety-five pages to make this proof. Based on extensive scientific authorities, he argued, "Long hours of labor are dangerous for women primarily because of their special physical organization. In structure and function," he told the Court, "women are differentiated from men." The brief went on, "Besides these anatomical and physiological differences, physicians are agreed that women are fundamentally weaker than men in all that makes for endurance; in muscular strength, in nervous energy, in the powers of persistent attention and application." As a consequence, overwork "is more disastrous to the health of women than of men, and entails upon them more lasting energy."[77] Moreover, the assault of long hours on women undermined the foundation of society itself:

> When the health of women has been injured by long hours, not only is the working efficiency of the community impaired, but the deterioration is handed down to succeeding generations. . . . The overwork of future mothers thus directly attacks the welfare of the nation.

A unanimous Court agreed with Brandeis and upheld the legislation. Justice David Brewer, writing for the majority, took the unusual step of mentioning Brandeis in the opinion and noted that his brief contained "a very copious collection" of authorities regarding the factual bases for the Oregon law. The Court observed that although the scientific opinions cited in Brandeis's brief were not, "technically speaking, authorities," they nonetheless signified "a widespread belief that woman's physical structure, and the functions she performs in consequence thereof, justify special legislation restricting or qualifying the conditions under which she should be permitted to toil."[78] In response to the concern that the Court might be perceived as "changing" the Constitution to follow changed public opinions or factual circumstances, the Court agreed that the Constitution's "permanence" was an essential component of a stable government. "At the same time," Brewer wrote, "when a question of fact is debated and debatable, and the extent to which a special constitutional limitation goes is affected by the truth in respect to that fact, a widespread and long continued belief concerning it is worthy of consideration. We take judicial cognizance of all matters of general knowledge."[79]

Although *Muller v. Oregon* marks an important juncture in constitutional law, the immediate decision fully accorded with the prejudices of the times. Its importance stems primarily from the form of advocacy Brandeis introduced in this and other cases, using what has come to be called the Brandeis Brief. This form of sociological jurisprudence would quickly take hold in the 1920s, especially among legal academics, and briefs today routinely amass social authorities in support of their legal argumentation. However, the scientific conclusion on which Brandeis distinguished the Oregon law in *Muller* from the New York law in *Lochner*—the inherent inferiority of women—was not controversial. Indeed, the social philosophy underlying Brandeis's brief—that women needed special consideration due to their inherent frailties—was endemic in the social Darwinist views of Spencer himself. Thus, while the nature of the brief was a radical departure from precedent, the science it contained was not. This, undoubtedly, contributed to the Court's enthusiasm for the brief. In a 1923 case, *Adkins v. Children's Hospital,*[80] for instance, the Court declined to follow *Muller* and instead relied on *Lochner* to strike down minimum-wage legislation for women. In *Adkins,* Felix Frankfurter, a protégé of both Holmes and Brandeis, argued the case and submitted an extensive and detailed Brandeis Brief in support of the legislation.[81] The Court argued that since 1908, when *Muller* was decided, the Nineteenth Amendment had been ratified, giving women the right to vote and ostensibly putting them on an equal footing with men. By this time, Brandeis was a member of the Court, though he did not participate in the decision. Holmes dissented. Holmes wrote sardonically that it "will need more than the 19th Amendment to convince me that there are no differences between men and women, or that legislation cannot take those differences into account."[82]

Muller illustrates a phenomenon that would become endemic to the Supreme Court's jurisprudence in the twentieth century. The Court adopted a sociological jurisprudence of convenience. Facts were listened to, and employed by, the Court when they supported the desired outcome. But, as in *Adkins,* they could be readily ignored if they were inconvenient. This use of facts was mainly implicit in the decisions of the nineteenth century, although sometimes, as with the *Dred Scott* opinion, it is plainly manifest. After the Brandeis Brief, however, facts increasingly became an integral component of the legal argument. Indeed, the Court employed facts in exactly this way, often marshaling them to support a decision much as it would have always cited original intent or precedent. If the facts did not support the desired result, then, as with original intent or precedent, the Court would distinguish or discount their relevance. Holmes observed on this general point, "Man believes what he wants to, and is moved only a little by reason. But reason means facts, and if neglected is likely or liable to knock a hole in his boat, but usually it is not big enough to swamp it and he sticks in an old hat and goes on."[83]

One of the pivotal insights Holmes offered regarding the real development of the law was his recognition that court decisions were not mere logical deductions from established premises. "It is the merit of the common law that it decides the case first and determines the principle afterwards. Looking at the forms of logic it might be inferred that when you have [a] minor premise and a conclusion, there must be a major, which you are always prepared then and there to assert. But in fact lawyers, like other men," Holmes observed, "frequently see well enough how they ought to decide on a given state of facts without being very clear as to the [reason]."[84] In constitutional law, the traditionally accepted reasons are authorities such as the text, original intent, and precedent. But legal authority is replete with ambiguity, and gives the Court room to maneuver. Facts, too, can be less than certain, though they sometimes can be largely unequivocal. With the Brandeis Brief and the school of sociological jurisprudence, the Court entered a new era, one that even today it is not entirely prepared to meet.

President Woodrow Wilson nominated Louis Brandeis to the Supreme Court on January 28, 1916. It ignited a firestorm. There were sundry reasons available to oppose the nomination, though very few that could be asserted publicly. In public, most opponents sought to label him a "radical" progressive. The more compelling reasons lay in private biases, including two in particular. First, Brandeis had become very active in the Jewish community and, somewhat controversially, had worked for the Zionist cause of establishing a Jewish state. If confirmed, Brandeis would be the first Jew on the Court. Second, Brandeis had made powerful enemies when, during a congressional investigation into the firing of a top official at the Department of the Interior in 1910, he demonstrated that then president Taft had employed an attorney general report that had been antedated to defend the decision. This business, known as the Pinchot-Ballinger affair, resulted in great embarrassment for Taft and a score of major government officials. A friend wrote to Taft, "When Brandeis's nomination came in yesterday, the Senate simply gasped. . . . There wasn't any more excitement at the Capitol when Congress passed the Spanish War Resolution."[85]

After a bruising battle, the Senate voted along party lines to confirm the nomination. President Wilson later commented that he could never again match the Brandeis appointment. "There is nobody else who represents the greatest technical ability and professional success with complete devotion to the people's interest."[86] Brandeis now joined Holmes on the Court. After he received the president's nomination, Brandeis had told the attorney general, "My views in regard to the Constitution are as you know very much those of Mr. Justice Holmes."[87] However, their brand of judicial restraint, their willingness to defer to legislative majorities and experimental reforms, and their devotion to an empirically informed jurisprudence were not shared by a majority of the Court. Very quickly, the line "Holmes and Brandeis, dissenting," became a mainstay of Court opinions.

Although Holmes and Brandeis generally agreed on how most cases should be decided, many differences remained between them. Substantively and philosophically, Holmes believed courts should refrain from invalidating legislative action because he thought that courts should not interfere with the political struggle that was manifest in legislation. For Holmes, "if the will of the majority is unmistakable, and the majority is strong enough to have a clear power to enforce its will, and intends to do so, the courts must yield . . . because the foundation of sovereignty is power, real or supposed."[88] Thus, if his "fellow citizens wanted to go to hell," Holmes declared, he would help them get there—"It is my job," he explained. He wished "that the dominant power should be wise." But, "wise or not, the proximate test of a good government is that the dominant power has its way."[89]

Brandeis and Holmes both firmly embraced Jefferson's philosophy that the Constitution was for the living. In contrast with Holmes, Brandeis had a Jeffersonian confidence in democratic wisdom and fully shared the Athenian ideal of the engaged republican populace. This meant, as Jefferson had put it, that "laws and institutions must go hand in hand with the progress of the human mind." And science was an integral and necessary component of the Constitution's meaning. Jefferson had said that as the mind "becomes more developed, more enlightened, as new discoveries are made, new truths disclosed, and manners and opinions change with the change of circumstances, institutions must advance also, and keep pace with the times."[90]

Brandeis sought, at every opportunity, to bring to fruition Jefferson's vision of the good Constitution. Legislative enactments, Brandeis believed, were worthy of deference because they more proximately reflected enlightened principles of society. More than Holmes, Brandeis believed that enlightened principles actually existed, and he was willing to have the Court enforce those values in those cases in which the engaged populace got it wrong. In *Meyer v. Nebraska*,[91] for example, the Court employed *Lochner*'s strong libertarian philosophy in a noneconomic sphere. The Court reversed the conviction of a teacher for teaching German in violation of a Nebraska law that prohibited the teaching of foreign languages to young children. The opinion was authored by Justice James McReynolds, the most reactionary member of the Court, both personally and philosophically. He wrote that liberty extended beyond property and contract cases, such as *Lochner,* and included personal and social rights:

> Without doubt, it denotes not merely freedom from bodily restraint but also the right of the individual to contract, to engage in any of the common occupations of life, to acquire useful knowledge, to marry, establish a home and bring up children, to worship God according to the dictates of his own conscience, and generally to enjoy those privileges long recognized at common law as essential to the orderly pursuit of happiness by free men.[92]

Brandeis joined the opinion, but Holmes dissented. Holmes generally did not believe the Court should act as a perpetual censor of legislative enactments, however reactionary or silly he might personally find them. Brandeis was driven more by outcomes, and *Meyer* differed from *Lochner* in important, substantive ways. Although Brandeis did not believe the Constitution should be used to safeguard corporate interests against legislative regulations, he readily accepted the Constitution's utility in protecting individuals when the legislature sought to regulate their personal conduct.

Each man also approached empirical jurisprudence differently. As Holmes put it in a letter to Felix Frankfurter, "[Brandeis] always desires to know all that can be known about a case whereas I am afraid that I wish to know as little as I can safely go on."[93] Holmes was a realist philosopher who, like Spencer, thought science informed philosophical principles, but he had no interest in actually collecting data. Brandeis was a social scientist who relished data and sought constantly to inform his philosophical views with the messy details of the empirical world. Brandeis constantly encouraged, even bullied, Holmes to leave his library to get a "real education" from exploring the world firsthand. He once encouraged Holmes to use his summer to educate himself by touring a textile mill, in order to see the reality of a worker's life. Holmes described the interaction to his friend Frederick Pollock: "Brandeis the other day drove a harpoon into my midriff with reference to my summer occupations. He said, 'you talk about improving your mind, you only exercise it on the subjects with which you are familiar. Why don't you try something new, study some domain of fact.' " Brandeis suggested the textile industry as a start toward getting "a human notion of how it really is." Holmes, who would remain with his books that summer, grumbled to Pollock, "I hate facts. I always say the chief end of man is to form general propositions—adding that no general proposition is worth a damn and have little doubt that it would be good for my immortal soul to plunge into the [facts], . . . but I shrink from the bore."[94]

While Holmes would shrink from gathering facts himself, he never discounted their necessity to the formation of the law. His expertise was philosophy and, he said, "theory is all that I can bring even to the law." Yet, he maintained, "theory sometimes leads one to keep in mind fundamental facts that one more versed in detail may forget."[95] Holmes's nineteenth-century approach was modeled on biology; Brandeis employed sociology and economics. Brandeis considered the detail imperative for the theory. He appreciated that the "economic and social sciences are largely uncharted seas," but they offered more than armchair theorizing could provide. Brandeis saw the law as a manifestation of man's will. Science could be employed to ensure rationality. Only scientific thinking could confirm that the means chosen indeed produced the desired ends of legislation or Court opinion.

While Holmes had a nimble and deep philosophic mind, Brandeis's brain was lightning fast, all encompassing, and prodigious. Brandeis's brain power was in the jet age at a time when most people were just beginning to drive cars. Over time, Brandeis brought his great intellectual powers to bear on Holmes. Former president and Chief Justice Taft, for instance, commented about Holmes: "I am very fond of the old gentleman, but he is so completely under the control of Brother Brandeis that it gives to Brandeis two votes instead of one."[96] Holmes's friend Nina Gray also expressed alarm, writing obliquely in a letter, "If only you stay thoroughly Anglo-Saxon." Holmes responded, "I am tickled at your [remark]." He said, "I take the innuendo to be that I am under the influence of the Heb's." He assured her that "I am comfortably confident that I am under no influence except that of thoughts and insights."[97]

Taft's comments and Gray's concerns somewhat overstate Brandeis's influence, since the two men generally agreed about outcomes, and this was true long before Brandeis joined the Court. But Brandeis did make a difference on Holmes's approach to the Court's business. His influence was in two main areas. First, he often influenced what form the argument took when they voted together, and second, and more important for posterity, Brandeis regularly encouraged Holmes to publicly dissent. Brandeis believed, especially in constitutional cases, that "since what is done is what you call statesmanship, nothing is ever settled."[98] Brandeis understood that yesterday's dissents are often tomorrow's holdings. Brandeis regularly strong-armed Holmes, persuading him to publicly announce his opposition to the Court. In 1927, Frankfurter said that these dissents "record prophecy and shape history."[99] In First Amendment cases, "Holmes and Brandeis, dissenting," usually signaled such a prophecy.

The modern doctrine of free speech evolved relatively slowly and its first statement was expressed by Holmes in a majority opinion that was not at all protective of speech. In *Schenck v. United States,*[100] the defendants were convicted of violating the Espionage Act of 1917 for distributing flyers calling on citizens to resist the draft. The flyer cited the Thirteenth Amendment to the Constitution and likened the draft to involuntary servitude. It went on to state, "If you do not assert and support your rights, you are helping to deny or disparage rights which it is the solemn duty of all citizens and residents of the United States to retain."[101] Before the Supreme Court, the defendants claimed that the flyers received First Amendment protection. The Court, with Holmes writing, disagreed.

Holmes admitted that in peacetime, the defendants' words would be protected. However, "[w]hen a nation is at war many things that might be said in time of peace are such a hindrance to its effort that their utterance will not be endured so long as men fight." Holmes wrote that the "question in every case is whether the words used are used in such circumstances and are such a nature as to create a clear and present danger that they will bring about the substantive evils that Congress has a right to prevent. It is a question of proximity and degree."[102] The test adopted by the Court was an empirical one, though in *Schenck* Holmes merely assumed it was met in affirming the convictions, since the jury below could not have applied a test that had not yet been created. Yet the clear-and-present-danger test would evolve into a strong speech guarantee through a set of inspiring dissents from Holmes and Brandeis that remade the law of free speech.

In *Abrams v. United States*,[103] the defendants were convicted under the 1918 amendments to the Espionage Act for urging the curtailment of the production of war materials by publishing leaflets that denounced the war and militarism of all types. Dissenting from the Court's affirmance of the convictions, Holmes, joined by Brandeis, belittled the influence of the defendants' leaflets: "Now nobody can suppose that the surreptitious publishing of a silly leaflet by an unknown man, without more, would present any immediate danger that its opinions would hinder the success of the government arms or have any appreciable tendency to do so."[104] Holmes then turned to the subject at hand, the meaning of "free speech" itself, and penned words that ever since would be repeated when the subject arose:

> [W]hen men have realized that time has upset many fighting faiths, they may come to believe even more than they believe the very foundations of their own conduct that the ultimate good desired is better reached by free trade in ideas—that the best test of truth is the power of the thought to get itself accepted in the competition of the market, and that truth is the only ground upon which their wishes safely can be carried out. That at any rate is the theory of our Constitution. It is an experiment, as all life is an experiment.[105]

In *Whitney v. California*,[106] Brandeis, joined by Holmes, again wrote separately from the Court's affirmance of the defendant's conviction for being "a member of an organization [created] to advocate, teach, aid and abet criminal syndicalism"—Anita Whitney was a member of the Communist Labor Party.[107] He added the following emphasis to Holmes's *Abrams* dissent:

> Those who won our independence believed that the final end of the State was to make men free to develop their faculties; and that in its government the deliberative forces should prevail over the arbitrary. They valued liberty as both an ends and a means. They believed liberty to be the secret of happiness and courage to be the secret of liberty. . . . Those who won

our independence by revolution were not cowards. They did not fear political change. They did not exalt order at the cost of liberty. To courageous,
self-reliant men, with confidence in the power of free and fearless reasoning
applied through the processes of popular government, no danger flowing
from speech can be deemed clear and present, unless the incidence of the
evil apprehended is so imminent that it may befall before there is opportunity for full discussion.[108]

While Holmes and Brandeis shared the view that the First Amendment
reaches dissonant opinions, their reasons for believing so were nearly
opposite. Holmes reached this conclusion through his libertarian philosophy, which continued to be informed by his cynical, pessimistic social
Darwinism. Brandeis reached the same conclusion through his republican
ideals, a worldview informed by hopeful optimism.

Holmes did not believe that setting speech free in the intellectual marketplace would produce truth, since he shared no pretensions that *truth*
could be had. Nor did Holmes necessarily believe that the public good
would be served by this liberal doctrine, though he hoped it might.
Holmes's opinion of speech mirrored his views in other areas, that the
crowd should have the opportunity to select their own fate. "If in the
long run the beliefs expressed in the proletarian dictatorship are destined
to be accepted by the dominant forces of the community," he wrote in
another dissenting opinion, "the only meaning of free speech is that they
should be given their chance and have their way."[109] In other words, as
he felt elsewhere, if the crowd wanted to go to hell, it was his job to
help them get there.

Brandeis, in contrast, exalted free speech because he thought it essential to good government. He believed in civic virtue and sought to reinforce republican principles, and was optimistic regarding the crowd's
chances. Like Jefferson before him, Brandeis looked to fifth-century Athens for inspiration. His opinion in *Whitney* was modeled on Pericles'
"Funeral Oration," and the line "they believed liberty to be the secret of
happiness and courage to be the secret of liberty" was taken directly from
it.[110] Pericles contended that only the active citizen would ensure freedom
and contribute to civic good. The quiescent citizen was a pawn of the
state and inevitably self-regarding. Athenians, Pericles declared, "decide
and debate, carefully and in person, all matters of policy, holding, not
that words and deeds go ill together, but that acts are foredoomed to
failure when undertaken undiscussed."[111] Brandeis attributed Athenian

ideals to the founders. It was they who embraced the principle that "public discussion is a political duty," and who, rather than fear tyranny and turmoil as a result, believed that only such liberty could guarantee the public good.[112]

While Holmes and Brandeis based their similar conclusions on different premises, common to both their outlooks was an empiricist's sensibility. The clear-and-present-danger test itself was strongly fact-based, requiring an evaluation of the contextual circumstances surrounding the speech and the probable consequences following its utterance. Moreover, Holmes's and Brandeis's respective justifications for the test were empirical. Holmes's thinking continued to be impressed by Darwinian principles and considered free discussion to be a component of the struggle for survival. Free speech should be protected because it permitted nature to take its course. Brandeis believed free discussion was an instrument of the good society. Free speech should be protected because it produced civic virtue.

As Holmes neared ninety, he asked Brandeis to please inform him when it was time for him to retire. He did not want to stay past his time, though, as most do, he hung on later than was prudent. He was slowing down precipitously and even slept on the bench from time to time. Although age had him in its clutches, he still cut a dashing figure. Elizabeth Shepley Sergeant offered this portrait of him:

> Here is a Yankee, strayed from Olympus. Olympians are reputed at ease in the universe; they know truth in flashes of fire, and reveal its immortal essence in cryptic phrase. . . . Oliver Wendell Holmes's tall and erect figure, which a ripe and white old age has scarcely stooped; his grand manner, at once noble and dazzling. . . . Watch his snowy head for a moment among his younger peers on the bench. Note the set of his shoulders in the gown. . . . The eyes, the most striking feature, give off sparkles of scintillating gray-blue, and have more skepticism and gentle malice than mercy in their depths.[113]

When the October 1931 term began, most of Holmes's brethren agreed it was time for him to retire. Brandeis, however, said he could not fulfill the appointed task of going to Holmes with this news. The job fell to Chief Justice Charles Evans Hughes, who went to visit Holmes at home on Sunday morning, January 12. It was a heart-wrenching moment, and after a long time Hughes left "with tears streaming down his face." Shortly thereafter, and "obviously by arrangement," Brandeis arrived. Holmes wrote in his letter of resignation, "the time has come and I bow to the inevitable."

After Holmes left the bench, Brandeis faced what Frankfurter called "a great personal void." He regularly visited Holmes throughout this time, as the man who seemed not to age declined quickly. Holmes would light up when Brandeis arrived, and the old warrior would embrace him, repeating, "My dear friend, my dear friend." When Holmes turned ninety-two, Brandeis sent him a copy of four lines from Goethe's *Iphigenie*:

> *Blessed is he who cherishes the meaning of his fathers*
> *Who, proud of their deeds, their greatness*
> *Entertains the listener, and quietly delights*
> *In seeing himself included at the end of this illustrious line.*

Early in March 1935, Holmes fell desperately ill with bronchial pneumonia. He rallied several times over the following days, but his strength waned and his friends expected the worst. He died in the early morning hours of March 6, two days before his ninety-fourth birthday, "more peacefully than anyone I've ever seen," his doctor told the press. At his funeral, Reverend Pierce aptly quoted Holmes himself to the congregated: "at the grave of a hero . . . we end, not with sorrow at the inevitable loss, but with the contagion of his courage; and with a kind of desperate joy we go back to the fight."[114]

Throughout his life, Holmes endeavored to transcend this world by achieving immortality through his work. In evaluating his corpus, he thought, "like the great artists, [he might] have succeeded in writing the definite and exact with a vista toward the infinite."[115] Emerson could have written his epitaph:

> THEY RECKON ILL WHO LEAVE ME OUT;
> WHEN ME THEY FLY, I AM THE WINGS;
> I AM THE DOUBTER AND THE DOUBT,
> AND I THE HYMN THE BRAHMIN SINGS.

5

"LET US NOT BECOME LEGAL MONKS":

Legal Realism and the Realistic Jurisprudence of the Supreme Court

> [T]he most significant (I do *not* say the *only* significant) aspects of the relations of law and society lie in the field of behavior, and that words take on importance either because and insofar as they are behavior, or because and insofar as they demonstrably reflect or influence other behavior. This statement seems not worth making. Its truth is absurdly apparent. For all that, it reverses, it upsets, the whole traditional approach to law. It turns accepted theory on its head.
>
> —KARL LLEWELLYN

When Oliver Wendell Holmes Jr. retired from the Court in 1932, legal commentators and the press speculated excitedly about his successor. There had not been a judge since John Marshall that reached his stature, both within the profession and among the general public. His seat was thought almost too big to fill. Only one name in the country enjoyed a reputation that placed him in the same company with Holmes. Justice Benjamin N. Cardozo, chief justice of the highest court in New York, the New York Court of Appeals, was considered by many to be the country's preeminent judge not already sitting on the Supreme Court. But a host of circumstances arrayed against him—he was a Democratic Jewish progressive from New York who would have to be appointed by a Republican president when one Jew and two New Yorkers already sat on the Court. President Herbert Hoover, to his lasting credit, ignored the superficial obstacles to a Cardozo appointment, and sent his name to the Senate. His nomination was approved without dissent. Although Cardozo's tenure lasted only slightly over five years, he marked an important transition between Holmes and the succeeding generation of jurists that would move the Court's jurisprudence in fundamentally new directions. Indeed, Cardozo would be succeeded by the best and the brightest from the New Deal generation, men like Hugo Black, Felix Frankfurter, and William O. Douglas.

Cardozo was a contemporary of Louis Brandeis, whom he joined on the Court. Cardozo was born on May 24, 1870, into a reputable family whose reputation tarnished badly just after he arrived. His father, Albert, was a New York trial court judge who owed his success to Boss Tweed's political machine out of Tammany Hall. Unfortunately, he paid this debt in a series of cases in which Tweed men or Tammany interests stood before him. When the scandal broke, Albert Cardozo and several other judges were accused of an assortment of misdeeds, from nepotism to having been influenced in specific cases. In one charge, the senior Cardozo was accused of appointing his wife's nephew, Gratz Nathan, to a number of commissions on an assortment of matters, including lunacy hearings and various city business. More egregious than this simple nepotism, he apparently split the fees paid to Nathan, conduct that alone merited impeachment and removal from office. Rather than face the charges, Albert Cardozo resigned his office on May 1, 1872. Benjamin turned two years old three weeks later.

From Benjamin's earliest recollections, the Cardozo name was thus indelibly stained with scandal and political corruption. The family did not meet ruin, however, for Albert's Tammany consorts did not forget him. He escaped discipline from the Association of the Bar and almost immediately joined Richard S. Newcombe, another Tammany crony, in law practice. Albert Cardozo soon regained some of his fortune, though never his reputation, in his practice with Newcombe. The Cardozo family, meanwhile, was initially required by these misfortunes to move to more modest lodgings. By 1877, they recovered enough to move to a stately home at 803 Madison Avenue, between Sixty-seventh and Sixty-eighth Streets. Although the young Benjamin enjoyed a financially secure childhood, the family fractured along numerous fault lines during his early years. In addition to his father's public woes, his mother suffered an assortment of mental problems, resulting in her commitment to a sanitarium. She subsequently suffered a stroke and was paralyzed for several years. She died in 1879 when Benjamin was just nine. Stepping into this breach, Benjamin's older sister, Ellen, known as Nell or Nellie, assumed responsibility for his upbringing. Benjamin and Nellie were unusually close. Benjamin never married and he and Nellie lived their lives together—facts that later were much commented upon by his biographers. When Benjamin was thirteen,

Albert Cardozo arranged to have Horatio Alger tutor him and his twin sister, Emily, in preparation for college entrance examinations. At fifteen, Benjamin moved a couple of dozen blocks north and west where he matriculated at Columbia University. His father died that same year.

Although Benjamin N. Cardozo followed his father's example in becoming a lawyer and later a judge, he differed from him completely in terms of judicial temperament. Indeed, Cardozo's life on the bench was as clean and free of political corruption as his father's had been tainted. It was as if he consciously sought to clean the slate dirtied by his father's fall and bring the Cardozo family name back into ascension. He was fabulously successful in doing so. Stephen Wise, commenting on the nomination of Cardozo to the High Court, remarked on this feat: "The glory of it will be . . . that [although his father] came under the malign influence of Tweed [and] made the name Cardozo synonymous with shame, [in] twenty years, Cardozo has effaced the memory of his father and his name can never more be used save in terms of reverence and honor. What an achievement for a man!"[1]

Cardozo's philosophy of law closely tracked that of Holmes. He was no radical, but agreed that formalistic logic alone could not resolve real cases. The judge, Cardozo believed, must know what sort of society he wanted to make before settling upon a legal rule. Rules were the means by which judges shaped, indeed engineered, society. Law does not subsist in an abstract firmament; it had to be molded and massaged for the purpose of serving greater sociological ends. The measure of a rule depended on its effectiveness in producing desired objectives. "Not the origin, but the goal, is the main thing," he said.[2] He added that there "can be no wisdom in the choice of a path unless we know where it will lead."[3] Cardozo held fast to Holmes's aphorism that "[t]he life of the law has not been logic: it has been experience." Like Holmes, he believed that logic was an essential tool, but sociology was the ultimate test of a rule's value for society.

Cardozo's was an enormously influential voice in twentieth-century law. His principal contributions were in the areas of private law, such as contracts and the law of negligence and trespass. More of his opinions in these areas appear in law school casebooks than any other judge's.[4] In addition, although he sat on the Court only briefly, his constitutional opinions are cited as frequently by federal courts as other well-known justices', including Brandeis, who served considerably longer.[5] His lasting success is attributable to several characteristics of the man and his work. Foremost, perhaps, Cardozo was a stylist. Not as pithy or erudite as Holmes, he nonetheless had a clear and poetic literary style that was both quotable and informative. It is no wonder that Cardozo is a favorite of modern law-book editors, since his writing both engages and instructs the reader. In addition, in many legal arenas, again mainly outside of constitutional law, Cardozo was an innovator and often set the law on a new path or redirected the path on which it traveled. Several cases in particular are landmarks, including the contracts case of *MacPherson v. Buick Motor Co.*[6] and the famous torts case of *Palsgraf v. Long Island Railroad Company.*[7] In constitutional law, too, his literary flair turned important cases into timeless precedents. Finally, Cardozo was famous for being contemplative about the process of judging itself. His best-known academic work, *The Nature of the Judicial Process,* was a brilliant exegesis on how judges decide cases.

Cardozo's *Judicial Process* was based on a series of lectures he presented at the Yale Law School. His lecture style was as well received as his writing. Professor Arthur Corbin described the scene at Yale:

> Standing on the platform at the lectern, his mobile countenance, his dark eyes, his white hair, and his brilliant smile, all well lighted before us, he read the lecture, winding it up at 6 o'clock. He bowed and sat down. The entire audience rose to their feet, with a burst of applause that would not cease. Cardozo rose and bowed, with a smile at once pleased and deprecatory, and again sat down. Not a man moved from his tracks; and the applause increased. In a sort of confusion Cardozo saw that he must be the first to move. He came down the steps and left, with the faculty, through a side door, with the applause still in his ears.[8]

In his lectures, Cardozo endeavored to describe in detail the process by which judges decide cases. Holmes had originally asked, What is the law in fact? He believed it to be nothing more, nor less, than what particular legal decision-makers did. In the context of courts, the law was merely the probabilistic prediction of judges' behavior. If the law is merely what judges do, Cardozo endeavored to provide a useful guide to this conduct. The process has two parts, he believed: "[The judge] must first extract from the precedents the underlying principle [of law] . . . [and] he must then determine the path or direction along which the principle is to move and develop, if it is not to wither and die."[9]

Cardozo thus joined Holmes in both accepting the existence of abstract legal principles and believing that their efficacy depended on experience. This was a marriage of nineteenth-century formalism and twentieth-century empiricism. If Holmes had built the philosophical bridge between the two centuries, then Cardozo paved the start of the road on the far side of the span.

Like Holmes, Cardozo was a reluctant inductee into the pragmatist and realist camps that were exploding across the legal frontier in the 1920s. Philosophical catch-phrases, such as pragmatism and legal realism, tend to have almost as many meanings as adherents. John Dewey himself, for instance, was both an early adherent of the school of pragmatism and uncomfortable with the term. The term *pragmatism,* as coined by Charles Pierce, identified the "experiential consequences" of abstract hypotheses.[10] Pierce's view of pragmatism was primarily fact- and science-based in that it demanded experimental or independent observational confirmations of experience. William James was most responsible for defining and popularizing the philosophical school. James, too, was concerned with the scientific realism of particular propositions or hypotheses. But James embedded a moral compass into his empiricism that allowed him to embrace subjectivity, while Pierce sought unadulterated objectivity. As John Dewey put it, "Pierce wrote as a logician and James as a humanist." James sought the "cash value" in empirical statements, their utility, in order that we might maintain "satisfactory relations with our surroundings."

Legal realism closely paralleled the main themes of pragmatism and, at the same time, evolved in several new directions. For instance, echoing James's demand for "cash value" in language, legal scholar and leading realist Felix Cohen derided the surplus of "supernatural concepts" in the law. He warned, "Any word that cannot pay up in the currency of fact, upon demand, is to be declared bankrupt, and we are to have no further dealings with it."[11] Realism was, like James's pragmatism, essentially empirical, but substantially informed by the progressive normative agenda.

Realism, however, was defined almost as much by what it was not as by what it was. It largely took shape as a rebuttal to nineteenth-century formalism. Formalists believed that a finite number of axioms could be discovered that would produce "correct" answers to specific legal questions. Justice Owen Roberts provided the classic statement of formalist jurisprudence in the 1935 case of *United States v. Butler*: "When an act of Congress is appropriately challenged in the courts as not conforming to the constitutional mandate, the judicial branch of Government has only one duty—to lay the article of the Constitution which is invoked beside the statute which is challenged and to decide whether the latter squares with the former."[12] Legal realism dismissed the talismanic power of logical deduction and replaced it with inductive empiricism—that is, knowledge based on experience. While formalists thought, as Blackstone had instructed, that judges merely declared the law, and do not *make it,* realists believed that the law was imbued with judges' personal, and even idiosyncratic, preferences. Law was a tool that produced social outcomes, and was within the control and under the guidance of mortal men, however much formalists sought to deny it. The more radical realists, for instance, quipped that how a judge decided a case on any given day had more to do with what he had for breakfast than anything in the statute books.

Realists additionally believed that judges were obligated to avow the corporal component of law. Legal realists set forth three related challenges to classical legal doctrine and the pat assumptions embraced by many. Legal realists claimed that unelected judges, not legislatures or "the people," largely choose the legal rules; second, they asserted, this reliance on the judiciary undermines, rather than reinforces, representative democracy; and, finally, they argued, outcomes are a product of will rather than abstract and neutral legal principle.[13] The realist challenge was fundamental and profound. If true, then ours is a government of men, not of laws. Law is not what courts say they do, it is what they do in particular cases. Thus, judges have great discretion to say what the law is, since the written word cannot sufficiently guide or restrain them. And the only way to measure the law's content and, implicitly, guide and restrain its direction is by studying law in practice. "A right," law professor Karl Llewellyn said, "exists to the extent that A can induce a court to squeeze, out of B, A's damages."[14] Reading cases and statute books could no longer be the lawyer's only task. As Brandeis had shown, lawyers had to collect data.

Holmes's exposition of what he called "the fundamental question"—"What constitutes the law?"—remains the best. He asked himself, if law is to govern society, what must society know about the law? More particularly, since good men mainly had little need to concern themselves with legal sanctions, Holmes asked himself, what does the bad man think constitutes the law? Formalist scholars, Holmes observed, mistakenly believed that law "is a system of reason, that it is a deduction from principles of ethics or admitted axioms or what not, which may or may not coincide with the decisions." But, Holmes stated,

> If we take the view of our friend the bad man we shall find that he does not care two straws for the axioms or deductions, but that he does want to know what the Massachusetts or English courts are likely to do in fact. . . . The prophecies of what the courts will do in fact, and nothing more pretentious, are what I mean by the law.[15]

Under the realist view, then, law was a function not of abstract theory but of social fact. Law evolved to account for and accommodate the demands of men and circumstances. Invariably, the law had to yield to the social context in which it operated, however compelling the abstract axioms that lay at its bottom. Roscoe Pound was an influential early expositor of realist philosophy. Born in 1870, the same year as Cardozo, Pound had been responsible for labeling the jurisprudential predecessor to realism, sociological jurisprudence. The most famous example of sociological jurisprudence was the Brandeis Brief. Pound was peculiarly well suited to the task of integrating the legal and the scientific. While studying law, he attended graduate school in botany, in which he received his doctoral degree in 1898. He continued to dabble in botany through-out his life, but focused primarily on the law. He became dean of the University of Nebraska's law school in 1903 and later moved on to become dean of the Harvard Law School, a post he held for twenty years. Pound succinctly explained the realist position on why law was contex-tually dependent:

> In a conflict between the law in books and the national will there can be but one result. Let us not become legal monks. Let us not allow our legal texts to acquire sanctity and go the way of all sacred writings. For the written word remains, but man changes. Whether laws of Mann or Zar-athustra or Moses, or the fourteenth amendment . . . or the latest legisla-tive discovery in Oklahoma, all laws tell us the same tale.[16]

Over time, though, legal realism fractured into several camps repre-sented by an assortment of colorful characters. Two in particular, Karl Llewellyn and Jerome Frank, are, together with Benjamin Cardozo and Roscoe Pound, worthy of note. Llewellyn was a Yale-trained lawyer who joined the Columbia law faculty in 1925 and remained there until 1951. In addition to his substantial contributions to scholarship on legal realism, Llewellyn tried his hand at poetry and reveled in what he called "an integration of the human and the artistic with the legal." Frank was trained at the University of Chicago and practiced both privately and for the government until he was nominated to the United States Court of Appeals for the Second Circuit by Roosevelt in 1941. In addition to his busy practice, Frank wrote extensively, especially concerning his belief that the law was imbued with Freudian psychoanalytic concepts and that its future success depended on coming to grips with the forces of the unconscious. Llewellyn and Frank represented the new, more radical wing of the realists. As is typically the case, they had little patience for the old ways—ways embodied by men like Pound and Cardozo.

In 1930, Karl Llewellyn opened fire on the old-guard realists when he published the article "A Realistic Jurisprudence—The Next Step." In somewhat overcooked prose, Llewellyn sought to lay a framework for what he conceived of as a new movement. It was one that sought to effectuate many of the basic principles Holmes had articulated almost a half century before. For instance, Llewellyn said that "real rules," if he had his "way with words, would by legal scientists be called the practices of the courts, and not 'rules' at all." He continued, saying that "statements of 'rights' would be statements of likelihood that in a given situation a certain type of court action loomed in the offing. Factual terms. No more."[17] The lawyer's job was to study the law in action. The lawyer's tools were no longer the black letter of reported cases, but the methods of social science. The lawyer's laboratory was no longer the dark library, but the light of the real world.

The young Turk Llewellyn had laid down the challenge to the first generation of Holmes's descendants, most famously represented by Pound. In his youth, Pound helped lead the revolution that Holmes and Brandeis both championed, the effort to shape law in light of experience. By 1930, however, Dean Pound had grown to suffer the ailments of age and position, conservatism and oracularity.

In "A Realistic Jurisprudence," Llewellyn had sought to pick a fight with the Harvard dean. To his delight, and Pound's everlasting regret, he was successful. Llewellyn pointedly accused Pound of being "caught in . . . an age that is passing." It was a charge that would stick. In his response to Llewellyn's challenge, Pound wrote "The Call for a Realist Jurisprudence," published in the *Harvard Law Review* in 1931. He criticized the new realists, saying that they were doing little beyond what had been done before. He also believed they overemphasized the "what is" questions, and failed to deal adequately with the problem of saying "what ought to be."

He agreed that "the gathering of statistics can show us much as to how justice is administered, and how and how far precepts are observed and enforced." But he rejected the idea that statistics could say how law "ought to be administered." He said that this "question of ought, turning ultimately on a theory of values, is the hardest one in jurisprudence." He thought it folly to try and make law "an exact science analogous to mathematics or physics or astronomy." Pound argued, "Faithful portrayal of what courts and lawmakers and jurists do is not the whole task of a science of law." He thought it simply impossible to divorce the question of what is done from what ought to be done. "The new realists," he charged, "have their own preconceptions of what is significant, and hence of what juristically must be. Most of them merely substitute a psychological must for an ethical or political or historical must."[18] The so-called new realists, he chided, have merely "an illusion of reality . . . [for] the significant question is the one excluded."[19]

Llewellyn responded to Pound in an aptly named article entitled "Some Realism About Realism," also published in the *Harvard Law Review*. Llewellyn agreed with Pound that if Pound's accusations were true, then "rebukes are needed." He stated, "Spare the rod and spoil the realist." The problem, as Llewellyn aptly demonstrated, was that Pound's characterization of the new realists was embarrassingly wide of the mark. It was little more than caricature. Indeed, before publishing his rejoinder, Llewellyn had written Pound several times asking him to name names, to say who among the new movement were guilty of the many offenses Pound itemized. Receiving no answer, Llewellyn looked for himself and in a withering critique found Pound's criticisms wanting. Pound had committed the ultimate offense against realism: he had ignored the facts.

According to Llewellyn, realism was a fabric of multiple conceptions. The essence of Llewellyn's realism had three basic aspects. First, law evolved. Law was not a set of fundamental axioms that, once discovered, could be applied to new contexts unerringly. The task of the realist was to study individual and institutional dynamics in the field, in an effort to formulate psychological and sociological theories of legal behavior. Second, law was functional. Realists conceived of law "as a means to social ends and not as an end in itself." It should not be concerned with meta-physical conceptions of "justice," "fairness," "good faith," or "prop-erty," but instead focus on how certain rules produce particular social outcomes. Third, Llewellyn argued for the *temporary divorce of Is and Ought for purpose of study*." If legal science was to be a member of the social sciences, it had to study law without preconception of what should be done. Later, wearing different hats, the realists could prescribe policy based on what the facts were.

Realism was a movement that, to be successful, had to fundamentally alter the way lawyers were trained and how they did their jobs. Jerome Frank, who was closely aligned with Llewellyn, argued that the very foun-dation of the legal citadel had to be rebuilt. The law schools, for instance,

> must become, in part, schools of psychology, applied to law in all its phases. In law schools, in law offices and law courts there must be explicit recognition of the meaning of the phrase "human nature in law." The study of human nature in law . . . may not only deepen our knowledge of legal institutions but open an unworked venire of judicial wisdom.[20]

A great divide had been opened between the descendants of Holmes.

Benjamin Cardozo, not one who ordinarily sought controversy, stepped into the abyss. He did so awkwardly and at some risk to his nomination to the Supreme Court. Holmes had retired on January 11, 1932. The news-papers filled with speculation on his replacement, with a resounding cho-rus calling for Cardozo. On January 22, Mark Sullivan summarized the sentiment in his syndicated column, writing that the "universality of the applause for Judge Cardozo constitutes a unique condition, almost a phe-nomenon."[21] Ordinarily, prospective nominees to the Court are counseled to avoid controversy during the twilight period before Senate confirma-tion. Cardozo, inexplicably, courted it. On the very day Sullivan's column celebrated his likely nomination, Cardozo gave a lecture entitled "Juris-prudence" in which he tried to mediate the feud between Llewellyn and Pound. In doing so, he stepped into a hornet's nest with his arms flailing.

Cardozo believed that the feud was unnecessary, since he believed that Llewellyn and Frank were members of the same school as Pound, as well as himself. Cardozo had written as much in a letter to Felix Frankfurter. "Recent talks with Llewellyn make me feel that the bark of the realists is worse than their bite, and that the differences are largely verbal." He told Frankfurter that he would try in his Bar Association address "to reconcile the factions and bring the contending groups together."[22] Unfortunately, Cardozo had little appreciation of the terms of the battle, or the personalities fighting it. For instance, he had considered addressing Frank's new book on realism, but decided against mentioning it at all, since he did not have the time to study it in detail. Frank, a proud and self-important man, would feel slighted by this treatment. He would have preferred the most violent criticisms to being ignored.

Cardozo began his lecture by describing the contributions of men like Holmes and Pound, "who strove to see the truth in the workings of the judicial process . . . and to report what they had seen with sincerity and candor."[23] He characterized what he called the "neo-realist" movement as part of an established and expanding realist tradition. But since the "new realists" saw themselves as a revolutionary departure from the old school of Pound, and as the rightful heirs of Holmes, this attempt at reconciliation was perceived as an insult. Unfortunately, Cardozo went even further, adding explicit affront to his implicit snub of the new realists. He criticized "the style that the faithful have appropriated for themselves," calling it "over-pretentious." He also discounted the more extreme positions marked out by some new realists, especially those who denied a role for logic and rational choice in judicial decision-making. He considered those realists who extolled ad hoc subjectivism as being out of the mainstream and described their writings as indicating "the derision and impatience that betray themselves here and there among the priests of the new gospel of juridical salvation."[24] Finally, Cardozo rejected the new realists' exclusive focus on what judges do, rather than what they say. Cardozo believed—not surprisingly, since he was a judge and had written famously on the judging process—that the explanations judges give remained a vital subject of study.

The so-called new realists, and especially Jerome Frank, were incensed with Cardozo's lecture. Frank, feeling personally impugned, believed that Cardozo had made light of the profound changes that he and his compatriots were bringing to the law. In a thirty-one-page letter that was accompanied by another thirty-one pages of his writings appended to it, Frank defended the revolutionaries, whom he called "sceptics." While Frank began the letter with a tribute to Cardozo's contributions to realism, he quickly settled into a detailed refutation of the lecture. He thought Cardozo underappreciated the amount of uncertainty in the judicial process, especially in the degree of discretion afforded at the trial level in finding facts. Moreover, he told Cardozo, the sceptics had merely recognized the uncertainty and caprice in the system; they did not applaud it. Frank then discussed his own work, and hailed the rational social planning afforded by the new "Enlightenment." Frank was angry and the letter accusatory. He believed that Cardozo had misjudged the new realist movement and, worse, largely ignored Frank's contributions to it.

Cardozo reacted by trying to smooth over the matter and by avoiding any direct confrontation. By this time Cardozo was on the Court so he could blame the workload for his inability to respond in detail. He wrote to Frank that he had time only to "skim over" the letter, but found it "full of interest and suggestion." He then deprecated his own work: "I am sorry that you have found so much to criticize in my address; but I do not think very highly of it myself and so I have no reason to complain that it is unsatisfactory to others." He told Frank that he had no intention to publish it in a law review. But he warned Frank, too, saying, "If you write about it, you will be investing it with an importance which I am quite ready to believe that it does not deserve."[25]

Frank was not mollified. In fact, by failing to give the letter more than a cursory read, Cardozo had thrown gasoline on Frank's simmering resentment. In attempting to avoid a fight, Cardozo had left the impression that Frank's ideas were not worth engaging. Frank would not forget the slight, and sought revenge after Cardozo's death when he published an anonymous critique of Cardozo's work.[26] He directed his venom at Cardozo's writing style, saying that "Cardozo attained eminence as a thinker not because but in spite of his style." Frank wrote that Cardozo "was a nice analyst with a zest, not always exercised, for following up all the implications of his ideas. But the clarity was in his thinking. His was not a lucid style."[27] Many years later, in an empirical study of Cardozo's reputation, Judge Richard Posner examined the sources of Cardozo's famed reputation. Among a long list, Posner singled out as most important his literary skills, a talent that lifted his opinions "out of the swarm of humdrum, often numbing, judicial opinions."[28] Posner also ascribed some of Cardozo's success to his being "saintly," in the sense that he was genuinely "nice."[29] The same cannot be said about Frank.

Given their belief in the value of a fact-based jurisprudence, the realists not surprisingly set out to collect data. Statistics were to be their salvation. By the late 1920s, realists were concentrated at three major institutions, the law schools of Columbia and Yale universities, and the institute for legal study at Johns Hopkins University. Under Langdell's brand of formalism, law professors across the country studied and taught cases as though they were the data on which the fabric of the law was woven. Realists, however, saw little value in court opinions beyond the outcomes they announced. The truth was to be had through experience, and statistics provided the window to it. At Yale, for example, Robert Hutchins and Charles Clark proposed in 1926 that the law school "perform distinguished public service by assisting in the solution of the most pressing problems of the law by scientific study of all procedure in its functional, comparative, and historical aspects."[30] They believed that the laws should reflect and be informed by social circumstances. This required the collection of data, and so the realists enlisted in the social sciences. Given that most of them had little or no training in statistics or social science research methods, the disaster that followed should have been entirely predictable.

As budding social scientists, the realists suffered from two serious faults. Foremost, although they were enthusiastic believers in the new art of statistical analysis, they had little understanding of it and even less patience to collect the data and conduct the analyses necessary to understand the extraordinarily complex phenomena in which they were interested. More problematic, the realists saw social science as a tool in the Progressives' political battles and as a tool for promoting their reform agenda. Past reform efforts failed, they believed, because of an absence of data. Therefore, data were needed to support reform efforts already in the works. Ordinarily, data collection reveals areas in need of reform. The realists already knew what needed reforming. The data merely filled in the details and confirmed the need for action. As Hutchins and Clark put it, "We regard facts as the prerequisite of reform."[31] The basic premise of their work was that if only the facts were known about extant social conditions, reform would naturally follow. Therefore, if research did not support immediate reform, it was not worth doing. The realists thought that data that did not conform to their view of society were little more than an "irrelevant jumble of figures."

Well representing the new faith in statistics were two of Franklin Roosevelt's brain trust, Felix Frankfurter, a protégé of Holmes and Brandeis, and William O. Douglas, a leading realist academic in the late 1920s. Frankfurter was born on November 15, 1882, in Vienna, Austria. He immigrated to the United States with his parents at the age of twelve, settling on the Lower East Side of New York. After attending the College of the City of New York, he moved to Boston to attend the Harvard Law School. He finished first in his class in each of his three years there. In 1906, he returned to New York for a short stint in private practice and then went to work for Henry L. Stimson, who was then the United States Attorney in New York. Frankfurter followed Stimson through a variety of political adventures, from a failed run for governor to Taft's cabinet, where Stimson was secretary of war.

In Washington, Frankfurter capitalized on an introduction by a former professor to develop a friendship with Holmes. He also met and befriended Louis Brandeis, a relationship that would develop into a close collaboration in future years. But he was destined, in the short term, to return to New England. In 1914, Frankfurter joined the Harvard Law School faculty. He later commented on his reaction to the job offer: "If I had received a letter from an Indian princess asking me to marry her, I wouldn't have been more surprised." Brandeis had quietly orchestrated the invitation and was alone among Frankfurter's friends in recommending that he accept it. Holmes advised against it: "Academic life is but half-life—it is withdrawal from the fight in order to utter smart things that cost you nothing except the thinking them from a cloister."[32] Holmes would be proved wrong—at least in Frankfurter's case.

Frankfurter pursued his Progressive reform agenda on two fronts. On one, he entered into a close collaboration with Brandeis whereby Brandeis, while on the Court, both supported him financially and collaborated with him intellectually in a multitude of efforts over the years, an arrangement not known to the public. Although the ethical guidelines for judicial behavior are more stringent today, even then this would have caused a considerable public stir. The battles on Frankfurter's second front were fought by the legions of his former students whom he placed in positions throughout the Roosevelt administration. These protégés, commonly referred to as "Felix's Happy Dogs," were scattered up and down the halls of power, and they all owed political debts to Frankfurter. But not all of Washington was happy with their presence, as expressed by George Peek's—the head of the Agricultural Adjustment Administration—comment:

A plague of young lawyers settled on Washington. They all claimed to be friends of somebody or other and mostly of Felix Frankfurter and Jerome

Frank. They floated airily into offices, took desks, asked for papers and found no end of things to be busy about. I never found out why they came, what they did or why they left.[33]

Frankfurter, despite being cloistered in Cambridge, Massachusetts, proved to be an enormously influential presence in Washington, particularly in the area of social policy. He owed this influence partly to his intellect and the force of his ideas, but primarily to his skills with people. He brilliantly cultivated relationships with two sets of people. First were his mentors, men such as Stimson, Holmes, and Brandeis. Frankfurter possessed the gift of flattery and consistently throughout his life developed relationships with powerful men by prostrating himself at their feet in dramatic displays of bootlicking. What self-esteem he lost in such obsequiousness he recovered in his relationships with a second group, his students. Although he genuinely cared for them and worked tirelessly to ensure their success both at Harvard and in their later careers, he demanded their unwavering loyalty and continued reverence. They must always remain his faithful students, never rising to be his peers. Unfortunately, Frankfurter's people skills did not extend to those who considered themselves his equal. This blind spot would compound the difficulties he would face during his tenure on the Supreme Court. One of the men who would be Frankfurter's chief antagonist on the Court had been one of his closest intellectual allies in the Roosevelt administration, William O. Douglas. Theirs was a feud that would last over twenty years.

Douglas was born in Maine, Minnesota, near the North Dakota border, in 1898. Shortly after his birth his family went west. They stopped first in Estrella, California, and then in 1904 moved to Cleveland, Washington, about fifty miles from Yakima. Douglas's father died that same year, and the family was forced to move to Yakima, where they suffered in abject poverty throughout Douglas's childhood. Compounding the travails of poverty, Douglas contracted infantile paralysis, which left him weak and vulnerable to the cruelties of his childhood acquaintances. When he recovered enough to begin a diet of exercise, Douglas built up his strength through mountain climbing and long difficult hikes in the wilderness. It was the beginning of a lifelong love of the outdoors and an insatiable appetite for adventure. His early experiences also contributed to a rugged independence and strength of character, as well as his regular displays of empathy for the poor, disabled, and disadvantaged— conditions he knew personally.

In his memoirs, Douglas looked back at his childhood and attributed much of his later success to the lessons and misery he suffered then. He believed that a turning point in his life was the oppressive sadness he felt after his father died, and the realization he came to as he stood at his father's graveside. At the funeral, Douglas observed years later:

> I happened to see Mount Adams towering over us on the west. It was dark purple and white in the August day and its shoulders of basalt were heavy with glacial snow. It was a giant whose head touched the sky.
>
> As I looked, I stopped sobbing. My eyes dried. Adams stood cool and calm, unperturbed by the event that had stirred us so deeply. Suddenly the mountain seemed to be a friend, a force for me to tie to, a symbol of stability and strength.[34]

After college, Douglas, with virtually no money in his pocket, hitched rides on freight cars across the country to attend law school at Columbia. There, he met Harlan Fiske Stone, who was then the dean and would later serve with Douglas on the Court. Douglas was initiated into the realist movement at Columbia when he served as Underhill Moore's research assistant. In fact, Columbia was a boiling cauldron of realist activity during the 1920s. In addition to Llewellyn and Moore, realist scholars and itinerant social scientists at Columbia included notables such as Herman Oliphant, Walter Wheeler Cook, Thomas Reed Powell, and Julius Goebel. After practicing for a short time, both in New York and Yakima, Douglas joined the Columbia faculty. Many of the Columbia realists, however, eventually moved to Yale, led by Douglas, after the insurgents lost the battle over Dean Stone's replacement.

At Columbia and Yale, Douglas's scholarship focused on corporate law and bankruptcy. Douglas had been greatly influenced by the work of Thorstein Veblen and Louis Brandeis, taking from the latter his lifetime skepticism of big business. His academic research was especially tailored to demonstrate the beauty of the small. At Yale, he ran the Business Failures Project, an ambitious research study in which he was given access, through Judge William Clark in Newark, to parties in bankruptcy proceedings. This project, however, demonstrated the daunting realities of the realists' efforts to collect data. Douglas ended up with incomplete data, and he hoped for conclusions that did not follow from the data that he did collect. Much of his work was in such a state of disorder that it was unpublishable. He began the project in 1928, expecting to expose the "functioning of the whole credit system of the country." By 1932, he had to settle for two modest publications. He eventually abandoned the project altogether.

Douglas's experience was far from unusual for the realists of the first part of the twentieth century. Almost to a man, they were primarily interested in affecting social policy. Douglas was first and foremost a reformer who wanted to fight the abuses of "predatory finance." Collecting data was an arduous and interminable commitment of time and resources. The payoff was not great, since most of the realists sought data not to test their hypotheses about the social world, but to confirm their conclusions about the need for new rules to transform a social world they believed they knew a priori existed. And when they were not proving the "obvious," they were testing the irrelevant. In an unusually sharp comment on his fellow travelers' empirical efforts, Llewellyn had this to say about the work being done at Yale and Johns Hopkins:

> I doubt whether in all of the quest for social science there has ever been such hastily considered, ill-planned, mal-prepared large-scale so-called research as was perpetrated by Cook and Oliphant at Hopkins. But it was at Yale that the nadir of idiocy was achieved when Underhill Moore "tested out" whether law has mystical operation by an elaborate observation, metering and statisticking of the non-effect on the parking practices of New Haveners of a change in the official traffic regulations which he had arranged to keep carefully from coming to the knowledge of any trafficker.[35]

Douglas's ambition, especially as a reformer, was ultimately vindicated when he was offered the opportunity to sit on the Supreme Court. He often told the story of how President Roosevelt pulled him off the golf course one Sunday morning in March 1939 to offer him the seat recently given up by Louis Brandeis. Ironically, the main obstacle to his joining the Court was the concern among many in Washington that Douglas was not western enough. It was widely believed that Brandeis's vacated seat should go to a westerner. Douglas had spent the greater part of his adult life in school, teaching, and practicing on the East Coast, but his western identity was complete. He deeply disliked the urban East, harboring a special contempt for New York City. Some years later, for instance, he dissented from an opinion denying a tax deduction for the winner of a business sales contest who had been awarded a trip to New

York for meetings and sightseeing. Douglas wrote that the trip could not be described as a valuable form of compensation, because no sensible person would choose to vacation in New York.

On the Court, Douglas was an iconoclast. He had been raised a realist and he brought those sensibilities with him to the bench. However, in the 1930s and after, the political climate began to change dramatically. These changes deeply affected realism itself and particularly the New Deal Democrats who had been educated in realist teachings.

When Holmes had inveighed against the Court's social Darwinist judicial activism, he was driven by a belief in deference to the legislative will. Brandeis, too, had revered judicial restraint, but only when state legislatures were passing socially responsible laws. Unlike Holmes, Brandeis had been more willing to invalidate legislative actions that trampled on individual rights outside the economic sphere. The only exception to this division between Holmes's and Brandeis's philosophies came about, in time, with Holmes's increasing willingness to be vigilant in protecting First Amendment values against government encroachment. On the whole, prior to the mid-1930s judicial restraint was associated with the belief in liberal progressive legislative reform. Judicial activism was represented by Spencerian social Darwinists who actively struck down social welfare legislation that protected the individual or small business from the predations of big business. In the 1930s, this switched.

The moment in time when the Court took its first steps into the modern era is indelibly linked with Franklin Roosevelt's infamous Court-packing plan. In the early years of the New Deal, a time when the federal government passed an abundance of social welfare legislation in an attempt to battle the Great Depression, the Court, dominated by social Darwinists, regularly struck down these laws, believing them contrary to natural principles of the free market. These onslaughts against New Deal legislation were led by the justices known as "the four horsemen"— Willis Van Devanter, James McReynolds, George Sutherland, and Pierce Butler. Justice Owen Roberts often joined these devotees of Herbert Spencer to constitute 5–4 majorities against federal legislation. Douglas despised the four horsemen for their narrow-minded mulishness. He also found much about them to dislike personally, even extending to their slow play on the golf links. The four regularly played together and Douglas sometimes found himself behind them on the course. He complained, "They were as slow as molasses, taking many shots and consuming what seemed like hours in putting."[36]

Roosevelt, incensed at the Court's intransigence, approached Congress and proposed a scheme whereby the president would have the power to nominate an additional justice for each sitting justice who turned seventy, up to a total of fifteen members. The ostensible justification for the proposal was Roosevelt's asserted desire to assist the Court by injecting young blood to help the aged and infirm do their jobs. Roosevelt badly miscalculated. His objective to pack the Court with justices who would endorse his programs was blatantly transparent. Roosevelt nearly admitted as much when he said, "[We have] reached the point as a Nation where we must take action to save the Constitution from the Court and the Court from itself." Roosevelt also did not anticipate Chief Justice Stone's deft response. In a letter to Congress, Stone informed the legislators that the Court was fully caught up on its business. The letter also pointed out the obvious flaw in Roosevelt's logic. Adding justices, as anyone who has sat on a deliberative committee knows, would multiply, not ease, the burdens on the Court.

Amid the ensuing uproar over Roosevelt's plan, the need for it disappeared. On March 29, 1937, Roberts abandoned the four horsemen. On that day, the Court upheld four acts involving social welfare reform and extensions of federal power, several of which dealt with the same subjects as laws struck down just months before. Presidential adviser, and later Court justice, Robert Jackson wrote, "What a day!" He cheered, "To labor, minimum wage laws and collective bargaining; to farmers, relief in bankruptcy; to law enforcement, firearms control. The Court was on the march." Roberts's change of mind is denoted in legal lore as the "switch in time that saved nine." As is often true, however, the story was rather more complicated than Roberts simply buckling under Roosevelt's pressure. In several cases, Roberts's change of heart had not been influenced by Roosevelt's court-packing plan, since his votes had been cast before its announcement, though the opinions were not published until after.[37] Nonetheless, a distinct sea change had occurred, one that was settled in August 1937 when Congress finally buried the plan and Justice Willis Van Devanter resigned. This gave Roosevelt the first of nine appointments he would make to the Court.

Roosevelt took advantage of Van Devanter's departure by appointing Hugo Black, a former Alabama senator and a staunch New Deal Democrat. Black would not disappoint Roosevelt and he developed a strict interpretive style that favored both broad federal remedial powers and occasional staunch protection of civil liberties. George Sutherland was the next horseman to leave, being replaced by Stanley Reed, from Kentucky, in 1938. Then, in 1939, Felix Frankfurter replaced Cardozo and that same year Douglas took Brandeis's seat. Black would later team with Douglas in case after case, and they especially came to be aligned against Frankfurter. With Black, Reed, Frankfurter, and Douglas joining the Court, New Dealers expected a group of brethren that would work hand in hand to realize the social and political values of the Roosevelt revolution. Although they were partly correct, they were mostly wrong.

When Frankfurter was nominated for the Court in 1939, there was no one in the country who had a more intimate knowledge of the Court's inner workings or of the history and doctrine that gave its pronouncements form and life. Douglas commented that Frankfurter was easily the most qualified man for the job. He had been a confidant of Holmes and Brandeis and was on intimate terms with Cardozo and Stone. He was as much of an insider as anyone not on the Court could be. He also was the foremost national authority on the system of federal courts and an expert on constitutional law. He had impeccable New Deal and Progressive credentials and had become popularly known for his critical assessment of the convictions of Sacco and Vanzetti. Frankfurter should have proved an enormous success on the bench, as the leader of Roosevelt's New Deal appointees. Frankfurter, too, believed that he was destined to lead the Court. He expected that his new colleagues would naturally defer to his greater knowledge, deeper experience, and superior intellect. When they did not, fur flew.

Frankfurter tended to treat his colleagues as somewhat dim-witted first-year law students. In one case, he courted Stanley Reed's vote, who he believed could not understand his position. Frankfurter told Reed, "It is the lot of professors to be often not understood by pupils. . . . So let me try again."[38] On another occasion, Frankfurter told Reed that at Harvard he taught his students that if they at first did not understand a statute they should read it a second or even a third time. He advised Reed to do likewise.[39] Although Frankfurter respected Douglas's intellect, he still tended to treat him in an obnoxiously professorial manner. Once, Frankfurter wrote Douglas a memo criticizing an opinion he wrote for the Court, stating, "I am bound to say that it is bad for both of us that we are no longer professors. Because if you were still a professor, you would have written a different elaboration and if I were still a professor, I would get several lectures out of what you have written."[40]

One of Frankfurter's most annoying habits was his tendency to pontificate during deliberations. Justice Potter Stewart recalled that Frankfurter "would speak for fifty minutes, no more or less, because that was the length of the lecture at the Harvard Law School."[41] Of all the justices, Douglas had the least amount of patience for Frankfurter's conference diatribes. He also developed a taste for getting under Frankfurter's skin at every opportunity. At one conference, Douglas told his collected justices that he had come into the conference agreeing "with the conclusion that Felix has just announced. But he's just talked me out of it." Whenever some incompetent attorney was fumbling through his oral argument, Douglas would send a note to Frankfurter saying that "this chap led your class at Harvard Law School." In one argument, in 1960, Frankfurter was blistering counsel with questions. Douglas decided to come to the poor man's aid and he began offering helpful answers to each of Frankfurter's questions. Frankfurter finally snapped, turning on the hapless lawyer: "I thought you were arguing this case." "I am," the attorney answered, "but I can use all the help I can get." This sort of behavior led Frankfurter to say that Douglas was one of "two completely evil men I have ever met."[42]

Frankfurter's faith in his own interpretations of case law bordered on the principle of justice infallibility. He had complete disdain for his liberal colleagues who, he believed, infused the law with their subjective preferences. He wrote in his diary, "When a priest enters a monastery, he must leave—or ought to leave—all sorts of worldly desires behind him. And this Court has no excuse for being unless it's a monastery."[43] Too many justices, he thought, bent the law for personal preference. In one opinion, he wrote, "It can never be emphasized too much that one's own opinion about the wisdom or evil of a law should be excluded altogether when one is doing one's duty on the bench." He accused Black of being "indifferent to the use he was making of cases, utterly disregardful of what they stood for, and quite reckless."[44] In a letter to Learned Hand, he wrote that Black "is a self-righteous, self-deluded part fanatic part demagogue, who really disbelieves in law, thinks it essentially manipulative of language."[45]

A constant source of dispute among succeeding generations of realists involved the question, Who were the rightful heirs of Oliver Wendell Holmes? This dispute lay at the core of the feud between Frankfurter and Douglas. Frankfurter had cut his teeth on the Progressives' disdain for the *Lochner* Court's judicial activism, and he considered himself, and his jurisprudence, as the rightful heir to Holmes. This, too, grated on his colleagues' nerves. Justice William Brennan reportedly commented, "We would be inclined to agree with Felix more often in conference, if he quoted Holmes less frequently to us." Like Holmes, Frankfurter thought the Court acted beyond its authority in second-guessing legislative judgments regarding the wisdom of programs like minimum-wage guarantees, maximum-hour limitations, or the multitude of social welfare reforms passed under Roosevelt. Unlike Holmes, he was not guided by a fully developed nihilistic theory of deference to the mob. Frankfurter came to his theory of judicial restraint more esoterically. He believed that the Court, with justices who were not elected by, or accountable to, the people, was obligated to defer to majoritarian choices exhibited by the political decisions reached by the legislative and executive branches. He believed that "holding democracy in judicial tutelage is not the most promising way to foster disciplined responsibility in a people."[46] Frankfurter trembled at the prospect of being governed by—or governing as— platonic guardians. According to one Court observer, Frankfurter's maxim was, "When in doubt, don't."[47]

It is impossible to say whether Holmes would have persisted on a Frankfurter-like course, a course of "deference, almost no matter what," if he had remained on the Court. Later in his career, Holmes moved away from this position somewhat, as evidenced by his increasing vigilance in protecting First Amendment freedoms against majoritarian incursion. But it was Brandeis who most clearly moved away from the strong version of judicial restraint. Brandeis deeply believed that the Court was duty-bound to protect certain basic liberties against majoritarian interference. However, according to Brandeis, the Court had little role in reviewing legislation that protected people from the predations of big business. The Court, thus, should be restrained when government acts on behalf of the public's general welfare. However, when government interferes with basic social and personal liberties, Brandeis followed his Progressive politics, believing the Court to be obligated to actively guard the individual from majority tyranny.

Justice Douglas was of the Brandeis school—with a vengeance. Douglas fervently embraced the role of philosopher king. He did not believe this role could be avoided. As a realist, Douglas had helped to expose the subjectiveness of judicial decision-making. As a justice, he fully embraced the latitude that this subjectiveness gave him. The Court had to tame two beasts, majority will and individual liberty, both of which sought to encroach upon the territory of the other. Persistent deference to majority will would unleash it to prey upon liberty. And always siding with liberty would undermine the very foundation of democracy, since it was premised on majority will. For Douglas, then, the Court would surrender its responsibility if it failed to actively reconcile the rights of individuals to be let alone and the privilege of the majority to govern as it deemed necessary. Judicial restraint, Douglas believed, constituted abdication of the very role invested in the Court by the Constitution.

For Frankfurter, such thinking was presumptuous and arrogant. He objected to the idea that the Court should adjust the Constitution to meet "the social arrangements and beliefs of a particular epoch."[48] He considered Douglas, along with Hugo Black and Earl Warren, to be "undisciplined by adequate professional learning and cultivated understanding."[49] They made decisions, Frankfurter cried, on the basis of "their prejudices and their respective pasts and self-conscious desires to join Thomas Paine and T. Jefferson in the Valhalla of 'liberty' and in the meantime to have the avant-garde of the Yale Law School . . . praise them."[50] For himself, he said, "As a member of this Court I am not justified in writing my private notions of policy into the Constitution, no matter how deeply I may cherish them or how mischievous I may deem their disregard."[51] The one "common-denominator" his activist colleagues shared, he said, "is a self-willed self-righteous power-lust."[52]

Frankfurter's strong version of judicial restraint ironically strengthened and deepened the progressive political agenda that he detested. It forced justices such as Black and Douglas, and later Earl Warren, William Brennan, and Thurgood Marshall—as well as a generation of legal scholars—to more fully justify their judicial activism. Frankfurter had sought to extend the tradition of Holmes and Brandeis as he saw it. But his vision was a crabbed and narrow view of the judicial role, one that mistook discretion for abdication. Yet he fought so strenuously for judicial abnegation that he forced his opponents to more forcefully defend their decisions. Only in time would this liberal activism win out and flourish with the Warren Court of the 1950s and 1960s. In the meantime, the 1940s would be a time of war, and civil liberties had to wait.

"ATTAINDER OF BLOOD":

Race and Eugenics in the 1940s

One element should be fundamental to all the compoundings of the social phar-
macopoeia. That element is blood . . . clean, virile, genius-bearing blood,
streaming down the ages through the unerring action of heredity. . . . What we
to-day need above all else is . . . a recognition of the supreme importance of
heredity.

—LOTHROP STODDARD

In May 1942, the United States Supreme Court heard oral argument in
Skinner v. Oklahoma, a case in which it considered the constitutionality
of an Oklahoma statute that provided for the forced sterilization of habitual offenders. Skinner had run afoul of the statute with his third robbery
conviction, one of which involved the theft of chickens. The Oklahoma
law was premised on the belief that criminal personalities were inheritable and that sterilization would stanch the flow of criminal traits in
subsequent generations. The Court invalidated the law on the basis that
it applied unequally to similarly situated offenders. Someone who robbed
more than $20 three times was subject to the act, but a person three
times guilty of embezzling the same amount was not. According to this
logic, the Court might have upheld the law if it applied to all habitual
offenders in an evenhanded fashion. The constitutionality of the basis for
the law—that certain tendencies of classes of habitual offenders are
inheritable—was not questioned. If the justices had considered this question, they would have been forced to reflect on whether scientific evidence
was available to support such a broad proposition regarding biological
determinacy, reflection that would have paid dividends when the Court
later confronted an analogous issue of racial determinacy. In May 1942,

Japanese-Americans were being displaced from their homes in the western states. When the Japanese internment cases came to the Court, the justices again chose not to evaluate the merits of the scientific proof. It was a failure that badly tarnished the Court's reputation and provides an important lesson on the need to understand, and critically evaluate, scientific evidence.

On December 7, 1941, without warning, the Japanese navy attacked the United States Naval Base at Pearl Harbor. At the very hour of the attack, Japanese diplomats were negotiating with the State Department ostensibly for the purpose of reaching a peaceful agreement between the two countries. That same day, the Japanese attacked Malaysia, Hong Kong, the Philippines, and Wake and Midway Islands. The next day the Japanese army invaded Thailand. In the following weeks the Japanese sank two British battleships and waged a successful campaign against Britain's great naval base on Singapore. Guam, Wake Island, and Hong Kong fell within a month. In March, Japanese forces established control over the Netherlands East Indies, Rangoon, and Burma. By early 1942, the Japanese Empire had successfully washed over the Pacific Islands and appeared to be spreading effortlessly east toward the American Pacific coast.

More ominous still, tens of thousands of Japanese living in the United States were thought to be poised as a "fifth column" of support for an invading imperial force. Rumors were rampant in December that Hawaii had fallen prey to such internal sabotage. Nazi invasions in Europe had been aided by fifth-column activities carried out by agents and sympathizers, so it stood to reason that at least as much could be expected from the Japanese. Indeed, this view was promulgated by high government officials. Secretary of the Navy Philander Knox told the press, "I think the most effective Fifth Column work of the entire war was done in Hawaii with the possible exception of Norway."[1] It was widely believed that, as a matter of human nature, Japanese-Americans would "identify" with others of "their kind" and that their loyalties would at best be mixed, and more likely stand squarely behind the invaders. A Japanese attack on the American mainland could likely be accompanied by concerted acts of sabotage from within. Indeed, in seeming preparation for such actions, Japanese-Americans had apparently "deployed" around sensitive military and industrial areas, undoubtedly ready to strike when the opportunity best presented itself.

California politicians led the way in raising the alarm about the strategic readiness of a Japanese fifth column. Earl Warren, California's attorney general and soon-to-be candidate for governor, described this "disturbing situation" to a select committee of the House of Representatives in February 1942. Population maps, he testified, showed that "along the Coast from Marin County to the Mexican border virtually every important strategic location and installation has one or more Japanese in its immediate vicinity."[2] For instance, a sheriff in one coastal county told Warren "that in his county Japanese farmers are working within a grenade throw of coast-defense guns"; and in another county, a sheriff warned him "that it is necessary to pass through the yards of three Japanese farmers to reach certain coast-defense installations."[3] Warren believed the danger was widespread and included American citizens. "I am concerned that the fifth column activities of our enemies call for the participation of people who are in fact American citizens, and that if we are to deal realistically with the problem we must realize that we will be obliged in time of stress to deal with subversive elements of our own citizenry."[4]

The Japanese presence around sensitive military areas could not be a coincidence. At least, according to Warren, the situation in Santa Barbara County could not be explained by coincidence alone:

> In the northern end of that county is Camp Cook where, I am informed, the only armored division on the Pacific Coast will be located. The only practical entrance to Camp Cook is on the secondary road through the town of Lompoc. The maps show this entrance is flanked with Japanese property, and it is impossible to move a single man or piece of equipment in or out of Camp Cook without having it pass under the scrutiny of numerous Japanese.[5]

California congressman Leland Ford wrote Secretary of State Cordell Hull a telegram in which he said, "I do not believe we could be any too strict in our consideration of the Japanese in the face of the treacherous way they do things." Ford was an early and ardent supporter of Japanese exclusion from the West Coast. He implored the secretary of state and the attorney general to remove "all Japanese, whether citizens or not, [to] inland concentration camps." He reasoned that, if truly loyal, Japanese-Americans would not protest being removed from their homes and interned behind barbed wire.[6] California governor Culbert Olson also favored evacuation. Perhaps most damaging, liberal congressman Jerry Voorhis accepted that evacuation was "a wise and proper move."[7] Earl Warren also ultimately resolved that evacuation was the only safe course. "I have come to the conclusion that the Japanese situation as it exists today in this state may well be the Achilles' heel of the entire civilian defense effort. Unless something is done it may bring about another Pearl Harbor."[8]

The Japanese on American soil, collectively known as Nikkei, were divisible into several categories. The Issei were born in Japan and had immigrated to the United States. Under the law at the time, they were ineligible for citizenship. The Nisei were first-generation and the Sansei were second-generation Americans. Nisei and Sansei were thus American citizens. A third category of note were the Kibei, American-born Japanese who returned to Japan for their educations. But whatever the generation, a general lack of assimilation was held up as strong evidence of their potential allegiance to Japan. Many Japanese-Americans attended all-Japanese schools where they undoubtedly would be indoctrinated into the ways of "their people." Given the experience of fifth-column activity in Europe, and the rumors of treachery in Hawaii, the presence of a "tightly knit racial group, bound to an enemy nation by strong ties of race, culture, custom and religion along a frontier vulnerable to attack constituted a menace which had to be dealt with."[9] Warren stated that "in some instances the children [of Japanese-Americans] have been sent to Japan for their education, either in whole or in part, and while they are over there they are indoctrinated with the idea of Japanese imperialism. They received their religious instruction which ties up their religion with their Emperor, and they come back here imbued with the ideas and the policies of imperial Japan."[10]

The Japanese, unlike most other immigrant populations, had not readily assimilated into the American populace. The apparent reasons for this were manifold. A principal reason, many American strategists believed, was a religious one. Before Buddhism arrived in Japan, Shintoism had been the predominant religion and had retained a very strong influence over Japanese culture. Shintoism's central teaching is singular: be loyal to one's ancestors. Many feared that this dictate might very well lead adherents in the United States to work on behalf of Japan.

Shintoism defies linguistic description and, indeed, is somewhat defined by that fact. It is conveyed from generation to generation by ritual and cultural practice. At its core, Shintoism is naturalistic. Virtually every natural phenomenon assumes a godlike status and is deified. Shintoism has over 800,000 such "nature deities," known as Kami. The chief god is Amaterasu—the sun goddess—from whom the imperial family is thought to descend. The religion originated around 500 BC and became institutionalized as part of the state apparatus with the Yamato Dynasty. Although not as codified as Western religions, Shinto tenets describe the High Plain of Heaven and the Dark Land, which is the foul land of the dead. Creation stories relate the lives of the Kami. In one, the divine couple of Izanagi-no-mikato and Izanami-no-mikato gave birth to the Japanese Islands. Their children, one of whom was Amaterasu, formed the several Japanese clans. Their daughter's descendants unified the country and the royal family embodied her spirit and ruled in honor of her legacy. Shintoists thus owe loyalty to the emperor as they owe fidelity to their religion.

When Buddhism arrived in Japan during the Nara and Heian periods (AD 710–1185), Shintoism became entangled with it and they have coexisted ever since. Shintoism, however, has always been identified first with Japan and Japanese nationalism. In the late nineteenth and early twentieth centuries, Shintoism was wielded as a weapon against foreign ideologies and increasingly symbolized Japanese uniqueness. In the 1930s, ultranationalists and militarists employed Shintoism to advance patriotic arguments. Religious faith became inextricably linked to Japanese militarism and the nation's imperialistic designs. Many American strategists, looking to Shinto practices and beliefs, assumed that Japanese-Americans who practiced the religion shared these beliefs, and that they were primarily bound to Amaterasu and her descendants, who were now waging war on the United States.

Distrust of Asians had a long history in California. Its roots, however, are as hard to discern as are the bases for any sort of racial hysteria and xenophobia. In the case of the Japanese, this bigotry may have been a product of complex factors, including at least some combination of fear of economic competition, diffidence toward strange manners or customs, and just plain old craven dislike of those who are different. Back in 1909, for example, Grove Johnson, the father and political opponent of the rising Progressive reformer Hiram Johnson, denounced the Japanese in language common to most prejudice:

I know more about the Japanese than Governor Gillett and President [Theodore] Roosevelt put together. I am not responsible to either of them.

I am responsible to the mothers and fathers of Sacramento County who have their little daughters sitting side by side in the school rooms with matured Japs, with their base minds, their lascivious thoughts, multiplied by their race and strengthened by their mode of life. . . . I have seen Japanese twenty-five years old sitting in the seats next to the pure maids of California. . . . I shudder . . . to think of such a condition.[11]

Much of the bigotry directed at the Japanese assumed the same tenor and reflected the same fears as the hate directed at all nonwhite "races." Mongrelization of the white race was a nightmare shared generally. Concerns about racial purity led many early-twentieth-century commentators to fear and loathing of Asians, in particular, because of their supposed excessively high birthrates. The "Asian hordes," which included both Chinese and Japanese, might, by sheer numbers alone, extinguish the white race. Studies at the time appeared to confirm that exactly this was happening, with one California report indicating that the Japanese birthrate was three times that of the white population. These numbers led Madison Grant, a prominent New York lawyer and civic leader, to warn about the "possibility of social sterilization." All of the "colored races," certainly, invoked this dread, but Grant saw "no immediate danger of the world being swamped by black blood." He did see, however, "a very immediate danger that the white stocks may be swamped by Asiatic blood."[12] He advised that unless the white man "erects and maintains artificial barriers [he will] *finally perish.*" White civilization, he warned, being coterminous with the white race, would perish with him.[13]

Demographic expert Lothrop Stoddard, writing in 1920 in his book *Rising Tide of Color,* thought that in the future, "in those better days, we or the next generation will take in hand the problem of race depreciation, and segregation of defectives and abolition of handicaps penalizing the better stocks will put an end to our present racial decline." Those "splendid tasks," he believed, "are probably not ours."

They are for our successors in a happier age. But we have our task, and God knows it is a hard one—the salvage of a shipwrecked world![14]

The prospect of the debasement of white American blood was understood as largely intractable but worth every effort to combat. The threat appeared on two fronts, with one coming from racial interbreeding and the second from the continued breeding of those considered inferior on any one of an assortment of bases. In the context of the Asian population, immigration controls and exclusion from citizenship were the primary weapons. They were, however, blunt instruments that could have only a limited and indirect impact on the perceived problem. Sharper and more direct tactics were employed against those in society considered defective, disabled, or degenerate in one or another way. A few months after Pearl Harbor, the Court heard arguments in *Skinner v. Oklahoma*,[15] in which it considered whether sterilization, the sharpest tool in the fight against debased blood, was constitutional when employed against "criminal degenerates." Just fifteen years earlier, in *Buck v. Bell*, the Court had upheld a Virginia law providing for the sterilization of mental defectives. That case left us with the infamous statement from Justice Holmes that "three generations of imbeciles was enough."

Sterilization of social outcasts was based on the principles of eugenics, a term coined in 1883 by Francis Galton, Charles Darwin's cousin. The term came from a Greek root meaning "good in birth" or "noble in heredity" and was used to denote "the science of improving stock." Eugenicists relied on a combination of Mendel's discoveries in plant heredity and general Darwinistic principles to support their argument that selective breeding of human populations could have beneficial consequences. Eugenicists theorized that there were genetic roots for an assortment of personality and behavioral flaws that troubled contemporary society, from criminal behavior to "hypersexuality." The basic tenets of eugenics provided that social, moral, and physical characteristics were inheritable, that the human race could be improved through selective mating, and that many ills of society could be eradicated by discouraging or preventing the reproduction of socially deviant individuals. Galton explained: "We may not be able to originate, but we can guide. The processes of evolution are in constant and spontaneous activity, some towards the bad, some towards the good. Our part is to watch for opportunities to intervene by checking the former and giving free play to the latter."[16]

Eugenics arrived just in time to be embraced by the Progressive movement. Progressivism, in very broad terms, sought to manage and control government and society through active and interventionist political strategies. Eugenicists in the Progressive Era used state police power to prevent reproduction of all manner of social deviancy. Henry Steele Commager, a historian and noted public intellectual, observed that Progressives "saw law not primarily as a concise body of principles regulating the relationship between the individual and his government but as a sprawling body of practices conditioning the conduct of the individual in his society."[17] Their objective was to improve the human condition through science. Modern biology, medical genetics, and biostatistics gave policy makers the tools to try to assuage the societal costs associated with the feebleminded, the insane, the criminalistic, the diseased, the blind, the deaf, the deformed, and the dependent—ranging from orphans to the homeless.

The sterilization solution to degeneracy and biological defect was embraced widely and by the mainstream. Theodore Roosevelt and Margaret Sanger supported the concept. H. G. Wells wondered if the human stock might be improved by "the sterilization of failures." Herbert Jennings, in his 1930 book *The Biological Basis of Human Nature,* called attention to the new "eagerness to apply biological science to human affairs." He observed, "Gone are the days when the biologist . . . used to be pictured in the public prints as an absurd creature, his pockets bulging with snakes and newts." He said, admiringly, "The world . . . is to be operated on scientific principles. The conduct of life and society are to be based, as they should be, on sound biological maxims!" He exclaimed, "Biology has become popular."[18]

In *Skinner,* the Court considered the constitutionality of the Oklahoma Habitual Criminal Sterilization Act. The law differed in several important respects from the one upheld in *Buck.* The Oklahoma law applied to the "criminalistic and other degenerate classes," while the Virginia law reviewed in *Buck* applied to the mentally disabled. Moreover, in *Buck,* the state was obligated to demonstrate that Carrie Buck was mentally impaired in a way that would likely be passed on to her offspring. No such proof was necessary in *Skinner.* Under the law, the state did not have to show that Jack T. Skinner possessed a hereditary criminal disposition. The only issue presented was whether he was a three-time felon guilty of crimes of "moral turpitude" as defined by the law. If so, he had amply demonstrated his criminal character, a character that could be expected to be handed down to his children and the children of his children.

In its brief to the Court, the state of Oklahoma pointed out the obviousness of the inheritability of behavioral characteristics and the still more obvious governmental justification to intercede in order to stem the flow of criminal tendencies from being "passed on to posterity." The Oklahoma brief "earnestly" submitted

> that there is not only reasonable, but almost certain, belief that children inherit the traits and characteristics of each and both of their parents, and to say that there is no reasonable relation or connection between the conferred criminal traits of one who has been thrice convicted and those which might be passed on through inheritance borders on the absurd, it being common knowledge that bad traits as well as good traits are inheritable.[19]

Most criminologists in the early part of the century concurred with the Oklahoma view that criminals were born rather than made. Society could best combat crime by preventing the reproduction of criminals. The preamble to Indiana's compulsory sterilization law asserted, "Whereas heredity plays a most important part in the transmission of crime, idiocy and imbecility . . ." Even though by 1942, the year *Skinner* was decided, this emphasis on heredity was waning in academic circles, and would soon recede almost entirely, it remained a central operating premise of the law.

In striking down the Oklahoma statute, the Court did not challenge the eugenic bases for the law, and indeed many of the justices apparently accepted them. The Court's opinion relied exclusively on the perceived unfairness of sterilizing robbers but not embezzlers. The Court said that a

> person who enters a chicken coop and steals chickens commits a felony; and he may be sterilized if he is thrice convicted. If, however, he is the bailee of the property and fraudulently appropriates it, he is an embezzler. Hence, no matter how habitual . . . his conviction, he may not be sterilized.[20]

The Court thus showed special solicitude for criminals, believing them worthy of equal treatment under the guarantee of "equal protection" afforded by the Fourteenth Amendment. Indeed, the Court applied the most rigorous level of scrutiny to Oklahoma's law: "Strict scrutiny of the classification which a State makes in a sterilization law is essential, lest unwittingly or otherwise invidious discriminations are made against groups or types of individuals in violation of the . . . equal protection of the laws."[21] Eugenic theory, the Court lamented, was not so finely tuned that it could draw distinctions between criminal types. If larceny was inheritable, wasn't embezzlement too? "We have not the slightest basis for inferring that the line [between larceny and embezzlement] has any significance in eugenics, nor that the inheritability of criminal traits follows the neat legal distinctions which the law has marked between those two offenses."[22]

Chief Justice Stone concurred in the Court's holding invalidating the Oklahoma law, but believed that a second clause in the Fourteenth Amendment, the Due Process Clause, should do the work. Stone believed that the law failed because it did not afford members of the specified class of larcenists the opportunity to show that their behavior was not inheritable. Stone accepted the asserted fact that crime could be inherited. This did not mean, however, that all criminal acts were a consequence of inheritance. He believed that Skinner should have had the opportunity to prove that he acted for reasons other than his genetic disposition. "A law," he wrote, "which condemns without hearing, all the individuals of a class to so harsh a measure as the present because some or even many merit condemnation is lacking in the first principle of due process."[23] But Stone did not doubt the legitimacy of the basic premise of the Oklahoma law, that the state has a compelling interest in preventing the degenerate seeds of one generation from proliferating in subsequent generations. He asserted, "Undoubtedly, a state may . . . constitutionally interfere with the personal liberty of the individual to prevent the transmission by inheritance of his socially injurious tendencies. . . . Science has found and the law has recognized that there are certain types of mental deficiency associated with delinquency which are inheritable."[24]

The second prong of the Progressives' eugenic agenda was race. In some ways, individual degenerates posed a less daunting challenge to Progressive policy makers, because the scale of the danger was much less. Race, and thus immigration, posed a more formidable obstacle. It was a futile effort to halt the propagation of biological defect through domestic sterilization programs if America's borders were open to degenerate races and defective individuals from abroad. In a prizewinning sermon, the Reverend Kenneth C. MacArthur warned, "At the present rate one thousand Harvard graduates of today will have only fifty descendants two hundred years hence, by which time one thousand Roumanian immigrants will have increased to one hundred thousand."[25]

Theodore Roosevelt warned of the dangers of excessive birthrates among nonwhites, calling it "the greatest problem of civilization which could lead to 'race-suicide.' "[26] The Progressives' ideology was forwarded by writers such as John Roger Commons. Commons was president of the American Economic Association, a professor at the University of Wisconsin, and confidant of Progressive Wisconsin governor Robert La Follette. In his book *Races and Immigrants in America,* he described "the basic qualities which underlie democracy" as "intelligence, manliness, cooperation." He cautioned that, if "they are lacking, democracy is futile." Proliferation of nonwhite races, he urged, could endanger democracy itself. "Race differences are established in the very blood and physical constitutions." He explained that these differences "are the most difficult to eradicate, and they yield only to the slow processes of the centuries." He continued:

> Races may change their religions, their forms of government, their modes of industry, and their languages, but underneath all these changes they may continue the physical, mental and moral capacities and incapacities which determine the real character of their religion, government, industry, and literature.[27]

While education and environment contributed to the definition of social institutions, Commons argued, "in a democracy race and heredity are the more decisive."[28] Inferior races, and defective individuals, threatened the very pillars of American democracy.

The Supreme Court had entered the fray over the definition of race in two cases decided in the early 1920s, *Ozawa v. United States*[29] and *United States v. Thind.*[30] The issue in both cases concerned the interpretation of a 1906 amendment to the naturalization law that limited citizenship to "white persons" and aliens of African nativity and persons of African descent. In *Ozawa,* the claimant was a Japanese alien and in *Thind* the claimant was a high-caste Hindu. The original Naturalization Act of 1790 restricted naturalization to free white persons and was subsequently expanded to include those of African descent after the Civil War. The question presented in each of the cases, therefore, was whether the claimants qualified as "white persons." The parties' briefs invited the Court to define "white persons" in accordance with prevailing scientific knowledge. The Court, however, found the "various authorities" to be "in irreconcilable disagreement as to what constitutes a proper racial division."[31] Justice George Sutherland observed, "Blumenbach has 5 races; Keane following Linnaeus, 4; Deniker, 29." The Court did not doubt the existence of racial divisions, but the justices were skeptical whether science could provide bright lines of division that lawmakers could rely upon. The Court thought the "explanation probably is that 'the innumerable varieties of mankind run into one another by insensible degrees,' and to arrange them in sharply bounded divisions is an undertaking of such uncertainty that common agreement is practically impossible."[32] Nonetheless, the Court held fast that both the law and common experience indicated differences among races of men. Legal classification might need to more sharply delineate what science had found to be fact, though the scientific taxonomies blurred at the margins of each category.

The Court set about solving this classification problem by noting that the claimants in *Ozawa* and *Thind* had argued that the original naturalization law had been directed at blacks and not Asians more generally. Although the Court did not disagree with this characterization, it thought it misrepresented the nature of the injunction the original framers had intended to construct. The Court explained that the "provision is not that Negroes and Indians shall be excluded, but it is, in effect, that only free white persons shall be included."[33] The Court further argued that "it is not enough to say that the framers did not have in mind the brown or yellow races of Asia. It is necessary to go farther and be able to say that had these particular races been suggested the language of the act would have been so varied as to include them within its privilege."[34] As regards those intended to be included as "white," the Court readily found that the framers would have counted those of the British Isles and north-western Europe as "bone of their bone and flesh of their flesh." Added to these, the Court said immigrants from eastern, southern, and middle Europe were similarly white, extending even to include "the Slavs and the dark-eyed, swarthy people of Alpine and Mediterranean stock." On the other hand, the Court held, those of "Asiatic stock" most certainly were not intended to be counted as white. The Court did not explain this conclusion. It merely assumed that it was intuitively obvious to all that Asians were not white.

The standard the Court adopted, then, was the "understanding of the common man." Science supported this obvious fact, though it could not neatly define the boundaries of the races. The Court acknowledged that common understanding might fail to distinguish racial types, at least in very close cases. Such cases, the Court said, must be evaluated on an individual basis. The naturalization law dealt with classes of people and in most cases racial identity was readily ascertained. In *Thind*, the Court said that "it cannot be doubted that the children born in this country of Hindu parents would retain indefinitely the clear evidence of their ancestry."[35] At the same time, the Court added, "it is very far from our thought to suggest the slightest question of racial superiority or inferiority. What we suggest," the Court emphasized, "is merely racial difference, and it is of such character and extent that the great body of our people instinctively recognize it and reject the thought of assimilation."[36]

The press also played a considerable role throughout the first half of the century in fanning the flames of bigotry based on the idea that racial characteristics were inheritable. In early 1942, a *Los Angeles Times* editorial commented that "a viper is nonetheless a viper wherever the egg is hatched. A leopard's spots are the same and its disposition is the same wherever it is whelped." In the case of the Japanese, concerns about race were compounded by cultural and religious ties that bound them to a foreign allegiance. A Japanese-American, the editorial announced,

> born of Japanese parents, nurtured upon Japanese traditions, living in a transplanted Japanese atmosphere and thoroughly inoculated with Japanese thoughts, Japanese ideas and Japanese ideals, notwithstanding his nominal brand of accidental citizenship, almost inevitably and with the rarest of exceptions grows up to be a Japanese not an American in his thoughts, in his ideals, and himself is a potential and menacing, if not an actual, danger to our country unless properly supervised, controlled and, as it were, hamstrung.[37]

Hearst newspapers were particularly vehement in their denunciation of the Japanese and their call to move them from sensitive coastal areas. War made possible the advocacy of every kind of extreme sentiment and prejudice. Henry McLemore, for example, a Hearst syndicated columnist, raged:

> I know this is the melting pot of the world and all men are created equal and there must be no such thing as race or creed hatred, but do those things go when a country is fighting for its life? Not in my book. No country has ever won a war because of courtesy and I trust and pray we won't be the first because of the lovely, gracious spirit. . . .
>
> I am for immediate removal of every Japanese on the West Coast to a

point deep in the interior. I don't mean a nice part of the interior either. Herd 'em up, pack 'em off and give 'em the inside room in the badlands. Let 'em be pinched, hurt, hungry and dead up against it. . . .

Personally, I hate the Japanese. And that goes for all of them.[38]

On February 14, 1942, Westbrook Pegler, one of the more colorful personalities in American journalism, a kaleidoscopic profession at the time, wrote that "we are so damned dumb and considerate of the minute Constitutional rights and even of the political feelings and influence of people whom we have every reason to anticipate with preventive action!"[39] Pegler was a former sports writer who turned to political commentary and journalism from the perspective of the Far Right. Pegler was a gifted wordsmith. What he lacked in judgment and perspective he made up for in wit. As a sports writer, for instance, he said of Lefty Grove that "he could throw a lamb chop past a wolf." Writing about the lively ball of his day, he said that "when you hold it between your thumb and forefinger, you can hear a rabbit's pulsebeat." He also wrote accurately that Knute Rockne "looks like a beaten up tin can."[40]

In turning his rhetorical skills onto politics, Pegler became, according to a Scripps-Howard poll in the 1940s, the most popular journalist of the time. A University of Wisconsin poll listed him as the best columnist in the nation in 1942. He won the Pulitzer Prize in 1941 for exposing labor union corruption. He also called FDR "a feeble-minded fuhrer," Eleanor Roosevelt "La Boca Grande" (the big mouth), Henry Wallace a "slobbering snerd," and J. Edgar Hoover "a nightclub fly-cop." He was an enthusiastic supporter of Joseph McCarthy and similarly hurled accusations of "Communist sympathizer" against his detractors. About the Japanese in California, he wrote in his February 14, 1942, column that they "should be under armed guard to the last man and woman right now and to hell with habeas corpus until the danger is over."[41]

Events immediately following the Japanese invasion of Hawaii appeared to confirm the fear of internal subversion. Military authorities reported unauthorized radio communications from areas along the West Coast as well as signal lights visible from just offshore. Virtually every ship leaving a West Coast port was reportedly engaged by enemy submarines. Only hostile shore-to-ship (submarine) communication could explain this expertly coordinated enemy activity. On December 9, 1941, Fourth Army Intelligence reported thirty-four Japanese ships off the California coast and two days later army headquarters ordered a "general alert of all units," because the "main Japanese battle fleet [was] 164 miles off San Francisco." Although these reports eventually proved false—the thirty-four ships turned out to be fishing trawlers from the Monterey fleet returning after hearing news of Pearl Harbor—they contributed to the sense of unease and insecurity on the Pacific Coast. Moreover, an FBI raid near Monterey netted a cache of over sixty thousand rounds of ammunition together with numerous rifles, shotguns, and maps. And, most ominously, one night shortly after Pearl Harbor, San Franciscans' sleep was disturbed by the sounds of low-flying aircraft. Military authorities informed a nervous citizenry that indeed the planes had been Japanese fighters.

Yet, despite rumblings of potential enemy action, such as the Japanese sortie over San Francisco and well-placed hostile agents, the enemy had yet to drop a single bomb, blow up a single installation, or attack a single military target on the American mainland. This quiet, however, did not necessarily signify a lack of danger. In fact, according to no less an authority than the respected columnist Walter Lippmann, the silence itself was particularly foreboding. Lippmann, ordinarily a careful and reasoned thinker, warned against complacency in his nationally syndicated column:

> It also is the fact that since the outbreak of the Japanese war there has been no important sabotage on the Pacific Coast. From what we know about Hawaii and about the fifth column in Europe, this is not, as some have liked to think, a sign that there is nothing to be feared. It is a sign that the blow is well organized and that it is held back until it can be struck with maximum effect.[42]

Earl Warren similarly found no comfort in the fact that no sabotage had yet occurred. For Warren, this was "the most ominous sign in our whole situation." He said it convinced him "more than perhaps any other factor that the sabotage that we are to get, the fifth column activities that we are to get, are timed just like Pearl Harbor was timed."[43]

Central to the effort to do something about the "Japanese problem" was General John DeWitt, who, at sixty-one, according to one historian, "was near the end of a long and undistinguished career."[44] DeWitt had spent three tours of duty in the Philippines where he was well schooled in anti-Japanese dogma. From the start of the century, diverse commentators, including V. I. Lenin, had predicted war between the United States and Japan over the Philippines. It was in this atmosphere, straight out of Kiplingesque folklore, that DeWitt was educated about the East. While DeWitt was slow to advocate complete exclusion, once convinced of its wisdom he quickly became one of its most outspoken and enthusiastic supporters. DeWitt was a weak-willed man whose views generally reflected those of the last person to whom he spoke. He commanded the U.S. Fourth Army charged with the defense of the West Coast, which placed him in command of Japanese internment. A later congressional commission said DeWitt had "caused more damage even than General Burnside in 1863, whose blundering with Vallandingham, the Ohio Copperhead, were the previous high in American military officiousness."[45] Clement Vallandingham had been a Democratic congressman from Ohio who was fervently critical of the Civil War and the Lincoln administration. He once declared, "The war is a bloody and costly failure. The dead, the dead, and the numerous dead—think of Fredericksburg. Let us make peace. Let the armies fraternize and go home." General Burnside, the military commander of Ohio, took personal affront at Vallandingham's attacks on the war effort. Burnside issued an order announcing that "all persons found without our lines who commit acts for the benefit of enemies of our country will be tried as spies or traitors." During the speech, Vallandingham tore up a copy of Burnside's order, proclaiming, "I have the most supreme contempt for [this] General Order . . . and I have the most supreme contempt for King Lincoln." He was arrested, tried by a military commission, convicted, and imprisoned for the duration of the war.

DeWitt clearly outdid Burnside. General DeWitt, like Burnside, pursued war aims largely untempered by good judgment. In his final report, DeWitt encapsulated his views as follows:

> In the war in which we are now engaged racial affinities are not severed by migration. The Japanese race is an enemy race and while many second and third generation Japanese born on United States soil, possessed of United States citizenship, have become "Americanized," the racial strains are undiluted. . . . It, therefore, follows that along the vital Pacific Coast over 112,000 potential enemies, of Japanese extraction, are at large today. There are indications that these were organized and ready for concerted action at a favorable opportunity. The very fact that no sabotage has taken place to date is a disturbing and confirming indication that such action will be taken.[46]

———

On February 19, 1942, President Roosevelt signed Executive Order 9066, which gave to the secretary of war "the power to exclude any and all persons, citizens and aliens, from designated areas in order to provide security against sabotage, espionage and fifth column activity." For a momentous decision, Roosevelt gave it little thought. Attorney General Francis Biddle, a strong opponent of the evacuation order, said that he did "not think [Roosevelt] was much concerned with the gravity or implications of his step. He was never theoretical about such things."[47] Most of his advisers, with the notable exception of Biddle, also favored exclusion. The president's conscience, Eleanor Roosevelt, a relentless activist in defense of civil rights, protested only once against the proposed plan, but without effect. Even Biddle, though he opposed the plan to the end, eventually capitulated to what he ultimately determined to be the inevitable. Biddle did not have the temperament to stand his ground and never seriously contemplated resigning in protest. He was considered an "Eastern upper-class snob in the grand style."[48] Indeed, his American roots went deep. One of his ancestors had been Edmund Randolph, the first attorney general of the United States. Even more striking, perhaps, one of his paternal forebears was burned as a wizard in Salem in 1692. Perhaps if he had reflected on the parallels between his ancestor's fate and his country's treatment of the Japanese, he would have stood more firm. Contributing to Biddle's capitulation was his admiration for, and deference to, the secretary of war, Henry L. Stimson.

Although the president's pen signed the order, and DeWitt's hand implemented it, it was Henry Stimson who was perhaps most responsible for the decision. Other than the president, he was the one man who had the power to stand up to the extraordinary pressure to remove those with Japanese ancestry from the West Coast. If he had said no, exclusion would not have occurred. Stimson had been situated at the heights of American government for most of the first half of the twentieth century. Like others before him, most notably Chief Justice Roger Taney, his spectacular career of public service was tarnished with a single profound act of bigotry. Unlike Taney, he had the good fortune not to become indelibly linked to this act; General DeWitt would instead suffer this misfortune.

Stimson started his government career in Theodore Roosevelt's administration and was secretary of war for Taft, secretary of state for Hoover, and secretary of war again for Franklin Roosevelt. He was a conservative Republican who advocated modernization, both in the public sector and in the armed forces. Roosevelt had made him secretary of war to help smooth the way with Congress in preparing the country to enter World War II. He performed his role well. He had broad and extensive experience with Japan in the decades preceding Pearl Harbor. He had governed the Philippines in the 1920s and, as secretary of state, strongly condemned the Japanese invasion of Manchuria in 1931, declaring it a violation of international law. Near the end of the war, it was Stimson who, after Roosevelt died, informed the new president, Harry Truman, of the existence of the atomic bomb. Stimson advocated using the bomb against Japan, but successfully argued against bombing the old imperial city of Kyoto, on the basis that destroying a national cultural treasure would violate the standards of civilized society.

Stimson's racial views were complex and reflective, but in the way of someone who cannot see beyond the refracted mirror image offered by his own experiences and background. A good illustration of his limitations in this regard comes from his diary entry in which he recounted his attempt to dissuade Archibald MacLeish, then working in the government's Office of Facts and Figures, from giving a speech advocating the integration of the army. Stimson's entry reflected his sympathy for the plight of blacks in American society, but this sympathy was tempered by his frank assessment, shared by many people of the time, of the facts of life as he understood them:

I gave [MacLeish] my life history, so to speak, on the subject because I have come in contact with this race problem in many different ways during my life. I told him how I had been brought up in an abolitionist family; my father fought in the Civil War, and all my instincts were in favor of justice to the Negro. But I pointed out how this crime of our forefathers had produced a problem which was almost impossible of solution in this country. . . . I told him of my experience and study of the incompetency of colored troops except under white officers . . . although we were doing our best to train colored officers. I pointed out that what these foolish leaders of the colored race are seeking is at the bottom social equality, and I pointed out the basic impossibility of social equality because of the impossibility of race mixture by marriage. He listened in silence and thanked me, but I am not sure how far he is convinced.[49]

The exclusion order affected nearly 120,000 Japanese residents of the western states, 79,000 of whom were American citizens. Families were uprooted after being given little time to make proper arrangements for their property and possessions. They were expected to leave with what they could carry. They sold what they could. The rest was lost:

On May 16, 1942, my mother, two sisters, niece, nephew, and I left . . . by train. Father joined us later. Brother left earlier by bus. We took whatever we could carry. So much we left behind, but the most valuable thing I lost was my freedom.[50]

Each family experienced the trip to the assembly center differently, but all suffered a sense of foreboding, financial insecurity, and loss of dignity. They were herded like cattle, families carrying their worldly possessions, people young and old treated as enemies of their own country. Grace Nakamura described her departure:

On May 16, 1942, at 9:30 a.m., we departed . . . for an unknown destination. To this day, I can remember vividly the plight of the elderly, some on stretchers, orphans herded onto the train by caretakers, and especially a young couple with 4 pre-school children. The mother had two frightened toddlers hanging on to her coat. In her arms, she carried two crying babies. The father had diapers and other baby paraphernalia strapped to his back. In his hands he struggled with duffle bag and suitcase. The shades were drawn on the train for our entire trip. Military police patrolled the aisles.[51]

Evacuees stayed at the assembly centers longer than expected, because of delays in construction of the relocation centers. Virtually all of the relocation centers were built from scratch for the purpose of housing evacuees. The camps were constructed according to a basic blueprint, including barbed-wire fences, watchtowers, and armed guards. The basic housing unit was a "block" of about twelve to fourteen barracks, a mess hall, showers, toilets, laundry, and a recreation hall. Barracks included rooms about twenty by twenty-five feet, each housing a family, no matter its size. Although the construction was new, it was poorly designed and shoddily built. Walls and floors began cracking at once and the wood warped almost immediately under the harsh weather conditions. The facilities were not built to withstand the brutal climate, which tended toward extremes in winter and summer. In desert camps, winter temperatures dropped to 35 degrees below zero and summer temperatures soared above 110 degrees. In many camps, dust and sand were significant problems. Congressman Leland Ford of California visited Manzanar, in east-central California, and observed that "on dusty days, one might just as well be outside as inside." Monica Stone, an inmate at Minidoka, in south-central Idaho, described the "rousing welcome by a dust storm" she and her family received. "We felt as if we were standing in a gigantic sand-mixing machine as the sixty-mile gale lifted the loose earth up into the sky, obliterating everything." Reaching shelter gave them little respite:

> At last we staggered into our room, gasping and blinded. We sat on our suitcases to rest, peeling off our jackets and scarves. The window panes rattled madly, and the dust poured through the cracks like smoke. Now and then when the wind subsided, I saw other evacuees, hanging on to their suitcases, heads bent against the stinging dust. The wind whipped their scarves and towels from their heads and zipped them out of sight.[52]

Although the United States was at war also with Germany and Italy, residents of German and Italian ancestry were not wrenched from their homes. There were intractable obstacles to evacuating German and Italian residents. A major problem was their sheer numbers. The Japanese on the West Coast were large enough that they appeared to present a viable threat, but not so many that they could not be displaced en masse. It would have been nearly impossible to evacuate all German- and Italian-Americans without massive disruptions to agriculture and industry.

The military also faced significant public relations difficulties with removal of Italian and German residents. Of particular concern, for example, was the fate of Joe DiMaggio's father. General DeWitt's aide, Colonel Bendetsen, raised this concern, telling DeWitt:

> there has been a great deal said in the papers about people like Joe DiMaggio's father, that is Italians who have never become citizens but concerning whom, it seems at least in the press, I don't know what their backgrounds are, there is no doubt as to loyalty. [James Rowe asked me] whether all of them need to be excluded.[53]

DeWitt answered emphatically,

No, you can't make an exception. If you start that you're in an awful mess. . . . I had one man speak to me about it the other day. He happened to be the editor, Mr. Patterson, I think of the *New York Sun*. He was in here and asked me about Joe DiMaggio's father, and I said, yes, he's got to go. You can't make a single exception because if you do that you're lost.[54]

Those higher in the chain of command than DeWitt, however, were more politically aware of the consequences of German and Italian evacuation. The day after 9066 was signed by the president, Henry Stimson wrote DeWitt a letter advising him, "In carrying out your duties under this delegation, I desire, so far as military requirements permit, that you do not disturb, for the time being at least, Italian aliens and persons of Italian lineage except where they are, in your judgment, undesirables or constitute a definite danger to the performance of your mission."[55] Joe DiMaggio's father was safe. This directive was extended to Germans as well, despite the fact that there were no famous German ballplayers whose fathers might be interned.

The Supreme Court considered the constitutionality of the Japanese evacuation from the West Coast in a series of decisions, principal among them being *Hirabayashi v. United States*[56] and the better-known *Korematsu v. United States*.[57] In the first decision, in 1943, the Court limited its analysis to the constitutionality of Gordon Hirabayashi's conviction under the congressional enactment enforcing Executive Order 9066, making it a misdemeanor for those of Japanese ancestry to be outside of their homes between 8:00 p.m. and 6:00 a.m. This curfew order applied also to German and Italian aliens, but only Americans of Japanese ancestry were arrested for violating it. In *Korematsu,* in 1944, the Court considered the broader issue of Japanese exclusion from the West Coast. Germans and Italians, as classes, were unaffected by exclusion. Both cases confronted the same basic issue regarding whether it was an affront to the Constitution to treat people differently based on ethnicity or race. The answer in both depended on the factual bases the government offered to justify its discrimination. In its brief, the government asked the Court to take judicial notice of the fact that at least some significant portion of second- and third-generation Japanese-Americans were primarily loyal to the Japanese Empire. The Court was not quite willing to go this far and required the government to at least articulate some empirical bases for its claim.

Gordon Hirabayashi was born in Seattle in 1918. His parents had emigrated from Japan, but had never afterward returned there. He was educated in the Washington public school system and at the time of trial was a senior at the University of Washington. He had never visited Japan, had no association with any Japanese there, and was of the Quaker faith. Fred Korematsu was born in Oakland, where he graduated from high school. He had worked in a shipyard as a welder until the war started, but lost his position when the Boiler Makers Union canceled his membership because of his race. He disregarded the evacuation order so he could remain behind with the Caucasian woman whom he planned to marry. He tried to escape detection by having plastic surgery on his nose and by changing his name. The attempt failed and he was arrested by the FBI.

An important aspect of judicial review of any government action concerns the degree to which the Court will be deferential to the government's reasons for acting as it did. In the context of allegations of discrimination, the amount of deference ranges from virtually complete to virtually none. All legislation discriminates on the basis of some characteristic or another. Legislation that regulates the business of making, fitting, and selling lenses and eyeglasses might benefit optometrists at the expense of opticians. Age requirements for driving or alcohol consumption discriminate on the basis of age. Laws that single out veterans for special treatment discriminate against nonveterans. In most cases, the Court does not strictly scrutinize the government's reasons for drawing distinctions among people. However, the Court has identified certain categories or classifications that receive special consideration. In particular, government actions that discriminate on the basis of race or gender deeply implicate the Equal Protection Clause of the Fourteenth Amendment. This sort of discrimination leads to higher levels of scrutiny, that is, close judicial review of the government's reasons for acting as it did. The first statement of this principle comes from possibly the most famous footnote in constitutional law, footnote four in the case of *United States v. Carolene Products*.[58] In that footnote, Chief Justice Stone wrote as follows:

It is unnecessary to consider now whether legislation which restricts those political processes which can ordinarily be expected to bring about repeal of undesirable legislation, is to be subjected to more exacting judicial scrutiny under the general prohibitions of the Fourteenth Amendment than are most other types of legislation. Nor need we enquire . . . *whether prejudice*

*against discrete and insular minorities may be a special condition, which
tends seriously to curtail the operation of those political processes ordinarily to be relied upon to protect minorities, and which may call for a
correspondingly more searching judicial inquiry.*[59]

Hirabayashi's case was decided one year before *Carolene Products*, so
he did not benefit from the solicitude seemingly bestowed by footnote
four. This is unfortunate, since one would be hard-pressed to imagine a
group better described as a discrete and insular minority—as footnote
four described groups needing special protection because they are
excluded from the political process—than the Japanese in 1941 and
1942. Therefore, the Court refused to closely scrutinize the government's
reasons for discriminating on the basis of Japanese ancestry. According
to the Court, the only question presented was whether government officials had "a *reasonable basis* for the action taken in imposing the curfew."[60] Indeed, this "reasonable basis" test is the most deferential level
of judicial review. It does not call upon the Court to independently evaluate the substantive bases—the factual foundation—for the curfew law.
Under this standard, the Court found easily enough that the curfew
passed muster: "That reasonably prudent men charged with the responsibility of our national defense had ample ground for concluding that
they must face the danger of invasion, take measures against it, and in
making the choice of measures consider our internal situation cannot be
doubted."

Citing only congressional reports and hearings testimony, the Court
found that "there [was] support" for the following propositions:

that social, economic and political conditions have prevailed since the close
of the last century, when the Japanese began to come to this country in
substantial numbers, which have intensified their solidarity and in large
measure prevented their assimilation as an integral part of the white population.

. . . that large numbers of children of Japanese parentage are sent to
Japanese language schools outside the regular hours of public schools in
the locality.

. . . that some of these schools are generally believed to be sources of
Japanese nationalistic propaganda, cultivating allegiance to Japan.

. . . that considerable numbers, estimated to be approximately 10,000 of American-born children of Japanese parentage have been sent to Japan for all or part of their education.

. . . that many of the children of Japanese parents hold dual citizenship, a fact that the military commander could have reasonably concluded would have bearing on the loyalties of persons of Japanese descent.

. . . that a large number of resident alien Japanese, approximately one-third of all Japanese inhabitants of the country, are of mature years and occupy positions of influence in Japanese communities. The association of influential Japanese residents with Japanese Consulates has been deemed a ready means for the dissemination of propaganda and for the mainte-nance of the influence of the Japanese Government with the Japanese pop-ulation in this country.

. . . that as a result of all these conditions affecting the life of the Jap-anese, both aliens and citizens, in the Pacific Coast area, there has been relatively little social intercourse between them and the white population.[61]

The Court made no attempt to verify the factual claims forwarded by the government or even to critically assess the data it did provide. More-over, the Court made no effort to conduct a more searching inquiry or consider that other motivations—illegitimate grounds—lay behind the discrimination. Justice William O. Douglas explained, concurring, that "we must credit the military with as much good faith in that belief as we would any other public official acting pursuant to his duties. . . . Where the orders under the present Act have some relation to 'protection against espionage and against sabotage,' our task is at an end."[62]

In times of great national crisis, or when the Supreme Court confronts a potentially controversial case, there is great pressure for the justices to stand together and decide cases unanimously. *Hirabayashi* was such a case. Justice Frank Murphy had planned to dissent, but the other justices impressed upon him the need for consensus during a time of national emergency. Nonetheless, Murphy felt impelled to write a separate state-ment to voice his concerns. In his concurring opinion, he wrote, "While this Court sits, it has the inescapable duty of seeing that the mandates of the Constitution are obeyed." He continued, warning as follows:

That duty exists in time of war as well as in time of peace, and in its performance we must not forget that few indeed have been the invasions upon essential liberties which have not been accompanied by pleas of urgent necessity advanced in good faith by responsible men.[63]

This consensus broke down, however, when *Korematsu v. United States* reached the Court in the fall of 1944.

That fall, the Allies had moved decisively, both in Europe and in the Far East. Hitler had been taken by surprise when the Allies landed on Normandy Beach in June, and over a million men and 500,000 tons of matériel began sweeping across Western Europe. On August 25, Paris was liberated and two months later the Germans were forced back to their prewar boundaries. In December, the Germans attempted one last offensive, driving through the Ardennes in an effort to split the British and American forces. About a week later, after the Battle of the Bulge, the Germans were at full retreat and the end of the war was imminent. Similarly, in the Far East, the United States was on the threshold of victory. The tide had turned in the Pacific war back in June 1942, at the Battle of Midway. In June 1944, the Americans had successfully landed on Saipan, and by July the island was in their control. Saipan provided a base from which B-29 bombing raids could reach Tokyo. On July 12, the Americans gained control of Okinawa, sealing Japan's fate.

By the time the Court heard oral argument in *Korematsu* in the second week of October and decided the case in the third week of December, the war's outcome was confidently known. Moreover, the Court knew that no substantial instances of sabotage or espionage had occurred in the United States in the nearly five months between the attack on Pearl Harbor and the main exclusion of Japanese-Americans from the Pacific Coast. Indeed, the Court knew categorically that no fifth-column activity had contributed to the events in Hawaii. The Roberts Commission, headed by the Court's own Justice Owen Roberts, had concluded that Japanese spies had provided information, but there was no evidence of espionage or sabotage. The Court was thus in a position to do the right thing, since the principal danger had passed and the facts as known to the military authorities at the time could be calmly assessed. The Court's failure was all the more tragic for this lost opportunity.

Unlike *Hirabayashi*, the Court in *Korematsu* promisingly announced that it would rigorously review the government's reasons for discriminating against Japanese-Americans. The Court was following the suggestion of *Carolene Products'* footnote four. Justice Black wrote the opinion for the Court, and stated at the outset "that all legal restrictions which curtail the civil rights of a single racial group are immediately suspect. That is not to say that all such restrictions are unconstitutional.

It is to say that courts must subject them to the most rigid scrutiny." Yet, almost immediately, the Court went on to ignore this injunction in favor of strict scrutiny and applied, in fact, the same deferential approach employed in *Hirabayashi,* relying on that case as authority for its holding. Justice Hugo Black asserted,

> Here, as in the *Hirabayashi* case, we cannot reject as unfounded the judgment of the military authorities and of Congress that there were disloyal members of that population, whose number and strength could not be precisely and quickly ascertained. We cannot say that the war-making branches of the Government did not have ground for believing that in a critical hour such persons could not readily be isolated and separately dealt with, and constituted a menace to the national defense and safety, which demanded that prompt and adequate measures be taken to guard against it.[64]

Justice Black did not restate the factual premises articulated in *Hirabayashi,* and instead simply accepted them as having already been settled as a matter of precedent. He added, however, the argument that proof of disloyalty, and therefore justification of internment, followed from the fact that five thousand Japanese-Americans "refused to swear unqualified allegiance to the United States and to renounce allegiance to the Japanese Emperor." Another "several thousand evacuees requested repatriation to Japan."[65]

Curiously, the Court limited its constitutional analysis to the evacuation order, never considering the conditions of the internment camps themselves or the prisoners who inhabited them. This meant that the Court was spared from asking why the camps were even necessary, if the "military necessity" was merely the need to exclude potentially disloyal Japanese-Americans from sensitive coastal areas. The Court thus did not confront the ugly reality that the camps were established largely because the interior states loudly objected to an uncontrolled Japanese migration. The Court chose instead to focus on the abstract niceties of equal treatment of a potentially dangerous class of nameless people, rather than confront the inhuman conditions of the camps and the suffering imposed in the name of military necessity.

In *Korematsu,* Justices Roberts, Murphy, and Robert Jackson, in separate opinions, all dissented. Justice Murphy, in particular, challenged the factual bases for the law. He believed that the "exclusion goes over 'the very brink of constitutional power' and falls into the ugly abyss of racism."[66] This racism was perpetrated, he asserted, "mainly upon questionable racial and sociological grounds not ordinarily within the realm of expert military judgment, supplemented by certain semi-military conclusions drawn from an unwarranted use of circumstantial evidence."[67]

The factual premises and sociological conjectures on which the exclusion order was based were simply not supported by the evidence. Japanese-Americans had not "deployed" around military institutions. In these locales, they represented the same proportion or less than their general population in the state.[68] The basic geographic pattern of the Japanese population had remained unchanged since 1910. In terms of proportionate statistics, Japanese-Americans were not present around military bases or secure coastal locations any more than German- and Italian-Americans. In real numbers, the San Francisco–Oakland area was, comparatively, virtually in German and Italian hands. In 1941, the Golden Gate Bridge was surrounded by 42,861 foreign-born Italians and 24,387 foreign-born Germans. In comparison, only 4,676 foreign-born Japanese resided in the area.

In regard to personal loyalty matters, the government's dual-citizenship argument also did not specially apply to Japanese-Americans. Both German and Italian law permitted dual citizenship for children of their citizens.[69] Other allegations of disloyalty were equally suspect or amenable to more narrowly tailored means than complete exclusion. For instance, only 0.4 percent of Japanese-Americans practiced Shintoism, with most of the rest being Christian. The threat of Shinto worship was also dramatically overplayed, since many adherents greatly admired aspects of American culture and practices. For instance, some Shinto temples hung portraits of Washington and Lincoln in reverence to their contributions to human advancement. Only about 2 percent of Japanese-Americans were Kibei—those who returned to Japan for their education. Because Kibei were educated in Japan, they had poor English skills and could often be easily identified. But the fact was that many Kibei contributed their knowledge of Japan and the Japanese language to support the American war effort.

In terms of the claimed menace of Japanese-American espionage, among the Allied vessels that carried the 2,004,234 tons of cargo sent to Hawaii from the West Coast in 1942–43, not one single ship was lost. In fact, there were no Japanese submarines or warships near the West

Coast during this time. In contrast, on the East Coast, 548 Allied merchant ships were sunk by German submarines. And, as regards the alleged Japanese sorties over San Francisco, San Franciscans at the time doubted the veracity of military reports of enemy planes, and there is no historical evidence that they ever occurred. A rumor surfaced at the time that the planes were actually American and had been dispatched to frighten the uncooperative locals into observing DeWitt's blackout orders. DeWitt lectured a gathering of San Franciscans that they did "not seem to realize we are at war." He said, "So get this:

> Last night there were planes over this community. They were enemy planes. I mean Japanese planes. And they were tracked out to sea. You think it was a hoax? It is a damned nonsense for sensible people to think that the Army and Navy would practice such a hoax on San Francisco.[70]

Finally, the cache of rifles, shotguns, maps, and sixty thousand rounds of ammunition—which was held up by the government as evidence of Japanese fifth-column activity—were in fact uncovered in a raid on a Japanese-owned sporting goods store. There was never any indication that this merchandise would be used for any purpose other than to be sold commercially.

Justice Murphy found no reasonable basis for the military's action discriminating against Japanese-Americans. He stated that the "factual" arguments were "largely an accumulation of much of the misinformation, half-truths and insinuations that for years have been directed against Japanese Americans by people with racial and economic prejudices—the same people who have been among the foremost advocates of the evacuation."[71] Murphy went on to say that such pseudo-sociology deserved no deference:

> A military judgment based upon such racial and sociological considerations is not entitled to the great weight ordinarily given the judgments based upon strictly military considerations. Especially is this so when every charge relative to race, religion, culture, geographical location, and legal and economic status has been substantially discredited by independent studies made by experts in these matters.

And General DeWitt's true colors were eventually displayed, this time before a House Naval Affairs Committee in April 1943:

A Jap's a Jap. It makes no difference whether he is an American citizen or not. I don't want any of them. We got them out. They were a dangerous element. The West Coast is too vital and too vulnerable to take any chances. They are a dangerous element, whether loyal or not. It makes no difference whether he is an American citizen. Theoretically, he is still a Japanese and you can't change him.[72]

History, of course, has passed judgment on DeWitt, though others have largely escaped the sort of condemnation that might be expected following the evacuation and internment of tens of thousands of American citizens. Roosevelt, Stimson, Warren, Lippmann, and many others were tainted by the decisions they made early in 1942, but their reputations survived largely intact. This is due in part to these men's other great works, and the reality that in war many sins are forgiven. One principal who received his comeuppance was Westbrook Pegler, the flamboyant Hearst columnist. In 1949, after reading a book review by his former friend Quentin Reynolds, Pegler wrote a column in which he called Reynolds, among other things, a coward, a war profiteer, and a moral degenerate. Reynolds brought a libel suit against Pegler and the Hearst Newspapers, in which the allegations appeared. The case came to trial in 1954, and Pegler withered under the intense cross-examination of Reynolds's famed attorney, Louis Nizer. The jury awarded Reynolds the largest sum ever granted for punitive damages up to that time. Henry Denker's 1963 play, *A Case of Libel*, was based on the Pegler–Reynolds battle. Pegler never recovered from the episode and spent his remaining years as a raging anti-Semite and bitter misanthrope who could not hold a job. He died of stomach cancer on June 24, 1969.

In Justice Murphy's view the sort of racism personified in men like Pegler, and displayed in various degrees by so many of that generation, should have been deemed an illegitimate basis for government action. In concluding his opinion in *Korematsu,* Murphy said he dissented "from this legalization of racism."

All residents of this nation are kin in some way by blood or culture to a foreign land. Yet they are primarily and necessarily a part of the new and distinct civilization of the United States. They must accordingly be treated at all times as the heirs of the American experiment and as entitled to all the rights and freedoms guaranteed by the Constitution.[73]

The other dissenters, Justices Roberts and Jackson, based their disagreements on somewhat more technical grounds. Roberts considered Korematsu's conviction unconstitutional on the ground that he actually confronted two military orders at the time of his arrest, one requiring him to remain in his residence and the other demanding his evacuation to an assembly center. Roberts accused the Court of hypothesizing a case for disposition that was not in fact presented, and he would have invalidated the conviction because of the conflicting state of the law. Jackson thought it was improvident of the Court to have taken the case in the first instance. He agreed that, on the merits, use of race violated fundamental tenets of our society. "Now, if any fundamental assumption underlies our system, it is that guilt is personal and not inheritable. Even if all of one's antecedents had been convicted of treason, the Constitution forbids its penalties to be visited upon him, that 'no Attainder of Treason shall work Corruption of Blood, or Forfeiture except during the Life of the Person attained.' "[74] Reliance on race, Jackson said, constituted an "attainder of blood." At the same time, he believed, if the war power were ever to fall "into irresponsible and unscrupulous hands, the courts wield no power equal to its restraint." He would not, he wrote, delude people into believing otherwise. "The chief restraint upon those who command the physical forces of the country, in the future as in the past," he observed, "must be their responsibility to the political judgments of their contemporaries and to the moral judgments of history."[75]

Forty years after President Roosevelt signed Executive Order 9066, the Commission on Wartime Relocation and Internment of Civilians, established by act of Congress, concluded that the order

> was not justified by military necessity, and the decisions which followed from it—detention, ending detention and ending exclusion—were not driven by analysis of military conditions. The broad historical causes which shaped these decisions were race prejudice, war hysteria and a failure of political leadership.[76]

Korematsu and *Skinner* marked the end of an era in the way the Court viewed the biological antecedents of human behavior. Although the Court did not itself rely on science in deciding these cases, it was deeply influenced by the cultural and societal setting in which these cases were situated. Internment and sterilization were societal solutions that had built into them deep premises regarding biological determinacy. The Court largely accepted these premises or felt constrained by wartime circumstances not to challenge them.

Society more generally, however, was coming to challenge the predominant position biology had been given in describing human populations, and cultural and experiential factors were rising to the forefront of academic studies. The work of Franz Boas in the 1920s and 1930s, in particular, contributed substantially to this change of perspective. In the mid-1930s, special blue ribbon panels were established to examine eugenic sterilization policies in both Britain and the United States. The American panel was organized by the American Neurological Association and headed by the Boston psychiatrist Abraham Myerson. Both panels concluded similarly that there was no established basis for eugenic sterilization. The American report stated, "There is at present no sound scientific basis for sterilization on account of immorality or character defect. Human conduct and character are matters of too complex a nature, too interwoven with social conditions . . . to permit any definite conclusions to be drawn concerning the part which heredity plays in their genesis."[77]

By the time of *Skinner,* in 1942, enforcement of state sterilization laws had fallen to minuscule proportions and by 1950 the practice had ended almost completely. The end of eugenics came with the revealed horrors of the Nazi death camps. Galton's dream of improving the stock of humanity had become a nightmarish crime against humanity of horrific proportions. The Nazis practiced experimental sterilization and wholesale murder with the shared hope of preserving racial purity and removing defectives and degenerates from the population. Auschwitz and Buchenwald came to symbolize affirmative eugenics policies. Eugenics, and the biological determinism on which it was based, became virtually forbidden subjects among mainstream scientists and policy makers. In the perennial debate, nature was out and nurture was in. The monumental cases of the 1950s would reflect this change, as social and environmental influences replaced biological considerations in setting the terms of the constitutional debate.

7

AUTOCRACY OF CASTE:

Brown v. Board of Education
and the Golden Age of Social Science

But it is said that these separate schools are for the benefit of both colors, and of the Public Schools. In similar spirit Slavery is sometimes said to be for the benefit of master and slave, and of the country where it exists. There is a mistake in the one as great as in the other. This is clear. Nothing unjust, nothing ungenerous, can be for the benefit of any person or any thing. . . .

Who can say that this does not injure the blacks? Theirs, in its best estate, is an unhappy lot. A despised class, blasted by prejudice and shut out from various opportunities, they feel this proscription from the Common Schools as a peculiar brand. Beyond this, it deprives them of those healthful, animating influences which would come from participation in the studies of their white brethren. It adds to their discouragement. It widens their separation from the community, and postpones that great day of reconciliation which is yet to come.

— CHARLES SUMNER (1849)

It is a maxim among these men, that whatever has been done before may legally be done again; and therefore they take special care to record all the decisions formerly made, even those which have through ignorance or corruption contradicted the rule of common justice and the general reason of mankind. These under the name of precedents, they produce as authorities and thereby endeavor to justify the most iniquitous opinions.

— JONATHAN SWIFT, *GULLIVER'S TRAVELS*

The law is tightly tethered to its past. Unlike science or art, for instance, novel or alternative approaches to problem-solving are actively eschewed by the law. Precedent, or, in Latin, stare decisis, establishes a presumption in favor of the status quo. In constitutional law, this may seem a strange tradition, since the current generation is as capable of reading the Constitution as those now gone. Precedent, then, gives credence to the views of past generations largely on the basis that they are past. Also important, certainly, is the fact that people may have grown to rely on whatever rule precedent has established. A certain comfort comes simply from a rule having deep roots in history. The past, however, can sometimes be a cruel oppressor whose practices are better left behind. This raises the question of whether the Court, using the Constitution, should ever—and can ever—be an instrument of change. In *Brown v. Board of Education*, the Court answered this question with a resounding yes.

The South had fought the Civil War principally in defense of the abstract notion of "states' rights." The war was, and still is, called in much of the southern United States the war between the states. The South held venerable the principle that the states were largely autonomous entities connected to one another in a loose confederation, mainly for purposes of trade and defense. The North, in contrast, had fought for the Union and a strong version of national sovereignty. The Civil War was tantamount to a war between descendants of Jeffersonian Republicans, with a fair measure of Patrick Henry's Anti-Federalism thrown in, and John Adams's and Alexander Hamilton's Federalists. And the Federalists prevailed. Among the North's spoils of victory were three constitutional amendments. The Thirteenth Amendment (1865) freed the slaves, the Fourteenth Amendment (1868) guaranteed the rights of due process, equal protection, and the privileges and immunities of United States citizenship, and the Fifteenth Amendment (1870) accorded freedmen the right to vote. These Reconstruction amendments codified the North's triumph and the principles for which the Union armies fought. Or so it seemed.

What was won on the battlefield was soon lost in the trenches of the courtroom. The first defeat occurred in a decision aptly named *The Slaughter-House Cases,*[1] decided in 1873. The underlying dispute concerned a Louisiana statute that granted the Crescent City Live-Stock Landing and Slaughter-House Company the exclusive right to conduct the business of livestock landing and slaughtering of animals for food in the city of New Orleans. New Orleans butchers challenged the law, arguing that it created "a monopoly and conferr[ed] odious and exclusive privileges upon a small number of persons at the expense of the great body of the community of New Orleans" and deprived "a large and meritorious class of citizens, the whole of the butchers of the city, of the right to exercise their trade, the business to which they have been trained and on which they depend for the support of themselves and their families."[2]

The principal legal ground asserted by the butchers was the claim that the Louisiana statute violated the privileges and immunities clause of the newly enacted Fourteenth Amendment. In short, they claimed a constitutional right not to be arbitrarily denied their livelihoods, a right that was enforceable against state legislatures by state and federal courts. The Supreme Court denied that such a right existed. The Court conceded that the Fourteenth Amendment had overturned the principal holding of the *Dred Scott* decision by providing that "all persons born or naturalized in the United States, and subject to the jurisdiction thereof, are citizens of the United States and of the States wherein they reside."[3] The amendment thus removed any doubt that the freed slaves would be citizens. Yet this very statement guaranteeing citizenship, the Court said, made clear that all Americans wear two citizenship hats. They are both citizens of the United States and citizens of the states wherein they reside. The Court noted that the constitutional provision guaranteeing no abridgment of citizens' privileges or immunities only speaks of those privileges of United States citizenship, not their respective state citizenship. The amendment provides that "no State shall make or enforce any law which shall abridge the privileges or immunities *of Citizens of the United States.*" Consequently, the Fourteenth Amendment did not make the federal government the guarantor of civil rights against state law infringement of those rights.

Prior to the Civil War and the passage of the Fourteenth Amendment, it was well accepted that the guarantees of the Bill of Rights, such as free speech and due process, applied exclusively to the federal government. Each state was responsible for guaranteeing the civil rights of its citizens from encroachment by state government. The federal government, under this conception of Federalism, did not intercede to defend Americans from the depredations perpetrated by their own state. This is one reason why slaves had no appeal to the federal courts for the conditions imposed upon them by the southern states. Chief Justice John Marshall, in 1833, had outlined this original understanding in *Barron v. The Mayor and City Council of Baltimore*:

> The Constitution was ordained and established by the people of the United States for themselves, for their government, and not for the government of the individual States. Each State established a constitution for itself, and in that constitution provided such limitations and restrictions on the powers of its particular government as its judgment dictated.[4]

In the *Slaughter-House* cases, Justice Samuel Miller, writing for the Court, asked incredulously, "Was it the purpose of the Fourteenth Amendment, by the simple declaration that no State should make or enforce any law which shall abridge the privileges and immunities of citizens of the United States, to transfer the security and protection of all of the civil rights . . . from the States to the Federal government? Such a construction," Miller warned, "would constitute this court a perpetual censor upon all legislation of the States." It would cause "so great a departure from the structure and spirit of our institutions," would so "fetter and degrade the State governments by subjecting them to the control of Congress," and would so radically change "the whole theory of the relations of the State and Federal governments to each other and of both of these governments to the people," that "we are convinced that no such results were intended by the Congress which proposed these amendments, nor by the legislatures of the States which ratified them."[5]

Thus, despite a civil war fought between the federal government and the states, won by Union forces, and fought in part to vindicate the civil rights of black Americans against state laws that oppressed them, the Court found no basic change in the structural relationship between the two governments. Amended by the Fourteenth Amendment, the Constitution, according to Justice Miller, afforded citizens no more protection against state tyranny than existed before the first cannonball fell on Fort Sumter. The opinion was adamantly opposed by dissenting Justice Stephen J. Field. Justice Field, the brother of David Dudley Field (who led the nineteenth-century codification movement) and Cyrus W. Field (who laid the Atlantic cable), was one of the most colorful justices to ever sit on the bench. Field had participated in the California gold rush as a frontier lawyer armed with pistol and bowie knife. His long-running feud with Justice David Terry, who was chief justice of the California Supreme Court when Field was elected to that court, led Terry to threaten Field's life. Many years later, in 1889, after Field had joined the Supreme Court, Terry attacked Field and was himself killed by a federal marshal assigned to guard Field. In the *Slaughter-House* cases, Field wrote that if the clause refers only "to such privileges and immunities as were before its adoption specially designated in the Constitution or necessarily implied as belonging to citizens of the United States, it was a vain and idle enactment, which accomplished nothing, and most unnecessarily excited Congress and the people on its passage."[6]

Deference to state sensibilities, a pre–Civil War conception of Federalism, guided the Court's hand and reversed with a few strokes of the pen a core component of the reforms won in that grim conflict. The banner of states' rights in the manner of *Dred Scott* would remain flying over the Court, and under its imprimatur the Court would permit the states great leeway to treat their citizens however they wished. The *Slaughter-House* cases laid the cornerstone of the apartheid that would pervade America in the first half of the twentieth century. The foundation for that edifice would be completed more than twenty years after the *Slaughter-House* cases in *Plessy v. Ferguson.*[7]

On June 7, 1892, Homer Adolph Plessy, a light-skinned black man (reportedly seven-eighths Caucasian), boarded the East Louisiana Railroad bound for Covington, Louisiana. He sat in the white coach, violating an 1890 Louisiana law mandating that blacks ride in separate railway cars. Plessy was arrested after refusing to move to the black car. The black community of New Orleans, possibly the most cosmopolitan in the South, decided to challenge the law and enlisted Homer Plessy for their test case. Plessy's counsel was Albion Tourgée, a prominent member of the Republican carpetbagger regime of North Carolina and a former judge. The law was entitled, "An Act to Promote the Comfort of Passengers," and mandated that "all railway companies carrying passengers in their coaches in this State, shall provide equal but separate accommodation for the white, and colored, races, by providing two or more passenger coaches for each passenger train, or by dividing the passenger coaches by a partition so as to secure separate accommodation."[8]

Before the Court, Plessy argued that segregation was arbitrary and a denial of the equal protection guaranteed by the Fourteenth Amendment. In his brief, he asked the justices to put themselves in his shoes, as if "by some mysterious dispensation of providence [they] should wake tomorrow with a black skin and curly hair." They, too, should imagine riding the rails and being told by the conductor to remove themselves from the white cars. "It is easy to imagine what would be the result," Plessy observed, "the indignation, the protests, the assertion of pure Caucasian ancestry. But the conductor, the autocrat of Caste, armed with the power of the State conferred by this statute, will listen neither to denial or protest. 'In you go or out you go,' is his ultimatum."[9]

The Court had little empathy. It stated that "the case reduces itself to the question whether the statute of Louisiana is a reasonable regulation."

On this general question, the Court compared the segregation of rail cars to school segregation, which was widely practiced when the Fourteenth Amendment was ratified. "We cannot say that a law which authorizes or even requires the separation of the two races in public conveyances is unreasonable, or more obnoxious to the Fourteenth Amendment than the acts of Congress requiring separate schools for colored children in the District of Columbia, the constitutionality of which does not seem to have been questioned, or the corresponding acts of state legislatures."[10]

The Court stated that the "underlying fallacy" of Plessy's argument was his "assumption that the enforced separation of the two races stamps the colored race with a badge of inferiority." According to the Court, "If this be so, it is not by reason of anything found in the act, but solely because the colored race chooses to put that construction upon it." Thus, the blame, if any, lay with the black community and not the state law. "If the two races are to meet upon terms of social equality, it must be the result of natural affinities, a mutual appreciation of each other's merits and a voluntary consent of individuals," the Court argued, and "legislation is powerless to eradicate racial instincts or to abolish distinctions based upon physical differences." The Court reasoned: "If the civil and political rights of both races be equal one cannot be inferior to the other civilly or politically. If one race be inferior to the other socially, the Constitution of the United States cannot put them upon the same plane."[11] Sixty-four years later, Professor Charles L. Black Jr. of the Yale Law School would say about this reasoning that "the curves of callousness and stupidity intersect at their respective maxima."[12]

The Court's impatience to reach a predetermined conclusion blinded it to the essence of Plessy's actual claim. It may have been, though the point is not obvious, that "legislation is powerless to eradicate racial instincts." But the Louisiana law was enacted to *maintain* "racial instincts." The law mandated segregation; it did not simply tolerate it. Justice John Marshall Harlan dissented in *Plessy,* and argued that the Fourteenth Amendment allowed the state to make no distinctions based on race. He stated, "In view of the Constitution, in the eye of the law, there is in this country no superior, dominant, ruling class of citizens. There is no caste here." He continued eloquently:

> Our Constitution is color-blind, and neither knows nor tolerates classes among citizens. In respect of civil rights, all citizens are equal before the law. The humblest is the peer of the most powerful. The law regards man

as man, and takes no account of his surroundings or of his color when his civil rights as guaranteed by the supreme law of the land are involved.[13]

Although the Court carefully avoided the subject, infused in *Plessy* is an acceptance of the racial inferiority of the "colored races." The Court preferred to put the matter more delicately, holding that the Constitution permits racial classifications, thereby acknowledging racial differences. But there was no gainsaying the reality of Jim Crow. Racial difference meant white superiority.

Ironically, just as the Court poured the concrete for the foundation of apartheid, the science of race was undergoing a fundamental reconceptualization. This revolution was particularly associated with the work of the great anthropologist Franz Boas, who, with others, emphasized the cultural and environmental contributions to perceived racial differences. Boas argued that the superior advancement of European civilizations was attributable, when considered over millennia, primarily to chance historical events. "In short," he said, "historical events appear to have been much more potent in leading races to civilization than their faculty, and it follows that achievements of races do not warrant us to assume that one race is more highly gifted than the other."[14] In rejecting traditional assumptions about racial achievement, Boas emphasized the relativity of standards of valuation and the functional environmental dissimilarities experienced by different peoples. Boas explained the apparent mental discrepancies in terms of varying cultural traditions and environmental influences.[15] European society's evaluation of primitive customs as "inferior" was due to its cultural vantage point and not any inherent value of the customs or objective scale of measurement. Boas urged his contemporaries to see that just as it was "impossible for us to appreciate their values without having grown up under their influence," so too "the value which we attribute to our civilization [was] due to the fact that we participate in this civilization, and that it has been controlling all our actions since the time of our birth."[16]

History is often transfigured by a combination of strong personalities, fortunate opportunities, fortuitous timing, and good luck. The history of desegregation is replete with all of these factors, with the first playing a predominant role. Certainly, even without the prodigious personalities who led the way, Jim Crow would almost certainly have ended eventually.

But the tale would have been very different and, in the context of race relations, how the story unfolds is almost as important as how it ends.

A towering figure in the earliest struggles against the institutional manifestations of racism was William Edward Burghardt DuBois. He was born in 1868, the same year that the Fourteenth Amendment became law. W. E. B. DuBois was raised in Great Barrington, a small town in Massachusetts, among only a small group of other blacks. He was slender and light-skinned, and he described himself as "a flood of Negro blood, a strain of French, a bit of Dutch, but thank God! no Anglo-Saxon."[17] He was educated at Fisk University, Harvard University, and the University of Berlin, and spent over seventy years writing and teaching in sociology and history. Foremost, he was a civil rights activist. He was a founding member of the NAACP and in his writing defined many of the principal themes of the black experience in America. He was the first editor of the NAACP's magazine *Crisis* and through it and his other writing and speeches set much of the early intellectual agenda for the civil rights movement.

Established around 1910, the NAACP would attract most of the major reformers of the first half of the twentieth century and served as the headquarters of most reform efforts. The impetus for the organization's early efforts was a strong opposition to the gradualism preached by Booker T. Washington. In addition to general lobbying efforts, the NAACP soon began a campaign in the courts against all institutional manifestations of discrimination. In 1915, the organization successfully challenged the grandfather clause used by many southern states to prevent blacks from voting. By 1920, membership had swelled to ninety thousand, half of which came from the South. In 1927 they won a suit against the all-white primary.

Walter White assumed the duties of executive secretary in 1930, and he would lead the organization for twenty-five years through its most tumultuous and glorious period. Perhaps his greatest contribution to the NAACP's success was his ability to attract talented and dedicated people to the cause. Possibly the most talented and accomplished recruit that Walter White hired was Charles Houston, the dean of Howard Law School. Houston joined the NAACP's reform efforts in 1935 and by his presence gave the effort instant credibility. Houston grew up in Washington, D.C.'s middle-class black community and attended Amherst, where he graduated with honors, and Harvard Law School. At Howard, he was known as demanding and unrelenting. Most of all, he was driven, expecting a complete commitment from himself and the same from his students. Thurgood Marshall, Houston's most famous student, described him as "hard-crust." Marshall recalled that, upon arriving at Howard, most students thought that Houston "was a mean so and so. He used to tell us that doctors could bury their mistakes but lawyers couldn't." But Houston impressed upon his students that they "would be competing not only with white lawyers but really well-trained white lawyers, so there just wasn't any point in crying in our beer about being Negroes." Although Howard was rough going—Marshall's class began with thirty but only about ten finished—Houston had a plan for his students. Edward P. Lovett, another of Houston's early students, said that "Charlie's view was that we had to get the courts to change—and that we could and should no longer depend upon high-powered white lawyers to represent us in that effort."[18] Houston "made it clear to all of us," Marshall stated, "that when we were done, we were expected to go out and do something with our lives."[19]

Houston, both in and away from Howard, played a pivotal role in shaping and leading early reform efforts. "He was," said one of his successors, "the Moses of [our] journey."[20] Tragically, he died before his work was done. He succumbed to a heart attack at the age of fifty-four, four years before the *Brown* Court vindicated his life's efforts. He received little recognition of his accomplishments, and today his name is known only to very few nonspecialists. But he led the way, making possible the successes that made names like Thurgood Marshall renowned.

First in the historiography of the civil rights movement stands Thurgood Marshall. He joined the NAACP in 1934 and became Charles Houston's indispensable associate when Houston joined the organization a year later. Marshall eventually became the leader of all litigation efforts at the NAACP, and the movement became associated with him and his thundering personality and imposing manner. His work earned him the title "Mr. Civil Rights." Born on July 2, 1908, Marshall was raised in a thoroughly middle-class section of Baltimore, and his experiences in this racially mixed environment deeply affected his lifelong belief that integration of the races, not separation, was the proper prescription for American society. Growing up, Marshall was not known as a serious student. He held science and math in particular contempt. His first introduction to the Constitution was as punishment for his many indiscretions at school. Marshall often told the story of how the principal of his grade school made him stay late to memorize different constitutional sections every time he broke the rules. He recalled, "Before I left that school, I knew the whole thing by heart."[21] An acquaintance of his described him as "happy-go-lucky on the face of it, always with some lie to tell, but he managed to get a lot of work done when nobody was looking."[22] Marshall had originally wanted to go to the University of Maryland's law school and not Howard's. But it was segregated and there was no use in even trying.

In the first several decades of the battle against segregation, the NAACP plan was adapted from a report prepared by Nathan Margold. The Margold strategy was simple and elegant. A frontal assault on *Plessy* was fraught with danger, because of both the precedent's lack of obvious vulnerability early in the century and the fear of what a new High Court endorsement of the *Plessy* holding would do to the fledgling civil rights movement. Margold proposed a flanking maneuver. The NAACP would attack *Plessy* by seeking specific enforcement of its holding—with a vengeance. Rather than clamor for integration, they demanded what the law supposedly guaranteed, truly equal facilities. *Plessy* promised separate but equal, so the NAACP insisted that this pledge be fulfilled. The disparities between white and black schooling were profound throughout the South. Whites received ten times as much per-pupil spending in South Carolina, five times as much in Florida, Georgia, Mississippi, and Alabama, and twice as much in North Carolina, Maryland, Virginia, Texas, and Oklahoma. Because these communities could not afford to maintain truly equal separate facilities, segregation would end simply by enforcing the law as it existed. This strategy appealed to Marshall's realist tendencies. Part of his success lay in his recognition of what battles could be won and thus which battles were worth fighting. Representative of this philosophy was a favorite Marshall story about his visit to a small Mississippi town where he considered staying overnight. "I was out there on the train platform," Marshall said, "trying to look small, when this cold-eye man with a gun on his hip comes up. 'Niggah,' he said, 'I thought you oughta know the sun ain't nevah set on a live niggah in this town.' So I wrapped my constitutional rights in cellophane, tucked 'em in my pocket . . . and caught the next train out of there."[23] But Marshall's and the NAACP's pursuit of the ultimate objective of ending Jim Crow never wavered. While the lawyers traversed an indirect course and fought only the battles thought winnable, their gaze remained fixed on the goal of full integration. Only with integration, Marshall believed, could blacks and whites succeed or fail based on their own abilities.

One of the first challenges brought under the Margold plan was a suit against the University of Maryland's law school in the case of *Murray v. Maryland*.[24] Houston and Marshall led the way. Maryland offered no legal education for blacks, but provided nominal scholarships so that eligible students could go to law schools outside the state, such as Howard Law School. Murray, however, wished to stay in Maryland. Murray won before the trial court, a victory celebrated by Baltimore's most famous man of letters, H. L. Mencken. He wrote that "there will be an Ethiop among the Aryans when the larval Blackstones assemble next Wednesday." As regards the university's suggestion that the Howard Law School constituted an equal opportunity, Mencken said, "the regents might just as well advise him to go to Addis Ababa or Timbuktu." He wrote that Murray "wants to get his training, not in Washington, but here in Baltimore, where the laws and procedures of Maryland are at the bottom of the teaching and where he plans to practice."[25] But Mencken did not favor school integration generally. He thought it imprudent to extend the mixing of races below the graduate level. This view was shared by many, and most of the NAACP's early efforts were directed at graduate education.

Because of the stark and dramatic inequalities that existed between black and white institutions, the Margold plan had enormous success when measured battle by battle. But there were too many battles to be fought. The Margold plan presented the danger of exhausting the NAACP's energies in fighting numerous skirmishes without substantially improving the prospects of winning the war. In retrospect, the Margold plan was a strategy with limited longevity. Moreover, it sprang from the core concession of *Plessy,* that separate-but-equal facilities could be constitutionally legitimate. Separation of the races affirmed the biological concept of black inferiority and the need felt among whites to maintain racial purity. But the science of race had fundamentally changed and it was no longer tenable to believe in the inherent superiority and inferiority of different races. Moreover, sociologists began to unmask the social and economic correlates of the principle of separate but equal. The racial bigotry at the core of the constitutional principle became increasingly clear and impossible to ignore.

In 1944, Gunnar Myrdal, a Swedish economist and sociologist, published his landmark indictment of American racism, *An American Dilemma*. The two-volume work was acclaimed as "the most penetrating and important book on our contemporary American civilization that has been written." Sociologist Robert Lynd said that, in the book, "we Americans are revealed clad in our patchwork 'American way,' attempting to live along with the vast and ugly reality of what Dr. Myrdal calls our 'greatest failure.' "[26] The manifestations of this failure were the variety of legal roadblocks the South constructed to block equality. The primary objective of these measures, according to Myrdal, was to avoid inter-marriage. More specifically, the means of segregation were tailored to keep black men from having sexual relations with white women. Their purpose was thus an ancient one and concerned the same fear that guided so many of the rules governing relations between blacks and whites during slave times. The laws' "relative significance" depended "upon their degree of expediency or necessity—in the view of white people—as means of upholding the ban on inter-marriage." Myrdal explained:

> In this rank order, (1) the ban on intermarriage and other sex relations involving white women and colored men takes precedence before everything else. It is the end for which the other restrictions are arranged as means. Thereafter follow: (2) all sorts of taboos and etiquettes governing impersonal contacts; (3) segregation in schools and churches; (4) segregation in hotels, restaurants, and theaters, and other public places where people meet socially; (5) segregation in public conveyances; (6) discrimination in public services; (7) politics; (8) justice and (9) bread winning and relief.[27]

Myrdal's study of the sociological and economic impact of American racism provided an important source of authority for the NAACP's offensive against the doctrine of segregation. After the Second World War, the realization set in among civil rights advocates that Jim Crow should be confronted directly. Two cases in particular operated as the transition from the Margold plan to a full frontal assault. One involved a Texas mailman who wanted to be a lawyer and the other an Oklahoma teacher with a master's degree who wanted to return to graduate school to earn a Ph.D.

In February 1946, Herman Marion Sweatt applied to the all-white law school at the University of Texas at Austin. He ended up in court instead. While his case proceeded to trial, the Texas legislature mandated the funding for a "first-class" Texas University for Negroes. Located in downtown Austin, the law school amounted to three small classrooms, a tiny library, and access to the state capitol's library across the street. Thurgood Marshall came to Austin ready for a fight. "I think we've humored the South long enough," he told a New York reporter, "and it's only by lawsuits and legislation that we'll ever teach reactionaries the meaning of the Fourteenth Amendment. . . . This is going to be a real showdown fight against Jim Crow in education."[28] At trial, the state objected to Marshall's attempts to use scientific evidence to show that segregation was scientifically unjustified and socially injurious. Marshall proffered the expert testimony of Robert Redfield, an anthropologist and lawyer from the University of Chicago and one of the most eminent scholars in the country. The state, however, argued that the testimony was irrelevant, since the suit only involved the state's educational offerings. Marshall erupted, saying, "We have a right to put in evidence to show that segregation statutes in the State of Texas and in any other state, actually when examined—and they have never been examined in any lawsuit that I know of yet—have no line of reasonableness. There is no understandable factual basis for classification by race, and under a long line of decisions by the Supreme Court, not on the question of Negroes, but on the Fourteenth Amendment, all courts agree that if there is no rational basis for the classification, it is flat in the teeth of the Fourteenth Amendment."[29] The judge permitted the testimony.

While Sweatt pursued equal protection in Austin, George W. McLaurin was engaged in a similar battle just north in Oklahoma. In 1948, he applied to the doctoral program in education at the University of Oklahoma and was denied admission because of his race. A federal district court ordered McLaurin's admission to the school, since there were no separate facilities available, much less equal ones. The state, however, responded by erecting a virtual bubble by which to keep McLaurin segregated within the department. In class, he was forced to sit in a row "reserved for Negroes," and he was provided a separate table to eat at in the cafeteria and a separate desk to study at in the library. Marshall explained his decision to take on McLaurin's case several years later: "The Dixiecrats and the others said it was horrible. The only thing Negroes were trying to do, they said, was to get social equality. As a matter of fact, there would be intermarriage, they said. The latter theory was the reason we deliberately chose Professor McLaurin. We had eight people who had applied and who were eligible to be plaintiffs, but we deliberately picked Professor McLaurin because he was sixty-eight years old and we didn't think he was going to marry or intermarry. . . . They could not bring that one up on us, anyhow."[30]

The Supreme Court heard both *Sweatt v. Painter*[31] and *McLaurin v. Oklahoma*[32] on the same day in April 1950. The brief quoted Myrdal's observation that "segregation and discrimination have had material and moral effects on whites, too." Myrdal found corroboration for "Booker T. Washington's famous remark, that the white man could not hold the Negro in the gutter without getting in there himself." Myrdal continued, as quoted in the *Sweatt* brief:

> Throughout this book we have been forced to notice the law, economic, political, legal, and moral standards of Southern Whites—kept low because of discrimination against Negroes and because of obsession with the Negro problem. Even the ambition of Southern whites is stifled partly because, without rising far, it is easy to remain 'superior' to the held-down Negroes.[33]

With *Sweatt* and *McLaurin*, Marshall and the NAACP entered a new phase in their struggle against Jim Crow. Under the Margold strategy the NAACP sought to hang the southern states on their own petard. The inequality that was manifest between black and white educational opportunities was thought to be enough to move the courts toward integration. And so it was, albeit in a limited way. By 1950, more dramatic strokes were needed. The NAACP decided that henceforth the aim in the education cases would be to obtain "education on a non-segregated basis and that no relief other than that will be acceptable."[34] Despite this strongly held view, the NAACP did not completely abandon the Margold plan. In *Sweatt* and *McLaurin*, Marshall argued in the alternative that the Texas and Oklahoma systems were inequitable in application and unequal in principle.

The Supreme Court, however, was not quite ready for radical change. The Court was unwilling to reconsider the continuing validity of *Plessy* itself. Chief Justice Frederick Vinson noted in *Sweatt* that "broader issues have been urged for our consideration, but we adhere to the principle of deciding constitutional questions only in the context of the particular case before the Court."[35] Although the Court held unanimously against the University of Texas in *Sweatt* and the University of Oklahoma in *McLaurin*, it rested its decision on the Margold-like ground that the state had failed to offer the complainants truly equal educational opportunities. In *Sweatt*, the Court found the makeshift law school established by Texas to be objectively inferior to the facilities of the white law school. Moreover, the black law school fell dramatically below grade in regard to the intangible qualities that make a law school great. Vinson explained that "a school's alumni, its prestige and influence, and its history were all to be considered when comparing it with any other school."[36] Implicitly, then, the Court recognized that Texas would never be able to create a fully formed all-black law school that could meet the venerable reputation of the University of Texas law school in Austin. Without specifically declaring Jim Crow's death, it was clear that segregation at the graduate level could never be equal. In *McLaurin*, the Court held that Oklahoma's practices violated "personal and present rights to the equal protection of the laws." McLaurin, the Court declared, "must receive the same treatment . . . as students of other races."[37] But these holdings were some distance from finding segregation to be inherently wrong, and the Court had yet to visit educational contexts involving children during their tender years. This battle would demand more ammunition.

The change of legal strategy from an indirect attack on *Plessy* to a direct assault on segregation was accompanied by a change in the emphasis of the scientific argument. Previously, Marshall had relied on systemic attacks on segregation, such as those offered by sociologists and economists. Such proof was not narrowly tailored to prove actual harm to named individuals. Sociology and economics could provide a broad indictment of segregation's effects, but these disciplines, by their very natures, could not make plain the pain felt by the individual men, women, and children who were its victims. In comparison, psychology and psychiatry offered a more particularized indictment of segregation. More important, these sciences tracked traditional legal conceptions of injury. If it could be scientifically demonstrated that the act of state-enforced segregation produced measurable harm, then no quantity of separation in education could ever be "equal."

Courts ordinarily evaluate empirical consequences one case at a time. Broad sociological and economic propositions are more usually the province of legislatures. In contrast and by necessity, courts are designed primarily to gather evidence regarding a specific incident or event. An accident victim, for instance, must prove both that the defendant was the cause of the injury and the fact and extent of the injury itself. Marshall believed that the same could be done in the school cases. "I told the staff that we had to try this case just like any other in which you would try to prove damages to your client." Marshall explained, "If your car ran over my client, you'd have to pay up, and my function as an attorney would be to put experts on the stand to testify to how much damage was done. We needed exactly that kind of evidence in the school cases."[38]

Social scientists had for years studied the effects of segregation on black schoolchildren. One young scientist studying this question was Kenneth Clark, an assistant professor in psychology at the City College of New York. Clark and his wife, Mamie, used the familiar technique of projective testing to evaluate segregation's effects. The best-known projective test is the Rorschach inkblot test, in which psychologists present subjects with an ambiguous inkblot and ask them to describe what they see. The subjects' answers are thought to provide a glimpse into their psyches. Rather than inkblots, the Clarks used dolls, two pink and two brown, which he bought for fifty cents at a five-and-ten on 125th Street in New York. Research employing these tests provided the basis for a paper Clark delivered to the White House Conference on Children and Youth in 1950. When Marshall heard about Clark's doll test he thought it "a promising way of showing injury to these segregated youngsters. I wanted this kind of evidence on the record."[39]

The notion to use Clark's doll studies was Robert Carter's. Marshall later recalled, "Bob gets all the credit for it."[40] Carter was one of the bright young men Marshall recruited to the NAACP during the war years. Like Marshall, he was a graduate of Lincoln University and Howard Law School. An associate described Carter as bright and a hard worker but not a philosopher like Howard dean Charles Houston. "He carried the heaviest burden, getting the work out and the briefs in on time. In that office, Bob Carter was the keel and Thurgood was—I don't know, the wind maybe."[41] But few on Marshall's team of lawyers shared Carter's enthusiasm for the dolls and most doubted that the dolls would help their cause. Spott Robinson "thought it was crazy and insulting to try to persuade a court of law with examples of crying children and their dolls."[42] William Coleman remembered that "of all the debunkers, I was the most debunking." Coleman had clerked for Justice Felix Frankfurter and didn't think the social science would impress the justices. "Jesus Christ," he said, "those damned dolls! I thought it was a joke!"[43] But Marshall delighted in the idea and believed that they should embrace anything that might advance their claims.

Marshall planned to use Clark's doll research in two ways. First, the research already done and published would provide the framework within which to understand segregation's effects. The fact that segregation was cancerous to the black communities that suffered its degradations would be demonstrated by this work. This use was akin to the previous use of sociological and economic research in showing the systemic effects and social consequences of Jim Crow. Now, however, Marshall sought to demonstrate the psychological injuries caused by Jim Crow just as one might demonstrate that chemicals in the water supply caused cancer. Marshall wanted to demonstrate that the children in the respective areas in which litigation was brought similarly suffered segregation's damaging effects. They were victims, just like any victim of toxic waste, poisoned by segregation. Inherent in Clark's methods, however, was the limitation that it was impossible to single out the percentage of psychological injury attributable to separate schooling and the percentage attributable to the segregation practiced throughout southern society. To Clark's credit, he was always careful to speak only of segregation's deleterious consequences and made no attempt to apportion blame to the schools.

In the case of *Briggs v. Elliott*,[44] brought in South Carolina, Clark received his introduction to the South. Clark remembered that they "settled in at the Boone house and had a real nice meal." Afterward, the group began discussing strategy for the following days. Clark eventually asked, "Who was going to go over to Clarendon County with me— Thurgood, or Bob or who?" They told him no one. "I thought they were kidding," he recalled, and said so. They responded, "No, we're here to prepare for the trial and—well, you know, it's dangerous over there." The next morning, Clark still thought they were teasing him when they introduced him to his driver, a young man from the South Carolina NAACP. He figured that "Thurgood or Bob is going to climb in with me." Instead, Marshall gave Clark a fifty-dollar bill and said, " 'Look, if you get into trouble over there, you might try showing this to them or their leader—it might help.' "[45]

Representing South Carolina was Robert Figg. A veteran newspaper editor once commented about Figg that, "if it came to a choice between arguing or following up a case and getting in a good round of golf, Bob Figg would probably have played golf. He was smart as a whip—and lazy as can be."[46] Somehow fitted between rounds of golf, Figg pursued a very busy legal practice and had a successful career in law, albeit entirely southern style. He served as a state solicitor in South Carolina for twelve years from 1935 until 1947, and thereafter practiced law privately, including his representation of the Clarendon County School Board. He also served as an adviser to South Carolina governor Strom Thurmond, and worked as a speech writer during Thurmond's presidential bid in 1948 on the Dixiecrat platform of segregation. He would later serve as dean of the University of Alabama law school, and led the school through a major expansion effort in the 1960s. Ironically, during Figg's tenure as dean, the Alabama law school admitted its first black students. Figg, however, never changed his view that the federal government had no right to legislate voting and civil rights.

At the *Briggs* trial, Marshall marched a parade of experts through the courtroom. But from the start it was not clear what legal question the social science would answer. There were two possibilities. One was whether the educational resources and opportunities were equal in the two school systems. On this issue, no one seriously contended that the separate school systems were even barely comparable. In every conceivable category the white schools were superior to the black schools. South Carolina actually took advantage of this fact. In an ingenious strategic move, the state conceded from the start that educational facilities for blacks did not equal those given whites. Figg hoped that this would end the matter and he figured the court would give the state time to equalize school facilities. And this was just what the court did, when it ordered the state to "remedy the disparity within six months."

The second, more subtle, empirical question concerned whether even equally well-funded separate schools could provide equal educational opportunities. For the NAACP, this was the whole ball game. But Figg argued strongly that this was not a proper subject for expert testimony. For instance, Robert Carter asked Ellis O. Knox, a professor of education at Howard, whether he believed "that Negro children attending a segregated school with facilities equal to the white schools in their community could obtain equal classroom instructional opportunities."[47] Figg objected to the question. Judge John Parker responded, "Well, what he's asking him is whether or not in his opinion it is discriminatory against the Negro children to segregate them in schools. That is what he's asking him. Why isn't that competent?" Figg's response:

> We think it's irrelevant and immaterial. It's been settled that the states can provide public schools and that they may provide separate schools for the different races. And his opinion is irrelevant and immaterial under the legal situation as laid down in the [Supreme Court's] decisions. That is a polit- ical matter for the legislature under our situation and not for witnesses on the witness stand.[48]

Parker overruled the objection and the witness was allowed to answer. Knox, however, was apparently bewildered by this colloquy and answered uncertainly that, in his experience, segregated schools never provided equal facilities to their black students.

Carter's other witnesses responded somewhat more on point. Dr. David Krech, for example, a social psychologist from Harvard, testified that "legal segregation hampers the mental, emotional, physical and financial development of colored children and aggravates the very prej- udices from which it arises." But the central witness was Kenneth Clark and his doll studies. Clark testified: "I have reached the conclu- sion from the examination of my own results and from an examination of the literature in the entire field that discrimination, prejudice and segregation have definitely detrimental effects on the personality devel- opment of the Negro child." Segregation, Clark explained, created "confusion in the child's concept of his own self-esteem—basic feelings of inferiority, conflict, confusion in his self-image, resentment, hostility towards himself, hostility towards whites," and a tendency "to resolve his basic conflict by sometimes escaping or withdrawing." Clark also reported to the court his findings in Clarendon County. He had inter- viewed sixteen black children there. On the question of whether the black doll was "bad or good," eleven of the children said "bad." When asked which doll was "nice," ten of the black children selected the white doll. Based on these data, Clark testified "that these children in Clarendon County, like other human beings who are subjected to an obviously inferior status in the society in which they live, have been definitely harmed in the development of their personalities." He found that "the signs of instability in their personalities are clear." He also warned that the damage was "likely to endure as long as the conditions of segregation exist."[49]

Figg, at first concerned about Clark's findings of fact, soon came to believe that they carried little weight. He said, "Once we determined that his testimony was based on very few children, that there were no witnesses to the tests, and that this was his own method and not a well-established one, I didn't press the matter. His numbers were small and unimposing, so why should I have pushed it? . . . Nobody took it seriously."[50]

With only a few exceptions, Figg's decision not to introduce countervailing social science research was followed by defendants in the several trials over segregation that were also occurring at the start of the 1950s. This decision was not specifically driven by the lack of data on the other side—though not much existed—nor was it obviated by the known weaknesses of the NAACP's data. Rather, it was determined largely by the reluctance of academic social scientists to testify against the NAACP. Many highly reputable social scientists believed that the existing data were scant and did not compel the conclusion that segregated schools caused particular diagnosable harms. For example, Dr. Elsa Robinson, a respected social psychologist at New York University's Graduate School of Arts and Science, was contacted by the NAACP and asked to participate in the case. After reviewing the research, she wrote back, "I have come to the conclusion that there is as yet no scientifically verified material of an empirical nature which bears directly on the issue."[51] But she never considered voicing these doubts publicly or in service to South Carolina.

Although the *Briggs* court had generously allowed the expert testimony on the injurious effects of segregation that occurred despite an equal allocation of educational resources, it ultimately agreed with the state that it was not a proper subject for it to decide the question of the constitutionality of school segregation. The court, with one judge dissenting, wrote that "it is a late day to say that such segregation is violative of constitutional rights." The court ruled that the "constitutional principle is the same now that it has been throughout this period; and if conditions have changed so that segregation is no longer wise, this is a matter for the legislatures and not the courts. The members of the judiciary have no more right to read their ideas of sociology into the Constitution than their ideas of economics."[52]

Judge J. Waties Waring dissented:

Segregation in education can never produce equality and . . . is an evil that must be eradicated. This case presents the matter clearly for adjudication, and I am of the opinion that all of the legal guideposts, expert testimony, common sense and reason point unerringly to the conclusion that the system of segregation in education adopted and practiced in the state of South Carolina must go and go now.

Segregation is *per se* inequality.[53]

The NAACP opened another front in 1951, this time in the northern city of Topeka, Kansas. The case was filed February 28, 1951, and was officially entitled *Brown v. Board of Education of Topeka*. The NAACP urged the social science research as fervently in *Brown* as it had in *Briggs,* though, ironically, Clark himself did not testify in the case. While Clark was missing from Topeka, his research was center stage. A virtual parade of experts, including psychologists, psychiatrists, education specialists, sociologists, and economists, testified in Topeka. Psychologist Horace B. English of Ohio State University testified that no evidence supported the existence of innate racial differences. He said, "If we din it into a person that it is unnatural for him to learn certain things, if we din it into a person that he is incapable of learning, then he is less likely to be able to learn." He explained that "there is a tendency for us to live up to— or perhaps I should say down to—social expectations and to learn what people say we can learn, and legal segregation definitely depresses the Negro's expectancy and is therefore prejudicial to his learning."[54] Another witness, Dr. Louisa Holt, a professor at Kansas University and formerly associated with the world-renowned Menninger Foundation in Topeka, echoed English's testimony and expressed particular concern regarding the fact that segregation was legally mandated. She said, "The fact that it is enforced, that it is legal, I think, has more importance than the mere fact of segregation by itself does because this gives legal and official sanction to a policy which is inevitably interpreted both by white people and by Negroes as denoting the inferiority of the Negro group."[55]

The trial court held unanimously for the Topeka school board on the basis that in the physical facilities, and in all other measurable respects, the segregated schools were comparable to the white schools. On the more basic question of whether segregation itself was so detrimental to black children as to render separate schools unconstitutional, the court, while persuaded by the NAACP's experts, considered it beyond the court's authority to decide the case in their favor. The court found explicitly that segregation caused psychological injury. In one of its nine findings of fact, the court stated:

> Segregation of white and colored children in public schools has a detrimental effect upon the colored children. The impact is greater when it has the sanction of law; for the policy of separating the races is usually interpreted as denoting the inferiority of the Negro group. A sense of inferiority affects the motivation of a child to learn. Segregation with the sanction of law, therefore, has a tendency to retard the educational and mental development of Negro children and to deprive them of some of the benefits they would receive in a racially integrated school.[56]

This finding of fact would reverberate all the way to Washington, D.C. Nonetheless, the court ruled in favor of Topeka, since it believed its hands were tied by precedent. The *Brown* trial court did not believe it had the authority to decide inconsistently with *Plessy*, even based on what it considered to be compelling empirical evidence of the detrimental effects of legally mandated separation of the races.

The one battlefront in which fierce resistance to the social science evidence was encountered was in Prince Edward County, Virginia. Virginia attorney general James Lindsay Almond Jr. said from the start that "we were going to create issues of fact, not just of law."[57] The Virginia strategy was twofold. It believed itself in the right both morally and empirically. On the moral side, Virginia took the position that whites had an obligation to "bring blacks along all in good time." Archibald Gerard Robertson, a leading partner of the law firm of Hunton and Williams in Richmond, which represented the state, observed years later, "After the War Between the States, this gentle, highly educated people, amid all its desolation and poverty, was trying to pull itself together, and we had loosed on us a horde of nigras who were utterly unprepared for freedom. It was the white people who paid the taxes and maintained civilization—the Negroes were an albatross around our necks, but we brought them up along with us and equalized the teachers' salaries and gave them as good schools as ours whenever we built new ones."[58] Attorney General Almond recollected similarly, though somewhat more candidly, "My forebears, people who were honest and Christian, felt kindly disposed to the nigra, but in no way wanted mingling and disapproved entirely of the amalgamation of the races because it would have endangered both. We believed strongly in separate schools, churches, and recreational facilities for the nigra. The Constitution called for equality, but it really wasn't there, and at the grass-roots level, people didn't favor it and didn't recognize the principle."[59] Virginia claimed simply that its tradition and practices were a matter of prerogative under American Federalism and were due respect by the national government and its federal courts. It would abolish segregation according to a timetable of its own choosing and in a manner conducive to the sensibilities of its citizens.

But Virginia intended to challenge tooth and nail the claims of Kenneth Clark and the assembly of experts that the NAACP had gathered. Chief counsel for the Prince Edward school board, and a partner at Hunton and Williams, T. Justin Moore would be the defendants' pit bull. He intended to go right to the heart of the NAACP's empirical argument that segregation itself inflicted harm. He told the court, "We are prepared to show by competent evidence that that sort of thing, at the present time at least, is purely speculative, that it is not based on a sound scientific basis, and we give notice to these gentlemen right now, if they don't already know it, that we intend to challenge that proposition if they attempt to present evidence on that, as has been done in some of these cases." He declared, "There is no foundation whatever for the fundamental theory on which this case is built—namely, that equal facilities and advantages cannot be provided regardless of the amount of money that is spent."[60]

Virginia sought out academics who might be sympathetic to their position. They found a star: Dr. Henry Garrett, born and raised in Virginia, and the chair of the psychology department at Columbia University in New York. He was past president of the American Psychological Association and a former adviser to the secretary of war. Although not a brilliant researcher or scholar, he was situated at the top of his profession and carried all of the accoutrements of mainstream success.

His views of blacks, however, were far from mainstream academic opinion. He considered blacks inferior intellectually, culturally, and physiologically. "Despite glowing accounts of ancient African achievements," he wrote, "over the past 5,000 years the history of Black Africa is a cultural blank."[61] He attributed the vast disparities between the races to biological factors, believing that only 10 percent of the difference could be traced to the environment. Garrett argued that while the average black's brain may not be smaller than the average white's, physiology demonstrated that blacks' brains were less complex and developed especially in the frontal lobes where abstract reasoning took place. He observed, "Given roughly the same opportunity and background, the Negro still performs less well than the white, even after 50 years of social progress, and the relative gaps remain as wide as ever."[62] Nonetheless, Garrett believed that educational resources should be divided equally between white and black, something Virginia counsel assured him that the state was making every effort to ensure. Despite the extraordinary pressure brought down upon him in New York, Garrett set off for Virginia to rebut the social science of desegregation. Virginia now had a formidable national figure willing to say that the science simply did not exist to conclude that segregation caused real and sustained harm.

Garrett proved an effective witness for the defense. He discussed the long tradition in America of separate schooling, ranging from gender to religion, all of which is accomplished without stigma or recriminations. He scored points questioning the value of Clark's doll studies, especially the fact that some students had shortly before gone out on strike protesting the conditions of the schools. Under the circumstances, Garrett testified, "you should be very much surprised" if the students' comments were not highly critical. Garrett also heaped scorn on a 1948 survey conducted by Isidor Chein and published in the *Journal of Psychology*. He called the Chein survey "blunderbuss" in character and said it was designed to get the very results obtained. Chein had sent a questionnaire to 849 social scientists specializing in the general area of developmental psychology and asked them a series of questions regarding their views concerning the effects of segregation. The survey was returned by 61 percent of the scientists. About 90 percent of the respondents agreed that "enforced segregation [has] detrimental psychological effects on members of racial and religious groups which are segregated, even if equal facilities are provided." Garrett commented about Chein, "I am surprised he did not select his sample well enough to have gotten a hundred percent [response endorsing the harmful effects of segregation]. . . . I would not like to make a bet, but I could wager that I would send a questionnaire and phrase it rightly and get almost any answer I wanted."[63]

Robert Carter had the unenviable task of cross-examining Garrett. He did not shine. As Carter himself admitted, "I was very tight," despite gaining permission from the court to allow Kenneth Clark to sit beside him at counsel's table. Carter said, "Mostly, I didn't want to give him a platform to make any more points than he already had. I didn't do very well with him." Carter did end up scoring a few points, though in general he was not well enough versed in the science. He asked Garrett whether "racial segregation, as presently practiced in the United States, and in Virginia, is a social situation which is adverse to the individual?" Garrett conceded that "in general, wherever a person is cut off from the main body of society or a group, if he is put in a position that stigmatizes him and makes him feel inferior, I would say yes, it is detrimental and deleterious to him." Nonetheless, Garrett maintained, "if the Negro child had equal facilities, his own teachers, his own friends, and a good feeling, he would be more likely to develop pride in himself as a Negro, which I think we would all like to see him do—to develop his own potentialities, his sense of duty, his sense of art, his sense of histrionics."[64]

To no one's surprise, the three-judge panel ruled unanimously for the state. The NAACP's Oliver Hill observed, "There was never any doubt about the outcome of the trial. We were trying to build a record for the Supreme Court." The court ruled that segregation rested "neither upon prejudice nor caprice nor upon any other measureless foundation." Separate schools had "for generations been a part of the mores of her people," and was even to be found in the Virginia Constitution. "We have found no hurt or harm to either race," the court concluded.[65]

The NAACP brought yet another case on the northern front in Delaware. There, Clark interviewed forty-one black children and found that three out of four of them, when asked, "Which of these dolls is likely to act bad?" picked the brown doll. Clark testified to the significance of this finding:

> Now, when you see that 100 percent of these youngsters correctly identify themselves with the brown doll . . . I think we have clear-cut evidence of rather deep damage to the self-esteem of these youngsters, a feeling of inferiority, a feeling of inadequacy—evidence which was further supported by the kind of things which the youngsters said: "I suppose we do act kind of bad. We don't act like white people."[66]

Clark's testimony in Delaware was buttressed by the clinical psychiatric testimony of Frederic Wertham, whom the court found to be "one of America's foremost psychiatrists." Wertham was a disciple of Freud, worked closely with Clarence Darrow on insanity claims, and was intently interested in the socioenvironmental causes of violence. He believed violent tendencies were a product of severe trauma produced by social and psychological circumstances, and that they did not have a biological genesis. Similarly, he believed that social circumstances, such as segregation, created observable pathologies and accounted for observed differences between blacks and whites. He testified that it was his "scientific opinion" that segregation affected blacks' mental health. It was "the fact of segregation in public and high school," he remarked, that "creates in the mind of the child an observable conflict, an unsolvable emotional conflict, and I would say an inevitable conflict." He found particularly at fault the message embedded in segregation rather than any physical disparity between the separate school systems. He testified:

> I have come to the conclusion that the physical differences in these schools are not at all really material to my opinion. In other words, if I may express it graphically, if the state of Delaware would employ Professor Einstein to teach physics in marble halls to these children, I would still say everything I have said goes: It is the fact of segregation in general and the problems that come out of it that to my mind is anti-education, by which I mean that education in the larger sense is interfered with. . . . Most of the children we have examined interpret segregation in one way and only one way—and that is they interpret it as punishment. There is no doubt about that. Now, whether that is true, whether the state of Delaware wants to punish these children, has nothing to do with it. I am only testifying about what is in the minds of the children.[67]

Clark's social science evidence, fortified by the psychoanalytic deductions of Wertham regarding the consequences of segregation, strongly influenced the Delaware court's decision. Chancellor Collins Seitz, the judge in the case, concluded that racial separation "creates a mental health problem in many Negro children with a resulting impediment to their education progress."[68] Nonetheless, he did not feel at liberty to invalidate segregated schools based on this evidentiary finding. Seitz believed that if these findings of fact were "given Constitutional recognition," then "the principle itself" of separate but equal "would be destroyed." The Supreme Court had still not overturned that principle as a matter of law and the

Delaware court felt itself bound by that principle, despite the fact that, as an empirical matter, separate schools invariably produced inequalities. Seitz explained, "I do not believe a lower court can reject a principle of United States Constitutional law which has been adopted by fair implication by the highest court of the land." He concluded, "I believe the 'separate-but-equal' doctrine in education should be rejected, but I also believe its rejection must come from that Court."[69]

Seitz went on to find, as a matter of fact, that the Delaware school system did not provide equal physical facilities or educational opportunities to blacks. The remedy he ordered was a significant victory for the NAACP, though not entirely satisfying, since it was in the vein of the old Margold approach. Integration was being ordered on account of physical disparities between the schools and not the inherent harms caused by segregation. He held that Delaware schoolchildren had to be given immediate equal access to the state's superior facilities. But considered from the perspective of the factual arguments made by the NAACP, this was a curious conclusion. The court believed that the physical disparity between the schools was legally sufficient ground upon which to tear down the walls of separation, but the psychological injury caused by the physical separation of the races was not. By emphasizing the physical disparities between the schools, rather than the psychological proof, the court's decision implied that Delaware could yet provide comparable facilities. The principle of *Plessy* remained intact, however unlikely it was that such physical equality could ever be achieved.

The Delaware court apparently recognized the different import of its relying upon the physical facts rather than the psychological proof. An opinion citing physical differences could be limited to the parties before the court. An opinion that rested on the corrosive effects of segregation in general, on the other hand, implicated segregation itself and its practice everywhere. Such an opinion would be seen as quite radical. But physical differences represented firmer ground on which to prove inequality compared to the perceived quicksand of psychological injury. To overturn *Plessy*, the Supreme Court would have to step into this quagmire.

When the Court agreed to hear the *Topeka* case in 1952 it also granted review in the South Carolina and Virginia cases. Later, the Court also added the cases from Delaware and the District of Columbia. The Court had a strategy in mind. By joining cases from a range of states, and especially not exclusively southern states, the Court hoped to deflect some of the regional ire that might be directed at Court-enforced desegregation. Justice Tom Clark later explained this plan: "We felt it was much better to have representative cases from different parts of the country. . . . If we got a number of states involved, especially some of them that were historically more liberal towards blacks, it would help [in not creating an anti-Southern impression]. . . . It would give us broader coverage."[70]

The decision to employ social science data in argument before the Supreme Court continued to stir disagreement on the NAACP team. For instance, one newcomer, thirty-year-old Columbia law professor Jack B. Weinstein, was scornful of the approach, recalling that he may have used the word *crap* to describe the doll tests. Weinstein, who later became a renowned federal trial judge known particularly for his opinions on scientific evidence, said he "thought it absurd to try to couch our argument in terms of dubious psychological data." He recalled, "I was afraid of it, frankly, especially since some of the Justices were well informed in the area and liked to dress up their opinions in terms of sociology." He would have preferred to build the case "on the general movement of the common law, historical evidence, and the trend of the nation in the wake of the Second World War." He said, "I didn't want us to build our case on a gimmick."[71]

By the time *Brown* arrived at the Supreme Court, the segregationists had a new champion. He was John Davis, one of the most accomplished appellate attorneys of the twentieth century. He had participated in over 250 cases heard by the Supreme Court. Writing to South Carolina's Figg about the social science argument, Davis said, "I think that I have never read a drearier lot of testimony than that furnished by the so-called education and psychological experts."[72] In the brief he filed with the Court, Davis challenged both the cogency of Clark's testimony in the cases below and its consistency with Clark's own 1947 published research. In particular, he pointed out that the earlier research, when it compared segregated southern schools to integrated northern schools, had found the southern black children to be *better* adjusted. "The southern children," Davis cited Clark, "in spite of their equal favorableness toward the white doll, are significantly less likely to reject the brown doll (evaluate it negatively), as compared to the strong tendency for the majority of the northern children to do so." Davis nailed down the point:

While these experiments would seem to indicate that Negro children in the South are healthier psychologically speaking than those in the North, Dr. Clark appears to disagree. In any case, the results obtained in the broader sample of experiments completely explode any inference that the "conflicts" from which Professor Clark's Clarendon County subjects were found to suffer are the result of their education in segregated schools.[73]

Davis further suggested that since the research indicated that a black child was psychologically preconditioned to racial awareness at a tender age, he might be better off attending schools with children of his own race rather than go to school "with children whom he regards as superior." But answering this question would take the "most careful and painstaking consideration" involving "study of the accumulated data which the most thorough, impartial and scientific research can supply." This evaluation, Davis argued, was not an appropriate one for the courts to make. Indeed, Davis's brief asserted, "this Court may judicially notice the fact that there is a large body of respectable expert opinion to the effect that separate schools, particularly in the South, are in the best interests of children of both races as well as of the community at large." Whatever the empirical truth of the matter, however, the courts were not the proper forums for determining these facts. These matters were more properly decided by state legislatures and educational authorities.[74]

Davis continued to press his attack on the social science research during oral argument before the Court. He told the justices that "much of that which is handed around under the name of social science is an effort on the part of the scientist to rationalize his own preconceptions. They find usually, in any limited observation, what they go out to find." Although much of his ire was directed against the research, he made clear to the Court that a venerable principle also supported the schools' claim. The constitutionality of segregation ultimately depended on the states' right to sovereignty over education. He asked, "Is it not a fact that the very strength and fiber of our federal system is local self-government in those matters for which local action is competent? Is it not, of all the activities of government the one which most nearly approaches the hearts and minds of people—the question of the education of their young?" He continued, imploring,

Is it not the height of wisdom that the manner in which [education] shall be conducted should be left to those most immediately affected by it, and

that the wishes of the parents, both white and colored, should be ascertained before their children are forced into what may be an unwelcome
contact?

I respectfully submit to the Court, there is no reason assigned here why
this Court or any other should reverse the findings of 90 years.[75]

During oral argument, the NAACP's Robert Carter asked the Court
to abide by the *Topeka* case's finding of fact that segregation had deleterious psychological consequences. He told the Court that the district
judge's fact-finding makes a reversal "necessary." He argued, "If there
[are inequalities] in fact, that educational opportunities cannot be equal
in law." Justice Hugo Black asked him whether that was "a general
finding or do you state that for the State of Kansas, City of Topeka?"
Carter's response was not well considered. He told the justices that "the
finding refers to the State of Kansas and to these appellants and to
Topeka, Kansas." But he added, "I think that the findings were made in
this specific case referring to this specific case."[76] Carter's response and
confusion were all the more surprising since the social science had been
his idea from the start. Black was troubled by the ramifications of limiting the empirical lesson to the single case of Topeka, as Carter had
suggested with his answer, and asked whether this meant that "then you
would have different rulings with respect to the places to which this
applies, is that true?" Carter then realized his blunder and backpedaled
furiously, abandoning volumes of social science testimony a little too
readily in his attempt. "Now, of course, under our theory, you do not
have to reach the finding of fact or a fact at all in reaching the decision
because of the fact that we maintain that this is an unconstitutional classification being based upon race and, therefore, it is arbitrary."[77]

Of course, if simply segregating on the basis of race was sufficiently
"arbitrary" to render the challenged policies unconstitutional, none of
the social science would have been needed in the first place. Carter had
misunderstood the import of Black's query. The NAACP had urged the
social science evidence on the Court in order to demonstrate two separate
factual matters. The original research, according to Kenneth Clark and
others, demonstrated that segregation negatively affected the psychological well-being of black schoolchildren. This fact was as true in Topeka,
Kansas, as it was in Richmond, Virginia. But the NAACP also wanted
to demonstrate that in each of the jurisdictions in which the litigation
took place, the children suffered just as the general research indicated

that they would. They thus took pains to conduct the doll tests in every locale to demonstrate the specific effects of segregation. Black was merely asking which level of proof, the general or the specific, the Court was being asked to recognize in fashioning a decision. After all, it was possible that segregation in some areas of the country did not follow the general pattern. For instance, while cigarettes cause lung cancer in some smokers, cigarette smokers do not invariably develop this illness. Similarly, the NAACP did not have to prove that segregation psychologically injured every child exposed to it. If segregation significantly increased the likelihood of injury, this fact would provide the legal authority to ban it as a denial of equal protection. The Court, as Carter should have fully appreciated, was not interested in creating a rule that would depend on a factual showing of segregation's harms in every new jurisdiction in which it would be applied. Rather than retreat so ignominiously from the social science, Carter would have been better served citing the general research and imploring the Court to fashion a rule barring segregation for this reason everywhere.

When Thurgood Marshall argued in the NAACP's rebuttal, Justice Frankfurter asked him about the import of the social science evidence. "Do you think it would make any difference to our problem," he probed, "if this record also contained the testimony of six professors from other institutions who gave contrary or qualifying testimony [regarding segregation's harmful effects]?" Marshall conceded the point, but insisted that there were no such "experts in the country who would so testify."[78] As in the cases below, the NAACP had addressed this general question by citing the 1948 survey conducted by Isidor Chein. That survey had been severely criticized by opposing witnesses and derided by many in the field as science by consensus. The survey's response rate was fairly low and one might suspect that scientists holding politically unpopular views would have been reluctant to return them. Nonetheless, Marshall found substantial comfort in Chein's findings and did not hesitate to bring them to the Court's attention. Marshall also told Justice Frankfurter that "even the witnesses, for example, who testified in the next case coming up, the Virginia case, all of them, admitted that segregation in and of itself was harmful." Frankfurter responded that, "of course, if it is written into the Constitution, then I do not care about the evidence. If it is in the Constitution, then all the testimony that you introduced is beside the point."[79]

When the justices met to deliberate the future of Jim Crow, they were deeply divided. Four of the justices—Black, Douglas, Harold Burton, and Sherman Minton—had clearly stated their intention to vote to end segregation. Stanley Reed said he would vote to affirm *Plessy*. Frankfurter was an almost certain fifth vote to end the practice, though at this time he was holding his cards close to his vest. Robert Jackson was a probable vote for *Plessy* and Fred Vinson and Tom Clark tended toward his view. The votes were thus apparently there to end segregation, but all of the justices feared the message and the consequences of a fractured Court. Vinson, as chief justice, was especially distraught at the prospect of a divided Court stepping so gingerly into the maelstrom that awaited. The situation needed a master politician, and that is what it got.

Felix Frankfurter proposed holding the case over until the following term by issuing a set of questions that the parties could address in reargument. The questions would have to be at least plausible and should not alert the parties that the Court's decision was already almost certain. Frankfurter drafted five questions to be posited to the parties and to be the subject of reargument during the 1953–54 term. In the memo to his colleagues that accompanied his draft questions, Frankfurter said, "Some give comfort to one side and some to the other, and that is precisely the intention." The first three questions asked about the history and original intention of the drafters and ratifiers of the Fourteenth Amendment. These questions would send both sides scrambling to employ historians and lawyers seeking the holy grail of original intent. The last two questions asked about the Court's remedial power if it were to overturn *Plessy*. Anticipating that this might suggest that the Court had reached a conclusion, Frankfurter said he thought that it was "not undesirable that an adjustment be made in the public mind to such a possibility." He continued, "I know not how others feel, but for me the ultimate crucial factor in the problem presented by these cases is psychological— the adjustment of men's minds and actions to the unfamiliar and the unpleasant."[80]

In September 1953, Chief Justice Vinson died, changing dramatically the balance on the Court. At Vinson's funeral, Frankfurter turned to his former clerk, Philip Elman, and said, "Phil, this is the first solid piece of evidence I've ever had that there really is a God."[81]

Earl Warren succeeded Vinson. During Warren's tenure, he would fundamentally change the Court's effect on American society and, just as important, its perceived role in that society. Warren was born on

March 19, 1891, in Los Angeles. His family moved to Bakersfield in 1894, where he lived until 1908 when he moved to the San Francisco Bay Area. "As I stood on the bow of the ferryboat," Warren later recalled, "I filled my lungs with refreshing air and said to myself, 'I never want to live anywhere else the rest of my life.' "[82] It was a pledge destined to be interrupted several times, including by service as governor in Sacramento and as chief justice in Washington, D.C.

Warren owed his early political success to the Progressive California governor Hiram Johnson. Warren always considered himself first a Progressive and second a Republican. In the 1952 election, Warren supported Eisenhower, and long before Vinson died Eisenhower and Herbert Brownell, the president's attorney general, had assured Warren of the first vacancy on the Court. They had all expected the first vacant seat to be Frankfurter's, but the center chair of the chief's opened first. At the press conference, Eisenhower extolled Warren's "middle-of-the-road philosophy" and predicted that Warren would maintain a steady course. But Eisenhower soon shared the lament of many presidents who came to regret their High Court appointments. Eisenhower later said that as president he had made only two mistakes and they were both sitting on the Supreme Court. (He considered William Brennan to be his second mistake.)

The Warren Court came to be recognized, and in some quarters vilified, for its defense of civil liberties and the rights of the accused. Warren, however, was not driven by any overarching theory of constitutional adjudication or high-minded understanding of the Bill of Rights. He was not an intellectual giant, though his impact on American law may rival John Marshall's. Warren was primarily interested in achieving the "right result," rather than, as Frankfurter preferred, crafting an elegant and authoritative judicial opinion. According to G. Edward White, a Warren biographer:

> The Bill of Rights, in Warren's jurisprudence, was a means by which governmental usurpations of individual freedom were checked. The rights enumerated in the Constitution were simply "the natural rights of man" or the "common law rights of Englishmen." The American legal system was "a mature and sophisticated attempt . . . to institutionalize" a "sense of justice" that was inherent in "the nature of man" and was manifested in a desire for freedom from "the terror and unpredictability of arbitrary force."[83]

Warren's jurisprudence was guided by a sense of right and wrong that transcended the concrete words of the Constitution's text. He believed ardently in John Marshall's view that the Constitution lived and breathed and, if it did not, the society it framed would die. This was a version of natural law. "In 'civilized society,' " Warren argued, "law . . . presupposes the existence of a broad area of human conduct controlled by ethical norms. There is thus a 'Law beyond the Law.' "[84] The Warren Court era, an era marked by a defense of fundamental rights and equality, effectively began with the decision in *Brown v. Board of Education*.[85]

In the Court's deliberations over how to decide *Brown,* it was quickly ascertained that Warren would provide the fifth vote to overturn *Plessy.* The difficulties lay not in how the case would be decided, but in what the Court would say, how many justices would join the decision, and how integration would be implemented without southern cities burning as a result.

Warren had come to the conclusion that the only premise that supported the principle of "separate but equal" was the belief in white supremacy. If the Court chose to follow that principle and uphold *Plessy* and its progeny, it could do so only on that basis alone. At the conference, Warren reportedly said, "I've come to conclude that the basis of segregation and 'separate but equal' rests upon a concept of the inherent inferiority of the colored race. I don't see how *Plessy* and the cases following it can be sustained on any other theory." This, Warren insisted, was not defensible. "I don't see how in this day and age we can set any group apart from the rest and say that they are not entitled to exactly the same treatment as all others. . . . I can't see how today we can justify segregation based on race."[86]

Frankfurter, too, in a memo to his files, expressed the impossibility of writing "into our Constitution a belief in the Negro's natural inferiority [or] in the desirability of segregating white and colored children during their most formative years." He went on, "To attribute such a view to science, as is sometimes done, is to reject the very basis of science, namely, the process of reaching verifiable conclusions. The abstract and absolutist claims both for and against segregation have been falsified by experience, especially the great changes in the relations between white and colored people since the first World War."[87]

If science could not be used to perpetuate segregation, it was far from clear that it should be employed to end it. The Court readily rejected any constitutionally cognizable differences between the races, but it was deeply divided over the proper place, if any, for the social science of segregation's detrimental effects. Justice Jackson, for instance, wrote in a memo that even if "all the woes of colored children would be solved by forcing them into white company, I do not think we should impart into the concept of equal protection of the law those elusive psychological and subjective factors." These factors, Jackson complained, "are not determinable with satisfactory objectivity or measurable with reasonable certainty. If we adhere to objective criteria the judicial process will still be capricious enough."[88] Jackson preferred to make plain the political basis for the decision and particularly the dramatically different world the Court found in 1954 as compared to the one in which Homer Plessy lived at the close of the nineteenth century. Of particular note was the changed public opinion attributable to the "awful consequences of racial prejudice revealed by . . . the Nazi regime," which had created "a revolution against the kind of racial feeling" that had led to Japanese internment the decade before and Jim Crow now.[89]

Jackson planned to write a separate opinion concurring in the outcome but setting forth his own reasons. Only Justice Stanley Reed intended to dissent. There was good reason to be greatly concerned about anything other than a unanimous opinion. One dissent and one concurrence would have given dissatisfied southerners a fissure against which they could direct their discontent. Unanimity would fortify the opinion against the inevitable claims that the Court had exceeded its constitutional warrant and had stretched the law to realize a political outcome.

The deliberations had begun in October of 1953. On March 30, 1954, Jackson suffered a serious heart attack and was hospitalized. Once again, it seemed that God was attentive to the Court's deliberations. Jackson would not have the strength to write a concurrence in *Brown* and he informed the chief that he would simply join the opinion of the Court. Warren then went to Reed and, as recalled by Reed's clerk, told him, "Stan, you're all by yourself in this now." Warren well understood what the decision meant to the South and was sympathetic to Reed's concerns, especially about implementation of the ruling. But he also firmly, though without bombast, told Reed, "You've got to decide whether [a dissent is] really the best thing for the country." Reed decided it was not and joined the opinion. Justice Frankfurter later sent Reed a gracious note thanking him for his decision. Frankfurter observed that "if the Segregation cases had reached decision Last Term, there would have been four dissenters—Vinson, Reed, Jackson and Clark. . . . That would have been catastrophic." Reed's decision not to create a rift had served his country's interests. "I am not unaware of the hard struggle this involved in the conscience of your mind and the mind of your conscience." Frankfurter added with a flourish, "As a citizen of the Republic, even more than as a colleague, I feel deep gratitude for your share in what I believe to be a great good for our nation."[90]

At 12:52 p.m. on May 17, 1954, Chief Justice Earl Warren stated to a packed courtroom, "I have for announcement the judgment and opinion of the Court in No. 1—*Oliver Brown et al. v. Board of Education.*"[91] The opinion was short, light on citations of authority, and did not explicitly overrule *Plessy*. The opinion did, however, reject the premises of *Plessy*. The *Plessy* Court had said that "the underlying fallacy" of the black complainant was his "assumption that the enforced segregation of the two races stamp the colored race with a badge of inferiority. If this be so, it is not by reason of anything found in the act, but solely because the colored race chooses to put that construction upon it." Warren, in prose more measured than it deserved, rejected this statement. "Whatever may have been the extent of psychological knowledge at the time of *Plessy v. Ferguson,* this finding [by the court below that segregation denotes inferiority and undermines educational achievement] is amply supported by modern authority. Any language in *Plessy v. Ferguson* contrary to this finding is rejected."[92] In footnote eleven of the opinion, Warren cited Kenneth Clark and other social scientists as representative of the modern scientific authority the Court relied upon. The footnote touched off a fierce debate.

Alexander Bickel, who had clerked for Justice Frankfurter the previous term, pondered the use of the footnote. He thought "it was a mistake to do it this way." He considered the doll studies to be weak and to have been thoroughly demolished by John Davis in his brief. "The Court was justified," he conceded, "to have included such references as a Brandeisian move, but it should not have been just dropped in like that." Bickel recognized that even a Brandeisian defense of the outcome, in which the best social science was brought to bear, would be seized upon by the "enemies of the opinion," and proclaimed "unjudicial and illegal." Bickel argued that the opinion "should have said straightforwardly that *Plessy* was based on a self-invented philosophy no less psychologically oriented than the Court was being now in citing these sources to justify the holding that segregation inflicted damage." Warren did not say this, according to Bickel, because he "wanted to present as small a target as possible." Warren "did not want to go out to the country wearing a Hussar's uniform."[93]

While Warren perhaps intended to present only a small target by placing the bulk of the social science in a footnote, it nonetheless garnered a great deal of attention—little of it good. Despite its being relegated to a note, the perception was that the science lay at the core of the decision. James Reston wrote in the *New York Times* that "relying more on the social scientists than on legal precedents, the Court insisted on equality of the mind and heart rather than on equal school facilities." He found the justices to be "most impressed by the testimonies of the effects of discrimination on personality development."[94] Warren, for his part, never could understand what all the fuss was about. "It was just a note, after all," he lamented years later in an interview.[95]

Whatever the utility of the social science, its sufficiency was quickly called into question. Even sympathetic critics, perhaps especially these critics, found the social science to be a weak reed on which to hang such an important right. As was to be expected, the research was meticulously scrutinized. It was not nearly good enough to withstand this sort of attention. A note in the *Yale Law Journal* reviewed the main effects found, which were as follows among black children from the North and the South:

	North	South
Prefer to play with white doll	72%	62%
White doll is "nice"	68%	52%
Black doll is "bad"	71%	49%

The Yale note observed that "these figures at first glance would seem to indicate that the South with its segregated schools provides a healthier environment for Negro children."[96]

Edmund Cahn, a prominent New York University law professor, similarly complained about the quality of Clark's science. Cahn focused especially on Clark's research methods, criticizing both the lack of representative sampling and the manner in which Clark collected his data. Moreover, Cahn accused Clark of interpreting his data in whatever way would corroborate his preexisting hypotheses. He complained, "If Negro children say a brown doll is like themselves, [Clark] infers that segregation has made them conscious of race; yet if they say a white doll is like themselves, he infers that segregation has forced them to evade reality."[97]

Clark responded to his critics about as effectively as his data allowed. He admitted that "on the surface," his "findings might suggest that Northern Negro children suffer more personality damage from racial prejudice and discrimination than southern Negro children." This interpretation, he argued, "would seem to be not only superficial but incorrect." He explained:

> The apparent emotional stability of the southern Negro child may be indicative only of the fact that through rigid racial segregation and isolation he has accepted as normal the fact of his inferior social status. Such an acceptance is not symptomatic of a healthy personality. The emotional turmoil revealed by some of the northern children may be interpreted as an attempt on their part to assert some positive aspect of the self.[98]

But with this argument, Clark effectively proved Cahn's criticism. Any result could have been interpreted in a way to prove his hypothesis. Clark simply found in his data what he was looking for. His doll tests were really no test at all, since no results would have falsified his hypothesis.

For African-Americans, *Brown* marked the first step off the parallel path that they had been forced to walk after *Plessy*. This would be an enormously important step toward equality. Ralph Ellison wrote a friend that in *Brown* "the Court has found in our favor and recognized our human psychological complexity and citizenship and another battle of the Civil War has been won."[99] While *Brown* was a momentous achievement in American race relations, the decision had even greater significance in the grand sweep of constitutional doctrine. Alexander Bickel wrote, "*Brown* was the beginning." It was the beginning of widespread societal change and of a dramatically altered role for the Supreme Court in saying what the law is. Historian David Garrow said *Brown* "singlehandedly marks the advent of the 'modern' or present-age Supreme Court."[100] It was the effective debut of Earl Warren, who led the Court for almost two decades. During this time the Warren Court greatly expanded constitutional protection of basic liberties and civil rights. *Brown* initiated the trend, to be greatly expanded over the next fifty years, of giving content to guarantees of due process and equal protection of the Fourteenth

Amendment. *Brown* also marked the start of the Court's modern approach to scientific authority and its use to support and justify constitutional outcomes.

What role the social science data ultimately played in the *Brown* decision has been a question of enduring interest to scholars and Court watchers of every sort. It is clear that the data had limited staying power. Subsequent cases barely mentioned the research as the Court struggled with the complexities and controversies surrounding implementation of *Brown* and its extension beyond the education arena. After *Brown,* the Court invalidated state-sponsored segregation in a variety of contexts ranging from golf courses to public parks and, ultimately, to the subject of *Plessy* itself, public transportation. The Court never cited any data in support of these outcomes and, in fact, none existed that would have supported them. The principle of separate but equal had been rejected in *Brown* and this ruling was now being implemented in social contexts well beyond education. An original basis for the ruling, the empirical proof of segregation's deleterious effects, appeared to recede quickly and disappear completely. But many observers have mistakenly equated the data's lack of importance in shaping the reforms of an integrated society with their lack of importance in the decision itself.

The problem inherent in crafting the *Brown* decision was that none of the usual authorities plainly supported the decision. The text of the Fourteenth Amendment was at best ambiguous. Original intent provided little guidance and, most scholars agreed, hurt the NAACP more than it helped. Precedent, even with the decisions in *Sweatt* and *McLaurin* moving slowly toward condemnation of separate but equal, was unhelpful, since *Plessy* remained good law. Structural arguments, such as Federalism, lent support to the segregationists, since they urged that states should have autonomy over matters such as education. Even contemporary values were decidedly split, with only about half of all voters believing that separate but equal was unconstitutional. Only academic constitutional scholarship was weighted in favor of the *Brown* result, and the Court has never been an enthusiastic taker of academics' advice on matters of constitutional interpretation. The social science evidence, therefore, supplied a much-needed major premise for ending segregation.

The Court employed the argument from fact, the deleterious consequences of segregation, to help establish the constitutional principle of equal access. But the true constitutional import of this fact is impossible to discern from the opinion itself. Although the Court cited the social science, it may not have actually relied on it. The best way to test this question is to ask what would happen if the facts changed, if segregated schools were not psychologically injurious. Would the result in *Brown* have been different? Just such a test arose not long after *Brown*.

In 1963, the county of Savannah-Chatham, Georgia, defended a desegregation suit on the basis that black children in that locale, unlike in Topeka, would not be psychologically harmed by attending segregated schools. The black plaintiffs responded to the claim by arguing that the fact had been "conclusively determined by the Supreme Court in *Brown* that segregation harmed black children." The trial judge, Judge Frank Scarlett, however, determined that a trial was necessary on the question of whether segregation had deleterious consequences. Tried without a jury, the court heard evidence from a host of experts, including Dr. Ernest van den Haag, a professor of social philosophy at New York University. Based on this testimony, the court found in the case of *Stell v. Savannah*[101] that "prejudices, whether ethnic, religious or racial, increase rather than decrease in proportion to the degree of non-voluntary contact between separately identifiable groups." The court said that this "is a psychological phenomenon which was noted in the time of Periclean Greece." Moreover, modern "studies made of actual inter-mixing of groups in classrooms confirm the predicted result that an increase in cross-group contacts increases pre-existing racial hostility rather than ameliorates it."[102]

The plaintiffs continued to insist that the question of segregation's effects was closed by the *Brown* decision. "The law is settled by the Supreme Court in the *Brown* case that segregation itself injures Negro children in the school system," they argued to Scarlett. Thus, they pointed out, "we do not have to prove that." Judge Scarlett disagreed. He explained that the lower court in *Brown* found that " 'segregation with the sanction of law . . . has a tendency to [retard] the educational and mental development of Negro children and to deprive them of some of the benefits they would receive in a racial[ly] integrated school system.' " The judge stated, "These are facts, not law," explaining:

> Whether Negroes in Kansas believed that separate schooling denoted inferiority, whether a sense of inferiority affected their motivation to learn and whether motivation to learn was increased or diminished by segregation was a question requiring evidence for decision. That was as much a subject

for scientific inquiry as the braking distance required to stop a two-ton truck moving at ten miles an hour on dry concrete.[103]

Thus, the *Stell* court concluded that whatever the state of the facts existing in 1954 in Topeka regarding the effects of segregation, the overwhelming weight of the evidence indicated that in 1963 in Savannah-Chatham County, Georgia, black and white children would mutually benefit from separate schooling.

The United States Court of Appeals for the Fifth Circuit summarily reversed the *Stell* district court. Judge Griffin Bell admonished the lower court, saying that "no inferior federal court may refrain from acting as required by [the *Brown*] decision even if such a court should conclude that the Supreme Court erred either as to its facts or as to the law."[104] Moreover, the circuit court discounted the importance of the social science evidence for the *Brown* result. "We do not read the major premise of the decision of the Supreme Court in the first *Brown* case as being limited to the facts of the cases there presented. We read it as proscribing segregation in the public education process on the stated ground that separate but equal schools for the races were inherently unequal."[105] The Supreme Court did not review the case.

Judge Bell's pronouncement that lower federal courts cannot depart from settled precedent is a little more complicated and much more ambiguous than he suggested. Without question, a lower court cannot ignore a higher court's interpretation of the law. This principle is a cornerstone of American jurisprudence, not just constitutional law. The binding effect of factual findings is rather less clear. Ordinarily, higher courts do not even make factual findings, since they are not established to hear witnesses and there is no provision for juries. Appellate courts are ordinarily deferential to lower court fact-finding, largely on the theory that the lower court actually sees and hears the witnesses and is in a better position to judge their credibility. In ordinary litigation, such as in a tort suit brought by a former flight attendant against a cigarette manufacturer, a court might be asked to determine whether secondhand smoke causes lung cancer. This fact is typically decided by a jury and does not apply to other cases in other jurisdictions. Also, the legal relevance of facts about things like secondhand smoke is established by ordinary statutes or judge-made common law. Constitutional facts are not so simple.

Most constitutional facts have importance and relevance beyond the particular case in which they are tried. This is why Justice Black asked Robert Carter during oral argument in *Brown* whether the Topeka trial court's finding that segregation was injurious was limited to Topeka or was more generally true. The answer given by the chief justice in *Brown* was that this fact had general application and need not be found anew in every case or for every party in the future. The Court had settled the matter in a legislative fashion and, indeed, these sorts of facts—facts that are instrumental to policy making (whether constitutional or otherwise)— are referred to as "legislative facts." It was as if the Court had found that secondhand smoke caused lung cancer and all claims would be settled under that determination without further consideration of individual cases. Segregation was deleterious as a general matter, and future litigants would only have to show that they were exposed to it, not that it had inflicted actual injury upon them.

The Court in *Brown* could have, if it had chosen, defined the legally relevant fact at the case-specific level. Under that scenario, future litigants would then have been required to demonstrate actual injury caused by segregation. But in constitutional law, even case-specific facts, ones that do not specifically apply to future cases, have important values attached to them. Facts that are particular to a case—such as whether the light was red or green when the plaintiff crossed at the intersection—are called "adjudicative facts." These facts are jurors' ordinary business. Robert Carter had initially defined the facts in *Brown* as adjudicative in nature— limited only to what was happening in Topeka—and Judge Scarlett in *Stell* had essentially done the same. This is why Scarlett felt free to determine the facts unfettered by what may have been true in 1954 or in the locale of Topeka, Kansas. In constitutional cases, however, adjudicative facts implicate basic constitutional values and thus have far-reaching implications. In the famous defamation case of *New York Times v. Sullivan*,[106] for example, the Court said that the First Amendment required the plaintiff government officials to prove that a defamatory statement was made with "actual malice" by the defendant, which the Court defined as having been made with knowledge that it was false or with reckless disregard of its being false. This is an adjudicative fact that must be determined on a case-by-case basis. But the standard set forth by the Court also implicates fundamental free speech values, since too rigid an enforcement of the *New York Times* standard would both interfere with the particular speaker's First Amendment right and possibly chill other speakers from exercising their rights out of fear of litigation. Even the most case-specific factual questions in the constitutional context have broad policy implications.

At the same time, there is—or ought to be—a strong awareness that there is always a substantial factual component to constitutional fact questions. It necessarily follows, then, that either the facts themselves or our knowledge of them might—and indeed are likely to—change over time. If a constitutional principle is truly tied to a factual premise, then perhaps lower courts should be permitted to hear new evidence that the facts are different than those upon which the constitutional rule was based. In short, if *Brown* was actually premised on the fact that blacks were disadvantaged by segregated schools, then subsequent and better research that indicated that blacks were advantaged by separate schooling should lead to reconsideration of the constitutional rule. The truth, however, is that we scoff at the *Stell* court's presumptuousness, because we know that the facts in *Brown* were merely a proxy for a judgment made on moral grounds. No new set of facts would change the decision. Not all constitutional cases that depend on factual premises will be so readily resolved.

The *Brown* decision illustrates a phenomenon that became common in the late twentieth century and will be a mainstay of twenty-first-century constitutional law. As science continues to mature it will produce an ever-expanding corpus of knowledge about the "real world," a world of special interest to Supreme Court justices. Constitutional principles do not exist in a vacuum. They are both framed by and framed for the affairs of a modern state. Yet facts have the frustrating tendency to change, either because our understanding of them changes or the facts themselves change in an evolving and technologically advancing society. This phenomenon has come to plague the modern Court and is an issue that the Court has yet to confront squarely or in any effective manner whatsoever. The proffered strategy thus far has been to ignore the issue, pretend that nothing odd is going on, and proceed with business as usual. This head-in-the-sand strategy was the one adopted in *Brown*. In the end, it was effective because eventually the country came to accept fully the legitimacy of the *Brown* result. The disputed facts did not have to sustain the decision once the basic principle had been established. In more controversial cases, however, attaching constitutional principles to disputed or changeable facts can be expected to create greater difficulties and more controversy. This is exactly what happened in the second most famous case of the latter half of the twentieth century. In *Roe v. Wade,* no consensus appeared after the initial decision guaranteeing a woman's constitutional right to an abortion. The facts supporting that right, as the next chapter illustrates, never receded into the background of received constitutional principle. They remain front, center, and hugely controversial today.

8

THE RIGHT TO BE LET ALONE:

Privacy and the Problem
of Defining Life and Death

The full scope of the liberty guaranteed by the Due Process Clause cannot be found in or limited by the precise terms of the specific guarantees elsewhere provided in the Constitution. This "liberty" is not a series of isolated points pricked out in terms of the taking of property; the freedom of speech, press, and religion; the right to keep and bear arms; the freedom from unreasonable searches and seizures; and so on. It is a rational continuum which, broadly speaking, includes a freedom from all substantial arbitrary impositions and purposeless restraints, . . . and which also recognizes what a reasonable and sensitive judgment must, that certain interests require particularly careful scrutiny of the stated needs asserted to justify their abridgment.

—JOHN MARSHALL HARLAN

In 1819, in *McCulloch v. Maryland*,[1] Chief Justice John Marshall observed that the Constitution was "intended to endure for ages to come, and, consequently, to be adapted to the various crises of human affairs." In order to accomplish this great task, the text could not specify how it should be applied to the many challenges known and the innumerable challenges that lay ahead. "To have prescribed the means by which government should, in all future time, execute its powers, would have been to change, entirely, the character of the instrument and give it the properties of a legal code." Although Marshall in *McCulloch* was interpreting the power-granting provisions of the Constitution, the lesson applies equally to the power-limiting provisions found in the Bill of Rights and the Fourteenth Amendment. The scope and content of such transcendent phrases as due process, equal protection, freedom of speech, and free exercise of religion are not self-evident or manifestly obvious.

Of all of the surpassing aspirations to be found in the Constitution, due process has proved to be the most enigmatic. Found in both the Fifth and Fourteenth Amendments, the clause guarantees that life, liberty, and property shall not be denied without due process of law. The Constitution's granting of concrete broad guarantees such as liberty has proven to be difficult and divisive, and has severely tested the proposition that the Court's legitimacy rests on its judgment rather than its will.

In 1879, Connecticut passed a law that made it a crime to use any drug, article, or instrument to prevent conception. This "uncommonly silly" law, as Justice Potter Stewart described it, was challenged twice before it was finally struck down in 1965 by a 7–2 margin. In *Tileston v. Ullman* (1943),[2] the Court held that the plaintiff lacked standing and, in *Poe v. Ullman* (1961),[3] the Court dismissed the challenge as not ripe, since the petitioner had not been prosecuted. Finally, in *Griswold v. Connecticut*,[4] the Court for the first time made explicit that the Constitution guaranteed *privacy*, a term nowhere to be found in the text. This right— in Justice Louis Brandeis's famous words, "the right to be let alone—the most comprehensive of rights and the right most valued by civilized men"—required invalidation of the Connecticut law. Professor Charles Black of Yale Law School, commenting on the Constitution's seeming silence on the issue of privacy, said this about *Griswold*: "If our constitutional law could permit such a thing to happen, then we might almost as well not have any law of constitutional limitations, partly because the thing is so outrageous in itself, and partly because a constitutional law inadequate to deal with such an outrage would be too feeble, in method and doctrine, to deal with a very great amount of equally outrageous material."[5] Although seven members of the Court agreed that the Constitution guaranteed privacy, and thus was not too feeble, there was considerably less agreement over where in the Constitution it was to be found.

Justice William O. Douglas wrote the opinion for the Court, joined by four others, infamously situating the right of privacy in the "penumbras" of specific guarantees of the Bill of Rights. He wrote that the First, Third, Fourth, Fifth, and Ninth Amendments implied protected "zones of privacy" that provided the basis for the right enforced in this case. Justice Arthur Goldberg, joined by Chief Justice Earl Warren and Justice William Brennan, agreed that the specific guarantees of the Bill of Rights cast penumbras that expanded their compass, but that the "language and history of the Ninth Amendment"—that "the enumeration" of "certain rights" in the Constitution "shall not be construed to deny or disparage others retained by the people"—supported judicial protection of unenumerated rights. Goldberg's approach was potentially much more expansive than Douglas's, since it buttressed the penumbral search for interstitial rights with the potentially vast scope of the Ninth Amendment. Justices John Marshall Harlan and Byron White also adopted a potentially expansive interpretation of the privacy right when they separated it entirely from the Bill of Rights. Harlan wrote that privacy was squarely to be found inherent in the guarantee of liberty and that it "stands . . . on its own bottom." The Connecticut statute failed, Harlan stated, because it violated fundamental values "implicit in the concept of ordered liberty." Harlan's extrapolation of the due process right would become the most influential over the succeeding forty years of its evolution. Justice White similarly employed the Fourteenth Amendment untethered by the Bill of Rights. He preferred the intrinsic balancing of determining whether the government's interests were sufficiently compelling to justify an infringement of a fundamental right.

The dissents of Justices Black and Stewart shared their colleagues' contempt for the Connecticut law, but each wrote to deny that they had the authority to question a state law on the basis of a nontextually based right. "I like my privacy as well as the next one," Black commented memorably, "but I am nevertheless compelled to admit that government has a right to invade it unless prohibited by some constitutional provision."[6] Black thought that the Court had no warrant to second-guess legislative decisions without specific textual authority. "Use of any such broad, unbounded judicial authority," he warned, "would make of this Court's members a day-to-day constitutional convention." Arrogating unto itself such dominion, Black stated, worked a "great unconstitutional shift of power to the courts which . . . will be bad for the courts and worse for the country."[7] Even more damning, he accused the majority of resurrecting *Lochner*-style substantive due process. At the start of the twentieth century, an ultraconservative *Lochner* Court invalidated health, safety, and welfare regulations in the name of due process. For Black, using due process now to effect liberal objectives was no more justifiable and would be a similar usurpation of the democratic process. Just as Justice Harlan's concurrence would reverberate through the majority opinions over the next several decades, so would Justice Black's reproach echo in the dissents of privacy's critics.

Griswold had invalidated a law that denied contraceptives to married couples. In 1972, in *Eisenstadt v. Baird*,[8] the Court extended this ruling to a Massachusetts law that made it a felony to distribute contraceptives to individuals. The Court thus made it clear that the right of privacy was not limited to the marital relationship, but was a right possessed by individuals. "If the right of privacy means anything," Justice Brennan wrote for the Court, "it is the right of the individual, married or single, to be free from unwarranted governmental intrusion into matters so fundamentally affecting a person as the decision whether to bear or beget a child."⁹ The Court clarified that privacy, like virtually all rights guaranteed by the Constitution, belonged to the individual and did not inhere in relationships such as marriage. The fact of marriage might influence the way a right manifests itself, but it does not affect the existence of the right itself. With *Eisenstadt*, the Court moved past the traditionally protected realm of the marital relation and began to slip down what all agree was, and is, a very slippery slope. Indeed, anticipating the next possible landing on that slope, Justice Brennan had purposely inserted the "bear or beget" language, knowing that *Roe* waited on the Court's docket. This is a process known in the law as "burying bones." As a clerk from that term recalled, "We all saw that sentence, and we smiled about it. Everyone understood what that sentence was doing."¹⁰

Although controversy surrounding abortion was hardly novel when the Court decided to tackle *Roe*, it can be said fairly that this decision gave the issue an injection of life impossible to have anticipated. *Roe* created entire industries either devoted to overturning the holding or dedicated to its survival. It ignited grassroots movements, some led by the Catholic Church, directed at the single-issue politics that adherents called "pro-life"; it energized the Republican Party in its struggle to regroup after Watergate; it produced an onslaught of regulations specifically directed at frustrating the Court's judgment; it provided employment for a multitude of lawyers and experts who fought the post-*Roe* battles litigating the onslaught of regulations directed at frustrating the Court's judgment; and it led to organized acts of vehement protest directed at patients, doctors, and clinics that ranged from simple harassment to terrorism and murder. At the same time, it also deflated the reform efforts of groups who had sought to rewrite what they considered to be draconian regulations, many of which had been on state law books since the mid-nineteenth century and reflected that century's sensibilities.

In the late eighteenth and early nineteenth centuries, when the Constitution was founded, abortion was an accepted practice, especially when performed on young, unmarried women. So long as the procedure occurred before quickening—the moment when the pregnant woman feels fetal movement (around sixteen to eighteen weeks)—abortion was not controversial. The choice of quickening as the point in time after which abortions were prohibited in common law was supported by several rationales. Foremost, as a practical matter, early-nineteenth-century science could not prove that a woman was pregnant prior to quickening, so prosecutions were not possible, or, at least, guilt for intentional performance of an abortion could not be proved.[11] Also on the practical level, abortionists were able to perform the procedure more safely before quickening and thus actively encouraged early intervention. And most religious doctrine adhered to the prevailing view. Many believers thought that the soul did not enter the body until quickening. The Catholic Church, for instance, did not forbid abortion at the start of the Republic, since it followed the Aristotelian view that the soul entered the body only at "animation." For males, animation occurred at forty days, while females became animated at eighty days.[12]

In the middle of the nineteenth century, a number of factors combined to change attitudes and led to more restrictive abortion regulations. As the century progressed, abortion became more commercialized and thus more public. At the same time, women increasingly sought fuller participation in social and commercial affairs. Compounding these changing circumstances, immigrant patterns began to shift from northwest Europe to southern Europe and the Far East. Many Americans became alarmed by the changing ethnic makeup of the country. Industrialization and modernization also began to challenge accepted societal norms. Together these social conditions produced increasing pressure to protect the family, womanhood, and traditional white Protestant values. The survival of white civilization might depend on it. In 1865, the antiabortion physician and activist Horatio R. Storer asserted that abortion is "infinitely more frequent among Protestant women than among Catholic." Looking to the great American expansion west and south, he feared that Mexicans, Chinese, blacks, Indians, and Catholics would settle in these areas, thus contributing to the mongrelization of the nation. "Shall these regions," Storer asked, "be filled by our own children or by those of aliens? This is a question our women must answer; upon their loins depends the future destiny of the nation."[13]

Around this time, physicians began to change their attitudes toward abortion, for both scientific and professional reasons. Scientific advances had begun to make clear that gestation was a process that did not permit neat categorization of stages of development. One stage merely merged into another. This new understanding of development profoundly undermined the traditional distinction between quick and nonquick fetuses. In the mid-1800s, physicians were also seeking to solidify their professional stature, especially against competitors such as homeopaths and midwives, who occupied a large part of the field. In the 1820s and 1830s, physicians came under fire as elitist and were forced to compete with a wide range of medical sects, collectively known as "Irregulars."[14] Physicians saw abortion regulation as an opportunity to help stabilize their professional standing while at the same time eliminating competition. Between 1860 and 1880, the nascent American Medical Association lobbied for state laws to situate abortion exclusively in the physician's domain and, in so doing, appealed to legislators' already well-developed xenophobia and sexism. Doctors asserted their domain, based on claims of scientific authority, over the definition of both life and death. It was a remarkably effective campaign. At the federal level, Congress passed the Comstock Law in 1873, which included regulation of abortion and birth control as part of an antiobscenity statute. By 1880, virtually every state banned abortion entirely, except when performed by a licensed physician to save the life of the pregnant woman. By the end of the century, abortion had been transformed from a private decision into a subject of "medical judgment."

Throughout most of the twentieth century, the laws remained relatively fixed, but abortion practice varied widely over time. Police and prosecutors did not always charge violators, and juries oftentimes refused to convict when they did.[15] In the 1930s, abortion clinics, staffed by licensed physicians, ran openly. During this decade, despite the still considerable risks associated with the procedure, historians estimate that approximately 800,000 abortions were performed per year. After World War II, however, hospitals began to tighten their practices by establishing physician review boards, which dramatically reduced the number of hospital abortions. Clinics also became the target of police raids, making abortions increasingly difficult to obtain. Death rates from abortion procedures doubled in the 1950s. As women were forced into "back alleys," and the death toll rose—especially among black women, who were four times more likely to die than white women—activists and physicians began to lobby for reform. These efforts led to new laws in nineteen states and produced such organizations as Jane, a Chicago-based group of self-trained abortionists who performed twelve thousand abortions between 1969 and 1973 without one fatality.[16] These reform efforts largely ended on January 22, 1973, when Justice Harry Blackmun announced the decision in *Roe v. Wade*.[17]

Justice Blackmun may have been the most scientifically curious justice to ever sit on the High Court, and had even considered a career in medicine at one time. He was raised in St. Paul, Minnesota, where his father owned a small grocery and hardware store. He majored in mathematics at Harvard College and attended the Harvard Law School. Before being appointed to the federal appellate bench in 1959 by President Eisenhower, he served for nine years as counsel to the Mayo Clinic, the world-renowned hospital in Rochester, Minnesota. Blackmun said that his time at the Mayo Clinic was the happiest of his life, because it gave him a foot in both camps—law and medicine. He was elevated to the Supreme Court by President Nixon after Nixon's nominations of Judges Clement Haynsworth and G. Harold Carswell were defeated. Blackmun was a close friend of Chief Justice Burger, whom he had known in Minnesota, and Burger had recommended him for the job. He was expected to vote similarly and consolidate the conservative bloc in Nixon's concerted effort to roll back the liberal Warren Court's precedents. Burger apparently shared this expectation, one that Blackmun at first did not disappoint. The two became known as the "Minnesota Twins" for their similar voting patterns. When Blackmun began to assert his independence, a move largely begun in *Roe* itself, it drove a wedge between the two men, both professionally and personally.

Jane Roe was the pseudonym for Norma McCorvey, who challenged the ultraconservative Texas law criminalizing abortion. The Texas law prohibited abortions except for the purpose of saving the mother's life. Constitutional law is littered with names made famous by their association with landmark decisions. It is typically the Oliver Browns of the world who lend their names to immortal legal principles that perhaps could be associated with any one of dozens of deserving people. It is fitting, then, that the pseudonymous Jane Roe should be the one who enjoys lasting fame. Norma McCorvey was a high school dropout who, at sixteen, married a twice-divorced sheet metal worker. She ran away from her abusive husband shortly before having her first child. She drifted for a time, and within a year was pregnant with a second child, which she gave up for adoption. A little over two years later, McCorvey was again pregnant and this time sought an abortion. She claimed that her pregnancy resulted from a gang rape, but later admitted that it resulted from a failed relationship. Under Texas law, however, she was prohibited in any case from obtaining an abortion. Her doctor gave her the names of two lawyers, Sarah Weddington and Linda Coffee, to consult, and the result was the filing of the landmark suit. Her contribution to history would have ended there, but in 2003 she emerged from obscurity to be featured on *Fox News* calling for the repeal of the *Roe* decision.

Roe was first argued in December 1971. Only seven justices heard argument, since Lewis Powell and William Rehnquist were confirmed too late to hear it. At the conference following the oral argument, the discussion and vote were somewhat confused and, more important, Chief Justice Burger's statements made it uncertain whether he intended to join the majority that agreed to invalidate the Texas law. Burger reportedly said, "I can't find the Texas statute unconstitutional, although it's certainly archaic and obsolete."[18] His comments were all of this type, both condemning the law as primitive and doubting the wisdom of invalidating it. The chief justice has the privilege of assigning opinions for the Court when he is in the majority, and Burger had hedged his position during the *Roe* discussion, apparently wishing to leave all of his options open. He eventually voted with the majority in *Roe*, but wrote a concurring opinion once again hedging his bets, though he would later say he regretted his vote in *Roe*. At the time, Burger said he did not tally the votes because he believed that the sentiment was ambiguous and that the writing should decide the division of votes. He assigned the opinion to Blackmun. The irascible Douglas, who thought Burger had voted to sustain the law, wrote a memo that not too subtly accused Burger of exceeding his authority. Douglas had counted a clear majority to overturn the Texas law, with Brennan, Stewart, Marshall, and Blackmun joining him to make the vote 5–2, with Burger and White in dissent. Burger denied the charge and stood by his recollection of the conference and the need to let the writing decide the vote. Blackmun set about drafting the opinion, a task on which he labored long and hard, but mostly without immediate success.

Blackmun's first draft concluded that the Texas statute was unconstitutionally vague, a ground that no one had urged at conference and one peculiarly designed to avoid the principal issue of whether the Constitution protects a right of reproductive choice. Justices Douglas and Brennan both informed Blackmun that a majority had voted to strike the Texas statute squarely on the constitutional merits, though they did so diplomatically so as not to alienate him. Brennan sent Blackmun a "Dear

Harry" letter. He wrote, "My recollection of the voting on this . . . was that a majority of us felt that the Constitution required the invalidation of abortion statutes save to the extent they required an abortion be performed by a licensed physician within some limited time after conception. I think essentially this was the view shared by Bill, Potter, Thurgood and me. My notes also indicate that you might support this view."[19] At the same time as Blackmun's initial effort was hitting the rocks, Burger proposed to hold the case over for reargument. Beyond the benefit of more time to sort out the details of the opinion, this would allow Justices Powell and Rehnquist, the recent appointees, to hear the case. Brennan, Douglas, and Marshall opposed this plan, being unsure that they would maintain a majority in a year. When Blackmun agreed that the case should be held over, however, Burger had the votes necessary for reargument. In the end, the delay did not affect the outcome, since Powell joined the majority and Rehnquist dissented. In fact, it arguably ended up strengthening it considerably, because *Roe* was decided with a full complement of justices.

Blackmun spent the summer of 1972 holed up in the Mayo Clinic library studying the science of pregnancy and the history of abortion. As Blackmun, perhaps more than any other justice, well understood, the law invariably depends on expertise of a wide variety of disciplines, including history, economics, and the multitude of sciences ranging from ecology to psychology. Blackmun decided to steep himself in the context and content of the science of gestation in order to situate whatever legal doctrine the Court would choose. Even if he might determine that medical science was irrelevant to the law that applied, he knew that he had to familiarize himself with the science to make that judgment. As it turned out, he found the science not just relevant, but determinative—at least insofar as the opinion read.

Blackmun's summer at the Mayo Clinic earned him a spate of criticism from Court watchers. Chief Justice Burger, concurring in *Roe,* registered his unease with Blackmun's heavy reliance on science. "I am somewhat troubled," Burger wrote, "that the Court has taken notice of various scientific and medical data in reaching its conclusion." Again hedging, he added, "However, I do not believe that the Court has exceeded the scope of judicial notice accepted in other contexts."[20]

Because the American judicial system is based on the adversarial model of conflict resolution, control of information flow is left largely to the case's parties, which mainly means that it is within the power of the lawyers. Of course, even the most ardent advocates of the adversarial process do not believe that judges have no role to play in managing the evidence. A multitude of rules of procedure and evidence have evolved, both in common law and by enactment of codes, which fairly strictly control the flow of information. Regardless, most lawyers believe that judges and juries should be passive recipients of information, and although rules such as hearsay or attorney-client privilege curtail what information enters the process, judges should not be empowered to go out and collect evidence on their own. The prospect of justices heading out to uncover facts on their own initiative is a picture that many lawyers find deeply disturbing. Such a process resembles inquisitorial systems in which government tyranny is prone to rear its ugly head.

However disturbing this picture, it is a necessary part of a judge's responsibility. Judges, especially Supreme Court justices, simply cannot rely on the parties to control the evidence regarding constitutional facts, at least to the extent that those facts are used to craft a rule that will be applied in other cases. Judges, certainly, have no business going out and interviewing witnesses to a traffic accident. But when factual propositions are forwarded as the basis for a legal ruling, as was the case in *Roe*, then judges must be able to look for, find, and analyze those facts. This is not to say that attorneys should not do as much as possible to educate the judges before whom they appear. But judges cannot be limited only to information parceled out by attorneys. Any alternative standard would leave constitutional decisions to the whim and incompetence of the attorneys who happen to be arguing the particular case. During oral argument in the *Brown* case, Justice Felix Frankfurter said to Thurgood Marshall, "In these matters this Court takes judicial notice of accredited writings and it does not have to call the writers as witnesses." Frankfurter added, "How to inform the judicial mind, as you know, is one of the most complicated problems. It is better to have witnesses, but I did not know that we could not read the works of competent writers."[21] Judges have an independent duty to investigate and evaluate the empirical bases for the law that their decisions set forth in the same way they are ultimately responsible for finding and interpreting the law itself. In his concurring opinion in *Roe*, Justice Stewart quoted Frankfurter regarding the factual foundation that supports principles such as liberty: "Great concepts like . . . 'liberty' . . . were purposely left to gather meaning from experience. For they relate to the whole domain of social and economic fact, and the statesmen who founded this Nation knew too well that only a stagnant society remains unchanged."[22] Blackmun's industry in going to the Mayo Clinic to determine the medical facts of the matter should be applauded. That is not to say, however, that he should have relied upon what he found.

The *Roe* opinion began with an extensive recitation of the history and sociology of abortion, both in America and in ancient times. In America, restrictive criminal abortion laws, Blackmun observed, were of "recent vintage." The ancients similarly did not consider abortion criminal. "Greek and Roman law afforded little protection to the unborn." In fact, Blackmun noted, the few prosecutions seem "to have been based on a concept of a violation of the father's right to his offspring." Blackmun also surveyed religious and philosophical opinion on the subject, again finding little disfavor until the modern era. Moreover, he outlined the intractable choices produced by the decision whether to end an unwanted pregnancy and the medical, physical, and psychological costs associated with the alternative of an unwanted offspring. More than the usual Court opinion, *Roe*'s introduction set the historical and sociological stage on which the abortion drama had played out. Also, more than usual, the opinion recognized the intense feelings the subject engendered and expressly acknowledged the justices' "awareness of the sensitive and emotional nature of the abortion controversy, of the vigorous opposing views, even among physicians, and of the deep and seemingly absolute convictions that the subject inspires."[23]

Blackmun next observed that the crux of the case involved a clash of principles between a woman's right to control her body and the government's interests in promoting health and protecting the potential life of the fetus. The woman's right, Blackmun stated, could be traced to the right of privacy that, though not explicit in the Constitution, could be found in Court precedent dating back to 1891. Recent precedents, especially *Griswold v. Connecticut,* had substantially reinvigorated that right. Somewhat lackadaisically, and almost as an aside, Blackmun located the right where Harlan had originally placed it, in the Fourteenth Amendment's Due Process Clause. The pivotal passage:

> This right of privacy, whether it be founded in the Fourteenth Amendment's concept of personal liberty and restrictions upon state action, as

we feel it is, or, as the District Court determined, in the Ninth Amendment's reservation of rights to the people, is broad enough to encompass a woman's decision whether or not to terminate her pregnancy.[24]

On the other side of the equation stands the government's interest in maintaining the woman's health and, more profoundly, the issue of the potential life of the fetus. Of greatest significance was the question of whether the fetus should be considered a "person" for Fourteenth Amendment purposes. Such a determination could have ended the debate, since the Fourteenth Amendment guarantees all persons the equal protection of the laws. It is true that the clause allows differently situated individuals to be treated differently. For instance, the Court considers a corporation to be a "person" for Fourteenth Amendment purposes, but corporations are not accorded guarantees identical to what individuals receive.[25] It would thus have been possible, at the start, to describe the fetus as a "person" without necessarily abrogating a woman's right to terminate her pregnancy. At the very least, however, concluding that the fetus was a person would have changed the constitutional calculus substantially. Blackmun, however, concluded as Justice Stewart had strongly urged him to do, that the Court did not have to determine when life began. If "those trained in the respective disciplines of medicine, philosophy, and theology are unable to arrive at any consensus," Blackmun explained, "the judiciary, at this point in the development of man's knowledge, is not in a position to speculate as to the answer."[26]

Any attempt to use science to answer the profound question of when life begins is doomed to fail. Elementary understanding of genetics and the so-called DNA blueprint have led some interlocutors in the abortion debate to claim that fertilization is the moment when life begins, since the DNA is set at that moment for all time hence. Dr. John Willkie, for instance, of the National Right to Life Committee, argued, "Contained within the single cell who I once was, was the totality of everything I am today."[27] Besides being incredibly deterministic philosophically, this belief about the power of DNA is basically incorrect as a matter of science. Dr. Charles Gardner, for instance, points out that a fertilized egg "is clearly not a prepackaged human being." He provides the following proof of his conclusion:

If a fertilized mouse egg from two white-furred parents goes through four cell divisions, the embryo will have reached the sixteen-cell stage. If this embryo is then brought together with a sixteen-cell embryo from two black-furred parents, a ball of thirty-two cells is formed. This ball of cells will go on to make a single individual with mixed black and white fur: one mouse with four parents, two white and two black. . . . A similar event sometimes occurs naturally in humans when two sibling embryos combine into one. The resultant person may be completely normal.

If the original embryos were determined to become particular individuals, such a thing could not happen. The embryos would recognize themselves to be different mice, or different people and would not unite. . . . They seem to recognize each other as early embryonic cells and nothing more. The only explanation is that the individual is not fixed or determined at this early stage.[28]

There is, Gardner says, "no blueprint." He explained, "Our genes give us a propensity for certain characteristics, but it is the enactment of the complex process of development that gives us our individual characteristics. So how can an embryo be a human being?" The pro-regulation response, however, is that even if an embryo is not fully human, its potential to become so is a compelling interest of government. Gardner retorts that this is "a strange kind of potential, having no determined path or blueprint to follow." "The fertilized egg cell," he said, "does not contain its fate, just as a grape seed does not contain wine."[29] Nonetheless, many states assert the overriding desire to give the grape seed the opportunity to become wine.

Despite his reluctance to answer the metaphysical question of when life begins, Blackmun found two junctures in the medical texts that could provide a framework around which to build the doctrine. The first important point was at the end of the first trimester, around twelve weeks, when the risks associated with the abortion procedure crept above the risks associated with childbirth. This fact, the Court ruled, gave the state a compelling interest in maternal health that would support regulations tailored to ensuring the health of the mother when obtaining an abortion. Thus, in the first trimester, when abortion was safer than childbirth, no regulations directed specifically at abortions could be passed. In the second trimester, as the risks of abortion increased past those of childbirth, the state could regulate to protect maternal health.

The second, and ultimately more controversial, juncture was at the end of the second trimester. The Court held that it was at this point— at viability—that the state's interest in the potential life of the fetus became compelling and the state could regulate, or prohibit entirely, the abortion procedure, except when it was necessary to preserve the life of the mother. Blackmun gave the following rationale for fixing the "compelling point" at viability: "This is so because the fetus then presumably has the capability of meaningful life outside the mother's womb. State regulation protective of fetal life after viability thus has both logical and biological justification."[30] The fetus, therefore, did not receive specific protection from the Constitution, as it might have if the Court had deemed it a "person" under the Fourteenth Amendment. Nonetheless, states, through their power to legislate for the general welfare, have a legitimate interest in protecting the potential life of a fetus. Just as a state can legislate to protect spotted owls, despite the fact that they are not protected by the Constitution, it can legislate to protect viable fetuses. At viability, according to the Court, this interest becomes compelling.

Justices Rehnquist and White dissented. Rehnquist observed that the Court cited Holmes's dissent in *Lochner* approvingly, but reached a result "more closely attuned to the majority opinion of Mr. Justice Peckham in that case." The strict scrutiny standard applied in both *Lochner* and *Roe,* Rehnquist argued, "will inevitably require this Court to examine the legislative policies and pass on the wisdom of these policies in the very process of deciding whether a particular interest put forward may or may not be 'compelling.' " The Court's opinion, Rehnquist declared, returns us to *Lochner* and "the heyday of the Nine Old Men, who felt that the Constitution enabled them to invalidate almost any state laws they thought were unwise."[31]

Roe met vehement resistance. Cardinal Krol, the president of the National Conference of Catholic Bishops, said, for instance, "It is hard to think of any decision in the two hundred years of our history which has had more disastrous implications for our stability as a civilized society."[32] Scholars, politicians, and newspaper editorials accused the Court of acting like a super-legislature in enacting an abortion code for the country under cover of the Bill of Rights. The Court's use of viability as the point at which states could regulate to save fetal life came in for particular scorn. John Hart Ely, a prominent liberal legal scholar, wrote that Blackmun's argument "seems to mistake a definition for a syllogism."[33] Blackmun never explained *why* viability mattered as a constitutional matter. Viability is defined medically as the point when a fetus might survive outside the womb, but Blackmun failed to say why such a statistical likelihood matters legally. Perhaps he thought it was intuitively obvious, though no one since

Roe has successfully explained the basis for this intuition. Viability was a juncture, certainly, but why should the fact that a fetus could theoretically survive outside the womb magically make the government's interest "compelling" only at that point, or at that point at all? Certainly, Blackmun did not contemplate that a woman could present herself in, say, the twenty-fifth week of pregnancy and demand either an abortion or that the state remove the fetus and maintain it using whatever technology was available. Under *Roe,* the state had the right at "viability" to coerce the woman to carry the fetus to term.

There are many other junctures that Blackmun might have used to set the outer limit of the right of reproductive choice, some of which might present a better argument for legal (or moral) line drawing. Early on, there is conception and implantation of the embryo, two fairly discrete events, but whose use would abrogate the right to abortion entirely. Further on, the emergence of motility—or quickening—is somewhat more amorphous but has the benefit of support at common law, among the ancients, and conforms to many religious practices. Motility actually begins early, around six to seven weeks, but is not strong enough to be perceived by the woman for more than two more months. Further still, around twenty-two to twenty-three weeks, the first neocortical circuitry develops, though in the cerebrum the mature brain cell pattern does not fully form until close to twenty-eight weeks. It is around this time, between twenty-eight and thirty-two weeks, that the morphophysiology and sleep patterns of the fetus resemble those of the full-term newborn. Finally, the most categorical event in pregnancy is birth. While some cultures view even birth as not the definitive juncture marking personhood, no one seriously argues in the United States that abortion-on-demand should be permitted until birth. In any case, in regard to the question of what significance different stages of prenatal development should have legally, it is clear, as one observer put it, that the subject is "a moving target."[34]

There were also many practical questions swirling around the Court's decision to attach a constitutional rule to contemporary medical science. Foremost, what if viability changed as technology improved? Just as was true in *Brown,* it is instructive to consider how important the fact cited was for the decision by asking whether the Constitution's meaning would change if the scientific facts were different. If viability occurred in the fourth week, for example, would a state have a sufficient justification to criminalize abortion after the first month of pregnancy? Justice Sandra

Day O'Connor had criticized the trimester framework for this very reason in the first abortion case she heard, in her dissent in *Akron v. Akron Center for Reproductive Health*.[35] She warned in her dissent that, due to recent advances in medicine, linking the constitutional framework in *Roe* to medical technology had set it "on a collision course with itself."[36] She predicted that the abortion procedure would become safer than childbirth well past the first trimester and that viability would continue to creep forward toward conception. Her first prediction was already proving true, since in 1983, when *Akron* was decided, abortion was safer than childbirth through week sixteen, four weeks later than at the time of *Roe*. But viability has proven to be more resilient to technological progress. The main difficulty is that fetal lungs don't develop until around the twenty-third week and scientists have yet to devise tools to maintain fetuses outside the womb before this time. Many believe that fetal lung development is a wall that technology will not scale. But technology has a way of surprising its doubters and scattered throughout the history of science are achievements once thought impossible made commonplace.

Viability, as an empirical matter, was never seriously developed or explained by the *Roe* opinion or any subsequent opinion of the Court. As Blackmun certainly knew, viability does not occur at some identifiable moment. Viability is a statistical estimate. On average, a fetus at twenty weeks might have less than a 1 percent chance of survival, at twenty-three to twenty-four weeks it increases to about 25 percent, at twenty-five weeks it is about 50 percent, and at thirty-two weeks it is over 90 percent. Given these probabilities, is a twenty-one-week-old fetus viable? Is a thirty-two-week-old fetus viable? The answers are not obvious and the Court made no attempt to provide any.

Whatever the fate of viability technologically, its legal relevance is also indefinite. Almost certainly, even if viability becomes possible in week four, no court that is being true to the legal principles behind *Roe* would curtail the right of reproductive choice after the fourth week of pregnancy. Four weeks would not be enough time for a woman to exercise her fundamental right to choose an abortion. Viability, in 1973, was an enormously convenient point in time for setting a compromise between two clashing principles. It was a political solution that was more or less arbitrarily set at twenty-four weeks. Indeed, Justice Blackmun originally chose instead the end of the first trimester in an early draft of the opinion he circulated following reargument of the case.[37] Blackmun wrote his colleagues in an accompanying memo, "You will observe that I have concluded that the end of the first trimester is critical. This is arbitrary, but perhaps any other selected point, such as quickening or viability, is equally arbitrary."[38] It was Justice Powell who initially raised the objection that the first trimester did not afford the woman sufficient time to exercise her fundamental right. Justice Marshall similarly voiced strong opposition to use of the first trimester. "I would be disturbed," he said, "if that point were set before viability, and I am afraid that the opinion's present focus on the first trimester would lead states to prohibit abortions completely at any later date."[39] Justice Blackmun responded that he was not wedded to using the first trimester. Any choice was arbitrary. Powell explained that viability provided something of a benchmark, a time, he thought, when "the interest of the state becomes clearly identifiable, in a manner which would be generally understood."[40]

In 1973, viability was thus a convenient stand-in for the compromise the Court struck in coming to terms with the woman's right to be let alone and the government's interest in protecting the potential life that grew inside her. There is nothing inherently salacious about choosing a convenient bright line, even if the exact point is chosen somewhat arbitrarily, to settle conflicting principles of law. The Court does it all of the time. Whether politically liberal or politically conservative, justices have no choice but to do it. The First Amendment protects pornography but not obscenity; the line between the two is somewhat arbitrarily set, based on a set of criteria that are entirely judge-created. The speech clause protects false statements made regarding public figures so long as the statements are not made with "actual malice," a standard that is somewhat arbitrarily defined as "with knowledge of their falsity or with reckless disregard for their truth." This criterion is not set forth in the Constitution; it was crafted by the Court in *New York Times v. Sullivan.* When the cases before it call upon the Court to look to the Constitution to reconcile fundamental rights with powerful government interests, the justices are repeatedly forced to establish rules or standards that resolve conflicts of basic principles. This necessitates line drawing and the process of locating just where that line will sit is very often largely arbitrary.

Selecting the end of the second trimester as the point at which states can prohibit abortion, except to save the life of the mother, may very well have been an inspired resolution of conflicting rights and interests. It permits a woman sufficient time to exercise her right of choice while recognizing that government has a legitimate and growing concern with the fetus as it matures toward personhood. The government's interest, undoubtedly, tracks the general unease in the United States with the prospect of aborting fetuses as they grow into a form recognizable as human. Most Western countries, in fact, have settled upon about eighteen weeks as the time within which a woman must exercise her right to an abortion. In short, the Court used viability, rigidly set at twenty-four weeks, as a proxy for a reasonable reconciliation of otherwise irreconcilable principles. Before viability, a woman can choose to terminate her pregnancy on demand; if she fails to exercise her rights in a timely fashion, the government can coerce her to carry the fetus to term. She has slept on her rights and, as a consequence, has lost them. There is nothing unusual about this sort of constitutional analysis, except that the Court failed to do it explicitly and instead hid behind the scientific veil of viability to achieve the very same result.

Just as in *Brown*, then, the *Roe* Court used science to disguise a policy choice. It did so for similar reasons in the two cases. In both *Roe* and *Brown*, the Court recognized its obligation as the ultimate protector of those rights guaranteed by the Constitution, but found itself on new ground that did not fully support the direction in which it sought to go. In difficult cases, often at the vanguard of society's evolution, the Court must breathe life into provisions that only dimly, if at all, speak to the exigencies of modern times. To protect against unreasonable government intrusion, it must sometimes go beyond the comfort of convention. While this places the Court in tension with the democratic tradition, the federal judiciary's countermajoritarian function is as much a part of the structure of American government as the right to vote itself. Nonetheless, the Court believes, rightly or wrongly, that its power derives from its perceived legitimacy, which, in turn, is thought to depend on its use of reasoned judgment based on neutral and nonsubjective principles. When the usual authorities, such as text, original intent, and precedent, are ambiguous, absent, or contrary to the direction the justices want to go, the Court employs arguments from fact and, if available, the research that describes those facts.

In *Brown*, however, it was readily apparent early on that no set of facts would ever change the basic holding mandating integrated schools. Relying on the fact of segregation's deleterious effects was a product of perceived rhetorical necessity. It was a makeweight to support a judgment that most Americans supported at the time and which has received nearly unanimous acclaim since. While more than half of the country, as indicated by Gallup Poll results, has consistently supported the outcome in *Roe,* it is not a large majority. Moreover, the minority voice, the so-called pro-life movement, has been loud and politically effective. An anti-abortion provision has been part of every Republican candidate's election platform since the first post-*Roe* presidential election in 1976. The Republicans have controlled the White House for eighteen years and counting since *Roe,* and they have masterfully held control of one or the other or both Houses of Congress for substantial periods of that time. In addition, much more so than with *Brown,* states relentlessly challenged *Roe,* both by enacting legislation that directly contradicted the Court's abortion decisions or by crafting barriers in sheep's clothing to make a woman's actual exercise of her liberty right as difficult as possible. Regulations such as exhaustive and heart-wrenching informed consent provisions, twenty-four-hour waiting requirements, bans on using Medicaid funds, spousal and parental consent or notification conditions, and viability testing have all been thrown in the way of women who have chosen to terminate pregnancies. Unlike after *Brown,* then, the Court felt virtually all the pressure that the political branches and states could bring to bear, and this pressure was all directed at the legitimacy of the Court's decision to step into and stir up the political cauldron of abortion. Whereas in *Brown* the premises of the decision, the Clark doll studies, could quietly recede into historical obscurity, the premises of *Roe* were given no such reprieve. If the Court was to continue to sustain *Roe* against incessant attack, it had to stand by the premises on which that outcome was based. Viability, however indefinite its constitutional roots might be, had the virtue of being grounded in scientific fact. But using viability as a rhetorical stand-in for the balance struck in *Roe* had certain unintended consequences. These consequences were manifest in a challenge to a 1989 Missouri antiabortion law in the case of *Webster v. Reproductive Health Services.*[41]

In *Webster,* the Court considered one of the multitude of state regulations passed in the decade following *Roe* that more or less openly defied that decision. No provision illustrated this fact better than the preamble to the Missouri statute that provided that life begins at conception. This pointedly contradicted the *Roe* Court's explicit statement that states could not adopt a particular theory of when human life begins as a basis for their abortion regulations. The *Webster* Court, however, on its way to nearly overruling *Roe,* held that this preamble had no operative legal effect and thus was not contrary to *Roe.* The Court also upheld another provision barring the use of state property for performing abortions. The most intrusive provision of the Missouri law, also upheld by the Court, was the requirement that physicians use medically appropriate tests to determine whether a fetus was viable when, in the doctor's judgment, the fetus was twenty or more weeks of gestational age. The statute provided that a twenty-week-old fetus was presumed viable, so these "medically appropriate" tests actually had to be used to disprove viability of fetuses older than twenty weeks. The standard tests used for assessing viability are gestational age, fetus weight, and fetal lung development, though they do not correspond in any meaningful way to whether a particular fetus will actually survive. These factors roughly estimate fetal maturity that roughly predicts survivability rates of premature births in general. About 30 percent of fetuses born at twenty-four weeks survive, but there is little science on what factors specifically predict which 30 percent will do so.

Shortly before *Webster* was decided in June 1989, most Court observers anticipated that the Reagan Revolution had finally achieved its long-stated objective of overruling *Roe.* It had been Reagan's campaign promise in the 1980 presidential race. During his two terms, Reagan had the opportunity to appoint three new justices to the Court, Sandra Day O'Connor (1981), Antonin Scalia (1986), and Anthony Kennedy (1988), as well as to elevate William Rehnquist to the center chair as chief justice. It was expected that these four would join Byron White, an original *Roe* dissenter, to finally bury the case. *Roe,* however, proved difficult to kill, mainly due to Justice O'Connor's strategic defection.

From the day that Justice O'Connor replaced Potter Stewart on the Court, she became the fifth vote that would decide *Roe*'s fate. She received her undergraduate and law degrees from Stanford University. She graduated third in her class (Rehnquist was first in the same class), but was unable to secure a legal job in the private sector because she was a woman. She worked first as a deputy county attorney in Arizona and then later moved into private practice. She served in the Arizona Senate and then as a state judge at both the trial and intermediate levels. Initially, O'Connor was widely believed to be pro-life. However, during her Judiciary Committee hearings, she refused to comment on how she would decide an abortion case if confirmed, and she had cast pro-choice votes in the Arizona Senate. Pro-life organizations asked President Reagan to withdraw her nomination. Jerry Falwell proclaimed that all good Christians should lobby their senators to vote against O'Connor. When asked about Falwell's call to arms, Arizona senator Barry Goldwater said that "all good Christians should kick Jerry Falwell in the ass."[22]

In her *Webster* concurrence, O'Connor interpreted the Missouri statute so that it would not directly implicate the *Roe* holding. It is a venerable, albeit usually ignored, principle of constitutional law that the Court should avoid deciding constitutional questions until they are squarely presented. O'Connor believed that the statute's provisions were sufficiently ambiguous that they could be read in a way that would allow them to be upheld without revisiting *Roe*. Thus, she stated, "there is no necessity to accept the State's invitation to reexamine the constitutional validity of *Roe v. Wade*." She explained, "When the constitutional invalidity of a State's abortion statute actually turns on the constitutional validity of *Roe v. Wade*, there will be time enough to reexamine *Roe*. And to do so carefully."[42] O'Connor clearly rebelled at the notion that history would record her as the deciding vote to invalidate a woman's constitutional right of reproductive choice.

Essential to her strategy, however, was her determination that the viability testing requirement was not inconsistent with the *Roe* trimester framework. If it conflicted with the trimester framework, the Missouri law could not be upheld without revisiting *Roe*. Chief Justice Rehnquist, writing for a four-member plurality of the Court, argued that the required twentieth-week viability test intruded upon the second trimester within which, according to *Roe*, the state could legislate for maternal health but not to protect the fetus. This put the Missouri statute, according to Rehnquist, in unalterable tension with *Roe* and should have undermined its continuing force. Although Rehnquist did not want to explicitly overrule *Roe*, preferring to gut it and leave it by the side of the constitutional road, he needed to convince O'Connor, the fifth vote, that the rigid *Roe* framework could not bend far enough to allow the Missouri viability testing requirement. O'Connor disagreed.

O'Connor argued that there is approximately a four-week "margin of error" in assessing gestational age so that a fetus believed to be twenty weeks old may be twenty-four weeks old and thus possibly viable. Missouri's twenty-week testing requirement, therefore, merely served the *Roe* framework's establishment of the twenty-fourth week and viability as the moment when states could legislate to protect fetal life. However, O'Connor insisted, it is not gestational age that is important under *Roe,* it is viability. O'Connor was thus making clear, given the substantial medical consequences Missouri imposed on women seeking abortions after twenty weeks, that viability had constitutional significance after all. Although she still did not say what significance it had, her opinion in *Webster* suggests that she was taking the facts very seriously indeed.

On the other hand, close consideration of O'Connor's position indicates that perhaps viability does not really have great independent constitutional relevance after all. O'Connor would not follow viability wherever it led if, say, technology permitted fetuses to survive outside the womb after the fourth week. However, since her prediction in *Akron* that the trimester framework would collapse in on itself, she had come to believe that fetal lung development will provide a natural barrier beyond which viability will not pass. The doctrine was secured by a seeming stability in medical technology. Moreover, viability cannot easily be abandoned for fear that the Court will suffer the lament that its abortion jurisprudence is subjective, nonneutral, and, even, *Lochner*ian. But there are significant costs associated with this approach. Under Missouri law, women are required after twenty weeks to undergo the cost, inconvenience, and risks associated with viability testing in order to measure an amorphous scientific fact that is little more than a proxy for a political compromise. Viability is a legal standard and not a factual finding, but Missouri requires the fact to be found anyway.

In *Akron,* the Court had confronted a similar problem. Statistics regarding maternal health were changing as technology progressed. Abortion was now safer than childbirth through week sixteen, not the week-twelve mark set in *Roe.* The *Akron* Court, however, did not amend the trimester framework. Instead, it abandoned the factual justification for the rule and now insisted that the "trimester standard . . . continues to provide a reasonable *legal framework* for limiting a State's authority to regulate abortions."[43] The first part of the trimester framework thus morphed from a rule based on scientific fact to legal fiat. Viability similarly is legally based but it is not as easily abandoned and there is, as of yet, no empirical need to discard it. But by continuing to treat it as a factual-scientific question, the Court forces women to undergo burdensome tests for no reason. It also misleads the Court's audience—lower courts, policy makers, and the public—regarding the true bases for its rulings.

———

The next major test of *Roe*'s continuing vitality came in 1992, in *Planned Parenthood of Southeastern Pennsylvania v. Casey.*[44] By 1992, the Reagan Revolution again had a voice, this time in the person of the first President Bush, and a distinct one with the appointments of David Souter to replace William Brennan and Clarence Thomas to replace Thurgood Marshall. The forces were now strongly arrayed against *Roe* as two of its most stalwart defenders were off the Court. Although Kennedy had yet to author an abortion opinion—he had joined the *Webster* plurality without writing separately—and O'Connor was proving reluctant to toll *Roe*'s death knell, this was a Court that included five members who had been selected specifically for their assumed opposition to *Roe* and two members who had dissented in *Roe*. The only certain votes to uphold *Roe* were Justice Blackmun, its author, and Justice Stevens. *Casey* looked like a sure rout.

In *Casey*, the Court confronted one of the most restrictive abortion laws in the nation and one, as the district court found, that included provisions that the Supreme Court had already held to be unconstitutional before they were passed. For example, the Pennsylvania law required physicians to give women seeking abortions detailed information regarding the risks and alternatives of the procedure, as well as materials describing and picturing the human characteristics of previable fetuses. Moreover, the statute provided that women had to wait twenty-four hours before proceeding with the operation. A virtually identical informed consent provision from Ohio had been invalidated in *Akron* in 1983. The *Akron* Court found that the Ohio informed consent provision was designed primarily to dissuade a woman from her decision, a purpose the Court found to be illegitimate. As for the twenty-four-hour waiting provision, the Court agreed with the lower court's finding that it had "no medical basis." The Pennsylvania provision adopted virtually jot for jot the scheme rejected in *Akron*. In addition, the Pennsylvania law included a spousal notification rule, which, subject to certain exceptions, prohibited physicians from performing abortions if the woman did not attest to the fact that she had informed her spouse of her intention to terminate the pregnancy. Finally, the Pennsylvania law mandated that minor women obtain parental consent, a provision that the Court had upheld in earlier decisions. These three provisions, the twenty-four-hour waiting period, parental consent, and spousal notification, presented a significant test of *Roe,* one that no sober observer thought it would pass.

As to be expected, the oral argument in *Casey* was alive with intrigue and vitriol. Kathryn Kolbert, of the ACLU, argued the case for the challengers. Her strategy was to present the Court with a stark choice: *Roe,* take it or leave it, but make it clear which was to be the case. In *Webster,* William Rehnquist had done all he could to bury *Roe* without eulogy or public notice of its demise. The ACLU anticipated that *Roe*'s passing would mean a rush of liberal Democratic activity, just as *Roe* had spurred conservative Republicans into action. They wanted to force the Court's hand, and, they hoped, snatch political victory from the jaws of jurisprudential defeat. Rehnquist, the most politically astute of the justices, wanted to jettison *Roe,* but without creating a political maelstrom for the Republicans. Overruling *Roe* in 1992 might be enough to usher the Democrats into the White House. When *Casey* was under consideration, in the spring of 1992, the first George Bush enjoyed soaring public approval ratings largely due to his success in the first Gulf War. Bill Clinton was the governor of a small state, with a seeming assortment of marital problems. Kolbert and the ACLU sought a clear statement and hoped, given the apparent inevitability of *Roe*'s doom, to create an election issue. In her brief and in oral argument she presented the matter in a plain and categorical fashion. The Court should either "resoundingly reaffirm *Roe,*" or else "forsake its historic role as guardian of constitutional liberties."[45]

At the argument, the justices were not enamored with Kolbert's strategy. They remained stonily quiet during her opening statement, and let her extol the brilliance of *Roe* and its strict scrutiny standard for seven long minutes without interruption. Her extreme position, in light of the forces arrayed against her, was met with uncomprehending silence. Justice O'Connor finally had enough: "You're arguing the case as though all we have before us is whether to apply stare decisis and preserve *Roe* in all its aspects." She lectured Kolbert that the Court had "granted *certiorari* on some specific questions in this case." Annoyed, O'Connor asked, "Do you plan to address any of those in your argument?" Kolbert diplomatically assured Justice O'Connor that she would. She never did. Justice Kennedy, perplexed by this strategy, said to her, "If you are going to argue that *Roe* can survive only in its most rigid formulation, that is an election you can make as counsel." Such an approach, Kennedy intimated, might not be the most responsible course to take. "I am suggesting to you that is not the only logical possibility in this case," he told her.

Kolbert's adversaries also received cool receptions from the justices. Ernest Preate Jr. represented Pennsylvania, and Solicitor General Kenneth Starr—later to become famous for another blood feud—weighed in for the United States. Preate sought to avoid a direct conflict with *Roe,* believing that a quiet *Webster*-like slip into the night was the preferred end for that tenacious authority. Blackmun contemptuously asked him at the start of his argument whether he had even read *Roe.* O'Connor peppered him with questions about the justification for the spousal notification provision, asking sarcastically, "Was its purpose to try to preserve the marriage?" Starr, when it was his turn, charged blindly ahead to kill the beast, arguing that "no credible foundation exists for the claim that a woman enjoys a fundamental right to abortion." Starr was met with questions from O'Connor, Stevens, and Souter asking him whether the government had now embraced the pro-life perspective and what sorts of regulations might follow if *Roe* were overturned. He did his best not to answer any of these questions. Souter, undeterred by Starr's prevarications, insisted on an answer as to what kinds of regulations the states could pass if *Roe* was overruled. Starr's basic answer was any law that was not arbitrary and capricious.

At the conference following the argument, Rehnquist steered discussion away from the question of whether *Roe* should be overruled, despite the fact that he surely believed that he had the votes to do just that. He still hoped to avoid stirring a hornet's nest by explicitly overruling *Roe.* He simply wanted a majority opinion to substitute for the opinion he wrote for the *Webster* plurality. He therefore led the discussion by saying that he thought all of the Pennsylvania regulations were constitutional, without challenging *Roe* itself. This scenario meant that two precedents would have to be overruled, *Akron* and *Thornburgh v. American College of Obstetricians and Gynecologists,*[46] but he apparently preferred this stealth approach to explicitly taking on the politically charged *Roe.* Justices White, Scalia, Kennedy, and Thomas agreed that the statute should be upheld, with Scalia advocating abandonment of *Roe*'s strict scrutiny approach in favor of the permissive rational basis test. Justice O'Connor repeated her reservations about the spousal notification provision and Justice Souter voiced somewhat broader and deeper concerns about the statute as a whole, agreeing that spousal notification was particularly suspect. Justice Blackmun "passed" at the conference, knowing that his antipathy for the Pennsylvania law was well known, but that voicing it would do no good. Justice Stevens said he would vote to strike both the twenty-four-hour waiting and spousal notification provisions. Rehnquist, finding himself in the seeming majority, assigned himself the opinion and set out to accomplish what he believed was long in coming.

In the Academy Award–winning movie *Forrest Gump,* Forrest says, "Now my mama told me that miracles happen every day. Some people don't think so, but they do." Well, perhaps they do.

Justice Souter had come to the bench with no agenda and no scores to settle. He had been described as the stealth nominee and little was known about his constitutional views beyond the assurances liberally peddled by his political mentors, Warren Rudman and John Sununu. He was born in Melrose, Massachusetts, but spent most of his early years in Weare, New Hampshire, which he described as "a town large in geography [and] small in population." It was a place where everybody "knew everybody else's business," Souter said, "or at least thought they did."[47] Throughout his life he excelled academically, and when he graduated from high school in 1957 he was voted "most sophisticated" and "most likely to succeed" by his classmates. He attended Harvard College, was awarded a Rhodes scholarship to attend Oxford University, and then went on to the Harvard Law School. He practiced law briefly but, as one of his colleagues observed, Souter "would seem to be a natural judge." Souter soon left private practice to become an assistant attorney general in the criminal division, and when Warren Rudman became attorney general he picked Souter to be his deputy. He was appointed attorney general in 1976 when Rudman returned to private practice. Two years later Souter was appointed to the bench as an associate judge of the New Hampshire Superior Court, a general jurisdiction trial court. In 1983, Governor John Sununu appointed him to the New Hampshire Supreme Court and in 1990 the first President Bush nominated him to the First Circuit Court of Appeals. Just three months later, the president named him for the High Court.[48]

At his confirmation hearings before the Senate Judiciary Committee, Souter demonstrated his intellectual acumen with detailed discussion of highly complex constitutional cases. At the close of his testimony, Senator Joseph Biden, the chairman of the committee, told him, "I . . . have been impressed with your knowledge. I have been impressed with your ability to articulate your position. I have been impressed with the ease with which you were able to make clear the purpose behind . . . a number of decisions, including even referring to the sense within those opinions that most would spend time in a law library having to look up. And you have done it off the top of your head." Although Souter demonstrated his keen intellect during the hearings, he gave little hint how he would vote on specific cases. The one hint that he did provide was his repeated statements indicating that John Marshall Harlan was his judicial hero and that he would seek to emulate him on the bench. For anyone paying attention, this was a telling sign.

Justice Harlan was an enigmatic character. Revered by conservatives, he felt himself almost duty bound to precedent. He also attempted to write opinions that would have limited reach, though he repeatedly exhibited sympathy for basic rights and fundamental fairness. In *Boddie v. Connecticut*,[49] for example, he invoked due process to support an indigent's right to avoid filing fees in divorce proceedings. However, Harlan made clear that the ruling was limited by the fact that states possessed a monopoly over divorces, thus limiting the future reach of the precedent. Yet, in *Poe v. Ullman*, four years before *Griswold*, he not only recognized the right of privacy, but described it in soaring terms. Liberty, he wrote, "is not a series of isolated points pricked out in terms" of the "specific guarantees elsewhere provided in the Constitution." Harlan believed that the Court must guarantee individuals "freedom from all substantial arbitrary impositions and purposeless restraints." Harlan, moreover, did not believe the constitutional text had talismanic power. The Court, he said, must approach "the text which is the only commission for our power not in any literalistic way, as if we had a tax statute before us, but as the basic charter of our society, setting out in spare but meaningful terms the principles of government."[50] Harlan's dedication to precedent and fidelity to a robust privacy right should have alerted conservatives to the possibility that Souter's vote on abortion might not be secure.

A greater problem with the conservatives' assessment, and this extends beyond their misjudgment of Justices Harlan and Souter, is a basic confusion about what "conservatism" means in the law. There is no simple answer to the question of what is a judicial conservative. Conservative politicians like to link conservative judging with the notion of judicial restraint. Along with motherhood, judicial restraint is one of those principles that public figures regularly extol, even if they don't quite understand it. Many conservative politicians, such as the second President Bush, tend to hold up Justices Scalia and Thomas as examples of good conservative judges. While surely conservative politically, Scalia and Thomas are two of the most activist judges ever to sit on the Court, as

measured by their proclivity to vote to strike down laws passed by popularly elected legislatures. Their conservatism lies in their desire to push
back the clock to some earlier era. They are judicial conservatives in
outcome, not in method. In Thomas's case, he would like to return most
of constitutional law to circa 1935 and, in some cases, he would send it
back to 1802. Unlike Justice Harlan, Justices Scalia and Thomas have
little use for precedent and they have been known to disregard half a
century of Court decisions with the flick of a pen. In his first year on the
Court, for instance, Thomas wrote a concurring opinion in *United States
v. Lopez,*[51] a case that overturned nearly fifty years of precedent, in which
he suggested that earlier decisions by justices such as Harlan Fiske Stone,
Oliver Wendell Holmes, and John Marshall were wrongly decided. For
any justice, but especially one in his first term on the Court, it is just
sound advice that if you write an opinion disagreeing with possibly the
three greatest minds ever to sit on the Court, you might want to sleep
on it before you send it to the printers. The conservatism desired by
Reagan and the two Bushes was a radical sort of conservatism that true
conservatives, such as Harlan, have always blanched at.

Harlan was Souter's starting point. Harlan had written that the "character of Constitutional provisions . . . must be discerned from a particular provision's larger context. And . . . this context is one not of words,
but of history and purposes."[52] In the case of abortion, *Roe* had been a
relatively straightforward extension of Harlan's opinion in *Poe v. Ullman*
and the holding in *Griswold*. It represented a flexible and determined
reading of the due process clause. A woman's right to make fundamental
decisions about her body and health was just the sort of right that Harlan
would have thought needed protection against arbitrary state intrusion.
Moreover, however embattled, *Roe* was still good law. Harlan needed
irresistible reasons before overturning precedent, even precedent with
which he strongly disagreed. Even if Harlan might not have joined *Roe*
in 1973, possibly believing it to be an overextension of due process, after
almost twenty years, he would need a better reason than his personal
dislike to overrule the decision.

Souter thus settled on his decision to not overrule *Roe,* believing this
course to be entirely consistent with conservative jurisprudential principles. In *Casey*, it was the so-called conservative bloc that displayed
activist tendencies in wanting to overturn settled precedent. More significantly, however, Souter was not satisfied simply to write an opinion
dissenting from the reversal of *Roe*. Taking a page from the playbook

of Justice Brennan, who was well known for his political acuity in establishing and maintaining alliances, Justice Souter went to talk with Justice O'Connor, a natural ally for his reluctance to overturn settled law. O'Connor received Souter's proposal enthusiastically, and was especially enamored with the prospect of pursuing a Harlanesque path on abortion. The two recognized, however, that the key to success lay with Justice Kennedy. With his vote, together with Blackmun and Stevens, they could control the Court's direction.

Kennedy was interested in their idea. It conformed well to the position that he was increasingly carving out for himself on the Court, one not unlike the role O'Connor saw for herself, as a principled centrist. Kennedy, even more than most of the Justices, was preoccupied with the Court's legitimacy, which primarily concerns the public's perception of what the Court is doing. Maintaining this legitimacy, in Kennedy's view, requires maneuvering between several rocky shoals, including fidelity to democratic decision-making, adherence to precedent, guarding fundamental liberties, respect for state autonomy, and adherence to neutral principles. Most important, legitimacy meant that the Court had to be perceived as deciding cases other than according to the justices' personal or political whim. Nothing would be more damaging to the Court's reputation than to allow the campaign to select anti-*Roe* justices to succeed. Such success, Kennedy believed, would breed mistrust among the citizenry and make the Court seem to be little more than a political organ like the legislative and the executive branches. Thirty years earlier, Harlan summarized the lesson that Kennedy now applied: "A basic change in the law upon a ground no firmer than a change in membership invites the popular misconception that this institution is little different from the two political branches of the Government. No misconception could do more lasting injury to this Court and to the system which it is our abiding mission to serve."[53] The Court's power lay in its judgment, and the perception that it was driven by political or personal motives would undermine that power. As Kennedy proudly said in one of the flag-burning cases, "The hard fact is that sometimes we must make decisions we do not like."[54] For the devout practicing Catholic justice who developed intellectual disdain for *Roe* while teaching a constitutional law course at a local law school in Sacramento, California, *Casey* would allow Kennedy to show just how principled he was and just how legitimate the Court was.

In the annals of Supreme Court decisions, the *Casey* opinion is remarkable for many reasons. Most remarkable, the primary opinion for the Court was jointly authored by Justices O'Connor, Kennedy, and Souter. They fully divided responsibility for drafting the joint opinion and then worked intimately together to smooth the result into a single statement. Justices Blackmun and Stevens each wrote separately, but united with the joint opinion's threesome to sustain the "central holding" of *Roe.* Chief Justice Rehnquist and Justices White, Scalia, and Thomas dissented, and explicitly called for the repudiation of *Roe. Casey,* an extremely long opinion even by the permissive standards of the modern Supreme Court, contains within its margins most of the major themes of constitutional law. Indeed, a course in constitutional law could be taught largely from the five opinions in *Casey* that discuss such mainstay topics as due process, equal protection, Federalism and states' rights, the institutional role of the Supreme Court in American government, and the role of precedent and tradition in defining constitutional values. It is an opinion in which the art of judging, in all its finery and tattered rags, is in full display.

The joint opinion begins, "Liberty finds no refuge in a jurisprudence of doubt."[55] The opinion states plainly, "After considering the fundamental constitutional questions resolved by *Roe,* principles of institutional integrity, and the rule of stare decisis, we are led to conclude this: the essential holding of *Roe v. Wade* should be retained and once again reaffirmed." The opinion paid tribute to the "promise of the Constitution that there is a realm of personal liberty which the government may not enter," relying largely on Justice Harlan's opinion in *Poe v. Ullman.* Echoing Harlan, the opinion cited the "inescapable fact" that "adjudication of substantive due process claims may call upon the Court in interpreting the Constitution to exercise that same capacity which by tradition courts always have exercised: reasoned judgment."[56]

Again following Harlan's lead, the joint opinion discussed at length the "prudential and pragmatic considerations designed to test the consistency of overruling a prior decision with the ideal of the rule of law." Some of these considerations included whether the old rule had proved unworkable or whether overruling precedent would impose a particular hardship on a group who had come to rely on it. Chief among these multiple considerations, the opinion stated, was "whether facts have so changed, or come to be seen so differently, as to have robbed the old rule of significant application or justification."[57]

The two historical precedents *Roe's* critics have most often compared it to are *Plessy v. Ferguson* and *Lochner v. New York*. Both of these cases, like *Roe,* came under intense attack and, in time, both were ultimately overruled. The joint opinion, however, distinguished these two lines of precedent primarily on the basis that it was the changing underlying facts that had compelled a new legal rule in those cases; but the same was not true in *Roe*. In *Lochner,* the opinion pointed out, "the clear demonstration that the facts of economic life were different from those previously assumed warranted the repudiation of the old law." Similarly, the empirical basis for *Plessy* was long extinct by 1954 and the *Brown* decision. The joint opinion observed, "The Court in *Brown* addressed these facts of life by observing that whatever may have been the understanding in *Plessy*'s time of the power of segregation to stigmatize those who were segregated with a 'badge of inferiority,' it was clear by 1954 that legally sanctioned segregation had just such an effect, to the point that racially separate public educational facilities were deemed inherently unequal."[58]

No such fundamental change in the factual underpinnings of *Roe* had occurred between 1973 and 1992. What change had occurred was relatively minor, as the *Casey* Court acknowledged: "advances in maternal health care allow for abortions safe to the mother later in pregnancy than was true in 1973, and advances in neonatal care have advanced viability to a point somewhat earlier." The opinion maintained that "the divergences from the factual premises of 1973 have no bearing on the validity of *Roe*'s central holding, that viability marks the earliest point at which the State's interest in fetal life is constitutionally adequate to justify a legislative ban on nontherapeutic abortion." Moreover, the opinion continued, "the soundness or unsoundness of that constitutional judgment in no sense turns on whether viability occurs at approximately 28 weeks, as was usual at the time of *Roe,* at 23 to 24 weeks, as it sometimes does today, or at some moment even slightly earlier in pregnancy, as it may if fetal respiratory capacity can somehow be enhanced in the future."[59]

The joint opinion thus continued to adhere to the factual referent of viability to describe both the relevance and scope of the woman's right. "The concept of viability," the opinion held, "is the time at which there is a realistic possibility of maintaining and nourishing a life outside the womb, so that the independent existence of the second life can in reason and all fairness be the object of state protection that now overrides the rights of the woman."[60] But then the opinion buried a bone, just in case viability should change factually, so that the right to abortion would not dim and vanish if technology should push viability too close to conception. The opinion stated, "The viability line also has, as a practical matter, an element of fairness. In some broad sense it might be said that a woman who fails to act before viability has consented to the State's intervention on behalf of the developing child."[61] For the first time, the Court identified what appeared to be the bottom line. Whatever the fate of the scientific concept of viability, women should be guaranteed a reasonable opportunity to exercise their fundamental right of reproductive choice.

This fail-safe statement, intended to protect the underlying policy judgment of *Roe,* actually illustrates the true difference between *Roe* and the contrasting authorities of *Plessy* and *Lochner.* In the latter two cases, the facts that "changed" were sociological or economic facts that reflected the very policy choice selected in the respective opinions. *Lochner* was premised on a belief in Spencerian social Darwinism that equality existed between labor and capital and that society could count on the efficiency of the marketplace to ensure that the fittest survive. The belief in the accuracy of this view waned in the first part of the twentieth century as the power and depravity of huge corporations and trusts became more and more evident. The Great Depression removed any doubt about the efficiency of free markets or about the need for government intervention. Similarly, the science of *Plessy* came to be understood, long before 1954, as a tissue of lies perpetrated to justify prejudice and maintain discrimination. In 1954, the Court rejected a worldview that had long since passed from civilized society.

The underlying sociology and economics of *Roe,* in contrast, had not changed by the time of *Casey* in 1992. If anything, *Roe's* original premises had only gotten stronger. A woman's right over her body stemmed not only from the liberty guaranteed by the due process clause, but also the equality of opportunity guaranteed by the equal protection clause. *Roe,* as much as *Brown,* was a product of its time and the increasing recognition that, as a matter of constitutional law, women should be treated equally. It is an old joke, but probably not entirely inaccurate, that if men got pregnant they would guarantee themselves the right of reproductive choice until about six months after birth. *Casey* plainly identified equality as a basis for the abortion right and explicitly discussed abortion as a component of women's status in American life. "The ability of women to participate equally in the economic and social life of the Nation has been facilitated by their ability to control their reproductive lives." The joint opinion continued, "The Constitution serves human values, and while the effect of reliance on *Roe* cannot be exactly measured, neither can the certain cost of overruling *Roe* for people who have ordered their thinking and living around that case be dismissed."[62] It was not the technology of neonatal care that had failed to change since 1973, it was the belief that women deserved equal protections of the laws and that they possessed a fundamental right to make the decision whether or not to bear a child for a reasonable period of time after becoming pregnant.

Despite their stated fidelity to *Roe,* Justices O'Connor, Kennedy, and Souter jettisoned most of the surrounding details of the earlier decision. They derided the trimester framework as a "rigid construct" and discarded it as not "part of the essential holding of *Roe.*" Instead of the trimester framework, the joint opinion articulated a new test. It provided that states could regulate nontherapeutic abortions before viability only to the extent that they did not unduly burden the fundamental right. Justice O'Connor had introduced the idea of an undue burden test as early as her dissent in *Akron* in 1983. In that incarnation, however, the test had two parts. First, if the regulation did not unduly burden the right, it was upheld unless the law was arbitrary or capricious. Second, if the law did constitute an undue burden, then the Court reviewed it under the classic and usually fatal strict scrutiny test. The new version had only one part: previability abortion regulations that were unduly burdensome were unconstitutional.

Since the meaning of the "undue burden" standard is not inherently obvious, the opinion sought to spell it out a little more clearly. According to the opinion, "A finding of an undue burden is a shorthand for the conclusion that a state regulation has the purpose or effect of placing a *substantial obstacle* in the path of a woman seeking an abortion of a nonviable fetus."[63] While this explanation is not terribly edifying, it makes it clear that a large proportion of the new rule is fact-based. Whether a particular regulation creates a substantial obstacle to a woman's exercise of her rights is an empirical question.

In some cases, the actual application of a standard such as the undue burden test clarifies how it might work in practice. Unfortunately, that was not true in *Casey.* The joint opinion applied the new test to the three main provisions of the Pennsylvania law, the twenty-four-hour waiting period, the parental consent condition for minors, and the spousal notification requirement. Joined by the dissenters, the joint opinion found that the informed consent–twenty-four-hour waiting provision was constitutional. In order to get to this result, however, the Court had to overturn two long-standing cases, *Akron* and *Thornburgh*. All of the justices, except Justice Blackmun, agreed that Pennsylvania's parental consent provision was constitutional. This was the one provision supported by precedent. However, joined by Justices Blackmun and Stevens, the Court concluded that spousal notification provisions were unconstitutional. Thus, having to wait a day to exercise a fundamental right and having to obtain parental consent are not unduly burdensome, but having to notify your spouse of your intention to exercise that right is an undue burden.

As regards the twenty-four-hour waiting provision, O'Connor, Kennedy, and Souter believed that the rationale was not arbitrary: "The idea that important decisions will be more informed and deliberate if they follow some period of reflection does not strike us as unreasonable, particularly where the statute directs that important information become part of the background of the decision." The Court found that, "because the informed consent requirement facilitates the wise exercise of that right, it cannot be classified as an interference with the right *Roe* protects."[64] Yet, after hearing extensive testimony on the subject, the trial court had reached a contrary conclusion. It found that for women without financial resources or who must travel long distances or have difficulty explaining their absence from work or home, the waiting provision was "particularly burdensome." Among numerous additional factual findings made by the district judge, he found that if the twenty-four-hour provision goes into effect, it

> will force every woman seeking an abortion in Pennsylvania to make a minimum of two visits to an abortion provider. Two trips to the abortion provider would subject many women to the harassment and hostility of anti-abortion protesters demonstrating outside a clinic. . . . Because most of plaintiff-clinics and plaintiff-physicians do not perform abortions on a daily basis, the mandatory 24-hour waiting period will result in delays far in excess of 24 hours. For the majority of women in Pennsylvania, delays will range from 48 hours to two weeks.[65]

The joint opinion, however, disingenuously observed that the lower court did not conclude that the increased costs and potential delays amounted to "substantial obstacles." "A particular burden is not," the three justices wrote, "of necessity a substantial obstacle."[66] Since the undue burden standard, now defined as a "substantial obstacle," was entirely new, the opinion did not explain how the district judge would have known that he should have used the magic words "undue burden" or "substantial obstacle," rather than "particularly burdensome."

The second provision, parental consent, was one of the most litigated and scientifically studied abortion regulations post-*Roe*. Under the Pennsylvania law, "an unemancipated young woman under 18 may not obtain an abortion unless she and one of her parents (or guardian) provides informed consent." As required by earlier case law, the Pennsylvania statute provides a judicial bypass procedure, whereby "a court may authorize the performance of an abortion upon a determination that the young woman is mature and capable of giving informed consent and has in fact given her informed consent, or that an abortion would be in her best interests." Because the Court had been "over most of this ground before," the joint opinion summarily dismissed the claim that parental consent provisions constitute an undue burden. Again, since the undue burden test was new, it was not obvious why the Court felt no need to apply it, even to a provision that passed muster under the old test. Additionally, the district court had found that this provision was particularly burdensome and, moreover, had actually used the magic words: "The requirement of parental informed consent for minor women seeking abortions adds significant expense and delay to the expense and delay already existing in the Act. Taken together," the lower court concluded, "the provisions of the Act, as applied to minors, will create layers of obstacles which would *unduly burden* a minor woman's ability to get an abortion."[67]

The ostensible purposes behind parental consent provisions include "the recognition and fostering of parent-child relationships, promoting counsel to a child in a difficult and traumatic choice, and providing notice to those who are naturally most concerned for the child's welfare."[68] Much like spousal notification provisions, parental consent was intended to help promote the good family. The Court recognized in its previous cases, however, that parental consent statutes could lead to problems in certain situations, especially including dysfunctional or violent families or where the pregnancy resulted from incest. Consent requirements also effectively gave parents veto power over the exercise of the right. In order to avoid these dire consequences, the Court had early on insisted that all parental consent and notification requirements be accompanied by the option of judicial bypass, allowing minors to obtain consent from their parents or petition the Court for permission to obtain the procedure. This seemingly compassionate allowance, upon greater reflection and after considering the research, turns out to be Kafkaesque in result.

In an extensive study of parental consent provisions, Professor Robert Mnookin found that, in the sample studied, "every pregnant minor who has sought judicial authorization for an abortion has secured an abortion."[69] In 90 percent of the cases, judges simply found that the minor was "mature." In all but five cases of the remaining 10 percent, the judges held that it was in the minor's best interest to have an abortion. And in those five, all of the young women eventually secured abortions. Brief reflection on these statistics reveals the obvious lesson. How can a judge rule that a minor is too immature to decide whether to have an abortion but that it is in her best interest to bear the child? One Superior Court judge, who reported that he once gave permission for an abortion to an eleven-year-old, complained that "the law puts judges in the ridiculous position of being rubber stamps."[70] It is for this reason that the trial court in *Casey* concluded that requiring a young woman to petition a court in order to obtain a surgical procedure that the court will grant almost as a matter of course, but without any guidance or counseling, was unduly burdensome. Indeed, such a scheme may be the very paragon of an undue burden. This is not to suggest that encouraging minors to obtain counsel from their parents is a bad idea or that states don't have legitimate and strong interests in facilitating family communications. But laws that burden fundamental rights—and the right is not diminished because the woman is not an adult—must be narrowly tailored to achieve their objective. Parental consent requirements that include judicial bypass allowances appear more attuned to interfering with the right to abortion than allowing the young woman to exercise it. Justice Marshall argued in an earlier case, "If the state truly were concerned about ensuring that all minors consult with a knowledgeable and caring adult, it would provide for some form of counseling rather than for a judicial procedure in which a judge merely gives or withholds his consent."[71]

The undue burden test gets stranger and stranger as we turn to the joint opinion's treatment of the spousal notification provision. The three justices found the factual findings of the lower court persuasive. They also cited additional social scientific studies that documented the dangers associated with spousal notification. "This information," the justices stated, "reinforce[s] what common sense would suggest. In well-functioning marriages, spouses discuss important intimate decisions such as whether to bear a child. But there are millions of women in this country who are the victims of regular physical and psychological abuse at the hands of their husbands." For these women, the opinion found, a requirement that they tell their husbands of their plans could trigger violence. Moreover, it does not matter that the affected group may be very small. "The analysis does not end with the one percent of women upon whom the statute operates; it begins there. . . ." The justices explained that "the proper focus of constitutional inquiry is the group for whom the law is a restriction, not the group for whom the law is irrelevant."[72]

The other justices registered varying degrees of astonishment at different parts of the joint opinion. Stevens and Blackmun agreed that the core of *Roe* should be retained, although Blackmun grieved over the loss of the remaining portions not deemed "central." Justice Stevens expressed bewilderment about how the opinion could invalidate spousal notification but sustain the waiting period. Both regulations affected a relatively small number of women seeking abortions, but affected them substantially. The district court had invalidated both provisions as "particularly burdensome" obstacles to the right to terminate a pregnancy. Finally, both lacked rational justifications. Spousal consent sought to legislate the good marriage and the waiting period presumed that women seeking abortions had yet to give their decisions serious consideration and thus should be forced to think about it some more, with the implicit message being that she made the wrong decision. As Stevens put it, the "mandatory delay thus appears to rest on outmoded and unacceptable assumptions about the decisionmaking capacity of women."[73]

Justice Scalia was considerably less charitable in his views of the cogency of the joint opinion. He began by stating unambiguously his opposition to the substantive due process right of an abortion. He compared abortion to bigamy, arguing that some issues fairly described as matters of liberty are, nonetheless, not protected by the Constitution. "I reach [the conclusion that abortion is not constitutionally protected] for the same reason I reach the conclusion that bigamy is not constitutionally protected—because of two simple facts: (1) the Constitution says absolutely nothing about it, and (2) the long-standing traditions of American society have permitted it to be legally proscribed."[74] Scalia, not known for his reticence, said he also had to "respond to a few of the more outrageous arguments in today's opinion, which it is beyond human nature to leave unanswered."[75]

He sneered at the joint opinion's "august and sonorous phrase," " 'Liberty finds no refuge in a jurisprudence of doubt.' " He said he would have understood finding such sentiments in a decision defending "the real *Roe v. Wade,* rather than the revised version fabricated today." He pointed out that "the shortcomings of *Roe* did not include lack of clarity." But, he said, "to come across this phrase in the joint opinion— which calls upon federal district judges to apply an 'undue burden' standard as doubtful in application as it is unprincipled in origin—is really more than one should have to bear."[76]

Scalia also criticized the joint opinion's retention of viability, which he decried as an arbitrary line. He accused the Court of being unable "to offer any justification for it beyond the conclusory assertion that it is only at that point that the unborn child's life 'can in reason and all fairness' be thought to override the interests of the mother." Scalia continued, asking, "Precisely why is it that, at the magical second when machines currently in use (though not necessarily available to the particular woman) are able to keep an unborn child alive apart from its mother, the creature is suddenly able (under our Constitution) to be protected by law, whereas before that magical second it was not? That makes no more sense than according infants legal protection only after the point when they can feed themselves."[77]

Finally, Scalia also could not fathom the joint opinion's undue burden test, which he described as rootless, or how it was applied in this case to sustain one particularly burdensome regulation but to invalidate another. Scalia said that "the approach of the joint opinion is, for the most part, simply to highlight certain facts in the record that apparently strike the three Justices as particularly significant in establishing (or refuting) the existence of an undue burden; after describing these facts, the opinion then simply announces that the provision either does or does not impose a 'substantial obstacle' or an 'undue burden.' " Scalia concluded, "Reason finds no refuge in this jurisprudence of confusion."[78] Scalia ended his opinion by comparing what the joint opinion sought to accomplish—"calling the contending sides of national controversy to end their national division"—with Chief Justice Roger Taney's similar quest in *Dred Scott.* Scalia predicted that similarly tragic results would be the consequence. Scalia then described the portrait of Taney that hangs prominently at the Harvard Law School, "an expression of profound sadness and disillusionment on his face." Taney also believed that he had called the opposing sides to accept "a common mandate rooted in the Constitution," as the joint opinion put it. Yet within two years Taney's reputation lay shattered, and he posed, "right hand hanging limply, almost lifelessly, beside the inner arm of the chair."[79]

As Scalia's taunt reveals, a primary goal of Justices O'Connor, Kennedy, and Souter in uniting to write the joint opinion was to finally be done with the subject. Abortion cases and abortion politics had plagued the Court for two full decades, from the moment *Roe* was first heard in 1972 until *Casey* was decided in 1992. Although, as illustrated by the five opinions, the Court was still badly divided over the issue, it was time to move on to other subjects. The nature of the undue burden test allowed states some leeway to enact regulations and was a flexible enough standard for lower courts to apply without being noticed on the general public's or the media's radar screens. Abortion was effectively buried in the federal judiciary's equivalent of the warehouse in which Indiana Jones stores the Ark of the Covenant at the end of the movie. Moreover, both sides could declare victory, often a prerequisite before armies can flee the field. *Roe* survived innumerable assaults and although bruised and battered, its central holding and main consequence remained intact. Also, for opponents of abortion, *Casey* permitted substantial regulation and produced a test so indefinite that lower federal court judges could do pretty much what they wanted with it. As long as the Republicans were stocking the federal judiciary, abortion regulations are likely to be received sympathetically. Largely proving Scalia wrong, the Court has not revisited the core issue of *Roe*'s continuing validity since *Casey*. Although laws regulating so-called partial birth abortions keep the issue on the front pages of the newspapers, the Court has shown little desire to rethink this area of the law.

The two decades spent wrestling with abortion was somewhat longer than the Court's usual infatuations with constitutional subjects. The Court regularly flirts with subjects for several years, typically over a span of five to ten, and then either solves the problem (or thinks it has) or throws up its hands, fashions a test of some sort, and leaves it to the lower courts to figure out. In the 1960s and early '70s, for example, the Court took on obscenity and the problem of distinguishing unprotected filth from protected filth. After numerous attempts, the justices finally realized, in Justice Potter Stewart's famous statement of exasperation, that they knew obscenity when they saw it but that they couldn't define it. Therefore, they devised the vague *Miller* test and thereafter left it to juries—the ultimate black boxes of the system—to do with it what they will. For the most part, unless you live in Cincinnati and you photograph crucifixes in urine, you don't have to worry about being prosecuted for obscenity. Many other subjects have similarly preoccupied the Court before it moved on to more pressing and seemingly more solvable concerns. Some of these subjects include busing, sexually violent predators, affirmative action, and religious symbols ranging from Christmas trees to menorahs.

Some subjects, however, the Court might visit and then decide to leave alone as not quite ready for decision. Many scholars believe that this would have been the wiser course with abortion, since legislatures had already begun reforming repressive laws of the nineteenth century. Allowing the democratic process to do its job is wise judicial statesmanship, or so the argument goes. Of course, if a fundamental right is at stake, then any delay on the Court's part constitutes a dereliction of its constitutional duties. There can be no blanket rule that democratic processes should be given free rein since, if a fundamental right is potentially endangered, the Court is obliged to step in. Whether or not such a right is at stake, of course, is very often the principal question presented.

The debate about the proper role of the Court in a democratic society has also occurred at the opposite end of life's spectrum from that of *Roe*. The subject of death and dying bears close constitutional similarity to abortion. One might wonder, if the Fourteenth Amendment is broad enough to include a right of reproductive choice—in which a mother has the discretion to kill the potential life of the fetus—must it not also be broad enough to include a right to kill oneself, at least under certain circumstances? The answer is yes and no and maybe. It turns out that death is every bit as complicated as birth, and the Court, possibly due to its experience on the one, has been somewhat reluctant to jump in too quickly on the other.

The Court's most extended discussion of the constitutional landscape of death and dying occurred in the 1997 case of *Washington v. Glucksberg*.[80] Plaintiffs were terminally ill patients and their doctors who claimed that the state of Washington's prohibition against "causing" or "aiding" a suicide offends the Fourteenth Amendment. More specifically, the plaintiffs claimed that a person who is terminally ill and mentally competent should have the right to choose what form his or her death would take and should necessarily have the right of a physician's assistance in exercising that right. Just as the right to terminate a pregnancy would not have much meaning without a doctor's assistance, the right to choose death would be greatly diminished without this professional help.

The first issue presented in most constitutional rights cases, and all due process cases, is what is the nature, or the definition, of the right in question. Although notions such as privacy, liberty, and autonomy present the abstract sense of what is at stake, they are too amorphous for the nuts and bolts task of due process analysis. At a sufficient level of generality, everything might fall within the realm of privacy or liberty, including personal drug use, bigamy, incest (with adults), and, even, bestiality. The objective in due process analysis is to determine whether the right being asserted is a fundamental right and thus one deserving of particular protection against state enforcement. Only a compelling government interest is enough to justify infringement of a fundamental right. To ascertain which rights are fundamental, the Court must search "our Nation's history, legal traditions, and practices." But this means that the Court must define the right before it begins searching. For example, at a sufficient level of generality, bigamy would be protected as part of the right to marry whomever you chose without interference by the state. But if defined too narrowly, then almost no right would be recognized. The Court would never have unanimously invalidated Virginia's anti-miscegenation law in the 1967 case of *Loving v. Virginia*[81] using a narrow definition of the right to marry, since our nation had a long tradition of banning interracial marriages. The *Loving* Court said, "Under our Constitution, the freedom to marry, or not marry, a person of another race resides with the individual and cannot be infringed by the State."[82] The right to marry was thus broad enough to ignore the nation's racial past, but not so broad that it would permit bigamy. Under the Court's precedent, the fundamental freedom to marry is limited to one person at a time. Thus, the definition of the constitutional question presented in the first instance is a matter of judgment.

In *Glucksberg*, the plaintiffs claimed that the right at stake could variously be described as "the liberty to choose how to die," or "the right to choose a humane, dignified death." Such a right undoubtedly finds deep support in our nation's history. The Court, with Chief Justice Rehnquist writing, said the right at issue was the "right to commit suicide which includes a right to assistance in doing so."[83] As so defined, the Court had little difficulty finding no basis in history to support such a right: "For over 700 years, the Anglo-American common-law tradition has punished or otherwise disapproved of both suicide and assisting suicide." For example, Henry de Bracton, one of the first legal-treatise writers, wrote in the thirteenth century, "Just as a man may commit felony by slaying another so may he do so by slaying himself." Rehnquist recognized that attitudes had changed considerably since Bracton lived— the state no longer confiscated a suicide's property—"but our laws have consistently condemned, and continue to prohibit, assisting suicide."[84]

The Court concluded that no general "right to die" exists in the Constitution. But this simple statement masks a great deal of complexity and *Glucksberg* will not be the final word. Indeed, the opinion was a study in avoiding the fine details of the issue. The Court wished to avoid stepping too far ahead of the nation, especially in this technologically challenging and swiftly evolving area. Chief Justice Rehnquist admitted as much: "Throughout the Nation, Americans are engaged in an earnest and profound debate about the morality, legality, and practicality of physician-assisted suicide. Our holding permits this debate to continue, as it should in a democratic society."[85] Justice O'Connor similarly invoked the prospect of democratic processes being permitted full opportunity: "Every one of us at some point may be affected by our own or a family member's terminal illness. There is no reason to think the democratic process will not strike the proper balance between the interests of terminally ill, mentally competent individuals who would seek to end their suffering and the State's interests in protecting those who might seek to end life mistakenly or under pressure."[86]

O'Connor, however, wrote separately to emphasize that the Court's holding did not foreclose later protection of a terminally ill patient's right to assistance in hastening death. The Court, she stated, merely found that the Washington statute prohibiting suicide was not invalid "on its face." This meant only that in most cases in which it is likely to be applied the law is constitutional. The Court's decision "does not foreclose the possibility that some applications of the statute might well be invalid." She explained: "Just as our conclusion that capital punishment is not always unconstitutional did not preclude later decisions holding that it is some-times impermissibly cruel, so it is equally clear that a decision upholding a general statutory prohibition of assisted suicide does not mean that every possible application of the statute would be valid." In particular, O'Connor contemplated a case in which a mentally competent person who is terminally ill and suffering excruciating pain seeks a physician's help to facilitate the end. "The liberty interest at stake in a case like this," O'Connor said, "is an interest in deciding how, rather than whether, a critical threshold shall be crossed." "Avoiding intolerable pain and the indignity of living one's final days incapacitated and in agony is certainly," she observed quoting *Casey,* " 'at the heart of [the] liberty . . . to define one's own concept of existence, of meaning, of the universe, and of the mystery of human life.' "[87]

Justice Souter also wrote separately to emphasize the interim nature of the *Glucksberg* decision. His opinion reads in part as an ode to Justice Harlan's perspicacity and in part as a master's-level thesis on Harlan's substantive due process jurisprudence as set forth in *Poe v. Ullman.* In essence, Souter put his finger on the crux of the matter, especially as regards reconciling Rehnquist's majority opinion finding no right to assisted suicide and O'Connor's presaging the next case down the line, which presents the sympathetic situation of the competent terminally ill patient in debilitating pain who wants to choose a dignified end to a dignified life. Souter wrote that the state has no interest in denying such an individual his or her choice of how to die. But the state fears the slippery slope that once a procedure is set in place that permits some to freely choose death, others will be encouraged or even forced into this choice. "The nub of this part of the State's argument is not that such patients are constitutionally undeserving of relief on their own account, but that any attempt to confine a right of physician assistance to the circumstances presented by these doctors is likely to fail."[88] According to Souter, "The case for the slippery slope is fairly made out here . . . because there is a plausible case that the right claimed would not be readily containable by reference to facts about the mind that are matters of difficult judgment, or by gatekeepers who are subject to temptation, noble or not."[89]

Whether the state is correct that compassionate assistance in dying ineluctably leads to involuntary euthanasia, Souter said, is an empirical question. Chief Justice Rehnquist cited and discussed at length a study from the Netherlands designed to test this hypothesis. According to Rehnquist, the 1990 Dutch study reported "2,300 cases of voluntary euthanasia (defined as 'the deliberate termination of another's life at his request'), 400 cases of assisted suicide, and more than 1,000 cases of euthanasia without an explicit request." More profoundly disturbing, Rehnquist reported that, in addition to those thousand cases, "the study found an additional 4,941 cases where physicians administered lethal morphine overdoses without the patients' explicit consent." Rehnquist concluded that the Dutch "study suggests that, despite the existence of various reporting procedures, euthanasia in the Netherlands has not been limited to competent, terminally ill adults who are enduring physical suffering, and that regulation of the practice may not have prevented abuses in cases involving vulnerable persons, including severely disabled neonates and elderly persons suffering from dementia."[90]

Justice Souter, however, found the empirical record more mixed. On the one hand, some commentators found that Dutch guidelines have "proved signally ineffectual; non-voluntary euthanasia is now widely practiced and increasingly condoned in the Netherlands."[91] Other researchers have found the opposite, that "Dutch physicians are not euthanasia enthusiasts and they are slow to practice it in individual cases." Souter concluded that he could not say with any "assurance which side is right." He also doubted "whether an independent frontline investigation into the facts of a foreign country's legal administration can be soundly undertaken through American courtroom litigation." Given the "nascent" state of the subject, "the most that can be said is that whichever way the Court might rule today, events could overtake its assumptions, as experimentation in some jurisdictions confirmed or discredited the concerns about progression from assisted suicide to euthanasia."[92]

This last statement raises a ticklish problem for the intersection of the Constitution and social fact. Souter believes that, on average, legislatures are to be preferred over courts for obtaining the facts necessary for a constitutional judgment. He believes them to "have more flexible mechanisms for fact-finding than the judiciary," as well as "the power to experiment, moving forward and pulling back as facts emerge within their own jurisdictions."[93] Souter recognizes that there will be times when courts will have to act regardless of this general institutional preference for legislative experimentation and fact-finding. He cited segregation as an example when the Court had to act irrespective of legislative study.

But ordinarily, he argued, the Court would be well advised to wait for development of the factual record.

Justice Souter's argument rests on two principal assumptions. One, the age-old belief that legislatures are better fact-finders than courts, is a dubious proposition at best. Even if legislatures are better able to conduct experiments and collect data, there is little reason to believe that these hotbeds of politics and special interests are better able to interpret the results of these experiments or implement the policies these outcomes recommend. The second and somewhat less dubious assumption is that constitutional law should be stable and that premising it on changeable facts would undermine its force. "An unenumerated right should not therefore be recognized," Souter argued, "with the effect of displacing the legislative ordering of things, without the assurance that its recognition would prove as durable as the recognition of those other rights differently derived." Souter continued, stating that the "experimentation that should be out of the question in constitutional adjudication displacing legislative judgments is entirely proper, as well as highly desirable, when the legislative power addresses an emerging issue like assisted suicide."[94] Souter believes that the Court's decision whether the right to die is constitutionally based should await state experimentation to determine whether there is a workable stopping point between assisted suicide and involuntary euthanasia. He stated that the Court should "stay its hand" until the state legislatures had ample opportunity to study the question.

Justice Souter missed the point. The existence of an unenumerated right to assisted suicide should not depend on whether procedural protections can be constructed to avoid having the right to die turn into the duty to die. This factual issue, the subject of the Dutch research and Souter's hoped-for subject of future American research, concerns the government's interest in curtailing the claimed right to die. The fundamental right to autonomy over death, if it exists, exists separately from the government's claimed reasons for regulating it. By analogy, states have often sought to regulate violent pornography on the basis that it makes consumers of it more prone to be violent. Violent pornography falls within the protection of the First Amendment's guarantee of free speech. This means, and the Court has so held, that violent pornography cannot be prohibited until the government demonstrates empirically that it causes violence. Thus, the right is protected first, and government claims of compelling reasons to permit regulation of it must be proved—a demand that might take considerable time and effort on the part of legislatures. Contrary to Souter's argument, this has not interfered with public officials studying the issue of the effects of violent pornography and, indeed, this topic has been the subject of substantial research attention as well as two presidential commissions. The free speech right exists, and will continue to be protected, until legislatures develop sufficient proof to demonstrate a compelling interest to justify infringements of that fundamental right. There is no reason why exactly the same sort of analysis should not apply to assisted dying.

Recognizing that the Constitution evolves as society—and, more particularly, our factual understanding of society—changes does not make the Constitution any less "durable" than Souter's institutional deference to legislatures in *Glucksberg*. In his universe, the Constitution "changes" if the legislative answer is that procedural protections can be instituted to ensure that assisted dying does not become forced euthanasia. At that point in time, the *Glucksberg* ruling would have to be "amended" to permit the right to die so long as it is accompanied by whatever procedural protections the states come up with to prevent involuntary euthanasia. In the alternative, the Constitution "changes" if assisted dying is protected today, but legislatures demonstrate tomorrow that procedural controls are ineffective. States would have demonstrated that they have a compelling interest in prohibiting all assisted suicides, because the practice cannot be limited to the small group in which it is appropriate. The only question is what is to be the default position. In the absence of sound empirical research one way or the other, does assisted suicide receive constitutional protection or does it not? Whether the right exists is not an empirical question. In *Glucksberg,* the Court answered this question in the negative. It is likely to have to return to it before long.

9

LIFTER OR LEVELER?:

Equal Protection in
the Land of Rugged Individualism

Once loosed, the idea of Equality is not easily cabined.

— ARCHIBALD COX (1966)

The Court confronts two basic problems when defining the equality guaranteed by the Constitution. The first is knowing when a problem of inequality exists and the second is knowing when it has been solved. The Fourteenth Amendment guarantees the equal protection of the laws, a dictate that has never been thought to ensure equal outcomes. At most, it guarantees equal opportunity. The Constitution does not warranty results. But what does according equal opportunity mean? Treating people equally, or fairly, does not mean treating all people the same. It is just as discriminatory to treat alike those who are different as to treat differently those who are alike. Competitors in a footrace are presumably treated fairly if they all begin from the same spot at the sound of the starter's gun. But does this race accord equal treatment to the deaf or physically disabled competitor? And if disadvantaged competitors are accorded due advantage, is the race still a race? More challenging still, equality is fundamentally at odds with liberty. The notion of equality uses the group as its litmus test, anticipating that those falling behind the group will be enabled to catch up, limiting the degree that others can be permitted to get too far ahead. Liberty applauds difference, while equality acclaims collective similarity. Equality lifts and levels, while liberty separates the wheat from the chaff. The Constitution guarantees you the liberty to follow your unique path in life and every other person the equality to share that path with you.

It is an abiding faith of American philosophy that all people are unique. We are all different, having been born to rich or poor parents, in urban or rural communities, with greater or lesser natural talents in math or music and with more or less generous physical and emotional endowments. The Constitution, however, does not guarantee equality when these sorts of differences are involved. For instance, I cannot claim discrimination in not being hired to be the director of a nuclear plant because I was born or bred with poor math skills any more than that my poor physical coordination permits me to claim discrimination in being excluded from the PGA Tour. Yet if my disability is a circulatory disorder (Klippel-Trenaunay-Weber syndrome), as was true with Casey Martin, I have at least a colorable claim to unfair treatment in not being allowed to use a golf cart—at least if the golf tournament is state sponsored, since the Fourteenth Amendment only applies to state action. (Golfer Casey Martin brought his claim under a federal statute, rather than the Constitution, though the basic considerations regarding the meaning of equality are mostly the same in both contexts.)[1]

The seeming key to measuring equality would appear to be distinguishing relevant differences from irrelevant differences where relevance is situation specific. Under this general guideline, relevant differences could legally be taken into account for purposes of discriminating among people and irrelevant differences could not. The trick lies in distinguishing the relevant from the irrelevant difference. In a footrace, the whole point—usually—is the running. A deaf competitor might validly argue that he or she should be accommodated, whereas the competitor with one leg might not. But this all depends on what the definition of a race is, which, in many contexts, from sports to jobs, is a somewhat arbitrary decision, usually based on traditions or practices emanating from a less enlightened time. In the case of Martin and the golf tour, the question of fairness concerned whether walking was an integral part of the game of golf. If so, it would be a relevant difference, and allowing Martin to ride would be unfair to the other golfers who, according to the rules, must walk. The alternative of allowing everyone to ride would solve the problem of equality, but it still might not be fair. It would be unfair, at least, to the golfers who had worked long hours to get into shape for a sport that did not allow players to ride. In effect, the walkers would argue, allowing everyone to ride would change the rules and effectively transform the nature of the game they played.

In the *Martin* case, the Court held that the PGA must accommodate Martin's disability and allow him to ride. The Court determined that walking was not an essential aspect of the game of golf. It found golf to be the same sport whether a player walked the pristine and gentle slopes of a course or rode a cart from shot to shot. The Court rejected the expert testimony of Arnold Palmer and Jack Nicklaus, both of whom said that the fatigue associated with walking eighteen holes over four consecutive days of a tournament inevitably affected *golfers' performances* and was an integral component of the competition. Instead, the Court found a physiologist's testimony to be persuasive:

> The fatigue from walking during one of petitioner's 4-day tournaments cannot be deemed significant. . . . A professor in physiology and expert on fatigue . . . calculated the calories expended in walking a golf course (about five miles) to be approximately 500 calories—"nutritionally . . . less than a Big Mac." What is more, that energy is expended over a 5-hour period, during which golfers have numerous intervals for rest and refreshment. In fact, the expert concluded, because golf is a low-intensity activity, fatigue from the game is primarily a psychological phenomenon in which stress and motivation are the key ingredients. And even under conditions of severe heat and humidity, the critical factor in fatigue is fluid loss rather than exercise from walking.[2]

Moreover, the Court concluded, allowing players to ride would not change the basic nature of the game. Golf, Justice John Paul Stevens stated, was merely "using clubs to cause a ball to progress from the teeing ground to a hole some distance away with as few strokes as possible." Shot-making, not walking, was the soul of golf. This fundamental aspect of the game is reflected in the very first of the "Rules of Golf," the Court declared, quoting those rules: " 'The Game of Golf consists in playing a ball from the teeing ground into the hole by a stroke or successive strokes in accordance with the rules.' Over the years," the Court observed, "there have been many changes in the players' equipment, in golf course design, in the Rules of Golf, and in the method of transporting clubs from hole to hole. Originally, so few clubs were used that each player could carry them without a bag. Then came golf bags, caddies, carts that were pulled by hand, and eventually motorized carts that carried players as well as clubs." The walking rule, the Court concluded, "is not an essential attribute of the game itself."[3] Mark Twain described golf as "a good walk spoiled." For the *Martin* Court, it was a good ride spoiled, too.

Historically, however, the Court has mainly avoided large-scale constitutional review of the equality of treatment afforded every group negatively affected by particular laws. It has done so by limiting the number of groups that receive judicial solicitude. Having been born into poverty or being slow in math are not classifications that receive substantive constitutional protection. If such classifications did receive close judicial attention, the Court would be very busy indeed. Virtually every law discriminates against one group or another, almost as a matter of course. As mentioned earlier, laws protecting spotted owls discriminate against loggers and minimum drinking ages discriminate against the young. Tax, social welfare, and zoning regulations all discriminate against easily identified groups. Interest-group politics is about winners and losers, and too broad a view of the Equal Protection Clause would mean that every group that lost in the legislative or administrative process would seek redress in the courts. Thus, the first order of business is identifying which groups qualify for heightened judicial attention.

The primary beneficiaries of the Fourteenth Amendment when it was adopted in 1868 were the newly emancipated slaves. At that time, the focus of the amendment was on ensuring equality of rights for African-Americans. Laws that explicitly drew lines based on race were invalidated, as in *Strauder v. West Virginia* (1879),[4] in which the Court struck down a law that denied African-Americans the right to sit on juries. From the start, race was broadly conceived, as illustrated by *Yick Wo v. Hopkins* (1886),[5] in which a law regulating laundry licenses, but that did not overtly discriminate against Chinese applicants, was struck down because it was almost uniformly applied to disadvantage them. In *Plessy v. Ferguson,*[6] however, the Court took a giant stride sideways, in holding that segregation in public transportation passed constitutional muster, so long as "equal" facilities were provided. The desuetude of Fourteenth Amendment protection that began with *Plessy* continued through the first half of the twentieth century.

In 1938, and marking the way for the rest of the twentieth century, albeit buried in a footnote, the Court in *United States v. Carolene Prod-*

ucts[7] stated that it would review with special care laws that imposed disabilities on "discrete and insular minorities." Although this designation clearly included African-Americans, the original beneficiaries of the law of equal protection, it also suggested a potentially broad expanse for the clause as well as considerably expanded powers for the Court. The more groups included and the more settings considered, the greater the Court's power to second-guess the decisions of the other branches of government and of the states—especially the states. Not long after *Carolene Products,* the Court held in *Korematsu v. United States*[8] that it would bring the highest level of review, strict scrutiny, to classifications based on race. Despite the Court's laxity in actually carrying out this test in *Korematsu,* strict scrutiny would become a potent weapon in the Court's arsenal. Indeed, in Professor Gerald Gunther's memorable words, for a time, this test was "strict in theory but fatal in fact."[9] Today, the test is somewhat less draconian in application. In fact, the test is no longer consistently applied from context to context. It is conceptually strict, but highly malleable in practice. Nonetheless, short of the few per se rules in constitutional law, it is as serious as the Court gets in reviewing the actions of the coordinate branches of government and the states.

As a practical matter, most legislatures no longer explicitly draw classifications that are intended to disadvantage blacks or other racial or ethnic minorities. Modern sensibilities have driven invidious discrimination underground. Still, many laws that do not discriminate on their faces have deleterious consequences that disparately affect one or more "discrete and insular minorities." Ordinarily, however, disparate impact alone is not enough to trigger close judicial review. Only when the totality of the circumstances surrounding the enactment or imposition of the law indicates that its purpose was discriminatory does the Fourteenth Amendment invalidate it. But proving purposeful discrimination often requires considerable work. This lesson is manifest in the short life and violent death by lethal injection of Warren McCleskey.

McCleskey was convicted of killing a white Atlanta police officer in 1978 during the course of a robbery and sentenced to death. His case would become one of the most significant challenges to the death penalty ever waged. It began, however, very much the way most of these sorts of cases begin, with a senseless murder, a hapless defendant, and a less than competent defense counsel. McCleskey's defense at trial rested on an alibi claim and he testified in his own defense. Unfortunately for his prospects, he had confessed to the crime and reportedly had admitted to a jailhouse informant that he had pulled the trigger. He even described to the informant his plan to fabricate an alibi that he had spent the afternoon of the robbery playing cards at his sister's house. On the stand, McCleskey told the jury that the police coerced his confession and he denied ever having met the prosecution's informant. But the state's case was too much, especially for McCleskey's anemic defense. His counsel, John Turner, had been retained by McCleskey's sister because she distrusted public defenders. Turner, a solo practitioner, was hired for the ridiculously paltry set price of $2,500. Turner proved worthy of his fee. He failed to interview witnesses, and he did not even look at the prosecution's case file—containing witness statements and police reports—until the Friday before the Monday trial. Because McCleskey claimed an alibi, Turner considered the evidence regarding the shooting to be peripheral to his defense strategy. The jury deliberated a mere two hours before returning a guilty verdict; after hearing little in the way of mitigating circumstances, they took only two hours more to decide that McCleskey deserved a sentence of death.

The appellate process in *McCleskey v. Kemp*[10] unfolded initially in the same routine fashion that the trial had gone, albeit with much-improved counsel. His appellate counsel, Robert Stroup, had volunteered to do a capital case pro bono, although his regular practice involved suing employers for race or sex discrimination. He thought it important that lawyers give something back to their communities and he figured that contributing his time to death penalty appeals would be a good way to do so. *McCleskey* was his reward. Stroup had the good sense to consult with the death penalty experts at the NAACP's Legal Defense Fund (LDF), who agreed to review his work and consult on the case. Stroup's pleadings employed the age-old strategy of alleging an assortment of errors, hoping that one might resonate with the appellate panels. None did. His best argument seemed to be the claim that McCleskey's trial counsel had provided ineffective assistance. While this may have been so, the claim is virtually impossible to win. The defendant must show not only that his counsel was incompetent, but that the outcome would have been different if he had received effective counsel. After exhausting his options with the Georgia state courts, Stroup filed a habeas corpus petition in federal court. Judge Owen Forrester, a Reagan appointee and former drug enforcement prosecutor, found nothing in McCleskey's petition that warranted relief and he denied the petition without even holding a hearing. Just then, fate stepped in and changed the course of the litigation, if not its eventual denouement.

Around the time McCleskey's petition reached Judge Forrester's courtroom, the results of an extensive study on the Georgia death penalty scheme became available. The research team was led by David Baldus, a University of Iowa law professor. The objective of the study was to examine every variable imaginable to determine which ones most influenced the death penalty decision. Many armchair psychologists had long hypothesized that race would be found to be a significant predictor of who received death sentences. And it was, but in a somewhat surprising way. After examining approximately 230 variables, and employing highly complex but well accepted statistical techniques, Baldus concluded that, *all things being equal,* "defendants charged with killing white victims were 4.3 times as likely to receive a death sentence as defendants charged with killing blacks." The basic sentencing rates for each category follow:

Race of Defendant	Race of Victim	Death Sentencing Rates
Black	White	.21 (50/233)
White	White	.08 (58/748)
Black	Black	.01 (18/1443)
White	Black	.03 (2/60)

Despite the obvious dangers of using the Baldus data in McCleskey's profoundly weak factual case—the killing of a police officer during a robbery in which the defendant confessed to the killing—the LDF decided to present the research to Judge Forrester. It was a substantial gamble, since novel claims, especially complicated scientific ones, are often colored by the trappings of the case in which they are framed. McCleskey's trappings stunk. Nonetheless, they filed a motion for reconsideration and request for a hearing with the Baldus data in hand. McCleskey's legal team, now joined by Jack Boger from LDF, claimed that Baldus's data indicated discrimination on the basis of race that violated both the Fourteenth and Eighth Amendments. Judge Forrester's curiosity got the better of him and he granted the hearing.[11]

In order to persuade the judge that they had considered every possible detail, Boger and Baldus conceived of the idea of inviting the prosecutor and the judge to suggest factors that they believed might explain the observed disparities. The prosecutor refused to go along, but Judge Forrester suggested several variables that he thought might explain why black defendants who killed whites were disproportionately sentenced to death. When Baldus ran these factors in his model, the factors actually increased the odds multiplier from the 4.3 originally obtained.[12] In the end, however, Judge Forrester was not persuaded. In rejecting McCleskey's petition, he criticized the data-gathering methods used by Baldus and his colleagues and challenged the reliability and validity of the statistics the researchers relied upon. In the inevitable law review debate over the *McCleskey* litigation, scholars—including Baldus and his colleagues—severely criticized Forrester's scientific and statistical acumen. He was accused of making basic mathematical errors and of not fully understanding the details of the underlying statistics or research methods. On appeal, the Eleventh Circuit Court of Appeals avoided the numerical quicksand in which Judge Forrester had sunk by assuming the validity of the Baldus data and conclusions. The appellate court concluded that, despite this assumption, McCleskey's conviction did not violate the Constitution. The next step was the Supreme Court.

Many of the justices were exceedingly fearful of agreeing to hear *McCleskey*. It combined two of the more emotionally charged and troubling issues that face the Court, race and capital punishment. Complicating matters further, the principal proof of a constitutional violation was a complex statistical study that lay well beyond most of their expertises. Justice Lewis F. Powell Jr., the eventual author of the *McCleskey* decision, told his biographer that he had little understanding of statistics and it was clear from his opinions that he had no interest in obtaining any.[13] In the 1978 case of *Ballew v. Georgia,*[14] for example, Powell had derided Justice Harry Blackmun's heavy reliance on social science studies to set the constitutional lower limit of jury size at six and compared statistics to numerology. However, since only four votes are needed to hear a case, Justices Brennan, Marshall, Blackmun, and Stevens—the four eventual dissenters—brought *McCleskey* to the Court's docket. Several of the justices' clerks, including one of Rehnquist's, urged that the Court retain a special master in order to assist them with the intricacies of the research. The justices declined this advice.[15]

The Supreme Court, hoping to avoid the embarrassment of the district court and following the lead of the circuit court, assiduously avoided any substantive evaluation of the Baldus study, though it offered gratuitous criticisms. Instead, the Court simply assumed the validity of the study's conclusions and held that the Constitution was not offended by the Georgia death scheme's discrimination on the basis of the race of the victim. Justice Powell's opinion for the Court examined the Fourteenth Amendment and the Eighth Amendment claims separately.

Justice Powell stated that "a defendant who alleges an equal protection violation has the burden of proving 'the existence of purposeful discrimination' " that " 'had a discriminatory effect' on him." Thus, "McCleskey must prove that the decision-makers in his case acted with discriminatory purpose."[16] This would prove hard to do. Statistical data, by their nature, are ill-suited to demonstrating particularized purposeful discrimination. Baldus's data indicated that juries in Georgia took race of the victim into account, effectively finding that killing a white person was more egregious than killing a black person. Since, by their nature, statistics summarize large amounts of data regarding populations, they can only illuminate the system as a whole, and can cast little light on individual cases. In addition, the three key decision-makers in capital cases—the prosecutor who decides whether to seek the death penalty, the jury who decides whether to impose it, and the judge who presides over the trial and who enters judgment when it is over—are not likely to admit that they discriminated. Since their deliberative processes are not open to public inspection, the stench of discrimination may never escape the inner recesses of the prosecutor's shuttered office, the black box of the jury room, or the judge's cloistered chambers. And even if researchers could put the decision-making process under a microscope, discriminatory intent might not be readily observable. When discrimination occurs, it may be largely unconscious, given that the explanation for Baldus's results appears to be that Georgia juries value white lives more than black lives. This sentiment is the sort that can lurk deep in the foundational values by which Georgians, and many others, measure events around them. In any case, Powell concluded that given the importance of upholding states' criminal laws against murder and the inevitable discretion inherent in carrying out these laws, more than a naked statistical showing was necessary to establish an equal protection violation.

McCleskey's second ground, that the Georgia scheme constituted cruel and unusual punishment, appeared to rest on firmer footing. Under the Court's prior cases, the death penalty could "not be imposed under sentencing procedures that create a substantial *risk* that the punishment will be inflicted in an arbitrary and capricious manner."[17] Precedent provided that a defendant did not need to prove that race affected *his* sentencing decision. The Eighth Amendment's concern was always the "sentencing system as a whole." The petitioner, therefore, could establish a constitutional violation by demonstrating a "pattern of arbitrary and capricious sentencing." This sort of systemwide perspective was and is especially well suited to statistical proof.

The Baldus study appeared to have substantiated just such a "pattern of arbitrary and capricious sentencing." Justice William Brennan, in his dissenting opinion, summarized some of the inferences that flowed from the Baldus study, as follows:

> For the Georgia system as a whole, race accounts for a six percentage point difference in the rate at which capital punishment is imposed. Since death is imposed in 11% of all white cases, the rate in comparably aggravated black-victim cases is 5%. The rate of capital sentencing in a white-victim case is thus 120% greater than the rate in a black victim case. Put another way, over half—55%—of defendants in white-victim crimes in Georgia would not have been sentenced to die if their victims had been black. Of the more than 200 variables potentially relevant to a sentencing decision, race of the victim is a powerful explanation for variation in death sentence rates—as powerful as nonracial aggravating factors such as a prior murder conviction or acting as the principal planner of the homicide.[18]

Confronted with this powerful demonstration of how race infects capital decisions, the Court decided to change the law rather than stop the practice. Ordinarily, the Court prefers to manipulate the facts when they prove inconvenient. In *McCleskey,* it was easier to change the law than dispute the facts. Justice Powell, therefore, accepted that "some risk" of racial prejudice might influence a jury's decision. But this was not enough. "At most," Powell stated, "the Baldus study indicates a discrepancy that appears to correlate with race."[19] One commentator observed that this statement was akin to saying that, "at most, studies on lung cancer indicate a discrepancy that appears to correlate with smoking."[20]

Justice Powell's opinion rejected the perspective of the prior case law in which merely a substantiated risk of arbitrary and capricious decisions in the system as a whole was deemed cruel and unusual. Instead, Powell turned the Eighth Amendment into a redundancy, finding that McCleskey could prevail only if he proved that racial considerations infected *his* jury—effectively the same standard as under the Fourteenth

Amendment. This requirement rendered the statistical proof irrelevant. "Even Professor Baldus," Powell stated, "does not contend that his statistics prove . . . that race was a factor in McCleskey's particular case."[21] Discounting this statistical risk, Powell argued that the sort of discretion that permitted variation in the infliction of capital punishment was basic to the criminal justice system. Indeed, Powell raised the concern that "McCleskey's claim, taken to its logical conclusion, throws into serious question the principles that underlie our entire criminal justice system." Powell then retreated behind a venerable standby, suggesting that data like those urged here "are best presented to the legislative bodies." "Legislatures," Powell asserted, "are better qualified to weigh and evaluate the results of statistical studies in terms of their own local conditions and with a flexibility of approach that is not available to the courts."[22] Of course, as is true in other contexts, this extolling of legislative numeracy begs the question entirely. If systemic discrimination constitutes cruel and unusual punishment, then the Constitution obligates the Court to invalidate state schemes that permit discrimination in the name of jury discretion. If it does not, then surely the legislature can consider the research data for what they are worth. But the fact that legislatures are presumed to be better consumers of empirical data than courts—a far from obvious proposition—says nothing about whether or not the Eighth Amendment was violated in Warren McCleskey's case.

The difficulty of proving purposeful discrimination has meant that most equal rights claims involving laws that do not explicitly employ race-based classifications are brought under civil rights statutes rather than the Constitution. Legislators learned long ago not to draw explicit distinctions based on race unless it is for the purpose of helping disadvantaged groups. Such affirmative action policies are discussed below. There remains one classification, however, that legislatures continue to employ.

On average, men and women differ physically, biologically, and temperamentally, and these differences have led to unequal treatment under the theory that the Constitution does not require legislators to treat differently situated groups alike. Or, at least, that used to be the law. Under traditional equal protection doctrine, if the differences were not real— that is, if they were the product of stereotype or bias—or if real differences were not relevant to the job, sport, educational opportunity, or task at hand, the Constitution prohibited discrimination. Thus legislators could classify only when groups manifested "real differences" and only when those differences were relevant to the job or opportunity that was the subject of the discrimination. In the context of gender classifications, however, the Court is increasingly willing to contemplate whether the job, sport, educational opportunity, or task at hand must change in order to permit equal participation.

Suppose that golfer Casey Martin had claimed that his disability meant that he hit the ball fifty fewer yards than the average player. Would he have been allowed to tee the ball fifty yards closer to the hole than the other competitors? Presumably not, since the Court probably would have considered the distance from the tee to the cup to be an integral part of the game. Yet distances are not set forth in the original Rules of Golf any more than the PGA's prohibition on using carts. Moreover, it would not be Martin's fault that he cannot hit the ball as far as the other players. In recreational golf, women and seniors are usually permitted to tee the ball closer to the hole than men. Despite the real differences between men and these physically unequal competitors, fairness might demand accommodation on the principle of an equal opportunity to participate. Perhaps women and seniors should be allowed to compete on the PGA Tour from tees that are closer to the hole.

On average, women hit the golf ball significantly shorter distances than men, though many women hit the ball farther than many men. At the professional level, shorter hitters generally do not fare as well. Assuming that the shorter distances women hit golf balls is a consequence of physiological differences, was it fair, for example, to require Annika Sorenstam to hit from the same tees as the men when she played at the Colonial Golf Tournament in June 2003? Most coverage of the event made a point of saying that Sorenstam would play from the same tees, thus indicating her willingness to play on equal terms with the men. But were these terms truly "equal" given the objective physiological differences between most men and most women? Demanding this sort of equality is like having two runners begin at the same point at the same time, but requiring one racer to wear heels while permitting the other to wear running shoes. To be sure, a truly outstanding runner could win a few races in heels, especially against lesser competition, but on average this runner will lose most of the time. Sorenstam, in 2003, was the best women's golfer in the world and while she may have been able to play competitively in a men's league, there were very few others who could have done the same. If professional golf were to break down all gender barriers, as race barriers were long ago demolished, would women as a group welcome this development?

When Sorenstam played the Colonial, some men did not think it was fair to allow her to participate at all, whatever tees she used, since men cannot play on the women's tour. They argued the unfairness of having one mixed league and one league for women only. In college athletics, this quandary is resolved by statute under Title IX's mandate that schools provide the same number of playing opportunities for women as they provide for men. In college sports the principle of separate but equal largely applies, presumably on the basis of basic physiological differences between men and women. This is so despite the fact that some of these differences might turn out to be a function of cultural differences in regard to what sports girls and boys play growing up and the manner in which they play them. Maintaining segregation may have the untoward effect of preserving gender differences. If women do not regularly compete at the highest levels of the men's game, then they will never truly have the opportunity to rise to those heights.

In sports, the physiological differences between men and women become relevant partly because of the rules of the respective games. Many sports privilege strength and speed over agility and wits. Male domination of sport historically led to the adoption of rules tailored to male conceptions of competition and success. These rules have effectively handicapped subsequent generations of women largely because they are women. For instance, women would compete much more effectively in soccer and ice hockey if the rules in these sports more strictly regulated physical contact. The rules of any game, of course, are not ordained from above. As the Court observed in regard to golf in the *Martin* case, the rules of different sports change all of the time and for a multitude of reasons. Whether the rules of a particular game should change or remain the same is, therefore, a choice. Admittedly, while the rules of professional sports may indeed be "socially constructed," only the most starry-eyed dreamer could expect any wholesale reconsideration of these rules with an eye toward making sports more gender-inclusive. But the same is not true for other traditionally male bastions of exclusivity, such as law, medicine, and the military. In them, the Court is more inclined to reconsider basic premises, premises that are the product of history and traditions imbued with male-dominated value choices.

Two possible models thus suggest themselves. In one, the Sorenstam model, women would be integrated into preexisting, and primarily male, paradigms and allowed to succeed or fail more or less on the same terms as men. In many contexts, at least at first, this model would mean that only a small percentage of women would participate, since the rules and standards of the model would have been tailored to men's abilities and sensibilities. The Sorenstam model, however, leaves open the possibility that the paradigm itself might change slowly over time. In golf, this might mean shorter golf holes with narrower fairways, which would negate men's physical advantage in hitting the ball greater distances. In the second model, the Title IX model, men and women would be segregated. Men and women would compete separately and, other than the occasional promotional matchup that would occur in sports—undoubtedly trumpeted as the "war of the sexes"—rigid separation would be maintained between men's and women's leagues. Maintenance of this model may depend on the view that participation is more important than integration. Sports, in general, seem to argue for segregation, because of physical differences, though, historically, physically demanding professions, such as police or firefighting, were largely segregated as well. Segregation permits each gender to become fully realized within these differences, and the sensibilities of one are not imposed on the other. But segregation also excludes the small percentage of women who would compete successfully in a "man's world." Thus, rigid segregation bars the Annika Sorenstams from the fields, links, and workplaces in which men compete. The Sorenstam model permits women to compete equally with men. In practice, this means that initially women must compete according to male models of success but that, over time—possibly considerable time—the models themselves might begin to change to reflect attributes more commonly associated with women. Outside of sports, the Sorenstam model has increasingly become the ascendant archetype for arranging male-female institutional relationships.

In 1839, the state of Virginia established the Virginia Military Institute (VMI) in Lexington, Virginia, an all-male four-year college with the avowed goal of educating "citizen soldiers," men prepared for "leadership in civilian and in military service." Today, VMI cadets wear uniforms very similar to those worn by the original classes. Life at the Institute is spartan in both accommodation and conduct. Cadets are given identical haircuts, live four to a room, submit to frequent surprise inspections, and drill and march to and from class. A special hell is reserved for and visited upon first-year students, known as rats. They are forced to stand in "rat lines" and suffer the invective and revilement slung by upperclassmen. This daily barrage of vituperation is an integral part of the adversative method, a pedagogical system designed to tear down the rat and reconstruct him as a leader of men.

Over the years, VMI graduates have distinguished themselves on fields of battle and in corporate boardrooms. Thomas "Stonewall" Jackson was a VMI professor and a notorious Confederate general. Jackson earned his sobriquet for his defense of a ridge at the First Battle of Bull Run, an action that helped turn imminent defeat into a Confederate rout of the Union forces. VMI cadets fought Union troops at New Market, Virginia, in May 1864, though they entered the battle only as the South's situation became desperate. Many of the cadets were only fifteen, and when General Breckinridge gave the command, he said, "Put the boys in, and may God forgive me for the order." During the war almost eighteen hundred VMI graduates (about 94 percent of the total at the time) fought for their country—Virginia. From the start, VMI never considered admitting women to its program, since they could not then serve in the military. It was a practice that persisted, however, long after women began serving in the armed forces and despite Congress's decision in 1976 to admit women to West Point, Annapolis, and the Air Force Academy.[23]

In early 1989, a Virginia high school student—whose identity is a closely guarded secret—wrote to the Justice Department complaining that VMI would not accept her application because she was a woman. The letter reached sympathetic eyes and the Justice Department sent a letter of inquiry to VMI asking about their "alleged" policy of discrimination. The Institute considered the Justice Department's inquiry tantamount to a declaration of war and they mobilized their forces in response. Indeed, the Institute actually fired the first shot by bringing suit against the Justice Department. VMI wanted to pick the field of battle and it chose a courtroom in nearby Roanoke. The litigation would last three years longer than the Civil War, but the end was similar. The North prevailed and imposed its ideas of equality on the South.

On April 4, 1991, a six-day trial began in the matter of *United States v. The Commonwealth of Virginia*. It was tried before Judge Jackson L. Kiser, a graduate of neighboring Washington and Lee law school. A total of nineteen witnesses testified, including four experts on education, one expert on college facilities, and one expert on human physiology. Several issues were tried. The first was whether segregated schooling provided educational benefits to students beyond what coeducational programs might provide. A second question of fact involved the value of the unique methods of instruction employed at VMI, a model referred to as the adversative or doubting method. The adversative method was based on the English public school and was once characteristic of all military instruction. The trial court explained, "Physical rigor, mental stress, absolute equality of treatment, absence of privacy, minute regulation of behavior, and indoctrination in desirable values are the salient attributes of the VMI educational experience."[24] An important and hotly disputed component of this second question concerned whether the rigors of the adversative method would be effective for women. Finally, the trial court considered the question whether admitting women would fundamentally alter the VMI experience and thus undermine the special pedagogical benefits the institution had to offer its students. The VMI case displayed a cascade of factual issues that squarely presented the question of the meaning of equality between the sexes.

Experts for both sides agreed that segregated education benefits some students and serves important government interests. For example, the trial court cited one study, not challenged by any expert, that "demonstrates that single-sex colleges provide better educational experiences than coeducational institutions." According to this study, "Students of both sexes become more academically involved, interact with faculty frequently, show larger increases in intellectual self-esteem and are more satisfied with practically all aspects of college experience (the sole exception is social life) compared with their counterparts in coeducational institutions."[25] The benefits of single-sex education were found to transcend graduation as well, increasing success in carrying out plans in law and business and having a positive effect on salaries.

On the question of the educational benefits of the adversative method for producing citizen soldiers, all of the experts left unchallenged the proposition that initially treating male students like rats was an effective first step in leadership training. The subsidiary matters of the method's suitability for women and whether women would destroy VMI's rat culture were vigorously debated. The government insisted that some women were capable of handling the rat line and that their presence would not destroy VMI's exclusive perdition. The government's expert, Professor Carol Nagy Jacklin, from the University of Southern California's psychology department, conceded that "there are some average differences between men and women," but, she testified, "the average differences between men and women are trivial compared to the very large differences within the group of men and the group of women."[26] VMI did not challenge the assertion that a small number of women might be able to handle the adversative method, but its experts vehemently attacked the argument that VMI would not be ruined by the inclusion of women. Professor David Riesman, for example, a world-renowned educational scholar from Harvard, testified for VMI. He stated unequivocally that "if women were admitted to VMI the whole program would collapse." He observed that "VMI concentrated on breaking students down," whereas women "need more support, [they] lose self-confidence earlier." He explained that, at least since middle school, "women become oriented to [be] cheerleaders." If women were admitted, Riesman testified, "VMI would have to change so much that it would be hard to see what would be distinctive about it."[27] It would destroy VMI and, more generally, contribute to the general homogenization of American society, which, he said, "would be destructive for the country" as a whole.

The trial court ruled in favor of Virginia and VMI on all counts. It found the evidence to be "virtually uncontradicted" that "substantial educational benefits flow from a single-gender environment, be it male or female, that cannot be replicated in a coeducational setting."[28] This separation limited the distractions inherent in the other sex's presence, and permitted teaching strategies to be tailored to the strengths of men and women, respectively. Moreover, the court found, single-sex education contributed to the diversity of educational opportunities offered by the state, thus serving an important government interest. This diversity was "further enhanced," the court said, by the adversative training VMI students received, a form of "instruction which was applauded by all of the educational experts who testified." Finally, the trial court was persuaded by the evidence that the adversative method was not generally appropriate for educating women and that, therefore, admitting women to VMI would unalterably undermine the use of that method. The court credited the opinion of Dr. Richard C. Richardson, a professor of education at Arizona State University and a former marine, who testified that the "nature of an experience that is growth-producing for a majority of women, according to the literature, is one that is supportive, is one that emphasizes positive motivation." Richardson agreed that some women prefer, and would prosper, under the adversative model. "But you [do not] design educational experiences around the exception," he stated. "You have to design them around the rule, and I think you would find that the doubting model . . . the adversative model . . . would have to be gradually adapt[ed] so that it incorporated more of the positive motivation, positive reinforcement."[29] The district court decided that the adversative model, an efficacious teaching method for men, was inappropriate for most women, and admitting women into VMI would necessitate softening the hard edges of that model.

The United States appealed. The Fourth Circuit Court of Appeals affirmed all of the factual findings made by the lower court, but reversed on the law.[30] The court of appeals agreed with the lower court's findings regarding the benefits of single-sex education, the inherent value of the adversative method for males and its manifest unsuitability for females, and that admitting women to VMI would fundamentally alter the unique benefits of the Institute. Opening VMI's doors to women, the appeals court said, would put an end to the adversative method, would require stopping the practice of denying cadets all privacy—which was found to be "essential to the leveling process"—and would mean altering the school's physical training requirements in order to accommodate women's lesser abilities. For example, when Congress made the decision to admit women to West Point, it directed the Academy to make whatever changes were necessary in the physical requirements of the school. West Point "identified more than 120 physiological differences that exist between men and women." Although West Point tried "to accommodate those differences to the minimal extent necessary," admission of women to the army's elite academy had led to fundamental changes in that school's requirements and culture. The Fourth Circuit observed, accordingly, that admitting women to VMI would "deny those women the very opportunity they sought because the unique characteristics of VMI's program would be destroyed by coeducation."[31]

Despite these findings of fact, the Fourth Circuit held that, as presently constituted, Virginia's support of VMI violated the Equal Protection Clause. The Institute provided a valuable opportunity to men that it did not offer women. It accorded men the chance to become citizen-soldiers, an opportunity denied women. Virginia failed to articulate a sufficiently important government interest to justify this disparity. The court, therefore, reversed the lower court's ruling and returned the case to the trial court so that Virginia could remedy this unequal treatment. The appellate court directed that Virginia could pursue one of several alternatives. It could stop funding VMI, which would make the Institute private and thus not within the Fourteenth Amendment's purview; VMI could admit women; or Virginia could establish a parallel program for women, comparable to VMI, that would share the objective of producing citizen-soldiers. Virginia chose the third option.

Virginia first had to determine what a separate but equal system might look like. Prior to *Brown v. Board of Education*,[32] states had sought to establish mirror-image segregated schools for blacks and whites on the assumption that "separate but equal" meant "the same, albeit in different places." This assumption, however, was built on the publicly espoused view that there were no biological or other "real" differences between blacks and whites that would require different pedagogical styles. The claimed need for segregated schools was—at least publicly—sociological. Segregationists argued that both races would benefit from being educated "among their own kind." However, underlying this sociological argument was the deeply held belief among segregationists that blacks were inferior to whites and that commingling the two would lead to the degeneration of the "white stock." Gender was different. Biological differences are manifest and the belief in temperamental differences is widely embraced. Unlike race, in which it became unfashionable to speak of inherent biological differences, no such prohibition attached to discussion of the sexes. Men and women were not the same and commentators from feminist scholars to right-wing pundits celebrated the differences— though not always same differences. The big question, though, was whether these differences were relevant to how men and women should be taught.

In a case decided in 1993, shortly after the first round of the VMI litigation, the Fourth Circuit laid out the basic blueprint it believed necessary to satisfy "separate but equal" in gender cases:

> Any analysis of [a parallel program] in response to a justified purpose must take into account the nature of the difference on which the separation is based, the relevant benefits to the needs of each gender, the demand (both in terms of quality and quantity), and any other relevant factor. In the end, distinctions in any separate facilities provided for males and females may be based on real differences between the sexes, both in quality and quantity, so long as the distinctions are not based on stereotyped or generalized perceptions of differences.[33]

Separate education thus could be established to attend to real differences between men and women, but could not be based on stereotype or bias. After the case was returned to Judge Kiser's courtroom, Virginia established a task force of leading educators to examine the feasibility and determine the content of any parallel program. The task force returned with a proposal, later adopted by the state, that would found a state-sponsored program for women with the objective of producing citizen-soldiers. The program would be located at the Mary Baldwin College, a small women's college in northwestern Virginia, and would be called the Virginia Women's Institute for Leadership (VWIL). The task force combined its own experience and expertise with an in-depth study of the literature on the "developmental psychology of women and the cognitive development of women."[34] The task force concluded that while men and women both respond positively to single-sex education, they are predisposed to responding differently to the same training models. Where men gain strength through competition, women blossom through cooperation. Moreover, it would be unrealistic to expect women to enter VMI and be able to treat men, and be treated by men, the way cadets historically behaved toward one another. Although they did not quite put it this way, task force members believed men were from Mars and women from Venus, and it would be detrimental to put them on the same planet together. Dean Heather Anne Wilson, for instance, commented: "Young men will paddle their pledges; they will brand them; they will make them consume alcohol and make them eat disgusting things. . . . Young women will give flowers, write poems."[35] These differences, the experts on the whole believed, were not inherent or biological, they were cultural. Mary Baldwin's dean, James Lott, testified, for instance, that "our society has encouraged young women . . . [to] define our sense of self in relationships so that leadership development in women will occur most effectively on building on that fact rather than building on another theory or hypothesis about the ways women learn."[36] Hence, the differences between men and women were not a product of nature, but differences they were.

Not surprisingly, Judge Kiser found the task force's conclusions persuasive. He observed, approvingly, that the "Task Force determined that a military model and, especially VMI's adversarial method, would be wholly inappropriate for educating and training most women for leadership roles." Instead, the task force recommended a "cooperative method which reinforces self-esteem rather than the leveling process used by VMI."[37] The task force found, based on the extensive literature on this issue, that VMI's adversative method would not only be inappropriate for women but was likely to be counterproductive. Citing the opinion of a task force member, Dr. Elizabeth Fox-Genovese, the court observed that "most women reaching college generally have less confidence than men."[38] A model intended to undermine excessive confidence, to instill humility and promote identification with the group rather than the self, would be harmful to most women students. The self-affirming method of VWIL, the district court observed, "will produce the same or similar outcome for women that VMI produces for men." Judge Kiser concluded: "If VMI marches to the beat of a drum, then Mary Baldwin marches to the melody of a fife and when the march is over, both will have arrived at the same destination."[39]

The United States again appealed the trial court's ruling. The government objected that the basic approach taken by the task force was misguided. The task force had designed, and Virginia sought to implement, a program that would appeal to statistical averages and the broad middle ground of normally distributed female characteristics. The Equal Protection Clause, according to the government, afforded every individual the right to participate if she was otherwise qualified. The government stated that women, however few might desire it, should have the opportunity to enjoy the rigorous training of the adversative method provided by VMI. "The fact remains," the government argued, "that men have [this] special educational opportunity available to them and women do not." Accordingly, "this suit was brought on behalf of those women who want to go to VMI precisely because it is such a demanding and challenging school. The remedial plan approved by the district court does nothing for them." Equal protection, the government claimed, was measured one person at a time. Virginia could not rely on propensities or statistical averages and thereby deny even one individual the right to an equal education. The Fourth Circuit, however, disagreed and this time affirmed the trial court. It found that the VWIL program satisfied the demands of the Equal Protection Clause.[40]

The Fourth Circuit quoted from the brief submitted by Mary Baldwin College, which argued that a mirror-image program would have been "easier to design and defend." "But it would have been a paper program," the brief stated, "with no real prospect of successful implementation."[41] Instead, the task force crafted a program that was tailored to women's pedagogical needs, a model that would produce women leaders.

The court highlighted the statement of Dr. Heather Anne Wilson, a task force member, who said that "the VMI model is based on the premise that young men come with [an] inflated sense of self-efficacy that must be knocked down and rebuilt." In contrast, she explained, what women "need is a system that builds their sense of self-efficacy through meeting challenges, developing self-discipline, meeting rigor and dealing with it, and having success."[42]

The Fourth Circuit ruled that equal protection does not require Virginia to treat women and men the same in this area. It stated, "Equal protection of the law requires persons similarly circumstanced be treated alike, but equal protection does not deny states the power to treat different classes of persons in different ways."[43] Of course, the classification, the court said, must be the product of "reasoned analysis," and not a "mechanical application of traditional, often inaccurate, assumptions about the proper role of men and women."[44] The task force, the court ruled, found that men and women, on the whole, benefit from different styles of learning and thus constitute "different classes of persons" for educational purposes. The task force recommendation was a product of an extensive scholarly literature and many years of experience with the subject, not bias or prejudice. The Fourth Circuit echoed the trial court's factual findings that men and women respond differently to different models of leadership education—with men responding better, on average, to the deprivations of the adversative method and women responding better, on average, to a reinforcing and affirming method. These differences, both the trial and appellate courts concluded, were "real," and not the mere product of stereotype. The Fourth Circuit added, in conclusion, that "if we were to place men and women into the adversative relationship inherent in the VMI program, we would destroy . . . any sense of decency that still permeates the relationship between the sexes."[45]

In light of the publicity the case generated and the importance of the issues presented, most scholars expected the Court to agree to hear *United States v. Virginia*.[46] There was similarly little surprise that Justice Ruth Bader Ginsburg would write the opinion for the Court. It must have appeared to her as the Pacific did to Lewis and Clark, a vista filled with every possibility, reached at the culmination of an extraordinary journey.

Joan Ruth Bader was born on March 15, 1933, in Brooklyn, New

York. She excelled academically, graduating at the top of her class in high school, college, and law school. She met Martin Ginsburg her freshman year at Cornell and, following her graduation and in his first year at the Harvard Law School, they were married. The next year, 1955, she enrolled there, too. She again excelled and was invited to join the prestigious *Harvard Law Review*. When her husband was offered a job in New York City after graduation, she transferred to Columbia for her last year, where she served on the *Columbia Law Review*.[47]

The legal world in the mid-1950s was not a hospitable environment for women. There were only nine women out of five hundred students in her Harvard class. Ginsburg also faced initial difficulty obtaining a judicial clerkship, despite esteemed Harvard professor Gerald Gunther's efforts on her behalf. Eventually, she succeeded in obtaining a position with Judge Edmund L. Palmieri in the Southern District of New York. Her sense of unwelcome is summed up by an often-told story about her first year at Harvard. Dean Erwin Griswold asked the women students at a Harvard dinner, as was his practice every year, how they could justify taking a place that rightfully belonged to a man. Ginsburg describes the query as an attempt at humor, but it made her defensive and uncomfortable. She described what happened: "In those days I smoked, . . . and when it came my turn [to answer] the ashtray I was sharing with . . . Herbert Wechsler slid . . . onto the floor . . . All I could think of to say was that my husband was in the second-year class and it was important for a wife to understand her husband's work."[48]

Ginsburg would eventually devote her energies toward remedying the sexist attitudes and practices that she confronted on a near daily basis during much of her early career. Her principal objective was to obtain the same kind of protection for gender that race received under the Fourteenth Amendment. She understood that it was an uphill battle, since the drafters could not have intended to include women within the scope of the Equal Protection Clause. Women did not even have the right to vote until 1920 with the passage of the Nineteenth Amendment, though the women's suffrage amendment was first introduced in 1868, the year the Fourteenth Amendment was ratified. As Ginsburg put it in 1987, while serving as a judge on the United States Court of Appeals for the D.C. Circuit, "The Constitution remained an empty cupboard for sex equality claims."[49] She, however, had much to do with filling that cupboard. She founded and was general counsel to the American Civil Liberties Union

Women's Rights Project. She cowrote the brief in the 1971 case of *Reed v. Reed*,[50] in which the Court invalidated a law that displayed a preference for men over women as the administrators of estates. *Reed* was the first case in which the Court struck down a law on the basis of gender discrimination. Ginsburg had urged the Court to employ the strict scrutiny test, thus putting gender on the same plane as race. The Court disappointed her when it used the rational relationship test and divided over the question of whether gender qualified for strict review. Over the next five years, Ginsburg litigated several cases and in each asked the Court for strict review of gender-based discrimination. The Court eventually settled upon a compromise of sorts, and in 1976 set forth an intermediate standard of review in the case of *Craig v. Boren*.[51]

The *Craig* decision is interesting for many reasons beyond its being the first to formally hold that gender classifications receive heightened scrutiny under the Fourteenth Amendment. It was a case in which a man complained of unequal treatment. Thus, the Court made clear from the start that, just as with race, it is the classification, not the disadvantaged status of the alleged victim of discrimination, that garners the Court's attention. In other words, white men receive as much equal protection as blacks and women, at least as measured by the tests the Court applies to laws that discriminate on the basis of their being either men or being white. Chief Justice Rehnquist once described the Constitution as color-blind, since racial classifications, whether favoring whites or nonwhites, received close judicial scrutiny. In effect, *Craig* made the Constitution gender-blind as well.

Curtis Craig brought suit challenging an Oklahoma law that prohibited men under twenty-one years of age from purchasing "nonintoxicating" 3.2 percent beer while permitting women over eighteen years of age to buy it. Oklahoma justified the discrimination on the basis of statistical studies indicating that young men account for a disproportionate share of drivers arrested for driving while intoxicated. Under the intermediate scrutiny standard, Justice Brennan, writing for the Court, dismissed the statistical studies as methodologically weak and of little use. Brennan, however, was unsure of his science and so he decided not to leave well enough alone and rest on his empirical critique. He added the following apologia:

> There is no reason to belabor this line of analysis. It is unrealistic to expect either members of the judiciary or state officials to be well versed in the

rigors of experimental or statistical technique. But this merely illustrates that proving broad sociological propositions is a dubious business, and one that inevitably is in tension with the normative philosophy that underlies the Equal Protection Clause.[52]

This was a remarkable statement. How could the Supreme Court possibly scrutinize whether a state law "was substantially related to" an "important governmental objective" unless it understood the empirical basis asserted by the state? The *Craig* Court basically invalidated a law passed by the democratically elected representatives of Oklahoma by rejecting a justification that, by Brennan's own admission, he did not fully understand. It was irresponsible decision-making.

The intermediate standard seems to have been born of the belief that many more gender classifications might be justifiable than classifications based on race. Under the original strict scrutiny standard, laws that discriminated on the basis of race were virtually always invalidated. Use of such an uncompromising test in the gender context might have endangered the sundry discriminatory government programs, particularly including the military, that the Court (at least in the 1970s) did not anticipate disturbing. This again depended—and continues to depend—on the view that race is always an irrelevant consideration (at least for negative action as opposed to affirmative action), but gender will sometimes be relevant. The Court had consistently recognized that "real differences" exist between men and women and that, on occasion, these differences justify differential treatment. In *United States v. Virginia*, however, Justice Ginsburg served notice that gender classifications would receive close review, and possibly as close as race classifications.

Ginsburg had also been involved in *Craig*, as an author of an amicus brief, but she always considered the case as something of an embarrassment and referred to it as "that beer case."[53] It is interesting to note that in her decision in *Virginia*, Ginsburg did not cite *Craig* even once, despite the fact that it was the first case to set the established standard of review. In contrast, Ginsburg cited *Reed v. Reed* numerous times. In *Virginia*, Justice Ginsburg would write the opinion that attorney Ginsburg had sought to have the Court write in *Reed*.

Ginsburg announced in the VMI case that, in order to prevail, Virginia "must establish an 'exceedingly persuasive justification' for the classification."[54] Under the Court's precedents, she explained, "the defender of the challenged action must show 'at least that the classification serves important governmental objectives and that the discriminatory means employed are substantially related to the achievement of those objectives."[55] Although Ginsburg framed the legal standard as being situated deep in the Court's precedent, Chief Justice William Rehnquist and Justice Antonin Scalia, concurring and dissenting, respectively—and most commentators since—considered *Virginia* to mark a significant departure from the earlier standard. Prior cases focused on the intermediate nature of the judicial review that would be brought to bear on gender-based classifications. This intermediate scrutiny was usually contrasted with the strict scrutiny that racial classifications received. Race-based classifications would only be upheld if the government could demonstrate that the means it chose were *narrowly tailored* to a *compelling* government interest. The rule in gender cases was less demanding. In gender cases, the means only had to *substantially relate* to an *important* government interest. In earlier cases, the phrase "exceedingly persuasive" merely described the difficulty of meeting the intermediate scrutiny test. It was not itself a test. In *Virginia,* Ginsburg elevated this phrase to the center of the inquiry, putting greater bite in the old intermediate scrutiny test and nudging it closer to strict scrutiny. Indeed, at the very time the Court was moving the scrutiny of gender classifications toward the strictest level, it was ratcheting down the level of scrutiny of racial classifications toward an "exceedingly persuasive" standard. This ratcheting-down was necessary to permit at least the possibility that certain affirmative action programs might pass constitutional muster. In short, without being entirely candid about it, the Court has recently made efforts to make its race and gender standards consistent with one another.

In *Virginia,* Ginsburg accepted the inescapable fact that "physical differences between men and women . . . are enduring: The two sexes are not fungible; a community made up exclusively of one [sex] is different from a community composed of both."[56] These "inherent differences," Ginsburg commented, "remain cause for celebration, but not for denigration of the members of either sex or for artificial constraints on an individual's opportunity."[57] In an interview following the Virginia decision, Justice Ginsburg stated that yes, she did believe "differences [between the sexes] exist on average." She emphasized, however, that these "differences should not determine what people do with their lives." She exclaimed, "Do I think there's a difference? Yes. Do I think it matters for most occupations in life? No."[58] Gender classifications cannot be used, she wrote in *Virginia*, "as they once were, to create or perpetuate the legal, social, and economic inferiority of women."[59]

Ginsburg stated that Virginia offered two basic justifications for maintaining single-sex education at VMI and for establishing a separate but equal institution at Mary Baldwin College. The first involved the benefits from single-sex education itself, and the diversity of educational opportunities that these programs brought to the state. The second justification Virginia offered against integration was that "the unique VMI method of character development and leadership training, the school's adversative approach, would have to be modified were VMI to admit women."[60]

Ginsburg was unimpressed with Virginia's claim that VMI exemplified the state's commitment to diversity. History, she observed, suggested quite another story. In 1839, when VMI was founded, higher education "was considered dangerous for women." The nation's first universities excluded women, including such venerable institutions as Harvard College and the College of William and Mary. "In admitting no women," Ginsburg stated, "VMI [also] followed the lead of the Commonwealth's flagship school, the University of Virginia, founded in 1819." Ginsburg quoted Thomas Jefferson, the University of Virginia's founder, to illustrate the sentiment toward women of the time. "Were our state a pure democracy," Jefferson stated, "there would yet be excluded from their deliberation . . . women, who, to prevent depravation of morals and ambiguity of issue, could not mix promiscuously in the public meetings of men."[61] Not until 1972 did the University of Virginia begin to admit women on an equal basis with men.

Justice Scalia, dissenting, found Ginsburg's reprimand of the founding generation tendentious. He complained that "much of the Court's opinion is devoted to deprecating the closed-mindedness of our forebears with regard to women's education, and even with regard to the treatment of women in areas that have nothing to do with education." He agreed that they were closed-minded, "as every age is, including our own, with regard to matters it cannot guess, because it simply does not consider them debatable." But in their defense, Scalia pointed out, "They left us free to change. The same cannot be said of this most illiberal Court," Scalia charged, "which has embarked on a course of inscribing one after another of the current preferences of the society (and in some cases only the counter-majoritarian preferences of the society's law-trained elite) into our Basic law."[62]

Notwithstanding Scalia's reprimand, Ginsburg concluded that Virginia's diversity rationale was not sufficient to justify continued exclusion of women from VMI. She said that "a purpose genuinely to advance an array of educational options . . . is not served by VMI's historic and constant plan—a plan to afford a unique educational benefit only to males." She concluded that "however 'liberally' this plan serves the Commonwealth's sons, it makes no provision whatsoever for her daughters. That is not equal protection."[63] Moreover, and in any case, Ginsburg pointed out, Virginia's claim of diversity benefited only one sex. The corresponding single-sex parallel program at VWIL utterly failed to furnish the advantages available to men at VMI. VWIL's military training was lesser, the standards for admission were lower, the number of Ph.D.-holding faculty were fewer, the curriculum offered was narrower, the alumni base was smaller, and the physical facilities were inferior. By every objective measure of academic quality, VWIL failed in comparison to VMI. Ginsburg went so far as to compare Virginia's program at VWIL to Texas's segregation of African-Americans in legal education prior to *Sweatt v. Painter*. The Texas law school in *Sweatt* had no independent faculty, no library, and no accreditation.[64]

Turning to the second issue, the effect that admitting women would have on the Institute's core program, Ginsburg summarized Virginia's argument: "Men would be deprived of the unique opportunity currently available to them; women would not gain that opportunity because their participation would 'eliminat[e] the very aspects of [the] program that distinguished [VMI] from . . . other institutions of higher education in Virginia.' "[65] The situation in Lexington thus had all of the earmarks of a Greek tragedy. Women desired and deserved entrée to the sacred grounds of VMI, but their presence would destroy the very sanctity that they sought.

Ginsburg explained that the lower courts' rulings maintaining separate institutions against equal protection challenge depended on " 'findings' on 'gender-based' developmental differences." But these findings, Ginsburg derided, merely "restate the opinions of Virginia's expert witnesses, opinions about typically male or typically female 'tendencies.' "[66] The lower courts' findings of fact, the research cited by the task force as indicating developmental differences between men and women, she thought, were products of stereotype and convention. Moreover, Ginsburg rejected the additional factual finding that placing women at VMI would fundamentally alter the adversative system and undermine the very unique contribution that VMI offered to the diversity of education in Virginia. She stated, "The notion that admission of women would downgrade VMI's stature, destroy the adversative system and, with it, even the school, is a judgment hardly proved, a prediction hardly different from other 'self-fulfilling prophec[ies] once routinely used to deny rights or opportunities.' "[67] Ginsburg, however, readily conceded that VMI would have to change aspects of its program with the admission of women: "It is uncontested that women's admission would require accommodations, primarily in arranging housing assignments and physical training programs for female cadets." She added, "There is no reason to believe that the admission of women capable of all of the activities required of VMI cadets would destroy the Institute rather than enhance its capacity to serve the 'more perfect union.' "[68]

Scalia found incredible Ginsburg's rejection of the two lower courts' findings of fact that developmental differences exist between men and women. To her statement that "these findings restate the opinions of Virginia's expert witnesses," he replied, "How remarkable to criticize the District Court on the ground that its findings rest on the evidence (i.e., the testimony of Virginia's witnesses). That is what findings are supposed to do."[69] Scalia said that the majority's holding could have saved everyone a lot of time and money by dispensing entirely with the bother of a trial. After all, argued Scalia, Ginsburg substituted her suppositions about the world for the opinions of a multitude of experts who had spent years researching these matters. "In the face of these findings by two courts below," Scalia wrote, "this Court simply pronounces that 'the notion that admission of women would downgrade VMI's stature, destroy the adversative system and, with it, even the school, is a judgment hardly proved.' " Without citing any evidence of its own, and indeed disregarding the United States' own experts who were unwilling to testify that VMI's adversative method was appropriate for most women, "the Court simply declares . . . that these professionals acted on 'overbroad generalizations.' "[70]

A basic question never fully answered in the VMI case was whether any publicly supported single-sex school could pass muster under the "exceedingly persuasive" standard. Scalia thought not and Ginsburg did not say. The answer would appear to be no. Suppose, for example, that a male student applied to VWIL after the Virginia litigation was over.

Despite losing the case, Virginia honored its commitment to Mary Baldwin College and established an all-women's leadership program to provide training in a nonadversative, but military-like, system, and no other school in Virginia provides the same. Under *United States v. Virginia,* it would appear that men, however few might be interested, should have the same opportunities for self-affirming leadership training as women. VWIL's uniqueness argues in favor of admitting male students. Moreover, the Court's perspective that equality is measured on an individual level, rather than by the group, would demand admission, for otherwise this applicant will be denied an opportunity equal to what women receive.

The difference between the majority opinion and the dissent largely involved different views about the compass of the "equality" guaranteed by the Fourteenth Amendment. Specifically, Ginsburg and Scalia disagreed over whether the state could legitimately legislate on the basis of group characteristics. Such laws, by definition, will be both overinclusive and underinclusive. Some individuals will be included when they do not have the relevant characteristics, and others will be excluded who do have them. Outside of the guarantees of the Equal Protection Clause, states legislate all of the time based on group characteristics or generalizations. For instance, laws mandating the minimum driving age as sixteen exclude fifteen-year-olds who are mature enough and fully capable of driving; and laws that allow twenty-one-year-olds to drink include many who are not mature enough to handle that responsibility. Scalia argued that government is allowed to legislate for the statistical average. Ginsburg's opinion measured equality one person at a time.

Scalia, therefore, agreed with Virginia's "what-was-best-for-the-group" approach to equal protection. This perspective, ironically, has its roots in the litigation strategy of Thurgood Marshall in the series of cases culminating in *Brown v. Board of Education.* Marshall primarily used Kenneth Clark's doll studies to show that, as a group, blacks were systematically disadvantaged by segregation. States like Virginia had argued in *Brown* that the Constitution did not provide groups-based remedies. Now, Virginia, though still in the service of segregated schooling, preferred Marshall's view that the Equal Protection Clause's perspective was groupwide, not individually based. Scalia made this point when he said, "there is simply no support in our cases for the notion that a sex-based classification is invalid unless it relates to characteristics that hold true in every instance."[71] For Scalia, VMI was substantially related to an important government interest because the school's adversative method was, as was apparently not generally challenged by the United States, an effective method for educating men to be citizen-soldiers. The fact that it did not suit most women's educational needs was attributable to differences between men and women and not any malevolent intent of the state. The *Brown* group perspective led to the opposite result in the VMI case since, unlike blacks and whites, there are "real" differences between men and women.

Ginsburg never denied that men and women differed as groups. Indeed, even her criticism of the experts who testified regarding developmental differences was fairly tepid. If pushed, she might have agreed that there is some validity to the findings that women generally respond better to an affirming educational experience and that men generally excel in a competitive atmosphere. She probably would not have considered these statistical differences to be "real" in any biological sense and, indeed, would probably attribute them to environmental differences in the way men and women are raised. In any case, it is clear that she did not consider the statistical differences to be relevant. She expressly rejected "the generalizations about women on which Virginia rests." She stated that the equality guaranteed by the Fourteenth Amendment was measured by the individual, not the group:

> VMI's implementing methodology is not inherently unsuitable to women; some women do well under the adversative model; some women, at least, would want to attend VMI if they had the opportunity; some women are capable of all of the individual activities required of VMI cadets, and can meet the physical standards [VMI] now imposes on men.[72]

For Ginsburg, then, as long as some women, presumably even just one woman, would benefit from VMI, the Fourteenth Amendment did not permit the state to deny them, or her, that opportunity. It is telling that Ginsburg accepted the prospect that VMI would change when women arrived. So be it. VMI's, and the district court's, error lay in emphasizing the means rather than the ends of the Institute's mission. VMI sought to produce "citizen-soldiers," individuals "imbued with love of learning, confident in the functions and attitudes of leadership, possessing a high sense of public service, advocates of the American democracy and free enterprise system, and ready . . . to defend their country in time of national peril." Ginsburg exclaimed, "Surely that goal is great enough to accommodate women, who today count as citizens in our American democracy equal in stature to men."[73] The end of producing citizen-soldiers was but one part of the inquiry. The means employed, the adversative method, also had to pass constitutional muster. The ends were of paramount importance, and if means were available to accomplish those ends that did not discriminate, Virginia was obligated to use those means.

Indeed, the factual debate that received little attention in this entire litigation was the pedagogical effectiveness of the adversative method itself. It was probably the factual issue that determined the outcome of the case, even though none of the parties addressed it in any substantial way. The United States took the untenable position throughout the litigation that the adversative method would not really be affected after women were admitted. More remarkably, it never argued that the adversative method itself was unnecessary for producing citizen-soldiers. The United States military academies had long ago abandoned this leveling method as anachronistic and not suitable for producing leaders, whether citizen or soldier. If West Point could train men and women without subjecting them to daily onslaughts of vituperation and degradation, why couldn't VMI? It is one of the great mysteries of this litigation why the government failed to make this rather obvious argument, given the adversative method's historical role at VMI and its centrality to the litigation. Philippa Strum, who wrote a well-regarded history of the VMI case, speculated that the decision not to challenge the pedagogical benefits of the adversative method was a political choice made in some dark corner of the White House or Justice Department.[74] However it came to pass, the empirical question presented regarding the adversative method did not escape the attention of the justices.

The unstated subtext of the holding in *United States v. Virginia* is that the adversative method is not necessary for, and may be counterproductive to, the claimed "important government interest" in producing citizen-soldiers. Indeed, Chief Justice Rehnquist, concurring, made this point explicit: "While considerable evidence shows that a single-sex education is pedagogically beneficial for some students, . . . there is no similar evidence in the record that an adversative method is pedagogically beneficial or is any more likely to produce character traits than other methodologies."[75] The majority opinion, however, was less candid about its skepticism. The uniqueness of the adversative system argued in favor of admitting women, Ginsburg said: "some women . . . do well under

[the] adversative model," and that "it is on behalf of these women that the United States has instituted this suit."[76] But it is doubtful that Ginsburg or the other justices, except Scalia, truly believed the adversative method was necessary to the production of citizen-soldiers or would wholly survive the admission of women. During oral argument, for instance, Justice Stephen Breyer asked Theodore Olson, who was representing Virginia, "Isn't it true that the district court judge never made any finding that there was a difference in the kind of leadership product, if you want to use that term, that VMI produces from what West Point or Annapolis or the other military schools [produce]?" Olson responded that this was correct, though the lower court found that "this methodology works for the people that go to that school." Breyer continued, pointing out that Olson's position was based on the premise that the adversative method "serves a distinct group of people." "You are not resting your case," Breyer said, "on the proposition that it is necessary to produce a distinctive kind of leader who is produced by it and can only be produced by it." Olson responded, "I agree with you, yes."

While Olson might not have realized it at the time, this concession ended his case. The objective of VMI was to produce citizen-soldiers who would be leaders in civilian and military pursuits. If there was more than one way to reach this objective, and the way chosen by Virginia excluded women while the other methods did not similarly discriminate, then VMI could not pass muster under the strict test, the "exceedingly persuasive" test, crafted by Ginsburg. While the objective of producing leaders might be exceedingly persuasive, the adversative method was hardly finely tailored to produce this outcome. The other military academies proved this to be so.

Although there was a good deal of teeth-gnashing and bluster about the option of going private, VMI's board of visitors voted to admit women on September 21, 1996. Yet it remains too early to say how this experiment in social engineering will turn out. Early on the head of VMI, General Josiah Bunting, pledged that the changes at the Institute would be minimal. While VMI might have to admit women, Bunting had no intention of changing the environment any more than was absolutely necessary. Ginsburg's opinion, Bunting declared, "says some women have the will and the capacity to succeed in the training and attendant opportunities that VMI uniquely affords."[77] If women wanted the adversative method, they would get it—good and hard. And, indeed, VMI was a distinctly inhospitable environment for women in the early years of integration. Over time, however, at least from the outside looking in, it appears that VMI is changing and becoming more accommodating to women. Their Web page, for example, features nearly as many pictures of women as it does men. As more women are admitted, one might predict that the very culture of the Institute will change. To the extent that at least some of the research relied upon in the Virginia litigation is accurate—that women respond to an affirming environment better than a disabling one—VMI should be expected to modify its environment to appeal to this population. Only time will tell.

In *United States v. Virginia,* the state of Virginia sought to maintain the all-male military college at VMI. In the parlance of the Constitution's Equal Protection Clause, the case presented the issue whether the state of Virginia had sufficient reasons to discriminate on the basis of gender. In the case, Virginia was discriminating against a historically disadvantaged group, and the Court ultimately interceded on behalf of that group to ensure an equal opportunity to participate. However, it would not have mattered, in terms of the kind of analysis brought to bear, if Virginia had sought to maintain an all-women's college. This is why Scalia's dissent announced the death of publicly supported single-sex education. In equal protection law, truly what is good for the goose is good for the gander. Scalia's prediction that publicly supported single-sex education was dead was based on the belief that the Court would not countenance segregation *for* women any more than it allowed segregation *against* women. Since the VMI case invalidated segregation against women, segregation to benefit women similarly should be prohibited. However, there remains a strong argument that benign discrimination should be considered in a fundamentally different way than the more malignant variety. When a state or the United States legislates to benefit a historically disadvantaged group, what is popularly known as affirmative action, the law must still survive the gauntlet of strict or exceedingly persuasive or intermediate scrutiny. But these tests essentially ask whether the government has good enough grounds for discriminating the way it seeks to. While Virginia's basis for discriminating against women was held to be insufficient, there may be better arguments for discriminating in favor of women or minorities that would sometimes permit affirmative action, despite the unequal standards used. It may be, then, that unequal treatment—affirmative action—is necessary to redress existing inequalities. At least, the Court has given us some reason to think so.

———

In June 1978, a badly divided Court invalidated the affirmative action program of the Medical School at the University of California, at Davis.[78] Allan Bakke wanted to be a physician and he twice applied to, and was twice rejected by, the UC Davis Medical School. Davis's admissions process was divided between regular admissions and special admissions for certain designated minority groups. Out of a total of one hundred positions in the entering class, sixteen were reserved for minority candidates. At the time of Bakke's first application, four of these special slots remained open. Being a white male, he was excluded for consideration in this category. He brought suit under both Title VI and the Equal Protection Clause. Although the Court issued six separate opinions, there were two main camps. The first was led by Justice John Paul Stevens who, joined by Chief Justice Warren Burger and Justices Potter Stewart and William Rehnquist, relied primarily on statutory grounds and Title VI's "broad prohibition against the exclusion of any individual" on racial grounds from a publicly funded program. Justice William Brennan led the second group, joined by Justices Thurgood Marshall, Byron White, and Harry Blackmun, and he focused on the constitutional grounds to find that under heightened (but not strict) scrutiny, the state could adopt race-conscious remedies to benefit "those least well represented in the political process" and who had suffered discrimination or disadvantage based on their race. Justice Lewis Powell, the deciding vote, wrote an opinion for the Court that was largely not joined by any other justice. Nonetheless, Powell did receive majority votes for his two principal conclusions, the first that the quota system employed by Davis was unconstitutional, and the second that universities could take race into account in their admissions decisions. Allan Bakke was admitted to the UC Davis Medical School, and one of the most controversial issues in American society was left in constitutional disarray.

The Court would not return to affirmative action in the educational context for twenty-five years. In the meantime, the Court shored up its equal protection jurisprudence outside the education context, most notably in employment cases. In case after case, the Court invalidated state affirmative action programs. The Court repeatedly emphasized that race-based classifications, whether designed to hurt or help minority groups, were presumptively unconstitutional. Only the most compelling circumstances would justify race-conscious decision-making and the means used would be carefully scrutinized to ensure that they were narrowly tailored to the accomplishment of any asserted compelling objectives. The Court stressed, however, that it did not intend to return to the days when strict scrutiny was inevitably fatal. It would closely inspect the objectives of the discriminatory action and check the empirical claim that the means chosen were narrowly tailored to achieve those ends.

But except in the narrow situation in which affirmative action was adopted to remedy particular past discrimination, the Court invariably invalidated state and federal efforts to discriminate in a benign fashion. Lower courts, with very few exceptions, similarly looked skeptically at race-conscious policies. Indeed, the Court's employment cases presented such a negative view of affirmative action that the United States Court of Appeals for the Fifth Circuit in New Orleans found in 1996 that the case of *Regents of the University of California v. Bakke* was "questionable as binding precedent."[79] In *Hopwood v. Texas,* the University of Texas School of Law claimed that its affirmative action program was narrowly tailored to produce a diverse class. Diversity, the state argued, was a compelling interest. Accordingly, racial diversity would contribute to the variety of ideas and experiences represented in the classroom and enrich the educational environment. The Fifth Circuit was unconvinced. Basing its ruling on the clear trend of Supreme Court cases following *Bakke,* the court held that diversity did not qualify as a compelling state interest.

In 2003, the Court finally returned to the subject of affirmative action in education in two cases involving the University of Michigan. The first, *Gratz v. Bollinger,*[80] concerned the university's undergraduate admissions policy of automatically granting all minority applicants twenty points toward their total admissions score. In effect, the Court determined, this policy "has the effect of making the factor of race . . . decisive for virtually every minimally qualified underrepresented minority applicant."[81] In a 6–3 decision, with only Justices Stevens, Souter, and Ginsburg dissenting from the holding, the Court held that the undergraduate affirmative action program failed to give the individualized consideration to each applicant that was required by the Fourteenth Amendment. In the second case, *Grutter v. Bollinger,*[82] however, Justices O'Connor and Breyer joined Justices Stevens, Souter, and Ginsburg to uphold the law school's more discretionary policy. *Grutter* thus establishes the standard by which all affirmative action programs will be measured in the future.

Justice O'Connor wrote the opinion for the Court. She found that flexibility was the hallmark of the law school's affirmative action policy. The single goal of the policy was to achieve a diverse student body, and the means chosen to produce that goal were tailored to allow discretion and judgment. The policy "requires admissions officials to evaluate each applicant based on all the information available in the file, including a personal statement, letters of recommendation, and an essay describing the ways in which the applicant will contribute to the life and diversity of the Law School."[83] The policy mandates that admissions officials combine hard factors, such as grades and standardized test scores, and soft factors, such as enthusiasm of recommenders and quality of the applicant's undergraduate institution. These factors are combined in an effort to assess the "applicant's likely contributions to the intellectual and social life of the institution."[84] Moreover, an express component of the law school's policy is to create diverse classes, and particularly emphasizes the "Law School's commitment to 'one particular type of diversity,'" that is, 'racial and ethnic diversity with special reference to the inclusion of students from groups which have been historically discriminated against, including African-Americans, Hispanics and Native Americans, who without this commitment might not be represented in our student body in meaningful numbers."[85] In order to make this commitment meaningful, the law school determined that it must enroll a "critical mass" of underrepresented minority students in order to ensure their active participation in the life of the institution.

The district court had held a fifteen-day trial, without a jury, in order to determine the extent to which race operated as a factor in the law school's admissions decisions, and noted that it had to determine, as a matter of law, whether the claimed benefits flowing from a diverse student body constituted a compelling state interest. Among an assortment of factual issues, the state's witnesses, both expert and lay, testified that (1) there was no minimum percentage of minority candidates admitted each year, (2) a daily tally of minority admittees was conducted in order to assess the school's success at amassing a critical mass of underrepresented students, (3) "critical mass" was operationally defined as the minimum number of students needed to ensure that underrepresented minorities would participate in classroom discussions and not feel isolated—however, no preestablished number or quota was set regarding what would constitute a "critical mass," (4) the purpose of the policy was not to remedy past discrimination, but to "bring to the Law School a perspective different from that of members of groups which have not been the victims of such discrimination," (5) Asians and Jews, two groups also historically victims of discrimination, were not included in the policy because they were already being admitted to the law school in significant numbers, (6) when a "critical mass of underrepresented minority students is present, racial stereotypes lose their force because nonminority students learn there is no 'minority viewpoint' but rather a variety of viewpoints among minority students," (7) minority group membership "is an extremely strong factor in the decision for acceptance," but it is not the predominant factor, and (8) abolishing a race-conscious policy would have meant that only about 4 percent of the 2000 entering class would have been underrepresented minorities, rather than the 14.5 percent actually part of that class.[86]

The district court ruled that the law school's policy was unconstitutional. It did not believe that *Bakke* mandated that racial diversity was a compelling interest, and, even if it were, the Court held, the law school had failed to narrowly tailor its program to achieve that interest. The Seventh Circuit Court of Appeals reversed, finding that *Bakke* indeed was binding precedent and had established diversity as a compelling state interest. Moreover, the appellate court said, the law school's use of race as a "plus factor," rather than as the predominant consideration, made it narrowly tailored. The Seventh Circuit, by ruling in favor of the Michigan Law School, created a split in the circuits between it and the Fifth Circuit, which had ruled against the University of Texas's affirmative action program, finding that *Bakke* was not binding precedent. This split increased the likelihood considerably that the Supreme Court would take the case.

In 2002, the High Court granted certiorari in *Grutter*. When its long-awaited decision was announced at the end of June 2003, Justice O'Connor explained that the Court agreed to hear the case in order to decide "a question of national importance." Specifically, the Court decided "whether diversity is a compelling interest that can justify the narrowly tailored use of race in selecting applicants for admission to public universities."[87] The Court said that, in 2003, it was, but cautioned that in all likelihood it would not remain so forever.

O'Connor's opinion stressed at the outset that the Equal Protection Clause "protects persons not groups." For this reason, classifications based on race can only survive if "they are narrowly tailored to further compelling governmental interests." But context matters, O'Connor stated. In particular, the Court has long recognized the "special niche" public education occupies "in our constitutional tradition." Indeed, somewhat paradoxically, O'Connor said that this special niche meant that " 'good faith' on the part of a university is 'presumed' absent 'a showing to the contrary.' " Thus, the Court would use strict scrutiny to closely review the law school's justification for discriminating, but would be deferential to that justification. O'Connor's stated standard of review is, therefore, something of a muddle. She maintained that the Court's review "is no less strict" for its deference to the university's better informed educational judgments regarding the benefits of a diverse class.[88] But how can this be so? The whole point of strict scrutiny is that it is not deferential. Saying that the Court will be deferential in its strict scrutiny review is akin to calling missiles peacekeepers. Some concepts just don't go together.

This does not mean that O'Connor's bottom line of deferring to universities regarding what is needed to meet pedagogical objectives is illogical or wrong. The Court has long recognized a constitutional dimension, grounded in the First Amendment, to educational autonomy. But this argument does not explain the meaning of "deferential strict scrutiny." Rather, it is an argument for creating an explicit university exception to traditional strict review, based on the principle that the First Amendment privileges educational autonomy even at the risk of certain constitutional costs. In effect, the First Amendment benefits of not second-guessing university decisions generally outweighs any anticipated constitutional trouble universities are likely to get into. The Court would not rubber-stamp university policies—after all, the Court did invalidate Michigan's undergraduate plan the same day it decided *Grutter*—but strict scrutiny was not called for. Under this education exception, then, the Court is reduced to the more deferential review standard of intermediate scrutiny or even the lesser rational basis test. And this was what O'Connor actually did, even if she told us she was doing something else.

O'Connor's standard of review led her to do little more than catalog the pedagogical benefits of a diverse student body as proclaimed by the law school. To the extent that these claims were based on research, she did not evaluate the quality of that research in any way. According to O'Connor, evidence demonstrated how the law school's admission policy "promotes 'cross-racial understanding,' helps to break down racial stereotypes, and 'enables [students] to better understand persons of different races.' " The presence of a critical mass of underrepresented minorities promotes a more robust educational experience, "because 'classroom discussion is livelier, more spirited, and simply more enlightening and interesting' when the students have 'the greatest possible variety of back-grounds.' " These evidentiary findings were buttressed, O'Connor said, by the law school's amici curiae ("friends of the Court"). These briefs highlighted the numerous studies that "show that student body diversity promotes learning outcomes and better prepares students for an increas-ingly diverse workforce and society, and better prepares them as profes-sionals."[89] O'Connor cited several sources but did not discuss what methods were used to study diversity, what data were collected to quan-tify its benefits, or whether their conclusions fairly followed the methods, principles, and data they employed. Moreover, as Justice Clarence Tho-mas noted in his dissent, O'Connor's heavy reliance on social science evidence was highly selective. "The Court never acknowledges," he stated, "the growing evidence that racial (and other sorts) of heteroge-neity actually impairs learning among black students."[90]

Just as Powell had concluded in *Bakke*, O'Connor found in *Grutter* that the experience of race could be considered a plus factor, but it could not be determinative. Its value was analogous to other soft variables traditionally considered, including artistic ability and geographical diver-sity. If growing up in Williston, North Dakota, might operate as an admissions plus, so might growing up black in Scarsdale, New York. O'Connor said that the "unique experience of being a racial minority in a society, like our own, in which race unfortunately still matters," is likely to affect one's views.[91] These experiences—whether of not being able to get a tractor started in the bitter winters of North Dakota or of not being able to hail a cab on the impersonal streets of New York—would enrich the law school classroom.

The linchpin of O'Connor's opinion in *Grutter* and its point of depar-ture from the undergraduate program struck down in *Gratz* was the individualized character of the assessment of the value of race as a plus factor. In *Gratz,* the Court complained about the inflexible granting of twenty points to applicants who were underrepresented minorities. In *Grutter,* in contrast, the race-based plus was never set forth categorically, insulating the law school's affirmative action program from judicial review. It is not unlike the decision in *McCleskey v. Kemp,* albeit to a very different result, in which juror discretion could mask discriminatory practice. One might wonder whether a Baldus-like study on the influence of race might demonstrate that race, though perhaps not the primary factor explaining the admissions decision at the law school, is one of the most powerful variables. Contrary to O'Connor's belief, pushing race under the table does not make it go away and may, indeed, give it greater operative force.

Similarly, the Court made much ado about the fact that Michigan, unlike the UC Davis Medical School, did not employ quotas. O'Connor assured the public on this point when she argued that the notion of "critical mass" did not set any absolute minimums.[92] But, of course, it did. At oral argument, the question as to whether critical mass operated to mask a quota arose several times. At one point, Justice Scalia rose in his seat to ask the law school's counsel, Maureen Mahoney, just what percentage would constitute a critical mass.

JUSTICE SCALIA: Is two percent a critical mass, Ms. Mahoney?

MS. MAHONEY: I don't think so, Your Honor.

JUSTICE SCALIA: Okay, four percent?

MS. MAHONEY: No, Your Honor, what—

JUSTICE SCALIA: You have to pick some number, don't you?

MS. MAHONEY: Well, actually, what—

JUSTICE SCALIA: Like eight, is eight percent?

MS. MAHONEY: Now, Your Honor.

JUSTICE SCALIA: Now, does it stop being a quota because it's somewhere between eight and twelve, but it is a quota if it's ten? I don't understand that reasoning. Once you use the term *critical mass* . . . you're into quota land?

MS. MAHONEY: Your Honor, what a quota is under this Court's cases is a fixed number. And there is no fixed number here. The testimony was that it depends on the characteristics of the applicant pool.

JUSTICE SCALIA: As long as you say between eight and twelve you're okay? Is that it? If you said ten it's bad . . . but between eight and twelve it's okay, because it's not a fixed number? Is that . . . what you think the Constitution is?

Critical mass was operationally defined as that number that is large enough to accomplish two basic objectives of the law school. It had to be large enough so that underrepresented minorities would not feel isolated and would participate fully in the life of the law school, and it had to be large enough to represent a diversity of views so that other students would understand that "there is no 'minority viewpoint' but rather a variety of viewpoints among minority students." Presumably, for this concept to pass any sort of critical review whatsoever, research would have to be available on what minimum percentage of a class would constitute a "critical mass." Is it one percent or twenty percent, or some number in between? But whatever minimum is needed to accomplish the purposes of a "critical mass" *is the quota.*

In the *Grutter* decision, the Court simply was not being candid about what it was doing. The idea of "critical mass" makes a good deal of sense, but to claim it is not a quota was disingenuous. The Court was unwilling to recognize this fact because the word *quota* has become associated with such negative connotations. One would prefer not to be a king or queen of them in any case. If the Court had leveled with the public and simply said that Michigan's critical mass was a quota, but that the school used it for very good reasons, the headlines the next day probably would have been, "Court Approves Quotas." This might have affected the nation's acceptance of the decision and implementation of similar programs elsewhere. Indeed, such headlines might have spurred legislative or popular initiatives like California's Proposition 209, which prohibited the use of race in state decisions in areas such as education, hiring, and contracts. *Grutter* stands for the principle that states can enact affirmative action programs in their universities, not that they must do so. California voters have declined this opportunity. If the Court had stated plainly that its decision upheld the use of quotas, many other states might have followed California's lead. Clearly, the Court preferred to avoid such bad publicity.

The quota issue haunts O'Connor's opinion in another respect as well. In a highly unusual, possibly unprecedented, move, the Court inserted a sunset provision into its decision. O'Connor wrote: "We expect that 25 years from now, the use of racial preferences will no longer be necessary to further the interest approved today." The reason, O'Connor explained, was that "a termination point 'assure[s] all citizens that the deviation from the norm of equal treatment of all racial and ethnic groups is a temporary matter, a measure taken in the service of the goal of equality itself.' "[93] Thus, in O'Connor's view, in a generation hence, all minorities should be able to compete successfully for admission to elite law schools like Michigan. Presumably, race might continue to produce experiences that would contribute to diversity, but she expects that today's underrepresented minorities will no longer need special consideration to gain admission. Although this injunction to a future generation is unlikely to be taken literally, it raises one of the fundamental questions that started this chapter. How do we know when we've succeeded in generating equal protection of the laws?

Quotas operate on the inherent belief that equal protection success can be measured by equal representation of different groups in whatever setting, work, school, or sports, is of concern. But this flies in the face of individualism and cultural diversity. If a particular cultural group, for example, does not value law as a professional choice, their lack of representativeness in law schools may be explained by lack of interest, not discrimination. And if a cultural group strongly values law, insisting on critical masses of all groups could operate to put a cap on their numbers in the law schools. We can be confident that so long as racism is endemic it will manifest itself in various ways. But just because every group is not represented in every segment of society in proportion to their numbers in society does not mean that discrimination is the cause.

A comparison of *Grutter* to *Virginia* is instructive. In terms of the underlying principles of equal protection law, the two are not consistent. In *Virginia,* the Court rejected the relevance of group characteristics; in *Grutter,* it found group differences to be dispositive. In *Virginia,* the Court rejected VMI's contention that admitting women into its adversative training method would destroy that model, despite the considerable social science that supported this judgment; in *Grutter,* the Court was deferential to the law school's contention that racial diversity would bolster its training methods, and used social science as window dressing to buttress this conclusion while ignoring any research that questioned it. In *Virginia,* the Court said it applied intermediate scrutiny, but actually employed the strict, exceedingly persuasive standard to strike down gender-based discrimination; in *Grutter,* the Court said it applied strict scrutiny, but actually employed a deferential standard to uphold race-based discrimination. Justice Thomas saw in these inconsistencies the majority's snobbery. "Apparently where the status quo being defended is that of the elite establishment—here the law school—rather than a less fashionable southern military institution," Thomas chided, "the Court will defer without serious inquiry and without regard to the applicable legal standard."[94]

The only way to reconcile *Virginia* and *Grutter* may be on the basis that their outcomes reflect the sort of world a majority of justices believe the Fourteenth Amendment was designed to create. Stated plainly, equality is an outcome-determinative notion. It is not driven by high principle or standards that can be applied consistently from abstract context to abstract context. In effect, the Fourteenth Amendment created a world, our modern world, in which both assimilation and diversity are celebrated. It mandates integration on the theory that all persons are created equal. This is the lesson of *Brown.* But *Brown,* taken to its natural conclusion, results in assimilation—it reflects the idea of America as the great melting pot. But in that melting pot, cultural differences eventually disappear. Since 1954 and *Brown,* homogenization has become a less attractive objective and movements from black power to Latin pride have displaced calls for assimilation. In order to maintain diversity, group differences must not only be recognized but encouraged. Yet how is the Court to decide when to require the melting pot and when to permit diversity? How does the Court decide whether it should permit the diversity of a segregated male military school or that of historically black colleges? Should North Carolina AT&T, a predominantly black college founded in 1891, whose principal mission is to serve the black community, be deferred to under *Grutter* or be required to more fully integrate under *Virginia*? The answer is not clear from the case law.

Equal protection is thus a function of what, to use Justice Ginsburg's phrase from Virginia, a "more perfect union" should look like. Inevitably, the answer to this question is, as Justice Scalia accused in *Virginia* and Justice Thomas accused in *Grutter,* a function of the majority's elitist attitudes. It is a world in which historically disadvantaged and underrepresented groups are given a chance to participate in all segments of society. In *Virginia,* this meant women are included in military-style education and in *Grutter* this meant that African-Americans, Native Americans, and Hispanics were admitted into a top-tier law school in greater numbers than their "objective statistics" might otherwise have justified. Equality thus is not just opportunity but also results. The Constitution does not guarantee truly equal outcomes. But where outcomes disproportionately disfavor certain historically disadvantaged groups, and given the irrebuttable presumption that "all men are created equal," unequal outcomes suggest unequal opportunity. As long as the United States remains a nation of groups that are defined by, and define themselves by, their race, gender, ethnicity, and sexual orientation, the Court will remain in this messy business. If the people ever become one undifferentiated mass, only then will the need for vigilance disappear. It is safe to say that there will always be the need for such vigilance.

10

IN THE SUPREME COURT WE TRUST:
Science and Supposition in the Religion Clauses

Neither a state nor the Federal Government can set up a church. Neither can pass laws which aid one religion, aid all religions, or prefer one religion over another. Neither can force nor influence a person to go to or to remain away from church against his will or force him to profess a belief or disbelief in any religion. No person can be punished for entertaining or professing religious beliefs or disbeliefs, for church-attendance or non-attendance. No tax, large or small, can be levied to support any religious activities or institutions, whatever they may be called, or whatever form they may adopt to teach or practice religion. Neither a state nor the Federal government can, openly or secretly, participate in the affairs of any religious organizations or groups and vice versa. In the words of Jefferson, the clause . . . was intended to erect "a wall of separation" between church and State.

—JUSTICE HUGO BLACK
EVERSON V. BOARD OF EDUCATION

In Genesis, God said to Abraham, "Take your son, your only son, Isaac, whom you love, and go to the region of Moriah. Sacrifice him there as a burnt offering on one of the mountains I will tell you about." Abraham dutifully followed God's instructions to the point when he "put forth his hand, and took the knife to slay his son." Just in time, however, God instructed Abraham to spare Isaac. Instead, a ram that had gotten caught in a thicket by his horns took Isaac's place on the sacrificial altar and was "offered up as a burnt offering." Abraham's willingness to take his son's life demonstrated his willingness to carry out the word of God and thus proved his abiding faith.

The parable of Abraham and Isaac was intended, as many stories of the Old Testament were, to impart lessons regarding man's relationship to man, man's relationship to God, and man's place in the natural world. The lessons of the Bible, for many of the faithful, were meant to be taken literally. Accordingly, Abraham actually escorted Isaac to Moriah, God actually created the universe in six days, and the great flood actually happened. But what significance should the Bible, or any other religious tract or set of beliefs, have in contemporary American society? Must government tolerate deviant religious practices, no matter how repugnant they might be to modern sensibilities? Surely, Abraham could be punished today for his behavior toward Isaac; but could a community also criminalize his sacrifice of the ram? And what role should God be allowed to play in civil government? Our trust in God is recognized on our currency; He is prayed to at the start of every session of Congress; and He is asked to save this honorable court every day oral argument is heard at the Supreme Court. Yet prayer, the Ten Commandments, and His teachings about man and nature have been systematically excluded from schools across the United States. How should the line between church and state be drawn?

The Constitution speaks to this testy matter in two clauses that are designed to, at once, keep religion out of government and government out of religion. Rather than Jefferson's wall, however, what separates church and state in America today seems more like the thicket that immobilized Abraham's ram.

In 1987, Ernesto Pichardo, a high priest of the Santeria religion, sought to establish a church in the City of Hialeah, Florida. It had the poetic name of the Church of the Lukumi Babalu Aye. The church would occupy a run-down yellow building almost directly across the street from City Hall. In order to obtain city approval for occupancy, the church had to obtain all of the necessary permits, including inspections of the building's plumbing system, electrical wiring, and fire safety. It also had to overcome local prejudice, for the people of Hialeah did not want Pichardo's kind in their midst. Santerians, it turns out, like Abraham before them, consider animal sacrifice an integral part of their religious practice.

Santeria is a combination of the Lukumi religion practiced in Nigeria and the Catholicism that slaves encountered in the New World. The religion's roots extend back over four thousand years. The modern form of the religion evolved over millennia in Cuba, where practitioners were targets of prejudice and repression. Today, there are approximately fifty thousand adherents of Santeria in southern Florida, and estimates of one hundred million worldwide. Santerians believe in one supreme God but

have adopted entities called "orishes," invested with supernatural powers. Church doctrine has "syncretized"—that is, combined or integrated—the identities of the orishes with the images of Catholic saints.
Orishes are powerful but not immortal, and depend greatly on animal
sacrifice to be effective in all of the domains in which their intercession
is sought.[1]

Santerians practice animal sacrifice to mark births, marriages, and
deaths, and to cure the sick and to initiate new priests. The list of animals
used in Santerian rituals is long, and includes chickens, pigeons, doves,
ducks, guinea pigs, goats, sheep, and turtles. Pichardo testified at trial
that between twenty and thirty animals are usually sacrificed during an
initiation rite, setting the annual number between twelve and eighteen
thousand. With the exception of healing and death rituals, sacrificed animals are cooked and eaten in celebration during the ceremony.[2]

The city of Hialeah, meaning "High Prairie," was incorporated in
1925 and is a suburb of Miami. It prides itself on its "family oriented
neighborhoods" but is best known for its famous horse track at Hialeah
Park. In addition, dog racing, hunting, fishing, and the Spanish sport of
jai alai are favorite local distractions. Hialeah is Florida's fifth largest
city, with more than 210,000 residents, and is similar to many southern
Florida cities. Hialeah's residents are predominantly Hispanic, largely
conservative and Republican, and fiercely proud of both their cultural
heritage and their success in the United States. People or practices that
threaten these hard-won qualities, or that endanger the community and
its family values, are resisted.

Not surprisingly, when Pichardo announced plans to open a church
in downtown Hialeah, the community did resist. While Santerian practices were well known in Hialeah, and widely detested, the religion operated mainly underground. Pichardo's plan to bring the religion into
public view ignited long-simmering resentments. The City Council
responded immediately by enacting a resolution that emphasized Hialeah's "great concern regarding the possibility of public ritualistic sacrifices" and enumerated the state laws that prohibited cruelty to animals.
The resolution declared its opposition "to ritual sacrifices of animals"
within Hialeah, and announced that any person or organization practicing animal sacrifice would be prosecuted. Officials decried animal sacrifice as "barbaric" and "medieval." Council member Julio Martinez,
for example, considered the practice to be "something out of the 15th

century."[3] Mr. Tarte, a lawyer representing residents seeking to shut the church down, said, "Santeria is not a religion. It is a throwback to the dark ages. It is a cannibalistic, voodoo-like sect which attracts the worst elements of society, people who mutilate animals in a crude and most inhumane manner."[4]

Not believing that existing laws were adequate, Hialeah's city council passed four ordinances designed to prohibit animal sacrifices. At the many public meetings at which the subject was discussed, tempers ran high. When Pichardo offered brief comments, he was taunted by the crowd. When Councilman Martinez pointed out that in prerevolution Cuba people were imprisoned for practicing Santeria, the audience cheered. Councilman Cardoso said that church members "are in violation of everything this country stands for." Councilman Mejides sought to distinguish Santerian practice from the analogous Jewish practice of kosher slaughter. Jewish tradition, he asserted, has a "real purpose." The "Bible says we are allowed to sacrifice an animal for consumption," Mejides explained, "but for any other purpose, I don't believe the Bible allows it."[5]

Hialeah city officials supported aggressive council action. The chaplain of the police department, for instance, called Santeria a sin, and described its religious practices as "foolishness," an "abomination to the Lord," and the worship of "demons." He told the council, "We need to be helping people and sharing with them the truth that is found in Jesus Christ." He exclaimed, "I would exhort you . . . not to permit this Church to exist." The city attorney echoed these sentiments, and summarized the consensus: "This community will not tolerate religious practices which are abhorrent to its citizens."[6]

The First Amendment of the Constitution, in conjunction with the Fourteenth Amendment, guarantees that states "shall make no law . . . prohibiting the free exercise [of religion]." One might naturally ask, then, what Hialeah thought it was doing. Pichardo thought that Hialeah's actions amounted to a modern-day inquisition. And so it seemed. The city had obviously responded to a religion it abhorred with vehemence and intolerance. It passed four ordinances in an effort to outlaw Santerian practices, rituals that all agreed were central to adherents' religious beliefs, beliefs that were sincerely held. But Hialeah officials adamantly denied waging a crusade against Santerians. The object of the laws, the city maintained, was not the banning of any one religion or even any general religious practice. The council's objective was the elimination of

the practice of animal sacrifice, for whatever reasons it might be performed, religious or otherwise. According to this view, because the law
was a law of general application, one that did not target religion, it did
not run afoul of the First Amendment's guarantee of free exercise.

In effect, the city of Hialeah was asserting that government has no
obligation to accommodate any religious practice. Period. For example,
if a state passed a statute criminalizing the possession and use of alcohol,
a church or synagogue, under this view, would have no constitutional
right whatsoever to an exception for sacramental use of wine. Similarly,
Hialeah claimed, the city could outlaw all sacrificial killing of animals,
as long as it did not specifically single out religious sacrifices. To be sure,
Hialeah could, if it so wanted, permit a religious exception—as is usually
done when prohibition statutes are passed—but Hialeah was not constitutionally obligated to do so. This perhaps somewhat surprising litigation
strategy, this severely cramped view of the meaning of the guarantee of
free exercise of religion, it turns out, comes from the pen of Justice
Antonin Scalia in the 1990 case of *Employment Division of Human
Resources of Oregon v. Smith*.[7] Although its days are likely numbered,
the decision in *Smith*—one of the most poorly reasoned decisions in modern constitutional law—remains the law to this day.

Alfred Smith was fired from his job with a private drug rehabilitation
organization because he ingested peyote "buttons" during a ceremony of
the Native American Church, of which he is a member. Peyote was a
Schedule 1 controlled substance and its use was illegal in Oregon; the
state provided no exemption for sacramental use. (Oregon has since
changed its policy and now provides an exemption for religiously
inspired use of peyote within the Native American Church.) Peyote buttons come from the peyote cactus, found primarily in the parched range-
land of the American southwest, particularly in Texas and northern
Mexico; the button contains the chemical substance mescaline. Users'
experience with the drug is decidedly mixed. It stimulates respiratory
changes and alters pulse rates. It is typically accompanied by vivid visual
and auditory hallucinations together with altered perceptions of time and
space. Some people experience extreme anxiety, even terror, and many
report severe nausea and vomiting. Peyote use in Native American religious practice is ancient, however, with adherents claiming that the practice extends ten thousand years into the past.

After being dismissed from his job, Smith applied to the Employment Division of Oregon's Department of Human Resources for unemployment compensation. The state determined that he was ineligible for benefits, because he had been discharged for work-related "misconduct." He brought suit, claiming that the Free Exercise Clause required Oregon to carve out an exception to its drug laws for those individuals who use peyote as a sincere and integral part of their religious practice in the Native American Church. The Supreme Court, with Justice Scalia writing, denied this claim.

Justice Antonin Scalia—"Nino" to his friends—was born in Trenton, New Jersey, in 1936, and was primarily raised in Queens, New York. He was the only child of two teachers, his father a professor of romance languages at Brooklyn College and his mother a schoolteacher. Scalia excelled in school, graduating as class valedictorian from Georgetown University and later *magna cum laude* from the Harvard Law School. He met his future wife, Maureen McCarthy, while at Harvard. They share a deep faith in Catholicism and have nine children, one of whom is a priest. After briefly practicing law, Scalia became a professor at the University of Virginia's law school, but interrupted his academic career in 1971 to try government service, eventually landing at the Justice Department's Office of Legal Counsel—the closest thing to an academic "think tank" one can find in government. In 1977, he returned to teaching, this time at the University of Chicago's law school. Five years later, President Ronald Reagan nominated Scalia to the U.S. Court of Appeals for the District of Columbia. While there, he gained a reputation as a strong advocate of limited congressional power, strict interpretation of statutes, rigid separation of powers, and a diminished view of the Bill of Rights. He was also known for his very active and engaging presence during oral argument, and his personality often shone brightly through his opinions. Despite being identified with a strong version of the conservative agenda, Scalia was confirmed unanimously (98 to 0) after President Reagan nominated him to the Supreme Court in 1986. His success with the Senate was largely attributed to the perception that he would not change the balance of power on the Court. He took the seat vacated when Justice William Rehnquist ascended to the chief justice chair, after Chief Justice Warren Burger retired from the Court. Of course, the next vacancy would be a different story. President Reagan's nomination of Judge Robert Bork, whose conservative views bore a close resemblance to Scalia's, ignited a fierce partisan debate in the Senate and the nation more generally. The demise of the Bork nomination and the eventual confirmation of Anthony Kennedy to the seat had a considerable impact on the development of constitutional law, especially in the area of religion.

In opinions bristling with energy and, more often than not, invective, Scalia has been a constant champion for a radical reorientation of government. He advocates a weak Congress and a strong executive branch, and believes that the Bill of Rights should have a limited domain, except when property rights are at stake. Above all else, perhaps, Scalia prefers bright-line tests and categorical rules, and holds in complete disdain the balancing tests that have found their way into almost every area of modern constitutional law. In many ways, *Smith* is the epitome of Scalia's crabbed conception of the Bill of Rights and his intense need for rules, no matter what the cost to liberty or doctrinal coherence.

The justices unanimously agree that the free exercise of religion means, at the very least, the right to believe and profess whatever religious doctrine one desires. The debate, then, revolves around religious *practices,* that is, conduct or behavior that accompanies or is a component of a person's religious beliefs. Indeed, if the Free Exercise Clause only guaranteed beliefs and the right to profess those beliefs, it would simply retrace the guarantees of free speech. For example, Catholics not only believe that sacramental wine represents the blood of Jesus Christ, but that an integral part of their religious obligation requires them to drink it. In *Smith,* the claim was that peyote embodied the supreme spirit and that adherents' exercise of their religion required ingesting this powerful drug.

Religious acts, as compared to religious beliefs, have the potential of running up against or contradicting certain societal rules. Beliefs are not ordinarily a fit subject for the criminal or civil law, but conduct is. If society deems a specific religious behavior objectionable, however, it cannot simply ban that behavior when it is engaged in for religious reasons. As Scalia put it in *Smith,* "It would doubtless be unconstitutional, for example, to ban the casting of 'statues that are to be used for worship purposes,' or to prohibit bowing before a golden calf."[8] More usually, religious practices, such as polygamy, alcohol and drug use, designated days of rest (other than Sunday), clothing or dietary restrictions for military personnel or prisoners, lifestyle choices, and so on, will conflict with laws that were not originally directed at a specific religion, but nonetheless effectively curb a religiously motivated practice. When a religious sect's practices violate our general societal norms, the question of constitutional guarantees gets quite murky.

The difficulty in the constitutional sphere, then, concerns those times when a religious practice is inconsistent with general laws that are passed without any particular religion in mind. Does the Free Exercise Clause mandate that religious practitioners sometimes be excused from societal laws? Scalia, in *Smith*, worried that "to permit this would be to make the professed doctrine of religious belief superior to the law of the land, and in effect to permit every citizen to become a law unto himself."[9]

The question of whether—and, if so, under what circumstances—someone can claim a religious exemption from a generally applicable law is very old. The first case presenting this issue was *Reynolds v. United States*,[10] an 1879 case in which the Supreme Court refused to find that the federal government was constitutionally obligated to allow Mormons to practice polygamy. In *Reynolds*, the Court held that although the government cannot interfere with a person's religious *beliefs*, it need not provide an exception for religious *conduct* so long as it has a rational basis for refusing such an exception. In this regard, the *Reynolds* Court observed, "Polygamy leads to the patriarchal principle, . . . which, when applied to large communities, fetters the people in stationary despotism, while that principle cannot long exist in connection with monogamy."[11] In 1961, in *Braunfeld v. Brown*,[12] the Court reaffirmed this approach when it held that Pennsylvania had no obligation to exempt a Jewish businessman from its Sunday closing law, despite the very significant, and possibly ruinous, effect it would have on his business. Justice Felix Frankfurter wrote the *Braunfeld* opinion over the forceful dissenting opinion of Justice William Brennan.

Just two years later, however, the Court changed direction dramatically when Justice Brennan wrote the opinion in *Sherbert v. Verner*.[13] In *Sherbert*, the Court ordered a state to pay unemployment benefits to a Seventh-Day Adventist, despite her unwillingness to work on Saturday (her Sabbath) as required by the state's unemployment compensation law. The claimant in *Sherbert* was arguably less disadvantaged than in *Braunfeld*—given that Braunfeld was effectively put out of business by the state's criminal statute while Sherbert was simply denied unemployment benefits. *Sherbert* essentially overruled *Braunfeld*. The new rule, crafted by Brennan, forced governments to allow exemptions to laws for those individuals exercising sincerely held religious beliefs, except when those laws served compelling interests and there was no less restrictive means by which to achieve that interest.

Since 1963, the compelling interest standard has been consistently applied and, indeed, expanded by the Court. Perhaps the most famous example is the 1972 decision in *Wisconsin v. Yoder*.[14] In *Yoder*, the Court held that the Amish were not required to send their children to public schools beyond the eighth grade in violation of their religious beliefs. The Court found that the state of Wisconsin had not shown compelling reasons to justify its *refusal* to grant a religious exemption. This holding greatly strengthened the free exercise right. Under the Court's previous rule, set forth in *Sherbert*, the government merely had to demonstrate compelling reasons for the general law, not for its decision to refuse a religiously based exemption.

With *Sherbert* and then *Yoder*, the Court established clear terrain for a successful free exercise challenge:

1. a demonstration of sincerity in wanting to conform to the religious practice;
2. a demonstration that the government's law poses a "cruel choice," placing a substantial burden on the religious practice involved; and
3. if the claimant has established steps 1 and 2, the government loses unless it can demonstrate (a) that the societal interest in not making an exception for the claimant's religious practice is compelling, and (b) that there is no less restrictive means to achieve the societal interest.

A perennial concern in free exercise cases is the fear that giving judges responsibility for assessing the weight or value of religious practices will result in their invading the very religious freedoms that the Free Exercise Clause was intended to safeguard. The background against which all religion issues must be measured is the second religion clause, the Establishment Clause, which prohibits government from making any "law respecting an establishment of religion." This clause is considered more fully later in this chapter, but it represents the belief that it is deeply troubling to have the government become so entangled with religion that it begins establishing or defining what tenets are central to a religion's practice. The Court, therefore, has held that the First Amendment prohibits a civil magistrate from engaging in what is known as a "centrality" test. In looking at whether there has been an assault on someone's free exercise of religion, a court cannot make assessments about the importance of a practice to a religion or of the harms that might befall a person forced to comply with a state's law.

In *Smith*, Justice Scalia had to determine the constitutionality of Oregon's refusal to make an exception to its drug laws for religiously inspired use of peyote. Under the Court's precedent, the applicable test amounted to a balance between the state's interest in not carving an exception to its general laws and the individual's right to freely practice his or her religion. But Scalia abhors balancing tests. He considers them unprincipled, unmanageable, and possibly uncivilized. He also believes that they invite judicial activism by permitting judges to infuse their values into the Constitution, cloaked as a search for the unwritten fundamental values of the founding fathers. Scalia has sought to eliminate all balancing tests at every opportunity. In *Smith*, he found such an opportunity and, more important, he found four justices to join his opinion.

Justice Scalia began his argument by reiterating the basic proposition that courts cannot be allowed to evaluate the spiritual importance or religious centrality of particular sectarian practices. Because this is the case, Scalia argued, if the "compelling interest" test is used, it would have to be applied "across the board, to all actions thought to be religiously commanded." "Any society adopting such a system," he warned, "would be courting anarchy, but that danger increases in direct proportion to the society's diversity of religious beliefs, and its determination to coerce or suppress none of them." To allow any constitutionally mandated exemptions is to require all of them. Such an approach, he believed, "required religious exemptions from civic obligations of almost every conceivable kind—ranging from compulsory military service to the payment of taxes."[15]

The only logical course of action that would avoid the slippery slope, Scalia maintained, would be to provide no constitutionally mandated exemptions. In *Smith*, Scalia asserted that laws of general application that incidentally burden the free exercise of religion *do not even implicate* the First Amendment. According to Scalia and the *Smith* majority, the First Amendment guarantee of free exercise of religion provides no protection—*none*—when a general and neutral law infringes religious traditions, observances, or practices. The legislatures are left the responsibility for carving out any exemptions—without safeguards from the Constitution. Scalia did not merely return to the 1879 standard of *Reynolds,* he went well beyond it. In *Reynolds,* the government at least had the obligation to have a rational basis for its decision not to provide any religious exemptions. Justice Sandra Day O'Connor, who concurred in the result in *Smith* but strongly disagreed with Scalia's radical reordering of such a basic right, wrote separately, saying, "It is difficult to deny that a law that prohibits religiously motivated conduct, even if the law is generally applicable . . . at least implicate[s] First Amendment concerns."[16] Yet, however difficult it was, Scalia denied exactly that.

Under Scalia's test, the only recourse individuals have to escape the "cruel choices" sometimes created by laws in which individuals must choose obedience to the state or to their faith is the political process. Scalia well understood "that leaving accommodation to the political process will place at a relative disadvantage those religious practices that are not widely engaged in."[17] Mainstream religions, of course, are likely to have the political muscle—no matter who is in the ruling majority—to obtain exemptions. Religious outsiders, or those not in the good graces of those in power, are out of luck. Scalia argued that this was a necessary result given the costs associated with what was, in his opinion, the only alternative: involving the judiciary in the process of evaluating which religious practices qualify, and which don't, under the First Amendment. The injury to minority religions, Scalia said, was "an unavoidable consequence of democratic government [that] must be preferred to a system in which each conscience is a law unto itself or in which judges weigh the social importance of all laws against the certainty of all religious beliefs."[18]

Justice O'Connor was incredulous. She wrote that "under our system of government . . . the First Amendment was enacted precisely to protect the rights of those whose religious practices are not shared by the majority and may be viewed with hostility." She made her point, stating, "The history of our free exercise doctrine amply demonstrates the harsh impact majoritarian rule has had on unpopular or emerging religious groups such as the Jehovah's Witnesses and the Amish."[19] To support her position, O'Connor quoted Justice Robert Jackson's justly famous statement of the Court's responsibility to protect basic rights:

The very purpose of a Bill of Rights was to withdraw certain subjects from the vicissitudes of political controversy, to place them beyond the reach of majorities and officials and to establish them as legal principles to be

applied by the courts. One's right to life, liberty, and property, to free
speech, a free press, freedom of worship and assembly, and other fundamental rights may not be submitted to vote; they depend on the outcome
of no elections.[20]

The effect of Scalia's *Smith* test is that no set of facts requires a constitutional exemption from a general law. In contrast, Justice O'Connor's
test—the traditional compelling interest test from *Sherbert/Yoder*—
requires a searching examination of the reasons why the government
believes no exceptions should be made. Unfortunately, O'Connor's application of the compelling interest test in this case ended up being little
more than a watered-down version of that ordinarily rigorous bar.
Oregon had argued that any exceptions would endanger its, and possibly
the nation's, war on drugs. Moreover, the state asserted, it had a legitimate and compelling interest in protecting users from the deleterious
effects of peyote. O'Connor accepted at face value Oregon's claims
regarding the great costs associated with making an exception for religious uses of peyote. She cited no research and considered no studies on
whether Oregon had any basis for its allegedly compelling justifications.
In effect, although not as profane as Scalia's approach, O'Connor's test
also violated the spirit of *Sherbert* and *Yoder* in ignoring the Court's
obligations to check the factual basis for the state's claims. The majority
essentially abdicated its responsibility for enforcing the substantive values
of free exercise.[21]

Justice Blackmun, joined by Justices Brennan and Marshall, dissented.
They agreed, foremost, that Justice Scalia's approach gutted the religious
freedom guaranteed by the First Amendment. For all intents and purposes, Scalia transformed the Free Exercise Clause into an equal protection guarantee that merely ensured that sects would not be actively
discriminated against. For Scalia, the First Amendment afforded no substantive protection to practice religion, only the procedural right to be
treated like everyone else. But being treated alike when you are different,
and especially when those differences involve fundamental matters of
belief, faith, and worship, constitutes an empty sort of equality. Blackmun wrote that Scalia held a "distorted view of our precedents" that led
him to consider the free exercise of religion to be "a 'luxury' that a well-
ordered society cannot afford and that the repression of minority religions [was an] 'unavoidable consequence of democratic government.' "[22]
Blackmun did not accept that "the Founders thought their dearly bought

freedom from religious persecution a 'luxury,' but an essential element of liberty—and they could not have thought religious intolerance 'unavoidable,' for they drafted the Religion Clauses precisely in order to avoid that intolerance."[23]

Justice Blackmun also strongly disagreed with Justice O'Connor's application of what he otherwise agreed was the correct test—that Oregon needed compelling reasons for not granting Native Americans an exception to use peyote. He pointed out, first of all, that the federal government and a multitude of states exempt Native Americans' use of peyote from their respective drug laws. It is somewhat difficult to argue that carving an exemption will undermine the nation's war on drugs when the federal government itself allows for the sacramental use of peyote. Indeed, Blackmun pointed out, in this case the state failed to evince "any concrete interest in enforcing its drug laws against religious users of peyote." Blackmun also found that the state's health interest was anything but compelling. He could find no evidence in the record "that the religious use of peyote has ever harmed anyone." Expert testimony supported the conclusion that peyote had beneficial consequences when used in Native American rituals. "There is considerable evidence that the spiritual and social support provided by the church has been effective in combating the tragic effects of alcoholism on the Native American population." Experts testified that, "[f]ar from promoting the lawless and irresponsible use of drugs, Native American Church members' spiritual code exemplifies values that Oregon's drug laws are presumably intended to foster."[24]

In the case of the Santerians in Hialeah, the city, taking a page from Justice Scalia's *Smith* decision, argued that its law punishing anyone who "unnecessarily kills an animal" is the epitome of a general and neutral prohibition. But Hialeah never argued that its laws were so general that they prohibited any killing of animals, since they allowed for hunting, fishing, extermination of pests, and euthanasia of sick or unwanted animals. The city's laws applied generally, however, to all *unnecessary* killings, which included sacrificial killings. But this claim highlights one of the inherent defects in Scalia's test. How does one recognize a general law when one sees one? The drug laws involved in *Smith*, for example, cannot be described as entirely general, since many drugs are permitted for medical purposes and many substances that might be considered "drugs," such as nicotine and alcohol, were not included. By necessity, all laws draw lines, and thus generality is always a judgment call. Under Scalia's test, so long as the general law in the text of the statute does not specifically prohibit a religious practice, it garners no judicial review. In the case of the Hialeah law prohibiting animal sacrifice, which Scalia found *did* violate the Free Exercise Clause, the problems lay in both the inartful drafting of the regulations and the multitude of statements on the legislative record explicitly attacking the Santerians. Scalia, in fact, wrote separately from the majority to say that a more artfully drawn prohibition would have gained his approval.[25]

Hialeah argued that its laws generally and neutrally prohibited the "unnecessary killing" of all animals, and were not limited to the Santerian practice of animal sacrifice. The use of the term "unnecessary," however, implied discretion, which, in turn, indicated that the law might be anything but "general" in practice. As Justice Kennedy noted in his decision for the Court, "one of the few reported Florida cases decided under [the applicable law] concludes that the use of live rabbits to train greyhounds is not unnecessary." In effect, then, "application of the ordinance's test of necessity devalues religious reasons for killing by judging them to be of lesser import than nonreligious reasons."[26] In Hialeah, sacrificing a chicken to save a loved one's soul is deemed "unnecessary," whereas killing a rabbit to hone a dog's competitive edge is considered "necessary."

If, as the Court found, a law is not general and neutral, and is directed at a particular religious practice that the community finds particularly abhorrent, the state can still justify the law if it has compelling reasons. The trial court in *Lukumi,* in fact, found that Hialeah had met this test. First, the court determined that animal sacrifices present a substantial health risk to both participants and the surrounding community. Animals were often kept in unsanitary conditions and their remains are sometimes dumped in public places. Second, the court determined that sacrifices had deleterious emotional and psychological consequences for children who witnessed them. Based on available research on modeling behavior, the court ruled that children who participated in the ceremonies could develop violent and other antisocial tendencies. Third, the trial court found that the method used in the sacrifices was unreliable and, together with the inhumane conditions in which many of these animals were kept, violated standards of basic decency. An assortment of experts testified that Santerian priests are not trained to kill animals efficiently and that the animals felt both pain and fear in the moments leading up to and during their slaughter. Finally, the trial court stated that the city had a compelling interest in restricting the slaughter or sacrifice of animals to areas zoned for slaughterhouse use. The court, however, did not explain how it reached this conclusion.[27]

The trial court cited extensive expert testimony to support its factual findings that the city had demonstrated compelling reasons for regulating animal sacrifice. For example, in regard to the city's claim that rituals injure children who witness them, the court was swayed by the testimony of Dr. Raul Huesmann, a research psychologist, who had done extensive work on the development of aggressive and violent behavior in children. The court was persuaded "that there is a correlation between the observation of violence by children, especially when conducted by persons of perceived high status, and the likelihood of the development of violent and aggressive behavior. The younger the child, the stronger the effect."[28] The court dismissed the Santerian expert, Dr. Angel Velez-Diaz, a clinical psychologist, who testified that while correlations exist between observing violence and committing violence, these findings could not be applied to predict effects on children observing ritualistic animal sacrifice.[29] For example, the correlations between television violence and violent behavior do not necessarily reflect a cause-and-effect relationship; it may be that violent children watch more violent television and not at all that violent television makes kids violent. Moreover, the ceremonial killing of animals in the context of religious observance cannot be said to be comparable to unsupervised television viewing or playing of video games. The trial court, however, said that Dr. Velez-Diaz had no research support for his opinions and thus found "the testimony of Dr. Huesmann more credible." The trial court concluded, accordingly, that the "governmental interest in guaranteeing the welfare of children is particularly strong."[30]

Oddly, although the majority opinion cited the trial court's findings of fact and noted the lower court's conclusion that these facts provided the city with a compelling interest to justify the law, the Supreme Court did not otherwise review the factual record. Justice Kennedy simply dismissed out-of-hand the city's claim and never mentioned the potential psychological effects on children who observe animal sacrifice. It appears that the charged legislative atmosphere that surrounded adoption of the challenged laws constituted a nearly *per se* violation. Ordinarily, the Court would consider an alternative ground that might sustain the city's action, such as the psychological consequences to children exposed to animal sacrifices, especially one that the trial court purported to rely upon for its decision. And given Kennedy's faith in psychological evidence, the failure is particularly conspicuous.

Although the city of Hialeah rested its basic argument on the *Smith* peyote decision, and many of the amicus briefs attacked Scalia's *Smith* test, the Court ultimately had no reason to revisit the *Smith* standard in *Lukumi*. As Justice Souter, concurring in *Lukumi,* observed, "Hialeah has provided a rare example of a law actually aimed at suppressing religious exercise."[31] Souter wrote separately, however, to urge the Court to overturn *Smith* at its first opportunity. Souter found *Smith* to be an aberration that neither followed from the history of the Free Exercise Clause nor comported with the Court's precedents interpreting it. He noted wryly, "it seems to me difficult to escape the conclusion that whatever *Smith*'s virtues, they do not include a comfortable fit with settled law."[32] Moreover, Scalia's test as set forth in *Smith* contradicted the original intent behind the clause and the historical reasons the founders placed it in the First Amendment. Souter stated, "the Clause was originally understood to preserve a right to engage in activities necessary to fulfill one's duty to one's God, unless those activities threatened the rights of others or the serious needs of the state."[33] This purpose supports the pre-*Smith* role of courts in evaluating the substantive basis for government's refusal to make exceptions to laws for religious exercise. Justice Souter concluded with the following powerful statement of what was at stake:

> The extent to which the Free Exercise Clause requires government to refrain from impeding religious exercise defines nothing less than the respective relationships in our constitutional democracy of the individual to government and to God. "Neutral, generally applicable" laws, drafted as they are from the perspective of the nonadherent, have the unavoidable potential of putting the believer to a choice between God and government. Our cases now present competing answers to the question when government, while pursuing secular ends, may compel disobedience to what one believes religion commands. The case before us [*Lukumi*] is rightly decided without resolving the existing tension, which remains for another day when it may be squarely faced.[34]

By any measure, *Smith* was a poorly decided case, one that had no basis in history, precedent, logic, or common sense. The Court split 5 to

4 when the case was decided in 1990. Only four members of the *Smith* Court remain on the bench in 2004, three from the majority (Scalia, Rehnquist, and Stevens) and one who dissented from the new rule set in the decision (O'Connor). Of those on the Court today, it is fairly certain that Scalia, Rehnquist, and Thomas would vote to affirm *Smith*; Justices O'Connor, Souter, Breyer, and Ginsburg are all probable votes for a return to the *Sherbert-Yoder* compelling interest rule. Only Stevens's and Kennedy's positions are unknown. Although Stevens joined the *Smith* majority, he has since become one of the most consistent liberal votes on the Court, and *Smith* is a most illiberal decision. Stevens has given no indication that he would rethink his *Smith* vote, but he could very well determine the Court's prospects for overturning the decision. Kennedy also has not indicated how he would vote regarding *Smith*, but has increasingly voiced opinions supporting a fairly expansive reading of the Bill of Rights. Moreover, in the religion arena, he has demonstrated a willingness to part company from Justice Scalia, particularly in the area of the Establishment Clause, the second pillar of religious freedom guaranteed by the Constitution. The rift between Kennedy and Scalia is perhaps best seen in *Lee v. Weisman*,[35] a 1992 case concerning school prayer at graduation ceremonies. In that case, Justice Kennedy wrote for a majority striking down the practice and Justice Scalia wrote a petulant dissent condemning both the decision and its author.

The very first clause of the First Amendment is not, like virtually all of the guarantees contained in the Bill of Rights, an individual freedom, such as free speech, due process, or the right not to be subjected to cruel and unusual punishment. The first clause provides that "Congress shall make no law respecting an establishment of religion." By keeping government out of the business of religion, the Establishment Clause is thought to protect religious institutions and the congregations that assemble under their luminescence. Unlike the Free Exercise Clause, in which religious practices inevitably get entangled with government regulations, it would appear that Jefferson's wall of separation would be easier to implement on the Establishment side of the religion equation. Government simply is enjoined from throwing its weight behind any sect or religious denomination; it is, and must remain, orthodoxly secular. In fact, however, the Establishment Clause cases may be more confused than their sibling Free Exercise Clause cases. *Lee v. Weisman* well illustrates the doctrinal chaos in this area.

Ironically, *Lee* concerned the city of Providence, Rhode Island. The father of Deborah Weisman, a Providence high school student, challenged the city's practice of permitting members of the clergy to offer invocation and benediction prayers as part of the formal graduation ceremonies for middle schools and high schools. The irony lay in the fact that Roger Williams, who founded Rhode Island, was the first to propound the view that strict separation of church and state would inure to the benefit of religion. Today, in contrast, many who argue for government support of religion, or the injection of religion into civic affairs, believe religion will be strengthened by government backing. Williams believed that just the opposite was true. He feared that government involvement in religion would lead to either the dilution of doctrine when the government sanitized it for general consumption, or the corruption of the pious by the power and worldly goods that grease the wheels of government. Government entanglement with religion, Williams maintained, would inevitably corrupt religion. "Worldly corruptions," Williams wrote, "might consume the churches if sturdy fences against the wilderness were not maintained."[36] It was this basic view, that "no law respecting an establishment of religion" be countenanced, that prevailed with the framers. Madison explained that "religion & Govt. will both exist in greater purity, the less they are mixed together."[37]

However attractive in theory a wall of separation between church and state might be, American tradition and practice contain no such clear demarcation between the two. Presidents, from Washington onward, have invoked the deity for guidance and strength. In *Marsh v. Chambers*,[38] the Court upheld the use of public funds to pay legislative chaplains who preside at the start of congressional sessions and on other selected occasions. Our currency displays God's name. In 1954, Congress amended the law codifying the Pledge of Allegiance to add the words "under God." Frankly, theism imbues modern American politics. While the United States may not be a "Christian nation," it is—at least to hear it from most politicians—a God-fearing and blessed one.

Despite God's ubiquity in American politics, the Constitution mandates that this association between religion and the state be strictly restrained. The outer limits of the infiltration of God into civil ceremony and daily life, however, are indistinct. While little danger exists that the Supreme Court will hold "In God We Trust" on our coins and paper money to be constitutionally repugnant, or that Thanksgiving will be abolished as an invalid establishment of religion, other situations may be closer calls. For instance, in 2003 a panel of the United States Court of Appeals for the Ninth Circuit found that the use of "under God" in the Pledge of Allegiance violated the Establishment Clause.[39] The Supreme Court agreed to hear the case, and a decision can be expected in June 2004. However the Court decides the particular case of God and the Pledge, the more important issue for constitutional law concerns what test it uses to set the line dividing church and state. Without Jefferson's proverbial wall, some verbal formulation is needed to demarcate this boundary. So far, consensus on a single test has eluded the Court, and this will likely continue long after the Pledge case is decided.

Over more than three decades now, the Court has used a hodgepodge of guidelines to govern its Establishment Clause case law. In 1971, the Court set forth a three-part test in the case of *Lemon v. Kurtzman*,[40] a unanimous decision authored by Chief Justice Burger that struck down state support of salaries of teachers of secular subjects in parochial and other nonpublic schools. The *Lemon* test mandated that for a law not to be an Establishment Clause violation, (1) it must have a secular legislative purpose, (2) its principal or primary effect must be one that neither advances nor inhibits religion, and (3) it must not foster an "excessive entanglement" with religion. Almost from its debut, the *Lemon* test was assailed by justices and scholars alike. Critics complained that the test is indeterminate and that decisions rendered under it are inconsistent. Yet, somehow, it survives. Justice Scalia likened the test to "some ghoul in a late-night horror movie that repeatedly sits up in its grave and shuffles abroad, after being repeatedly killed and buried." The *Lemon* test, Scalia wrote, "stalks our Establishment Clause jurisprudence . . . frightening the little children and school attorneys."[41]

Lemon, as Scalia's image suggests, carries along with it the scars of many battles, but like the late-night horror monster, these scars have only made the creature more frightful. The most heralded modification of *Lemon* has been Justice O'Connor's "endorsement" test, set forth in *Lynch v. Donnelly.*[42] Her test effectively collapsed the first two elements of *Lemon*—purpose and effect—into a single factor of constitutional concern: "Endorsement sends a message to nonadherents that they are outsiders, not full members of the political community, and an accompanying message to adherents that they are insiders, favored members of the political community."[43] O'Connor's endorsement test was adopted by a majority of the Court in 1989 in *County of Allegheny v. ACLU*.[44] The endorsement test is essentially empirically based, since it asks, for example, whether a reasonable observer would consider a Christmas display at city hall to be a "government endorsement" of religion. The Court, however, has never looked for data on the answer to the endorsement question, and instead relies on intuition and common sense.

Another modification of *Lemon* occurred in the *Lee v. Weisman* case. In *Lee,* Justice Kennedy explained that the school's principal, Robert E. Lee, chose Rabbi Gutterman to give the invocation and benediction at Deborah Weisman's middle school graduation ceremony. In addition to selecting the clergyman, the principal gave the rabbi a copy of the "Guidelines for Civic Occasions" and advised him that the prayer should be nonsectarian. Kennedy found that by doing so the principal interjected himself into "the business" of "compos[ing] official prayers." Arguably, this amount of entanglement was enough to violate the *Lemon* test and thus the Constitution, since there is simply no such thing as a generic prayer, at least from the perspective of the nonbeliever. Believers too might object, since whatever form of prayer government chooses will offend those who would prefer a different form. But the facts here were not close. With *Lee,* the Court chose not to revisit, as many had wanted it to do, the continuing validity of the *Lemon* test. "The government involvement with religious activity in this case is pervasive," Kennedy said, "to the point of creating a state-sponsored and state-directed religious exercise in a public school."[45]

Kennedy, however, felt obliged to push further, since the Court had upheld a similar kind of "prayer" for legislative sessions in *Marsh* without applying *Lemon* at all. In *Marsh,* a key consideration was the long history and settled tradition of legislative chaplains, a practice that effectively excepted them from the general rule. The question, then, was how was *Lee* different from *Marsh?* Kennedy found the answer in modern psychology.

The obvious difference between *Marsh* and *Lee* is the audience. In the former, the audience consisted of legislators, while in the latter it was composed of students, faculty, and parents. In issues of separating the secular from the sectarian, the school setting has always been reviewed with special vigilance. For one thing, schoolchildren are a captive audience, so that, unlike the legislators in *Marsh,* objectors cannot readily stand up and leave. And even if a student has the right to walk out, the school context does not lend itself easily to such behavior. However, in *Lee,* the school argued, and Deborah's father conceded, that the graduation exercises were not mandatory; students could obtain their degrees without attending the ceremony. But Kennedy was unwilling to grant any relevance to this fact. "To say a teenage student has a real choice not to attend her high school graduation is formalistic in the extreme."[46]

Although public schools did not exist at the founding of the republic, they have assumed a central place in American society. This fundamental and indispensable role was explicitly recognized in *Brown v. Board of Education* and is a basic fact of modern American life. Public schools have become an integral part of, and a sustaining force for, the republic itself. This role includes the basic proposition that church and state are separate. Writing in 1948, Justice Frankfurter made this point eloquently:

> The sharp confinement of the public schools to secular education was a recognition of the need of a democratic society to educate its children, insofar as the State undertook to do so, in an atmosphere free from pressures in a realm in which pressures are most resisted and where conflicts are most easily and most bitterly engendered. Designed to serve as perhaps the most powerful agency for promoting cohesion among a heterogeneous democratic people, the public school must keep scrupulously free from entanglement in the strife of sects.[47]

Justice Kennedy described the issue as involving the experience of the student who objects when the people surrounding him or her stand and bow their heads in prayer. Kennedy crafted his argument around the principle that "at a minimum, the Constitution guarantees that government may not coerce anyone to support or participate in religion or its exercise, or otherwise to act in a way which establishes a state religion or religious faith, or tends to do so."[48] The situation presented here could effectively coerce nonbelieving students. The state's position was that a student had the choice to sit or stand. The state conceded that the situation imposes some pressure on the nonadherent to stand, but nonetheless, it argued, standing connotes nothing more than due respect for others and the sentiments being expressed. Kennedy saw it otherwise. "In a school context," he observed, this pressure "may appear to the nonbeliever or dissenter to be an attempt to employ the machinery of the State to enforce a religious orthodoxy." The pressure on the student to

conform to state-sponsored religious orthodoxy, he stated, "though subtle and indirect, can be as real as any overt compulsion."[49]

Prayer in the graduation ceremony, Kennedy stated, gives the student
only the choice of participating or protesting. Turning to several empirical studies, he observed that "Research in psychology supports the common assumption that adolescents are often susceptible to pressure from
their peers towards conformity, and that the influence is strongest in
matters of social convention."[50] Psychological research demonstrated a
corrosive effect on children of the social pressures to conform, in this
case, to government-sponsored prayer. Therefore, Kennedy said, "we
think the State may not, consistent with the Establishment Clause, place
primary and secondary school children in this position."[51] But Kennedy
cited only three studies, and none of them specifically researched the
question before the Court.[52] The studies were empirical investigations of
general issues concerning peer pressure and adolescents' conformity to
peers and parents under different circumstances. Kennedy made no effort
to explain the relevance of the studies to the case and, indeed, did not
even summarize the studies' methods or findings.

Justice Scalia was apoplectic. He objected foremost to the Court's
"laying waste" to "a tradition that is as old as public school graduation
ceremonies themselves," and which "is a component of an even more
longstanding tradition of nonsectarian prayer to God at public celebra-
tions generally."[53] What provoked his ire even more, however, was the
"psychological coercion" test Kennedy employed to reach his result.
Scalia found it an "embarrassment" that "our Establishment Clause jurisprudence . . . has come to require scrutiny more commonly associated
with interior decorators than with the judiciary." Indeed, he found that
"interior decorating is a rock-hard science compared to psychology practiced by amateurs."[54] He continued, saying:

> A few citations of "research in psychology" that have no particular bearing
> upon the precise issue here, cannot disguise the fact that the Court has
> gone beyond the realm where judges know what they are doing. The
> Court's argument that state officials have "coerced" students to take part
> in the invocation and benediction at graduation ceremonies is, not to put
> too fine a point on it, incoherent.[55]

Smelling blood, Justice Scalia continued to press his point, since he
believed the "psychological coercion" test to be "the very linchpin of the

Court's opinion." Scalia completely rejected expansion of the concept of coercion to include psychological and social pressures. Coercion, Scalia maintained, meant a threat of real penalty. He said that actual coercion is "readily discernible to those of us who have made a career of reading the disciples of Blackstone rather than of Freud."[56] Scalia contrasted the subtle pressures suffered by the students in this case to those experienced by students in *Virginia Board of Education v. Barnette,*[57] in which the Court held that reciting the Pledge of Allegiance could not be required. In *Barnette*, failure to recite the Pledge "resulted in expulsion, threatened the expelled child with the prospect of being sent to a reformatory for criminally inclined juveniles, and subjected his parents to prosecution (and incarceration) for causing delinquency."[58] Scalia commented that Kennedy's assertion that the subtle pressures in this case were "the 'practical' equivalent of the legal sanctions in *Barnette* is . . . well, let me just say it is not delicate and fact-sensitive analysis." He found the Court's opinion to be as "intriguing for what it does not say as for what it says." "It does not say," he remarked, "that students are psychologically coerced to bow their heads, place their hands in a Durer-like prayer position, pay attention to the prayers, utter 'Amen,' or in fact pray." Perhaps, he said, "further intensive psychological research remains to be done on these matters."[59]

Intending to show the absurdity of Kennedy's psychological coercion test, Justice Scalia asked how the Court could fail to mention that just prior to the rabbi's invocation, all those assembled stood to recite the Pledge of Allegiance. Scalia asked, "since the Pledge of Allegiance has been revised . . . to include the phrase 'under God,' recital of the Pledge would appear to raise the same Establishment Clause issue as the invocation and benediction." Scalia reasoned that, "[i]f students were psychologically coerced, moments before, to stand for . . . the Pledge," then, logically, he concluded, the Pledge "ought to be the next project for the Court's bulldozer."[60]

The Court agreed to hear a case in 2004 out of California in which both the trial court and the Ninth Circuit Court of Appeals held that the "under God" language in the Pledge violated the Establishment Clause—thus bringing to fruition what Justice Scalia had meant to be an absurd and extreme example in his *Lee* dissent. But Scalia will not hear the case. Scalia's enthusiasm for his own rhetoric led him to make certain ill-considered remarks about the lower court's holding in the Pledge of Allegiance case. At a Knights of Columbus dinner, Scalia complained that the Supreme Court had created a jurisprudence that mandated that "the government may neither favor nor disfavor any particular sect of religion or religion in general." But, he pointed out, "never mind that this is contrary to our whole tradition, to 'in God we trust' on the coins, to Thanksgiving proclamations, to [publicly funded] chaplains, to tax exemptions for places of worship, which has always existed in America." The Court's philosophy, Scalia went on, "enabled a district court in California to hold, with some plausible support in the opinions of the United States Supreme Court, that it is unconstitutional to say in the Pledge of Allegiance 'one nation, under God.' " Scalia's comments ran afoul of the ethical prohibition proscribing judges from commenting on pending cases. Scalia subsequently recused himself, a move that could result in affirming the circuit court's decision to remove the phrase "under God" from the Pledge. As it turns out, God was inserted in the Pledge of Allegiance in 1954 partly at the urging of the Knights of Columbus as a rebuttal to the Godless communism that appeared to threaten Western democracy on every front. It seems appropriate, then, that the Knights might play a role in determining if God is excised or remains in our oath of loyalty to God and country.

While graduation prayers might seem to be a relatively benign, albeit still invalid, attempt by government to insinuate religion into the schoolhouse, states have been known to employ more insidious methods to give schoolchildren "the word of God." Perhaps the most famous example of this is the recurring crusade by some state legislators against the teaching of evolution in public schools. In 1982, Louisiana passed a law, the Balanced Treatment for Creation-Science and Evolution-Science in Public School Instruction Act, which provided that evolution could not be taught in public schools unless equal time was accorded creation science. Under the statute, schools had the option of teaching both of the "scientific" theories, or teaching neither of them. The legislation was challenged by parents, teachers, scientists, and many religious leaders as an unconstitutional establishment of religion by the State. In 1987, the Supreme Court invalidated the law in the case of *Edwards v. Aguillard.*[61]

In an opinion authored by Justice Brennan, the Court found that the primary purpose of Louisiana's act was to advance religion, running afoul of the first prong of the *Lemon* test.[62] As a practical matter, however, asserting that an act's purpose violates the Constitution does not usually reap enough factual evidence to invalidate a statute. Legislative intent is notoriously difficult to pin down, since there may be as many intentions as there are legislators. Not all states keep assiduous records of legislative debates, and, even when such records exist, politicians cannot always be trusted to express their true purposes—especially if they know that the "wrong" purposes will result in the law's invalidation. This appeared to be the very strategy adopted by Louisiana legislators and, indeed, was the approach behind the national movement advocating the enactment of similar balanced treatment acts.

Paul Ellwanger, a respiratory therapist, without degrees in science or law, drafted the act that was used by Louisiana legislators, and which served as a model for a nearly identical law passed in Arkansas. Arkansas's law was invalidated in 1982 by a federal judge after a ten-day trial.[63] In its opinion, which held that the teaching of creation science in public schools violated the Establishment Clause, the Arkansas trial court quoted a letter from Ellwanger to State Senator Joseph Carlucci of Florida outlining the best strategy to avoid constitutional complications:

> It would be very wise, if not actually essential, that all of us who are engaged in this legislative effort be careful not to present our position and our work in a religious framework. For example, in written communications that might somehow be shared with those other persons whom we may be trying to convince, it would be well to exclude our own personal testimony and/or witness for Christ, but rather, if we are so moved, to give that testimony on a separate attached note.[64]

This might be an effective strategy—if it does not get discovered by the courts. The state decided not to appeal the decision, so the Supreme Court never had the opportunity to hear the case.

In addition, the fact that a legislative policy is strongly supported by religious groups does not mean it should automatically be adjudged to advance religion unconstitutionally. Such a standard would have doomed abolitionist legislation of the nineteenth century and many humanitarian laws of the twentieth. Justice Scalia, dissenting in *Edwards,* commented, "we surely would not strike down a law providing money to feed the hungry or shelter the homeless if it could be demonstrated that, but for the religious beliefs of the legislators, the funds would not have been approved."[65] Today, religious activists advocate the balanced treatment acts, Scalia pointed out, "but yesterday's resulted in the abolition of slavery, and tomorrow's may bring relief for famine victims."[66]

Louisiana defended its law on the basis of two arguments. The state contended, first, that "creation science" really is a science, and, second, that "evolution-theory" is not. Louisiana's claim boiled down to the position that "creation science" was at least as scientific as "evolution-science" and that whether they were each a patchwork of guesses and faith or could be considered scientific did not matter. They should be treated similarly and, as the statute mandated, either taught together or not taught at all.

Louisiana maintained that creation science was, in fact, a bona fide science. The basic belief holds that life appeared abruptly in the fossil record and has remained relatively static through time. Orthodox creation science embodies four basic tenets:

(1) that a divine Creator created the world from nothing ("ex nihilo");
(2) that the Creator fashioned distinct "kinds" (or "types") of plants and animals that cannot give rise to new "kinds";
(3) that a "worldwide flood" or "Deluge" formed fossils and other paleontological and geological phenomena; and
(4) that the universe had a "relatively" recent inception (within the past 10,000 years).[67]

The theory, the state asserted, did not depend on biblical authority. According to the "hundreds and hundreds" of scientists cited by the state, creation theory accords better with the facts than does evolution. Moreover, the state claimed that only two viable theories existed: either a creator deposited life whole on the planet or it evolved as Darwin first posited. Teaching creation science, the argument goes, would highlight the flaws allegedly replete in evolutionary theory.

At the same time, Louisiana also asserted that evolution was a mere theory, and might be better described as a "guess" or even a "myth." As myth, it has become a central tenet of "secular humanism," which the Supreme Court has described in other cases as tantamount to "religion." Through this reasoning, the teaching of evolution is itself unconstitutional as a violation of the Establishment Clause.

In the end, the Court held that the Louisiana law violated the Establishment Clause solely on the basis that the legislature had a sectarian purpose in passing the law, despite a dearth of legislative history suggesting religious motivation. Louisiana was no Hialeah. As part of a well-orchestrated plan, Louisiana legislators expressly and repeatedly rejected the suggestion that religion lay behind the statute. With no smoking gun, Justice Brennan could only presume that but one motivation was behind this enactment. Yet, since the trial court had invalidated the law on summary judgment, no trial had been held. There was no battle of the experts in the lower courts, though the record was quite complete thanks to the many briefs filed by interested parties in the case. Brennan never made a factual finding, nor did any judge below, that "creation-science" was not science. Justice Scalia criticized him for this, accusing the Court of narrow-minded illiberality for rejecting "creation-science" without considering the evidence for it:

> [We cannot] say (or should we say) that the scientific evidence for evolution is so conclusive that no one could be gullible enough to believe that there is any real scientific evidence to the contrary, so that the legislation's stated purpose must be a lie. Yet that illiberal judgment, that Scopes-in-reverse, is ultimately the basis on which the Court's facile rejection of the Louisiana Legislature's purpose must rest.[68]

The bottom line for Scalia was that there was no trial, and therefore no factual record, on which the majority could base any statement that creation science was or was not science. "Perhaps," Scalia said, "what the Louisiana Legislature has done is unconstitutional because there is no such evidence, and the scheme they have established will amount to no more than a presentation of the Book of Genesis." But without a trial, "we have no basis on the record to conclude that creation science need be anything other than a collection of scientific data supporting the theory that life abruptly appeared on earth."[69]

The trial court gave two reasons for its decision to grant summary judgment and invalidate the law without a trial.[70] The principal basis was the court's rejection of the state's claim that at least one genuine issue of material fact was in dispute: "the definition of science."[71] The court said it would "decline the invitation to judge that debate," explaining that "whatever 'science' may be, 'creation,' as the term is used in the statute, involves religion, and the teaching of 'creation science' . . . involves teaching 'tailored to the principles' of a particular sect or group of sects. . . . While all religions may not teach the existence of a supreme being," the court asserted, "a belief in a supreme being (a creator) is generally considered to be a religious tenet." Moreover, the court said it was disinclined to make the people of Louisiana pay "the very considerable needless expense . . . of a protracted trial."[72]

An interesting phenomenon of the *Edwards* case was that despite the fact that no trial was held on the definition of science or the merit of creation science as science, the Court had before it incredibly rich information on these subjects. Both sides in the controversy marshaled their supporters to submit amicus briefs arguing the merits or demerits of "creation science" and evolution and to debate the nature of science. Opponents of the law included seventy-two Nobel laureates and seventeen state academies of science who signed a lengthy brief on the very definition of science. One of the strongest and most vehement arguments came from the National Academies of Science (NAS), the preeminent organization of scientists in the United States. The NAS brief declared categorically that "Creation science is not science." It does not meet any of the criteria for science and instead relies upon "supernatural means inaccessible to human understanding."[73]

The NAS also did not shy away from defending evolution and decrying the Louisiana slight of referring to it as "guesswork" or "myth." In a scientific defense, they provided a wonderful sense of the rigor brought to the subject of evolution by scientists:

> The degree of similarity in the sequence of nucleotides in DNA (or of amino acids in proteins) can now be precisely quantified. For example, the protein cytochrome-a in humans and chimpanzees consists of the same 104 amino acids in exactly the same order, whereas that of rhesus monkeys differs from them by one amino acid, that of horses by 11 amino acids, and that of the tuna by 21 amino acids. The extent of derivation corresponds to the time interval since fish, mammals, and human ancestors appeared in the geological record, i.e., the degree of divergence reflects the time that has passed since the respective lineages branched out from a common ancestry. Thus, inferences from paleontology, comparative anatomy and other disciplines as to the evolutionary history of organisms can be tested by examining the sequences of nucleotides in the DNA or the sequences of amino acids in proteins. The potential of such tests is overwhelming. Each of the thousands of genes and proteins provides an independent test of evolutionary history.[74]

Although never expressed in so many words, Justice Brennan relied on the surplus of credentialed authority, conveyed through numerous amicus briefs, to conclude that "creation-science" was religion, not science. He simply could not accept Louisiana's claim that "creation-science" was merely one more subject in the lexicon of knowledge that the state was permitted, indeed obligated, to impart to its students. If creationism were not so completely imbued with religious tenets, Louisiana's argument might have had merit.

In many respects, the argument over "creation science" and evolution represents the intersection between the two principal clauses of the First Amendment, religion and speech. Louisiana tried to frame the debate as one of speech. The Court has described the First Amendment as creating a marketplace in which all ideas are welcome. In the marketplace of ideas, truth is thought to win out through the open competition of alternative points of view. The speech clause, therefore, encourages full participation of competing perspectives, even when government is a participant in the debate. While the religion clauses operate on the basis that government participation in religious establishment threatens individual freedom, in the realm of free speech the theory is that individual freedom is advanced by the unfettered airing of all competing viewpoints. In regard to speech, more is usually better.

11

SHOUTING FIRE:

The Moral and Empirical Consequences
of Free Speech

Pasties and a G-string moderate the expression [of nude dancing] to some degree, to be sure, but only to a degree. Dropping the final stitch is prohibited, but the limitation is minor when measured against the dancer's remaining capacity and opportunity to express the erotic message.

— JUSTICE DAVID H. SOUTER
BARNES V. GLEN THEATRE (CONCURRING)

No area of constitutional law is more fact sensitive than the First Amendment guarantee of freedom of speech. At the same time, no area of constitutional law is as doctrinally confused. One is hard-pressed to find cases so muddled, and court decisions so inconsistent, as those attempting to articulate the contours of this most basic right. Perhaps there lies a connection between these occurrences. Essential to the application of virtually every one of the multitude of doctrines contained in those few words—"Congress shall 'make no law' abridging the freedom of speech"—are factual questions, many of which are amenable to scientific test.

Although the Constitution speaks in absolute terms, that Congress (and, by interpretation, all government actors) shall make no law, the reality is rather less categorical. The rule is perhaps more aptly phrased, "Congress shall make no law abridging freedom of speech unless it has good enough reasons for doing so." These reasons tend to be, as often as not, empirical. The Supreme Court has told us that government can regulate "fighting words" that will cause fights, obscene photographs that cause moral depravity, child pornography that causes injury to children, and words that advocate imminent lawless action that will likely provoke violence or produce illegality.

The First Amendment is nearly ubiquitous in modern American society—it applies to subjects ranging from abortion protesters to the zoning of adult bookstores. But, for whatever reasons, scientific issues seem to arise disproportionately in cases involving sex, perhaps best illustrated by the Court's several run-ins with nude dancing. What Marlene Dietrich said about sex in America apparently applies equally to the Supreme Court. "Sex. In America an obsession. In other parts of the world a fact."[1]

Americans spend more money at strip clubs than at Broadway, off-Broadway, regional, and nonprofit theaters, at the opera and ballet, and at jazz and classical music performances—combined.[2] Nude dancing establishments attract over ten million patrons per year who collectively spend upwards of three billion dollars on this form of entertainment.[3] Despite the popularity of these businesses among citizens, municipalities continue to enact ordinances attempting to regulate them. Such regulations ordinarily assume one of two basic forms. The more common type are zoning laws that exclude strip clubs from residential districts or keep them some distance away from schools and churches. A second and increasingly popular tool is the application of general indecency laws, such as public nudity bans, to live nude dancing clubs. In conception, these two approaches present very different constitutional issues, since zoning laws merely segregate nude dancing establishments from decent society, whereas indecency statutes prohibit an entire class or form of speech. Over time, however, the Court has begun to merge the constitutional analyses that apply in these different cases and, in doing so, has entangled the law. A central ingredient in the Court's muddle is the science of nude dancing or, more precisely, the science of its effects.

An early and oft-used form of regulating sex shops, or what are known in genteel society as adult entertainment establishments, was zoning, which corralled adult businesses in one area to minimize their impact on other neighborhoods and separate them from schools, churches, and proper society more generally. Zoning also has the effect, probably unintended, of giving consumers a sort of mini-mall of sex shops, making shopping much more convenient. The central case setting forth the current standard for evaluating zoning of adult establishments, including strip clubs, video parlors, adult shops, and adult bookstores, is the 1986 decision in *City of Renton v. Playtime Theatres, Inc.*[4] Chief Justice William Rehnquist wrote the opinion for the Court.[5]

Renton, a suburb of Seattle, with a population of approximately

32,000, had enacted an ordinance prohibiting any " 'adult motion picture theater' from locating within 1,000 feet of any residential zone, single or multiple family dwelling, church, or park, and within one mile of any school." The Renton City Council passed this ordinance on the basis of a Seattle study that indicated that adult establishments had negative secondary effects on the neighborhoods in which they were located. In particular, the Seattle study reported that adult shops contribute to neighborhood blight, including higher crime rates and lower property values.

It was a new issue for the Court, but Chief Justice Rehnquist noted the Court's previous holding in the case of *Young v. American Mini Theatres, Inc.,*[6] in which the Court had upheld Detroit's zoning of adult theaters. No majority rule, however, had emerged from that decision. In *Young,* Detroit had similarly found a causal connection between adult-oriented businesses and blighted neighborhoods. The city of Detroit dispersed the theaters in order to minimize their effects, while the city of Renton put them all in the same neighborhood, with roughly the same objective in mind.

Rehnquist described the Renton ordinance as "content-neutral," since its focus was on the secondary effects of the speech and not the speech itself. Under established First Amendment case law, regulations that discriminate on the basis of the content of speech only pass muster if the government has compelling reasons to justify the law. Under Rehnquist's theory, regulations directed at secondary effects—that is, laws whose purpose was avoidance of blighted neighborhoods—were content-neutral. The argument was that Renton cared about what went on outside these theaters, not inside. "The appropriate inquiry" for content-neutral regulations, Rehnquist stated, "is whether the . . . ordinance is designed to serve substantial governmental interests and allows for reasonable alternative avenues of communication."[7] A content-based regulation, in contrast, which targets the primary effect of the speech—here, an erotic message—would have to be justified by compelling government interests and the nonexistence of a more narrowly tailored alternative. Ordinarily, moral outrage alone does not qualify as a compelling interest; moreover, the narrowly tailored requirement demands that government not employ regulatory means that cut too broad a swath through speech.

Renton's claim rested on the empirical proposition that adult entertainment establishments created conditions that led to increased crime, such as prostitution, rape, assaults, and public intoxication. But Renton did not conduct any studies testing this hypothesis. Instead, the city relied on research studies conducted in Seattle, and the generalized anecdotal experience of the city council members. Chief Justice Rehnquist said that this was enough. He stated that a city need not conduct original research before acting in this context. "The First Amendment," according to Rehnquist, "does not require a city, before enacting such an ordinance, to conduct new studies or produce evidence independent of that already generated by other cities, so long as whatever evidence the city relies upon is reasonably believed to be relevant to the problem that the city addresses." He concluded, "that was the case here."[8] He did not explain why it was reasonable for Renton to rely on the Seattle study—and did not consider either the methods or principles of the study or the reasons it could be generalized to the situation in Renton.

In constitutional law, the standard of review for a fact like the relationship between nude dancing and blighted neighborhoods depends on the reading of the Constitution. Notably, the Court rarely says explicitly what standard of proof applies to constitutional fact-finding. For more ordinary facts, such as guilt in criminal cases or liability in civil cases, courts employ well-known standards of proof, the two best known being "beyond a reasonable doubt" and "by a preponderance of the evidence." But the Court has not provided similar guidelines for what standards should apply to constitutional facts. The Court has never, for instance, said that a state or city must demonstrate that adult establishments cause diminished property values or crime by a preponderance of the evidence, or any other level of proof. Instead, the Court buries fact questions deep in its more general jurisprudence and leaves its audience to guess what the test is. It was for this reason that Rehnquist could so easily skirt the factual question regarding proof that nude dancing theaters caused secondary effects. Such vagueness breeds irresponsibility, both on the part of courts and on the part of governing bodies that pass laws supposedly buttressed by those facts.

Most immediately, the law that applies to constitutional facts must be defined. As set forth by the Court, laws that infringe the First Amendment's guarantee of free speech are categorized as either content-based or content-neutral, and the amount of judicial scrutiny any law receives depends on which category it falls into. As a matter of basic constitutional law, content-based laws are rigorously reviewed and can only pass muster if the state has compelling reasons to justify the discrimination; content-neutral laws, in contrast, such as a law banning all roadside advertising, apply to all messages equally, and they receive much less rigorous review.

The term "content neutral," while it sounds innocuous enough, can be extremely misleading, as in the context of zoning regulations of adult entertainment. These laws are, in fact, drafted to apply to certain kinds of speech based on its content, that is, its erotic message. After all, it is the charged eroticism that lawmakers presume causes increases in crimes such as prostitution, rape, and assault. On the face of such ordinances, then, cities like Renton appear to be discriminating against certain kinds of speech, a result that is ordinarily a core concern of the First Amendment. The secondary effects theory, however, changes the focus from the face of the statute to the legislative objective. The city of Renton claimed that it did not object to the erotic message of adult entertainment; it merely sought to avoid the increased crime and decreased property values associated with this kind of speech. Moreover, Renton argued that the erotic message was not censored, but rather merely moved to another part of town. Rehnquist agreed that the regulation's limited impact was an important consideration. The First Amendment, he said, requires only "that Renton refrain from effectively denying respondents a reasonable opportunity to open and operate an adult theater within the city."[9] The relatively lenient judicial review in the *Renton* zoning case, therefore, was attributable to the city's claim that its focus was the secondary effects of the speech, not its message, together with the non-absolute nature of the regulation. Here the Court gave the city of Renton, if not a free pass on judicial scrutiny, then certainly a discounted ticket, by accepting the city's contention that it was merely regulating the places in which the erotic message could be displayed in order to lessen the unintended consequences of the speech. The critical foundation of the city's claim was, of course, the factual premise that adult entertainment establishments cause neighborhood blight.

Rehnquist's statement that the city need only "reasonably believe" the evidence it purportedly relied upon, and that there would be no substantive judicial evaluation of the proffered research to assess validity, reliability, or even relevance, should mystify, if not alarm, free speech advocates. But it gets worse yet.

An alternative means of regulating certain kinds of adult businesses, in particular nude dancing clubs, is to apply ordinary indecency laws to them. This was the subject of the 1991 decision in *Barnes v. Glen Theatre, Inc.*[10] Indiana enacted a statutory requirement that dancers at strip clubs not go beyond pasties and G-strings when they performed.[11] The requirement was a component of Indiana's general prohibition on nudity in public. The challenger of the law was the proprietor of the Kitty Kat Lounge who argued that this prohibition violated the dancers' right to free speech.

The initial question presented in these cases concerns whether nude dancing can fairly be defined as speech. The Court has, at least through the twentieth century, taken a very broad view of what qualifies for First Amendment protection. Although political debate represents the core of First Amendment concern, books, photographs, paintings, performance art, and dance have all been readily included under the amendment's umbrella. The Free Speech Clause thus extends not only to speech, but to all forms of expressive conduct, like dance. That dance can be speech is not considered controversial by the Court. Indeed, the Book of Psalms directs, "Praise Him with . . . dance." The French poet Stéphane Mallarmé said that a dancer, "writing with her body . . . suggests things which the written work could express only in several paragraphs of dialogue or descriptive prose." Nonetheless, Chief Justice Rehnquist commented that "nude dancing of the kind sought to be performed here is expressive conduct within the outer perimeters of the First Amendment, though we view it as only marginally so."[12]

Barnes presents a very different case than *Renton*. Indiana claimed simply that it objected to nudity in public and any curtailment of speech was merely incidental to this general prohibition. In fact, Indiana had a long history of forbidding its residents from exhibiting their " 'privates' in the presence of others," as the Court put it. Rehnquist traced this prohibition back to at least the mid-nineteenth-century.[13] Indiana's public nudity law is analogous to Oregon's drug law in *Smith*, which was found to only incidentally affect religious practices. In both cases, laws of general application that did not target constitutionally protected rights nonetheless burdened those rights in certain applications. Unlike Scalia's spartan approach in the religion arena, however, the Court has pursued a different approach to laws of general application in free speech cases. The current test comes from a case involving the celebrated practice of draft card burning that was so popular in the 1960s.

In 1968, in *United States v. O'Brien*,[14] David O'Brien was convicted of intentionally burning his selective service registration certificate in violation of a law that criminalized the intentional destruction or mutilation of the cards. In front of a large crowd on the steps of the South Boston Courthouse, O'Brien set fire to his draft card in protest against the Vietnam War. He claimed that his criminal conviction violated the First Amendment because his act had been protected symbolic speech. With Chief Justice Earl Warren writing, the Court disagreed that O'Brien was entitled to full First Amendment protection for his act of defiance. Warren explained that "when 'speech' and 'nonspeech' elements are combined in the same course of conduct, a sufficiently important governmental interest in regulating the nonspeech element can justify incidental limitations on First Amendment freedoms."[15] O'Brien's act fell within the coverage of the First Amendment, but the law he violated by carrying out his act did not get the kind of strict scrutiny that, say, a law criminalizing war protests would have received. The law, the Court found, was content-neutral, because it was directed at the nonexpressive conduct of draft card destruction. That O'Brien used this act to convey a message brought the matter within the First Amendment, but because the law was not aimed at those who destroyed draft cards to send a message, but rather at all who destroyed or mutilated the cards, it did not raise the same constitutional concerns as laws that target speech. In order for a law to pass muster under the *O'Brien* test, therefore, the government must demonstrate (1) an important or substantial interest in the objective of the law, (2) that the regulation is unrelated to the suppression of speech, and (3) that the restriction on speech is no greater than is essential to the furtherance of the government's interest. In *O'Brien*, Warren found that the law banning the burning of draft cards met these requirements, on the basis of the government's strong interest in raising and supporting an army and the administrative needs that the draft cards served.

O'Brien figures prominently in First Amendment case law, because so many laws have the incidental effect of proscribing someone's means of expression. A law prohibiting camping in city parks, for instance, operates to prohibit protesters who want to sleep in a city park to protest government homeless policies, and a litter ordinance might preclude the posting of leaflets on telephone polls. At the same time, *O'Brien*'s reach has been limited by the Court in important respects, especially when there is no other relevance to the prohibited conduct than the message it expresses. For example, the Court has twice struck down flag burning laws, on the basis that this form of protest, unlike the incineration of draft cards, does not entail conduct that is sometimes symbolic and sometimes not. Burning American flags is always symbolic. The only non-symbolic reason for burning an American flag is that it is thought more respectful to destroy a worn or tattered flag than to throw it away. Flag protection acts invariably permit this ceremonial disposal of flags, and penalize other destructive acts as constituting desecrations.

Determining whether, and if so how, the *O'Brien* test applied to the Indiana nudity law was not a straightforward exercise. As increasingly occurs with the modern Court, the justices were badly divided in *Barnes*. Five justices agreed that the Indiana law could constitutionally require dancers to cover up, as it were, with pasties and G-strings. Only three of these five—Chief Justice Rehnquist and Justices O'Connor and Kennedy—could agree on a rationale for this outcome. Justices Scalia and Souter both concurred in the result, but each had his own theory as to why the law should be sustained. Justice White, joined by Justices Marshall, Blackmun, and Stevens, dissented.

Rehnquist's plurality opinion applied the *O'Brien* test to Indiana's public indecency statute. The important government interests served by the law, he said, were "public morals and public order." Nudity, Rehnquist pointed out, is not always expressive conduct, though admittedly someone walking naked down Main Street in South Bend would be making a statement of sorts. But, taken to an extreme, all conduct may be seen as expressive at some level. Driving down Main Street in an SUV is just as much a statement as walking it nude, albeit of a rather different sort. The plurality, however, had no intention of sliding down that slippery slope. Rehnquist also did not consider it constitutionally relevant that the law was being applied to the expressive act of dance. The same had occurred in *O'Brien,* and the Court there found no constitutional violation because the general law served substantial government interests unrelated to speech. Here, Rehnquist observed, the "perceived evil that Indiana seeks to address is not erotic dancing, but public nudity." This evil, the plurality concluded, was a sufficiently important interest to sustain the law and the law's application to nude dancing.[16]

Justice Scalia, as he has been inclined to do, applied his own special brand of constitutional interpretation. He adopted exactly the same approach to free speech that he had employed in the free exercise (peyote) case of *Employment Division of Human Resources of Oregon v. Smith,* but this time he did not get four additional votes. In fact, he did not get any. It was his view that "the challenged regulation must be upheld, not because it survives some lower level of First Amendment scrutiny, but because, as a general law regulating conduct and not specifically directed at expression, it is not subject to First Amendment scrutiny at all."[17] As impoverished as Scalia's approach is, it actually makes more sense in speech cases than it does in religion cases. When legislators pass general laws that are not directed at speech or religion, it may be that they have simply overlooked the incidental effects of those laws. To be sure, they might not have any inclination to create exceptions for draft card burners and peyote users. But, at least in the speech area, general laws rarely cut off all speech outlets. O'Brien, for example, might not have been able to burn his draft card to protest the war, but he could have burned the American flag, shouted "fuck the draft," or worn a black armband. O'Brien did not need the beneficence of the majority to be heard. In contrast, Smith's religion obligated him to ingest peyote, and a general law insensitive to that religious duty effectively shut down his only means of worshiping according to his faith. As a practical matter, then, Scalia's stunted view of liberty would be less pernicious in speech cases than in religion cases. It would be less pernicious, but pernicious all the same.

Justice White, dissenting, found little to admire in the chief justice's plurality opinion. White argued that the Indiana law was not, in fact, general in theory, general in practice, or supported by adequate justification.

Justice White pointed out that Indiana's nudity law, on its face, prohibits nudity only in public. There was no suggestion that it extended to nudity in private homes. In other cases in which the O'Brien principle had been employed, the laws were general in that they applied wherever the conduct took place. In O'Brien, for example, burning draft cards was actionable whether it occurred in the privacy of one's home or before cheering throngs. Similarly, in the analogous situation of the general drug laws considered in the Smith peyote case, White pointed out, the state's "interest in preventing the use of illegal drugs extend[ed] even into the home."[18] Indiana, White asserted, did not enact a truly general law, as that concept is understood in the case law. And if it had, White said, it would certainly have been struck down as too intrusive.

Justice White also pointed out that, however general Indiana might claim the statute is in applying to all public nudity in theory, the record indicated that it was not in practice applied in a general fashion. As one state witness admitted, "No arrests have ever been made for nudity as part of a play or ballet."[19] White stated that Indiana conceded "that the evils sought to be avoided by applying the statute in this case would not obtain in the case of theatrical productions, such as *Salome* or *Hair*."[20] The anti-nudity law was thus wielded selectively. In practice, the state applied it to expressive conduct that it found offensive, and permitted expressive conduct of which it approved. This discrimination based on content, White argued, demanded close scrutiny of the reasons Indiana offered to justify its actions.

Justice White also argued that the Indiana law was not supported by adequate grounds. He said that there were only two possible justifications for Indiana's law against nude dancing. The first, he observed, supported the general anti-nudity component, which forbids nudity in parks, on beaches, and at hot dog stands. This purpose, White said, was "to protect others from offense." But this objective could not be behind application of the nudity ban to nude dancing, since obviously patrons of nude dancing clubs do not need protection, and in fact pay a lot of money to see what Indiana deems offensive at the beach. In the case of draft card destruction statutes or drug laws, the purpose behind the general statute applied to all its applications, whether they were expressive or not, and whether they occurred in public or in private.

Justice Scalia rejected Justice White's contention that public offense lay behind the public nudity prohibitions. Scalia believed the rationale was more basic, that legislative majorities are permitted to pass laws in defense of morality alone. It was not any particular witness to the nudity that was the concern of the law, Scalia contended, it was the moral health of the state. Scalia observed, "The purpose of Indiana's nudity law would be violated, I think, if 60,000 fully consenting adults crowded into the Hoosier Dome to display their genitals to one another, even if there were not an offended innocent in the crowd." This admittedly disturbing activity is prohibited not because of any harm to others, Scalia said, but because it is "considered in the traditional phrase, '*contra bonos mores*,' i.e., immoral." In American society, Scalia pointed out, "such prohibitions have included, for example, sadomasochism, cockfighting, bestiality, suicide, drug use, prostitution, and sodomy."[21]

The alternative ground supporting the Indiana law, according to Justice White, was one specific to the application of the law to nude dancing. This basis included the secondary effects of "prostitution, sexual assaults, criminal activity, degradation of women and other activities which break down family structure."[22] It was Justice Souter, concurring, who had argued that this secondary effects basis was sufficient to uphold Indiana's nudity law in this case. Justice Souter, then in his first term on the Court, wrote a separate opinion solely to posit this secondary effects argument, despite the fact that the state had never raised it and Rehnquist's opinion for the Court never mentioned it.

Souter began by saying that he agreed with the application of the *O'Brien* test to these facts. But, he believed, the plurality's conclusion would be buttressed by "the State's substantial interest in combating the secondary effects of adult entertainment establishments of the sort typified by [the Kitty Kat Lounge]." Souter said that Indiana might have shared the same concern that motivated the cities of Renton and Detroit in earlier cases. "It therefore is no leap," he asserted, "to say that live nude dancing of the sort at issue here is likely to produce the same pernicious secondary effects as the adult films displaying 'specified anatomical areas' at issue in *Renton*."[23] Souter was not bothered by the fact that, under this scenario, Indiana would have been relying on Renton's findings, which in turn had relied on Seattle's findings, that adult establishments cause neighborhood deterioration. Souter observed, "In light of Renton's recognition that legislation seeking to combat the secondary effects of adult entertainment need not await localized proof of those effects, the State of Indiana could reasonably conclude that forbidding nude entertainment of the type offered at the Kitty Kat Lounge . . . furthers its interest in preventing prostitution, sexual assault, and associated crimes."[24]

The problems with Souter's analysis are manifold. Foremost, Indiana never claimed that prevention of secondary effects provided the rationale for its law. Indeed, because Indiana does not record legislative debates or supply legislative history, there was no evidence indicating the reasons for the nudity ban. At trial and on appeal, Indiana proceeded entirely on the theory that it could enforce its specific law requiring dancers to wear pasties and G-strings on the basis of the important government interest underlying its general nudity law. *O'Brien* and *Renton* are based on entirely different lines of doctrine. Souter's analysis confused the two.

White believed that moral disapproval lay at the bottom of Souter's analysis: "That the performances in the Kitty Kat Lounge may not be high art, to say the least, and may not appeal to the Court, is hardly an excuse for distorting and ignoring settled doctrine."[25] White argued, moreover, that the quality of the speech was beyond the Court's competence to judge:

> While the entertainment afforded by a nude ballet at Lincoln Center to those who can pay the price may differ vastly in content (as viewed by judges) or in quality (as viewed by critics), it may not differ in substance from the dance viewed by the person who . . . wants some 'entertainment' with his beer or shot of rye.[26]

Souter's secondary effects argument was primarily relevant as a justification for curbs on nude dancing. At best, his argument is only tangentially pertinent to a general nudity ban. Secondary effects are central in cases like *Renton,* in which the neutrality, such as it is, derives from the fact that the objective of the law is not the speech but the unintended consequences of that speech. Renton's law applied to speech on its face, since it singled out adult-oriented businesses for special disfavor. Moreover, unlike the Indiana statute that prohibited an entire category of speech, the ordinance in *Renton* simply moved the affected businesses, it did not censor their message.

The more basic defect in Souter's secondary effects analysis, however, was the one endemic to the doctrine itself. Souter noted that the Court in *Renton* did not require the city to produce any studies demonstrating the claimed effects of the offensive speech. So long as the reliance was "reasonable"—whatever that means—Indiana, like Renton, could base its prohibition on studies done by other cities. No court, however, has yet reviewed these research studies to determine their scientific validity. Assuming the analysis of the Court in *Renton* stands, no court will ever have the opportunity to do so. The secondary effects doctrine, it turns out, is hopelessly circular. The reason that full First Amendment protections do not apply in these cases is that the speech allegedly produces secondary effects. But we really do not know if the alleged secondary effects are real, because courts have not scrutinized the research studies reporting their existence. Courts do not scrutinize the studies that report secondary effects because full First Amendment protections do not apply. Hence, the mere allegation of secondary effects, ostensibly supported by "empirical studies," is enough to eviscerate First Amendment protection.

The *Renton* no-review-of-scientific-studies rule is wrongheaded and the product of ignorance. Justice Souter, himself, declared this to be so. Justice Souter's mea culpa came in the 2000 case of *City of Erie v. Pap's AM,*[27] in which the proprietors of "Kandyland" claimed that a city ordinance that banned nude dancing violated their First Amendment right of free speech. The case was seemingly analogous to *Barnes* and came to the Court primarily because the Pennsylvania Supreme Court could not figure out what rule should apply, since there was no majority opinion in the earlier case. Significantly, however, the case differed from *Barnes* in that the city specifically stated in the law's preamble that the nudity ban was enacted "for the purpose of limiting a recent increase in nude live entertainment within the City." Furthermore, according to the preamble, this activity provided "an atmosphere conducive to violence, sexual harassment, public intoxication, prostitution, the spread of sexually transmitted diseases and other deleterious effects." Erie appeared to be enlisting Souter's concurring opinion in *Barnes* to justify its nudity ban. Souter, however, no longer believed what he wrote in his first term on the Court.

Justice Souter parted company with his opinion in *Barnes* specifically on the question of whether a city can justify a ban on nude dancing without providing empirical research to support its law. In *Barnes,* he had cited *Renton,* the case in which the Court had ruled that a city could rely on the research studies conducted by other cities to justify zoning regulations. In *Erie,* though, Souter maintained that "mere conjecture" was not "adequate to carry a First Amendment burden." He still believed that an intermediate level of scrutiny was appropriate, rather than some stricter standard. Nonetheless, he asserted, what the cases make plain "is that application of an intermediate scrutiny test to a government's asserted rationale for regulation of expressive activity demands some factual justification to connect that rationale with the regulation in issue."[28] He said, "What is clear is that the evidence of reliance must be a matter of demonstrated fact, not speculative supposition."[29] The city councilors in this case, Souter observed, failed to look at the evidence purportedly showing a connection between nude dancing establishments and the incidence of prostitution and violence. Moreover, he suggested, there was good reason to doubt that such a connection was supported by the research available.

Souter's frank admission of his error in *Barnes,* where he had been alone in finding that Renton's permissive secondary effects test was sufficient to meet the intermediate standard of *O'Brien,* was refreshing. He added in *Erie* that "careful readers" will realize that his demand for an evidentiary basis was inconsistent with his concurrence in *Barnes.* "I should have demanded the evidence then, too," he conceded. He continued, "my mistake calls to mind Justice Jackson's foolproof explanation of a lapse of his own, when he quoted Samuel Johnson, 'Ignorance, sir, igno-rance.' " Souter concluded, saying, "I may not be less ignorant of nude dancing than I was nine years ago, but after many subsequent occasions to think further about the needs of the First Amendment, I have come to believe that a government must toe the mark more carefully than I first insisted. I hope it is enlightenment on my part, and acceptable even if a little late."[30]

In *Erie*, the Court again divided badly, with only a plurality of four—in an opinion authored by Justice O'Connor and joined by Chief Justice Rehnquist and Justices Kennedy and Breyer—agreeing on the reasoning of the case. At issue was Erie's "public indecency ordinance that makes it a summary offense to knowingly or intentionally appear in a 'state of nudity.' " To comply with the ordinance, as was true in *Barnes*, dancers were required to wear, at a minimum, pasties and G-strings. Justice Souter joined the plurality opinion in one respect, to agree that the proper test was *O'Brien*, thus being the fifth vote for that proposition. But he dissented from the Court's analysis of the factors of the test as applied to the facts in *Erie*. *Erie* presents the same difficulty as did *Barnes*, a badly divided Court articulating no clear standard by which similar future cases can be analyzed. Justice Scalia remained steadfast in holding to his idiosyncratic explication from *Barnes*, but he picked up a vote this time out, with Justice Thomas agreeing. Justice Stevens, joined by Justice Ginsburg, dissented.

Incredibly, O'Connor's plurality opinion largely adopted Souter's *Barnes* concurrence, the one he now disavowed. As in *Barnes*, the key to the secondary effects approach was the question whether the nudity ban furthered "an important or substantial government interest," the second factor of the *O'Brien* test. The plurality held that this standard was met using exactly the same specious reasoning Souter now found so ignorant:

> Because the nude dancing at Kandyland is of the same character as the adult entertainment at issue in [*Renton*], it was reasonable for Erie to conclude that such nude dancing was likely to produce the same secondary effects. And Erie could reasonably rely on the evidentiary foundation set forth in [*Renton*] to the effect that secondary effects are caused by the presence of even one adult entertainment establishment in a given neigh-borhood.[31]

As regards whether there was any reason to believe that Erie's regulation would be effective in combating secondary effects, O'Connor observed that "it is evident" that the regulation would have the required efficacy.[32] Justice Souter said that "this ipse dixit is unconvincing."[33] But ipse dixit—which, roughly translated from Latin, means, "because I said so"—was pretty much all the plurality had.

The plurality's seeming ignorance about the nature of the scientific method, and the need for empirical data when social fact issues arise, is surprising in this day and age. It is true that for 200-plus years the Court has demonstrated remarkable insensitivity to empirical questions. Its factual jurisprudence is slapdash, sloppy, and, too often, supercilious. Yet the Court has demonstrated in nonconstitutional cases some facility with the subject of science. Most notably, in the evidentiary context, the Court constructed an elaborate scheme by which to measure the scientific and technical bases of proffered expert testimony.

In the landmark case of *Daubert v. Merrell Dow Pharmaceuticals, Inc.*,[34] the Court, with Justice Blackmun writing, held that trial court judges must be gatekeepers when litigants proffer scientific expert testimony. In the subsequent case of *Kumho Tire Co. v. Carmichael*,[35] the Court extended this gatekeeper function to all expert testimony, whether it was based on scientific, technical, or other specialized knowledge. The basic rule of *Daubert*, and now the Federal Rules of Evidence, is that expert testimony is not admissible unless the trial court finds, by a preponderance of the evidence, that the basis for the proffered expert testimony is reliable and valid. The *Daubert* Court suggested that in making this determination judges consider several questions, including: (1) is the basis for the opinion testable and has it been adequately tested?; (2) is the error rate associated with the opinion or technique acceptable?; (3) is the research on which the opinion is based published in a peer-reviewed journal?; and (4) is the basis for the opinion generally accepted in the pertinent field? These criteria are not intended to be exclusive and trial courts are encouraged to consider whatever factors might be useful to determine the reliability and validity of the proffered expert evidence.

The natural question to ask is, how would the studies used to justify municipal banning of nude dancing fare under the Supreme Court's own test of scientific validity? The short answer is not well, not well at all. In an amicus brief filed by the First Amendment Lawyers Association in

Erie, Dr. Daniel Linz, a well-respected psychologist at the University of California at Santa Barbara, provided an extensive evaluation of the principal studies relied upon by cities that regulate adult entertainment under the rule set forth in *Renton.* Linz outlined the criteria necessary to ensure "that a scientifically valid study of secondary effects has been conducted."[36] He found four to be crucial. Researchers must make certain that, (1) the comparison neighborhood is truly comparable, especially on the outcome variables of interest, such as crime or economic circumstances, (2) a sufficient period of time is studied "both prior to and following the establishment of an adult entertainment business," (3) the crime rate is measured consistently and police surveillance is similar across the neighborhoods in the study, and (4) the survey techniques employed are proper.[37]

Linz next analyzed in detail the four principal studies that cities had relied upon to demonstrate negative secondary effects. These included Los Angeles, CA (1977), St. Paul, MN (1978), Phoenix, AZ (1979), and Indianapolis, IN (1984). His conclusions are numbing. He described the St. Paul study as "the most methodologically sound of all of the empirical research" that he reviewed. It employed most of the standards Linz recommended and was considered fairly exemplary of how this research ought to be done. The only problem with it was that "it found absolutely no relationship between sexually oriented businesses and neighborhood deterioration."[38] The only relevant factor found to correlate with neighborhood blight in the St. Paul study was the presence of an establishment selling alcohol. Linz next found that the Los Angeles study also had been erroneously cited as finding effects when the authors themselves never made such claims. The only finding of an effect in the Los Angeles study was an alleged relationship between crime and "clusters of adult entertainment businesses." The study suggested that when adult shops become highly concentrated in an area, or operate several types of businesses under the same roof, crime increases as a result. But Linz dismissed this finding as wholly untrustworthy, because "the researchers failed to adhere to even the most basic and rudimentary professional standards."[39] The police found high levels of criminal activity, but they used no comparison neighborhoods (i.e., without adult shops) and admitted that they stepped up police surveillance during the study period. The Los Angeles result could simply be a function of the police looking for more crime and finding it. Finally, as regards the Phoenix and Indianapolis studies, Linz found the methods they used to be woefully inadequate and many of the findings to be, at best, equivocal. Indeed, one finding in the Indianapolis study suggested that areas with adult shops had fewer secondary effects than a comparable area with no adult shops.

In summary, Linz found that three of the four studies most often relied upon by cities, and thus by courts, would utterly fail even the most forgiving *Daubert* analysis. The one study that arguably would pass muster under *Daubert* found no secondary effects associated with adult entertainment establishments. As regards the Detroit study cited in *Young v. American Mini Theatres, Inc.*, which was cited approvingly in *Renton*, Linz found that it did not even qualify as empirical research.

The *Erie* plurality's abdication of responsibility for reviewing the factual bases for laws is usually explained in terms of deference to legislative bodies and their purported superior fact-finding capabilities. But deference to legislative fact-finding is completely out of place when fundamental rights, such as speech, are at stake. In the 2002 case of *City of Los Angeles v. Alameda Books, Inc.*,[40] Justice O'Connor, writing for a plurality (including Chief Justice Rehnquist and Justices Scalia and Thomas), upheld a Los Angeles ban on multiple-use adult establishments.[41] The ordinance essentially prohibited book shops from having video arcades under the same roof. It was based exclusively on the Los Angeles (1977) study that indicated "that concentrations of adult businesses are associated with higher rates of prostitution, robbery, assaults, and thefts in surrounding communities."[42] Dr. Linz had found the methods used in this study to be utterly unprofessional and woefully inadequate. But O'Connor adopted the *Renton*-styled review of the research—virtually none at all—and explained that despite this being a First Amendment case, the Court should be deferential to the city's fact-finding. She said, "we must acknowledge that the Los Angeles City Council is in a better position than the Judiciary to gather and evaluate data on local problems."[43] But, to say the least, this explanation explains nothing. It may very well be that the City Council is in a better position to *gather* research on the subject at hand, but it is certainly not the case that it is better positioned to *evaluate* that research. Evaluating research data does not depend on knowledge of the surrounding area or experience and expectations regarding what the data might indicate. Arguably, the City Council is exactly the wrong group to trust with this task. Even if the Council members can be trusted not to impose their biases, their expectations coupled with political pressures are likely to color their view of the data. And, in any case, the First Amendment exists for the very purpose of erecting a bulwark against majority tyranny over speech that is disfavored. The rule in *Alameda Books* effectively turns the First Amendment on its head. O'Connor placed the burden on the challengers of a law that on its face discriminates on the basis of the content of speech. This is exactly the reverse of what the Constitution should require.

Justice Stevens, in dissent in the *Erie* case, was flabbergasted by the plurality's approach to the subject. First of all, he pointed out, the decision had the effect, unlike in *Renton,* of fully banning a category of speech. Nude dancing conveyed a different message than dancing in pasties and a G-string. Whereas in *Renton* the establishments were moved to avoid the secondary effects, the Court here completely silenced these dancers. And this is true even if, as O'Connor maintained, the difference between dancing nude and dancing in pasties and a G-string was de minimus. (She did not, by the way, cite any research for this proposition either.) Moreover, Stevens pointed out, *Erie* differed from *Renton* in another important respect. In *Renton,* the city chose a remedy, zoning, that was reasonably related to the problem of secondary effects it sought to avoid. In *Erie,* the city required dancers to cover up with pasties and G-strings. But there was no research, and none should be expected, to show that secondary effects would be ameliorated by having the dancers "cover up." Stevens put it this way:

> In what can most delicately be characterized as an enormous understatement, the plurality concedes that "requiring dancers to wear pasties and G-strings may not greatly reduce these secondary effects." To believe that the mandatory addition of pasties and a G-string will have any kind of noticeable impact on secondary effects requires nothing short of a titanic surrender to the implausible.[44]

12

THE HOUSE THAT THE COURT BUILT:

The Future of Science at the Supreme Court

A *constitution* states or ought to state not rules for the passing hour, but principles for an expanding future. In so far as it deviates from that standard, and descends into details and particulars, it loses its flexibility, the scope of interpretation contracts, the meaning hardens. While it is true to its functions it maintains its power of adaptation, its suppleness, its play.

—BENJAMIN N. CARDOZO

Visitors to Monticello, Thomas Jefferson's home in Charlottesville, Virginia, are told that he never quite completed its construction. Throughout his life, Jefferson modified and added to the house in both major and minor ways. In particular, Jefferson integrated the latest science and technology into the preexisting structure. For instance, in the main entrance hall he installed a seven-day clock with two sets of cannonball-like weights that hung along the two sides of the room. Jefferson had originally designed the clock, however, for a house in Philadelphia, and when the weights arrived in Charlottesville, the builder, Peter Sprock, discovered that the ropes for the great clock were longer than the height of the entrance hall. Jefferson's ingenious solution was to allow the weights to descend, as he put it, "naked until they got to the floor, where they then entered a square hole and continued down to the cellar floor."[1] Although Jefferson might have rebelled at the analogy, the history of the Constitution, like his beloved Monticello, is the never-ending story of the building of the American form of government. And like Jefferson's stately home, necessity and changing times have sometimes required cutting holes in the Constitution's floor so that the latest inventions could be installed.

Constitutional law is primarily art, not science. But it is not art in any abstract sense, for it must be fully grounded in the day-to-day affairs of state. It is art more in the sense that the carpentry of building houses is art. The master carpenter, like the Supreme Court justice, must begin with some objective in mind and have the education, training, skills, and imagination to build the structure that will meet that objective. The carpenter must keep in mind many considerations as he or she goes about the business of construction. Foremost, the structure must be sound, which requires an understanding of the tools, materials, and engineering principles necessary to keep the house standing and in good repair. The structure should also be aesthetically pleasing. A house must give its occupants the security of a sound structure, offer the amenities they desire, and be beautiful to look at.

Constitutional law is the same. In constitutional terms, a successful structure guarantees life, liberty, and the pursuit of happiness. The success of the rules and standards declared by the Supreme Court can only be measured on the basis of whether they withstand the test of time. But constitution building is not a one-time task. It is a work in progress. Supreme Court justices, past and present, labor on a structure whose foundation and basic outline was laid by the framers. From John Marshall forward, justices have labored on the constitutional house we live in today. Like all houses, it needs constant maintenance and, from time to time, the tearing down of walls and the building of new ones.

Many scholars, and perhaps most of the justices, would disagree that the Supreme Court has societal objectives in mind when it interprets the Constitution. But the Constitution is too vague and indistinct to supply a picture of what sort of society the United States should be, much less a blueprint of how to build it. To be sure, the justices are not free to make up objectives out of whole cloth, and the text, history, tradition, and precedent with which the Court deals limit the Court's freedom somewhat. The Court cannot tear down the existing framework, and major structural repairs are usually accomplished only over long periods of time. But there is simply no question that the Court sets forth objectives, whether strictly or loosely based on the constitutional text, and then crafts rules and standards that are thought to advance or achieve those stated objectives. For example, the holdings in *Brown v. Board of Education, United States v. Virginia* (VMI), and *Grutter v. Bollinger* (affirmative action) all shared the goal of advancing equality. The success of these cases can only be measured by how the justices operationally defined "equality" and whether the rules pronounced in these cases led to the outcomes sought.

———

But equality might be measured in many different ways. In *Plessy v. Ferguson*, for instance, the Court accepted a segregationist definition, believing that separate could be equal. In the *Brown* and VMI cases, the Court rejected this vision, ruling that segregation of the races in the one and the genders in the other had failed to achieve true equality. The Court has largely embraced an equality based on integration. This fits well with the melting pot metaphor that has long described the American ideal. We are a country of immigrants who have, generation after generation, integrated into an American identity. But integration has a cost. As many first-generation Americans know well, the second and third generations often lose much of their old-world identity. The children of a marriage of a Chinese-American woman and an Italian-American man are Americans in the truest sense of that term. They may indeed identify with, and be proud of, their heritage, but if they were to visit China or Italy they would immediately understand their American identity. The world the *Brown* case sought to bring about was a world of diminished diversity. Some African-American leaders recognized this from the start, and questioned the objectives of *Brown* as a result. My Jewish grandmother voiced similar fears when I was growing up, regularly warning of the dangers of assimilation. It is not that all vestiges of group identity are lost, but they are prone to dilution. To take a sportive example, the number one condiment sold in the United States today is salsa. This fact is a great testament to a minority group's cultural influence. But as a good friend who is Mexican-American pointed out to me, American salsa "is nothing like the real thing." The Americanized version of this Mexican classic has little of the bite of true salsa. Likewise, children of Chinese and Italian parents may retain many of their parents' ancestral characteristics, but they are nothing like the real thing.

Only by answering the question, what sort of society does the Constitution contemplate, can rules and standards be crafted to get us there. Is integration or diversity the ultimate goal? The rules the Court adopts must be tailored for one or the other, and it is unlikely that the two ends can coexist. In *Grutter*, the success of *Brown*'s integrationist objectives was measured. The state's compelling interest in its affirmative action program was based largely on society's failure to yet realize the objectives of *Brown*. In a fully integrated society, one in which every individual truly has equal opportunities regardless of race, the disparities found at the Michigan law school should not have been as marked. Or, at least, that was the Court's empirical judgment. And *Grutter* itself will be measured, as the opinion put it, by the next generation of Americans.

Of course, the Court is only one part of a very rich constitutional structure involving an interplay between it and the two coordinate branches of the federal government, the Congress and the president, and the state governments that constitute our federalist system. Every state and federal official has an obligation to uphold the Constitution. This duty necessitates their interpreting the Constitution at some level. While the Supreme Court may have the last word on every constitutional question, the more political branches and the states usually begin the debate and contribute substantially to the subject of constitutional meaning. Article III of the Constitution limits the Court's power to cases or controversies brought to it. Unlike the Congress, for example, the Court has no power to pursue a particular agenda as it sees the need. For instance, when Ian Wilmut announced that he had successfully cloned a sheep, Congress and the president, as well as many state officials, responded swiftly by holding hearings, commissioning studies, and waxing poetic about the sanctity of human life. Nothing was heard from the Court, though it is likely that the justices held strong views about the matter.

At the same time, although the Court cannot act without a case to decide, in reality it has tremendous discretion to set its own agenda. The Court chooses its docket from among thousands of cases on appeal from the state and federal courts below. If the Court wants to reach a controversial issue, it rarely has to wait too long for a case or controversy to wind its way up the ladder. De Tocqueville wrote that "scarcely any political question arises in the United States which is not resolved, sooner or later, into a judicial question."[2] Cloning might take a little time, but eventually the Court will be confronted with one or more constitutional questions arising from this and similar genetic technology. These challenges are likely to run the constitutional gamut. Reproductive technologies, such as genetic screening and cloning, implicate the due process right of privacy. Use of DNA in crime prevention, such as DNA data banks containing offender profiles, raises the privacy concerns of the Fourth Amendment. And the science of eugenics is likely to reappear, albeit with a different appellation. The science of behavioral genetics might one day permit us, among other things, to design babies, enhance ourselves, and identify those among us who are prone to violence. Not long ago, I had the opportunity to explore this last possibility with a large group of federal judges.

In July 2001, I was invited to be on a panel at the Ninth Circuit Judicial Conference in Sun Valley, Idaho. The conference is an annual event in which most of the appellate and trial court judges of the Ninth Circuit— comprising California, Oregon, Washington, Nevada, and Hawaii—meet to hear speakers on the pressing issues of the day and to press the flesh with one another. The panel was organized by Judge Robert Jones, a federal district court judge in Portland, Oregon. Judge Jones is a leader in modernizing the law to deal with emerging science and technology, both in terms of courtroom practice and in shaping the contours of the law. His courtroom was one of the first in the nation to become fully electronic, thus allowing experts to testify without having to travel to the trial and allowing attorneys to effortlessly display electronic presentations. Judge Jones also has been a trailblazer in the substantive uses of science. In the silicone breast implant litigation, for example, he assembled a panel of experts to help him evaluate the available research on whether implants were associated with autoimmune disorders. His panel concluded, as all independent groups have since, that the research did not indicate an association between implants and these disorders. In his highly informed and comprehensive opinion, Jones excluded expert testimony on the systemic effects of silicone implants, since it did not meet the minimum reliability and validity requirements set forth by the Supreme Court and the rules of evidence.[3]

In Sun Valley, Jones organized a group of scholars to consider the future of genetic evidence. My role was to consider the possibly disturbing scenario in which genetic information might be used to predict future violence. It appears increasingly likely that genes are related to behavioral predispositions.[4] Whether or not this relationship turns out to be robust remains to be determined. It would surprise me if some statistical relationship did not exist between genes and sexual violence. Other factors, however, from the environment to a myriad of possible physiological factors, are likely to play a large, if not a larger, role in the expression of such violence. My assignment was to examine the law's likely response to the hypothetical discovery of a set of genes that is positively correlated with sexual violence. Simply put, if genes predict violence, then in what ways could—and should—the law take this into account?

The law, of course, already asks experts to predict future violence in a vast variety of settings. A person's likelihood of committing violent acts in the future is relevant to probation, parole, civil commitment, and capital sentencing decisions. In recent times, prediction of violence has played an especially large role in the civil incarceration of so-called "sexually violent predators." The Supreme Court has been very active in this area, having decided five cases between 1997 and 2003, on issues ranging from community notification statutes, such as Megan's law, to civil commitment. The two most important decisions on the commitment of sexual offenders are a pair of cases from Kansas, *Kansas v. Hendricks*[5] and *Kansas v. Crane.*[6] The two cases are heavy on scientific speculation and short on empirical data.

In 1984, Leroy Hendricks was convicted of taking "indecent liberties" with two thirteen-year-old boys. He served ten years of his sentence and was slated for release to a halfway house when the state successfully petitioned to have him civilly committed under Kansas' Sexually Violent Predator Act (SVPA). Under the Kansas law, which was modeled on a Washington state law, a person can be civilly committed if he is found to be "mentally abnormal" and "dangerous." The Kansas statute defined mental abnormality as "a congenital or acquired condition affecting the emotional or volitional capacity which predisposes the person to commit sexually violent offenses in a degree constituting such person a menace to the health and safety of others."[7] The concept of dangerousness contained in this definition was not further defined, and neither the statute nor the Court said how likely the future violence had to be to qualify someone for indefinite incarceration in a mental health facility.

Hendricks challenged his commitment on the basis of three constitutional provisions, the Due Process, Ex Post Facto, and Double Jeopardy Clauses. The Court found that none of these provisions was infringed. The Court concluded that the civil commitment of sexual offenders was not punitive in nature and, because of the prerequisites of "mental abnormality" and "dangerousness," the statutes would not cast too wide a net. These laws apply only to those who cannot control their violent propensities and, therefore, present a danger to the surrounding community. Absolutely essential constitutionally, however, was the Court's finding that those civilly committed were not being punished for things done in the past. They were merely being locked up for their own good and the good of the community for the things they were likely to do in the future. If civil commitment laws were found to be "punitive" in intent or when applied, they would violate both the Double Jeopardy and Ex Post Facto Clauses. The criminal laws apply to past bad acts, and once a person has been punished for past conduct he cannot be punished again for that conduct. It also follows that a person cannot be punished for future conduct, since he can hardly be held responsible for an act not yet committed.

The Court stated that the Kansas commitment law was presumptively not punitive because the legislature had evinced no punitive purpose. Moreover, the law was not punitive because it applied to a group of offenders who were "mentally abnormal," that is, only those who lack volitional control. The logic of the Court's view was straightforward: there are two bases for imposing punishment under the criminal law, retribution and deterrence. Because the statute applies only to those persons who lack volitional control, neither goal of the criminal law is served. A person who lacks volitional control cannot be said to be "responsible" for his actions and he is unlikely to be deterred by the threat of confinement. At least, that was the Court's theory in *Hendricks*.

The easily anticipated problem with the Court's approach was the question of what "lack of control" meant as a practical matter. After the *Hendricks* decision was handed down, the lower courts in several states expressed confusion regarding the new test and they divided on just how much control was necessary before someone could be deemed committable. Minnesota, for instance, adopted a weak volitional control test that largely dispensed with the volitional control factor altogether. In contrast, Kansas courts read the *Hendricks* decision as mandating a strong volitional control test, and limited commitments to only those persons who lacked "total control." The Court agreed to hear another Kansas case, *Kansas v. Crane*, in order to clarify the *Hendricks* test.

Michael Crane, a convicted sex offender, was committed by a trial court under the Kansas sexually violent predator law. On appeal, Crane argued that his commitment was unconstitutional because the state had failed to demonstrate that he lacked control over his behavior. The state argued that Crane's proclivity for sexual violence was sufficient by itself to commit him under *Hendricks* and that no explicit finding of fact regarding volitional control was necessary. The Kansas Supreme Court reversed Crane's commitment, ruling that the Supreme Court in *Hendricks* made it abundantly clear that there were two prerequisites for involuntary civil commitments under the Constitution, dangerousness and mental abnormality, with the latter defined as lack of volitional control. Therefore, according to the Kansas Supreme Court, trial courts must find as a matter of fact both that the defendant lacks substantial volitional control over his violent behavior and that he is likely to be violent.

In *Crane*, the Supreme Court agreed to decide the thorny issue of the meaning of volitional control. It adopted a middle position on the question. The Court held that complete lack of control need not be demonstrated, but that some lack of control was required. Justice Stephen Breyer wrote for the Court. He explained that "an absolutist approach is unworkable." Such a demand, Breyer said, "would risk barring the civil commitment of highly dangerous persons suffering severe mental abnormalities." At the same time, Breyer recognized, not requiring any showing of lack of control would undermine "the constitutional importance of distinguishing a dangerous sexual offender subject to civil commitment 'from other dangerous persons who are perhaps more properly dealt with exclusively through criminal proceedings.' "[8] If a person can control his behavior, civil commitment potentially becomes a "mechanism for 'retribution or general deterrence'—functions properly those of criminal law, not civil commitment."[9]

Breyer, however, was reluctant to define with any "mathematical precision" the meaning of lack of control. He said that "it is enough to say that there must be proof of serious difficulty in controlling behavior."[10] Lamenting his inability to draw a brighter line, Breyer stated that "the constitutional safeguards of human liberty in the area of mental illness and the law are not always best informed through bright line rules."[11]

Not surprisingly, Justice Scalia dissented, joined by Thomas (the author of *Hendricks*), finding Breyer's failure to establish a more definite standard lamentable: "This formulation of the new requirement certainly displays an elegant subtlety of mind. Unfortunately, it gives trial courts, in future cases under the many commitment statutes similar to Kansas' SVPA, *not a clue* as to how they are supposed to charge the jury." According to Scalia, the proper standard has a singular requirement, albeit with two elements. The Kansas statute, he argued, "conditions civil commitment not upon a mere finding that the sex offender is likely to reoffend, but only upon the additional finding (to be found by proof beyond a reasonable doubt) that the *cause* of the likelihood of recidivism is a 'mental abnormality or personality disorder.' " Thus, "the very existence of a mental abnormality or personality disorder *that causes* a likelihood of repeat sexual violence in itself establishes the requisite 'difficulty if not impossibility' of control."[12]

Justice Scalia's approach, while seemingly simpler, solves none of the ambiguity. The confusion lies in the term "mental abnormality." Scalia uses this term in a way that makes his approach hopelessly circular. Justice Scalia expects jurors to determine when the mental abnormality has caused lack of control. The Kansas statute, however, *defines* mental abnormality as a "loss of emotional or volitional control." Contrary to Scalia's understanding, mental abnormality does not cause lack of control, it is defined by it. Everyone who is mentally abnormal lacks control and everyone who lacks control is mentally abnormal. Scalia's test is no test at all.

In the end, the problem lies in the vacuity of the term "mental abnormality," which the Court has defined as "inability to control behavior." This standard comes from the law's fundamental assumption that people have free will. This is a quaint philosophical notion, but one that has no correlate in science. Scientists, by trade, are materialists, believing that human decisions are a product of the brain and its interaction with the body and world that surround it. The science of the mind simply has not advanced far enough to permit experts to know with any confidence what decisions are "controllable" and which ones are not. Breyer, himself, recognized the inherent difficulty of speaking in terms of lack of volitional control. He quoted a well-regarded handbook: "The line between an irresistible impulse and an impulse not resisted is probably no sharper than that between twilight and dusk."[13]

Scientists have no operational definition for free will. It is not something that exists physically; it cannot be measured. Free will is a philosophical conclusion, not a physical reality. People do have more or less impulse control and their reasoning faculties may be greater or less, but these traits remain elusive and, in any case, the Court did not employ them to give content to the term "mental abnormality." And even if scientists could say that a particular present behavior was a product of a lack of impulse control, this is a far cry from saying that some future violent act will occur and be a product of this same mental defect. In fact, it is hardly obvious that those lacking control are of greatest concern. Those who cannot control their behavior are readily identified and caught. The child in middle school who cannot control himself is the one who slaps his neighbor while his teachers are looking. It is the child who waits until his teachers turn their backs that should most concern us. He *can* control his behavior.

Scientific research on predicting future violence, therefore, ignores the notion of free will. Instead, scientists build statistical models using factors that are associated with future violence. This research is not aimed at discovering the neurophysiological causes of violence, but rather at finding correlates of future violence. The single best predictor of future violence is past violence. Other factors associated with violence include alcohol and drug use, marital status (single), socioeconomic level (poor), educational achievement (low), and scores on particular psychological tests. These factors cannot be said to cause violent behavior, nor do they indicate a lack of control, but they do permit modest predictions of future dangerous conduct. Since "lack of control" and "mental abnormality" more generally are devoid of meaning, scientific research is devoted exclusively to the second factor found necessary by the *Hendricks* Court: dangerousness.

In Sun Valley, Judge Jones wanted to consider the prospect of adding genetic information to the mix of sociological and psychological data that today are the common currency of violence prediction. At this point in time, predictions of violence are very weak, with rates of predicted recidivism of around 30 percent being sufficient to civilly commit sexual offenders. In other words, given a group of one hundred offenders whom experts predict will be violent, about thirty will in fact be violent. This means, of course, that seventy would not be violent, and thus will be deprived of their liberty only because they fit the profile. The incarceration of such large numbers of "innocent" people, I believe, is due to the fact that few people count them as "innocent." Virtually all those falling within the purview of predator statutes have served time in prison for sexual offenses. But it is important to note that there is no constitutional reason why only those who have committed prior offenses should be subject to commitment as sexual predators. Under the *Hendricks* decision, anyone proven to be prone to future violence who "lacks control" of this behavior could be committed. Thus, if the right tests were available, states need not wait until a person actually commited any offense at all. Indeed, a prior offense requirement potentially creates a constitutional problem, since this fact raises the concern that the civil commitment is being used to punish the offender for his past bad act and not truly out of concern for his future behavior in violation of the Double Jeopardy and Ex Post Facto Clauses.

The availability of genetic evidence has the potential of dramatically changing the manner in which preventive detentions occur in this country. Suppose that sometime in the future a seventeen-year-old high school dropout, whom we will call Steven Victor Perle, is tested for the presence of thirteen genes whose combination is known to dramatically increase the likelihood that he will sexually assault a child. The state seeks to commit this young man as a sexually violent predator. According to the state, the defendant not only has the thirteen genes indicating high risk, but also has traditional risk factors such as alcohol and drug abuse, little formal education, is not married, and earns an income below the poverty line. The defendant, however, has never been arrested for, or convicted of, a sexual offense. He was expelled from high school for a variety of reasons, including poor grades, grabbing and verbally harassing female students, and allegedly exposing himself to children at a nearby middle school. Other than expulsion from school, these allegations never resulted in any formal action. Based on his genetic, psychological, and sociological profile, the state's experts predict that Perle is 85 percent likely to commit a sexual offense in the next two years. Without the genetic information, the likelihood rate drops to about 30 percent.

Should the state be allowed to commit Perle based on this sort of evidence? There are only two differences between the proof posited in the hypothetical case of Steven Perle and what occurs in the typical predator commitment case. One is in his favor and one is against. On his side is the fact that he has yet to commit any crime. Arrayed against him, the likelihood statement of 85 percent far exceeds the estimates current technology typically can offer, or on which courts usually rely. The factor in his favor, however, is irrelevant, since civil commitments must be based on likelihood of future bad conduct, not anything done in the past. The genetic evidence is highly relevant, but raises profound questions about the moral tenor of American society. We need not use every tool science creates. But the decision whether or not to use any particular tool should be well informed, and not guided by knee-jerk reactions to hot-button terms such as "genetic engineering."

When the Perle hypothetical was presented in Sun Valley, the judges and other participants expressed great skepticism regarding the proof. Although no formal poll was taken, Judge Jones did ask for a show of hands. The attendees overwhelmingly agreed that reliance on genetic evidence to predict future violence was inappropriate. From their comments and questions, it was clear that many were troubled by any use of genetic evidence against someone, at least until that person had an opportunity to demonstrate that he could not resist his genetic destiny. The general view seemed to be that the psychological and genetic profile was not sufficient, because he had not yet done anything wrong.

But civil commitment is not about whether someone has *done* something wrong; it is only about—it can only be about—whether someone *will do* something wrong. Under the Constitution, past acts are subject to the criminal laws. Under current commitment doctrine, evidence of past sexual offenses is relevant only to prove likelihood of future bad acts. Today, the best predictor, by far, of future behavior is past behavior. Someday, however, genetic evidence may provide strong evidence of future behavior. When that day arrives, the Court will have to decide what can be done with it.

Under the Court's interpretation of the Constitution, genetic evidence carries none of the constitutional baggage concerning double jeopardy that is associated with past sexual offenses. Yet it remains troubling. Experience with past eugenics programs, in particular, is sobering. Much of the hesitation revolves around historical abuses and the fact that past claims for the science far exceeded what the research supported. But these are objections to the process of using such proof, not to the use of the proof itself. Another possible objection could be the generalized nature of the proof—that is, "85 percent of all those with this psychological and genetic profile will commit violent acts." Yet the best evidence used today for predicting violence are profiles that are general in this very way. Genetic information would simply add a factor to those already relied upon—such as past conduct, alcohol and drug use, and so forth. Adding genes to the model would not fundamentally change the way predictions are made; their addition would only increase the models' accuracy.

At least for now, however, using genes to predict future behavior is likely to be disfavored by the Courts. The principle reason appears to be repugnance toward the deterministic model implicit in such use. Of course, there is great irony in this. First of all, the Court's commitment cases, in which the state must prove lack of volitional control and dangerousness, are highly deterministic. Second, the scientists the courts rely upon in these cases are all determinists. Although we rebel at the notion that our destinies lie in our genes, it is likely that they will come to occupy a greater and greater role in courts of law. The great challenge will be integrating the future research on genetic predispositions with the law's notion of free will. This will demand a sophisticated understanding of the science and considerable creativity in the law.

Privacy doctrine arises in an assortment of areas of the law. As in the previous example, control over one's genetic information might fall within a sphere of constitutionally protected privacy. Similarly, reproductive rights, from contraceptives to abortion, fall within the right of privacy defined in cases like *Griswold v. Connecticut* and *Roe v. Wade*. The more common view of privacy, however, involves an individual's right to be free from government scrutiny. This issue raises modern concerns of "Big Brother," and the fear that government has the interest, and the tools, to see and know "all." Indeed, when Louis Brandeis described privacy in *Olmstead v. United States* as the "right to be let alone—the most comprehensive of rights and the right most valued by civilized men,"[14] he was speaking of the Fourth Amendment. The Fourth Amendment is meant to be a bulwark against government intrusiveness. It has not always been a steady defense of our freedoms.

In *Olmstead*, the Court ruled that the Fourth Amendment's protection against warrantless or unreasonable searches and seizures did not extend to an illegal federal wiretap. Brandeis dissented. Chief Justice William H. Taft, writing for the Court, concluded that conversations are not protected by the Fourth Amendment and that no trespass on Olmstead's home or property had occurred. According to Taft, the Constitution merely protected things, not persons. He thus read the guarantee literally, since the new technology of wiretaps did not involve a physical incursion and thus did not resemble the sort of searches that the Fourth Amendment was designed to stop.

Unlike many of the Constitution's liberty guarantees that were based in English legal history, the Fourth Amendment has a uniquely American heritage. Among the many grievances held by Americans prior to their declaring independence, one that cut especially deeply, was the English practice of issuing general search warrants. General warrants were conferred by Parliament on customs officials through Writs of Assistance and were an effort to stem the rampant smuggling operations that arose in the colonies to avoid the empire's restrictive trade laws. The writ permitted English officials great latitude and ultimate discretion since the warrants did not have to identify the people covered or specify the property to be searched. Also, these warrants were not limited by probable cause requirements so that officials did not have to articulate the bases for their suspicions.

Unfortunately, while the Fourth Amendment was intended to interpose some standard between government officials' discretion and their invasive actions, its text is not a model of drafting clarity. The first clause bans "unreasonable searches" and the second sets forth the criteria for issuance of a warrant. The amendment states a preference for warrants, but tolerates warrantless searches that are reasonable. The main ambiguities of the amendment, then, concern when a search or seizure has occurred and under what circumstances a search or seizure is justified despite being conducted without a warrant. Advancing technology has primarily affected the first ambiguity, since during the drafters' time they could barely have imagined the telephone, much less wiretaps; and the prospect of machines being able to "look through" walls would have been completely incomprehensible.

Brandeis argued in dissent in *Olmstead* that the Fourth Amendment created a general right to individual privacy and was not limited to property or material things. In *Katz v. United States*,[15] the Court adopted Brandeis's more expansive vision of the amendment. The government in *Katz* sought to introduce evidence of the defendant's wagering activity by introducing transcripts of his telephone conversations while using a public telephone booth. The FBI eavesdropped on the conversation by attaching a recording device to the exterior of a phone booth Charles Katz regularly used. The trial court, following *Olmstead*, found that no search had occurred, because the government's devices had not penetrated the wall of the booth. The Supreme Court reversed, and in so doing completely reoriented Fourth Amendment law. Justice Potter Stewart, writing for the Court, said that "the Government's activities in electronically listening to and recording the petitioner's words violated the privacy upon which he justifiably relied while using the telephone booth and thus constituted a 'search and seizure' within the meaning of the Fourth Amendment."[16] Justice John Marshall Harlan wrote separately to reinforce the point that the Fourth Amendment protects people, not places. His formulation has since become the standard statement of the test: "there is a two-fold requirement, first that a person have exhibited an actual (subjective) expectation of privacy and, second, that the expectation be one that society is prepared to recognize as 'reasonable.' "[17]

The *Katz* test is readily adaptable to changing technology, since it can evolve with changing times and changed sensibilities. It expressly incorporates the most modern ideas of privacy by querying subjective intent and contemporary values. In practice, however, it suffers certain significant limitations. First of all, the test is hopelessly circular, since a person's reasonable expectations necessarily depend on what legal standards apply. Hence, if the Court had allowed the listening device in *Katz*, a reasonable person would have no expectation of privacy in a phone booth. The government could be listening in. More problematic still, the Court's cases after *Katz* display a remarkably naive and unrealistic view of what ordinary people expect regarding their privacy. For instance, in a California case, the Court allowed an aerial observation of marijuana plants growing inside a backyard surrounded by a ten-foot fence. The Court said that the plants could have been seen by "a policeman perched on the top of a truck or a two-level bus," so the owner had no actual expectation of privacy.[18] In another case, the Court concluded that a person sitting on a bus boarded by several armed drug enforcement agents, with another agent standing guard near the door of the bus, was not "seized," since he would believe that he had the right to leave anytime he wished.[19] These, and many other examples, suggest that the justices have little concept of the realities of day-to-day life. And the Court has never made any attempt to buttress its myopic experiences with sociological data on the subject of reasonable expectations of privacy.

In *Kyllo v. United States*,[20] the Court considered a technological innovation several orders of magnitude beyond the devices in *Olmstead* or *Katz*. In *Kyllo*, the Court asked "whether the use of a thermal-imaging device aimed at a private home from a public street to detect relative amounts of heat within the home constitutes a 'search' within the meaning of the Fourth Amendment."[21] With Justice Scalia writing, the Court made clear that *Katz*'s approach would continue to be used. In short, the Court found, people in their home have reasonable expectations that their activities that generate heat will not be spied upon by the police without adequate grounds. This was true even though the thermal-imaging device used in *Kyllo* could not distinguish "intimate details" inside the house. The device in question could not actually "see" through walls. Scalia said that "limiting the prohibition of thermal imaging to 'intimate details' would not only be wrong in principle, it would be impractical in application, failing to provide a workable accommodation between the needs of law enforcement and the interests protected by the Fourth Amendment."[22] Scalia explained that the sophistication of the imaging device was not necessarily associated with the degree of intrusion on privacy perpetrated by the government's snooping. For instance, Scalia said, the imaging device involved here, which was relatively crude, could disclose "at what hour each night the lady of the house takes her daily sauna and bath—a detail that many would consider 'intimate.' "[23] A "much more sophisticated system," Scalia observed, "might detect nothing more intimate than the fact that someone left a closet light on."[24] It was clear, however, that Scalia's opinion was written in anticipation that much more powerful imaging devices were on the horizon. Scalia, as he is inclined to do when he can, sought to draw as bright a line as possible. Especially affecting Scalia's decision was the fact that the imaging device was used on a private home, a sanctuary receiving particularly strong constitutional protection. Scalia stated, "We have said that the Fourth Amendment draws 'a firm line at the entrance to the house.' That line, we think, must be not only firm but also bright—which requires clear specification of those methods of surveillance that require a warrant."[25] This outcome, Scalia said, "assures preservation of that degree of privacy against government that existed when the Fourth Amendment was adopted."[26]

Although the Court in *Kyllo* adopted a strong rights-protective stance, it is unlikely that it signals a softening of the Court toward criminal defendants and the use of sophisticated technology in their apprehension. For future surveillance technologies, the Court, as it did in *Kyllo*, can be expected to hold to a firm boundary around a person's home. Many of the newest technologies, however, designed to "sniff out" drugs and bombs, or identify terrorists or illegal aliens when they travel, are likely to get a warmer reception from the Court. How the Court, and the other branches of government, eventually balance the newest invasive technologies with our ancient right to be let alone will say much about what sort of nation this is. It will also further impress upon the Court the need to be conversant with the latest technology and scientific research.

For both the casual observer and the interested researcher, the Court's fact-finding processes may seem a complete mystery. Indeed, for a topic that appears to play such a large role in establishing the context and setting the scene for constitutional law, the justices seem to take a surprisingly lackadaisical approach to the subject. There are no rules or procedures that apply to the manner in which constitutional facts come to the Court; they arrive in the trial record, in amicus briefs, and in independent research, and are the product of intuition, speculation, and anecdotes of the justices themselves. The Court also has no set or systematic criteria by which to measure constitutional facts. The justices do not employ any of the usual standards of proof, such as the preponderance of the evidence standard. They sometimes defer completely to legislatures' fact-finding, and in other cases they defer not at all. These systemic defects would seem to have particular impact on lower courts that are charged with the responsibility of applying the Court's rules and standards and must evaluate cases with complex facts. Moreover, there is no mechanism in place for reconsidering constitutional facts as they themselves change, or our knowledge of them changes.

In light of the many questions that writing this book raised, I decided to ask the justices themselves what they thought about these matters. I contacted all nine justices to request an interview on the subject of this book. Three of the nine agreed—Justices Stevens, O'Connor, and Breyer. I spoke with each justice separately. The other six justices declined my invitation. I would single out Justices Souter and Ginsburg for their particularly kind refusals. The remaining justices said that they either never grant such requests or, in one case, do grant such requests but had no intention of doing so in my case.

The most disheartening finding in my research, though it was something I had anticipated from having taught the subject, was the haphazard way constitutional facts come to the Court's attention. This is especially surprising given the well-ordered way that facts are developed in ordinary litigation, where rules of evidence, such as the rules against hearsay or character evidence, regulate the facts that jurors hear or judges consider in making decisions. Justice Breyer told me that constitutional facts "are different." They are "not the sort of facts that lower courts are concerned about or decide," Breyer said. Of course, although Breyer was correct that the Supreme Court is the ultimate arbiter of constitutional meaning, clearly constitutional facts regularly are decided by trial and lower appellate courts. In the VMI case, for instance, the Virginia district court held a six-day trial to resolve constitutionally relevant facts such as whether the adversative training method was appropriate for women and whether Mary Baldwin College's alternative program was comparable to the education provided by VMI. Trial courts similarly held extensive trials on the constitutional fact questions in *McCleskey v. Kemp*, in which the defendant claimed that the Georgia capital sentencing scheme discriminated on the basis of the race of the victim, as well as in *Casey v. Planned Parenthood*, in which the claimants argued that the Pennsylvania law created obstacles to the exercise of the fundamental right of reproductive choice. In the landmark case of *Brown v. Board of Education*, trial courts in several states held extensive hearings on the constitutional question of whether segregated schools were equal to integrated ones.

Justice Breyer, however, insisted that it would be "very rare that facts will be found in lower courts in constitutional cases in ways that are specific or [that] we would have to reconsider." He pointed out, in particular, that most constitutional facts are "legislative facts," which means that they are facts that are relevant to the formation of legal rules or that help establish the Constitution's meaning. These facts primarily come to the Court's attention, Breyer said, through amicus briefs. Amicus briefs, however, are not the product of adversarial processes, though the many sides interested in a Supreme Court decision typically have their views expressed through these tracts. Indeed, in many controversial cases, such as the affirmative action cases decided in 2003, or an abortion case such as *Casey*, the Court can receive more than fifty briefs from "friends of the Court." Justice Breyer pointed to these as being a particularly rich source of data upon which the Court may rely.

Justices Stevens and O'Connor are somewhat less ardent supporters of amicus briefs. Although such briefs may represent a wide range of views, since they have not been tested through the adversarial process, they come to the Court without having been put through the grinder of cross-examination. O'Connor expressed a strong preference for facts that percolated up through the process and were part of the trial record. Stevens agreed, observing that "basically, we rely on the record." Both readily conceded, however, that the Court routinely was forced to go to the briefs for relevant facts and important research findings. Stevens, for example, referred to the University of Michigan affirmative action case in which there were both an extremely robust trial record and extraordinarily helpful briefs from amici. O'Connor noted that, admittedly, it is a "stretch to make statements based on briefs" when there is no trial record, "but sometimes we do that." She acknowledged, for instance, the rich briefing in the Louisiana "creation science" case, which came to the

Court after the trial judge invalidated the Louisiana statute on summary judgment.

Given the complexity of some of the science and technology the Court must consider, I asked each of the three justices whether they use, or thought they should use—when the case called for it—a court-appointed expert or special master. Each of them told me how they had the benefit of such assistance in a limited way in a recent Internet pornography case. The justices had gone up to the stately Supreme Court library, surrounded by the rich mahogany shelves and tables, to be given a demonstration of the kinds of computer software available to screen pornography in order to protect children when they use the Internet. Other than that, all three justices were fairly adamant that it would be highly unusual for the Court to use independent experts. Justice Breyer mentioned the recent case of thermal imaging, in which technology is able to "see" heat-generating objects behind solid walls as the most likely sort of case to engender the Court's use of independent experts or technical advisers. Breyer specifically said that he could not imagine the Court, for example, enlisting the assistance of a statistician to help the justices understand multiple regression analysis, a statistical tool used in *McCleskey v. Kemp*, in which the Court found no constitutional violation despite statistics showing that death sentences were correlated with the race of the victim. Justices Stevens and O'Connor each echoed this sentiment, with O'Connor emphasizing just "how unusual" such a practice would be.

A recurring issue in constitutional cases concerns what level of deference the Court owes to legislators and whether legislatures institutionally are better fact-finders than courts. All three justices were quick to express their trust in legislative fact-finding, with Justice O'Connor emphasizing the deference owed to federal and state legislatures. She explicitly premised this deference in the interview, as she did in the *City of Erie* nude dancing case, on the basis that legislators are better fact-finders than courts. She pointed out that they can commission studies and hold hearings on factual questions that underlay proposed legislation. Justice Stevens initially agreed that it was the "traditional role" of the Court to accept the fact-finding of Congress. Upon reflection, however, Stevens said that he thought that there were some matters on which judicial hearings might be superior. He explained that the legislature excels when the factual issue is not well defined and there may be a need "to roam around" and consider many possible domains. Courts, he suggested, might be better on average when the factual questions are well defined and a trial court can hold hearings, subjecting the evidence to cross-examination and applying the other attributes of the adversarial process. He added that, as a general matter, he believes that appellate courts should "give respect to lower courts' fact-finding." Trial courts have the advantage of being able to judge witness credibility in person. Stevens stated, "I am very big on giving deference to the lower-court judge who has heard the witnesses."

Possibly the most vexing issue confronting fact-finding in constitutional cases is the prospect of changing facts, either because the facts themselves change or our knowledge of them changes. I asked each of the justices about this. Justice Breyer questioned the premise of the question, saying that it was "very rare that general sociological facts will give you a specific answer to a legal problem." I raised the case of *Brown v. Board of Education*, in which the Court had explicitly stated its reliance on the doll studies and the social science evidence of Kenneth Clark and others. Justice Breyer agreed with much of the academic literature that indicates that the reliance was not actual. "It did not take sociological evidence," Breyer told me, "to tell this Court that racial segregation was deleterious to black schoolchildren." I brought up the example of viability, identified in both *Roe* and *Casey*, as setting the point in time when the government interest in the life of the fetus became sufficiently compelling to prohibit the right to abortion. Viability is defined, at least in the case law and the medical literature, as a medical fact—the time at which a fetus would likely survive if removed from the womb. He maintained that the facts in *Roe* and *Casey* did not establish the constitutional rule. "The facts of *Roe* and the trimester framework," he said, "really didn't rely on the medical facts, they were merely informed by them. They supported them."

Justice Breyer did say that the Court must take into account changing facts, changing circumstances, and changed understanding of the facts that supported the Constitution's structure. He illustrated his point by discussing his dissent in the highly controversial decision in *United States v. Lopez*. In *Lopez*, in an opinion by Chief Justice Rehnquist, the Court, for the first time since 1937, invalidated a federal statute on the basis that Congress did not have the power to enact the law because it exceeded its authority under the Commerce Clause. The law made the possession of a gun within a school zone a federal crime. Although the Court's precedents had interpreted Congress's power expansively under the Commerce Clause, as extending to all matters that substantially affected interstate commerce, Rehnquist held that the clause extended only to economic activities. According to Rehnquist, possession of a gun in a school zone does not qualify as an economic activity. Justice Breyer, joined by Justices Stevens, Souter, and Ginsburg, dissented. Breyer wrote first that "the Court must give Congress a degree of leeway in determining the existence of a significant factual connection between the regulated activity and interstate commerce—both because the Constitution delegates the commerce power directly to Congress and because the determination requires an empirical judgment of a kind that a legislature is more likely than a court to make with accuracy."[27] Breyer made the additional point in *Lopez*, "Having found that guns in schools significantly undermine the quality of education in our Nation's classrooms, Congress would also have found, given the effect of education upon interstate and foreign commerce, that gun-related violence in and around schools is a commercial, as well as a human, problem." He concluded, "Education, although far more than a matter of economics, has long been inextricably intertwined with the Nation's economy."[28]

Justice Breyer told me that *Lopez* well illustrated how a changed understanding of facts may affect constitutional interpretation. Whatever the original meaning of the Commerce Clause in 1789 as regards what activities qualify as "commercial," it is clear that today education surely fits within "the definition of what is economic." At the very least, as his *Lopez* dissent makes plain, it is entirely rational for Congress to so find as a matter of fact.

Justices Stevens and O'Connor somewhat more readily conceded that there may be times when constitutional rules or outcomes change due to changing factual circumstances. O'Connor, of course, had made this exact point in several of the abortion cases in which she expressed concern that the medical facts could fluctuate over time, facts on which the edifice of reproductive rights were built. When asked about this, she told me that her views had remained the same and that she recognized that the Court might one day need to modify the rule if the facts change. She brought up the Michigan affirmative action case as illustrative of a ruling that very much depended on a contextual understanding of education involving underrepresented students. In *Grutter v. Bollinger*, O'Connor, writing for the Court, identified the importance of the empirical judgment made by the university that "diversity will, in fact, yield educational benefits."[29] Moreover, O'Connor noted that while today the facts were clear that using race was necessary to "further an interest in student body diversity," the Court expected "that twenty-five years from now, the use of racial preferences will no longer be necessary to further the interests approved today."[30] It will be the social scientists of 2028 who will tell us whether Justice O'Connor's prediction has come true.

Justice Stevens agreed that if a constitutional rule is premised on empirical facts, then the rule should change when the facts, or our knowledge of the facts, change. He, too, pointed to the affirmative action case of *Grutter* and observed that the facts in cases like this could take the Court in different directions. It may be, he said, that research might justify the use of race beyond the graduate-school level. Moreover, he emphasized, the record in the Michigan cases was very strong that "minority candidates do well once they are in—so [there is] little concern of stigma attaching."

Stevens cautioned, however, that not all facts are relied upon so fully that, if they were to change, doctrine would necessarily follow suit. Like Breyer, Stevens cited *Brown* as an example in which the facts played merely a supporting role. Therefore, he told me, changing circumstances would not affect the rule there. The facts in *Brown*, and many other constitutional cases, he said, are really mixed questions of fact and law. There is an unmistakable empirical component, but the values infused in the determination of the facts may demand a particular result despite changed circumstances. Although Justice Stevens did not use this example, this could occur if viability changed from the current estimate of about twenty-four weeks to some earlier point. The fact of viability became so intertwined with the constitutional value of a woman's fundamental right of reproductive choice that changed factual circumstances might not eviscerate the right. The facts of the matter may become irrelevant if the constitutional value remains.

Constitutional facts, and the scientific research that sheds light on those facts, have an uncertain role at the Supreme Court. The Constitution is an eminently practical document. In interpreting its meaning, the Court must take into account the nature of things, both as they are and as they might be. One would think that after more than two hundred years the Court would have developed a sophisticated apparatus for dealing with constitutionally relevant information about the empirical world. One would expect to find, for instance, elaborate procedures in place by which the justices could be apprised of the latest technology and the most recent research available on a given subject. The Court's docket is replete with subjects on which data should be forthcoming, from the viability of fetal life to the demarcation of death, and from discrimination in capital sentencing to discrimination in education. Moreover, one would expect that after more than two hundred years, the Court would be able to say which party bears the burden of proof in particular constitutional contexts and under what circumstances the Court should be deferential to legislatures.

Yet the Court's constitutional fact jurisprudence is erratic; each justice appears to make it up as he or she goes along. The Court's fact-finding is guided by no comprehensive vision anchored in constitutional theory. Its fact-finding is rootless and is little more than a product of chance and circumstance. The Court repeatedly expresses fidelity to the belief that legislatures are better fact-finders than courts. However, this is probably inaccurate as an empirical matter and, in any case, is unsound as a matter of constitutional principle. Abdication of all constitutional fact-finding to the political process would be an abandonment of the Court's historical role. If the judiciary were to be truly deferential, then legislators could prohibit abortion after the first trimester by "finding" that "viability" occurs at twelve weeks, or prohibit violent song lyrics by "finding" that they cause listeners to be violent. Constitutional facts are integrally related to constitutional values. Ignorance of facts leads ineluctably to disregard of constitutional values.

Still, there is reason to be hopeful. Science and technology today are so pervasive that the Court cannot continue its slapdash ways. The Constitution's framers were products of the Enlightenment. They expressly sought to bring the science of their time into the document that would govern the times to come. Subsequent generations of lawyers and judges have failed to carry forth this mandate. This state of affairs may change with the next generation of lawyers. It is not that lawyers and judges will suddenly volunteer to join a new enlightenment. They will be forced to do so. The scientific revolution is everywhere; it cannot be ignored with impunity. If the Constitution is to "endure forever," its guardians will have to read it in light of the science of today and be prepared to incorporate the discoveries of tomorrow.

NOTES

PREFACE

1. Ralph Ketcham, *James Madison* (Charlottesville: University of Virginia Press, 1990), 297.

1. THE LESSON OF LEECHES

1. Richard Brookhiser, *Founding Father* (New York: Free Press, 1996), 198–99.
2. John Marshall, *The Life of George Washington*, vol. 2 (n.p.: Walton Book Co., 1980).
3. Ibid., 520.
4. Roy Porter, ed., *Cambridge Illustrated History of Medicine* (Oxford: Cambridge University Press, 1996), 58.
5. Ibid., 122.
6. Ibid.
7. Brookhiser, *Founding Father*, 199.
8. Marshall, *George Washington*, 521–22.
9. *Helvering v. Hallock*, 309 U.S. 106 (1940), 119–21.
10. Oliver Wendell Holmes Jr., "The Path of the Law," *Harvard Law Review*, 1897, vol. 10, 457, 469.

2. IF MEN WERE ANGELS

1. Bernard Bailyn, ed., *The Debate on the Constitution*, vol. 1 (New York: Library of America, 1990), 164.
2. Bernard Bailyn, ed., *The Debate on the Constitution*, vol. 2 (New York: Library of America, 1990), 596.
3. Ibid., 165.
4. Forrest McDonald, *Alexander Hamilton* (New York: W. W. Norton, 1982).
5. Bailyn, *Debate on the Constitution*, vol. 1, 33.
6. Bailyn, *Debate on the Constitution*, vol. 2, 765–66.
7. Bailyn, *Debate on the Constitution*, vol. 1, 164.

8. James Morton Smith, ed., *The Republic of Letters*, vols 1–3 (New York: W. W. Norton, 1995), 445.
9. Saul Cornell, *Anti-Federalism and the Dissenting Tradition in America* (Chapel Hill: University of North Carolina Press, 1999), 2.
10. Smith, *Republic of Letters*, 1.
11. Ibid., 37.
12. Ibid., 38.
13. Alf J. Mapp Jr., *Thomas Jefferson* (New York: Madison Books, 1989), 313.
14. Ibid.
15. Smith, *Republic of Letters*, 51.
16. Ibid.
17. McDonald, *Alexander Hamilton*, 35–36.
18. Ibid., 36.
19. Jack Rakove, ed., *James Madison: Writings* (New York: Library of America, 1999), 92–93.
20. Bailyn, *Debate on the Constitution*, vol. 1, 131.
21. Ibid.
22. McDonald, *Alexander Hamilton*, 36.
23. Bailyn, *Debate on the Constitution*, vol. 2, 418.
24. Jean Edward Smith, *John Marshall* (New York: Henry Holt, 1996), 121.
25. Ralph Ketcham, ed., *The Anti-Federalist Papers and The Constitutional Convention Debates* (Denver: Mentor Books, 1996), 231.
26. McDonald, *Alexander Hamilton*, 28.
27. Bailyn, *Debate on the Constitution*, vol. 1, 490.
28. Thomas Hobbes, *Leviathan* (1651), pt. 1, chap. 13.
29. McDonald, *Alexander Hamilton*, 61.
30. Ketcham, *James Madison*, 297.
31. Alexander Hamilton, John Jay, and James Madison. *The Federalist*, no. 10 (Norwalk, Conn.: Easton Press, 1979), 56.
32. Ketcham, *James Madison*, 71.
33. Rakove, *James Madison*, 31.
34. Moses I. Finley, ed., *The Legacy of Greece* (Oxford: Clarendon Press, 1981), 22.
35. Donald Kagan, *Pericles of Athens and the Birth of Democracy* (New York: Free Press, 1998), 54.
36. Finley, *Legacy of Greece*, 28.
37. Hamilton et al., *Federalist*, no. 10.
38. Ibid.
39. Ibid.
40. Ibid.
41. Finley, *Legacy of Greece*, 11.
42. Ibid.
43. Bailyn, *Debate on the Constitution*, vol. 2, 596.
44. Hamilton et al., *Federalist*, no. 6, 27.
45. Bailyn, *Debate on the Constitution*, vol. 2, 605.
46. Ibid., 450.

47. Ibid., 762.
48. Bailyn, *Debate on the Constitution*; vol. 1, 170–71.
49. Smith, *Republic of Letters*, 450.
50. Ibid., 458.
51. Ibid., 523.
52. Bailyn, *Debate on the Constitution*, vol. 1, 227.
53. *Encyclopedia of New Jersey*, see http://www.scc.rutgers.edu/njencyclopedia/databaseSpecificFiles/Articles/Stevens.asp./.
54. Bailyn, *Debate on the Constitution*, vol. 1, 227.
55. Ibid., 437.
56. Hamilton et al., *Federalist*, no. 9, 50.
57. Bailyn, *Debate on the Constitution*, vol. 1, 457.
58. Ibid., 199.
59. Ibid.
60. Ibid.
61. Bailyn, *Debate on the Constitution*, vol. 2, 768.
62. Ibid., 130.
63. Hamilton et al., *Federalist*, no. 10, 58.
64. Ibid., 59.
65. Ibid.
66. Bailyn, *Debate on the Constitution*, vol. 1, 894.
67. Ibid.
68. Ibid., 892.
69. Ibid., 61.
70. Ibid.
71. Smith, *Republic of Letters*, 501.
72. Bernard Schwartz, *A History of the Supreme Court* (New York: Oxford Univ. Press, 1993), 16.
73. Smith, *Republic of Letters*, 15.
74. Ibid., 1.
75. Ibid., 280.
76. Henry Adams, *History of the United States during the Administration of Thomas Jefferson* (New York: Scribner's 1886), 132.
77. Smith, *Republic of Letters*, 12.
78. Ibid.
79. *Marbury v. Madison*, 5 U.S. 137 (1803).
80. *McCulloch v. Maryland*, 17 U.S. 316 (1819).
81. McDonald, *Alexander Hamilton*, 201.
82. Hamilton et al., *Federalist*, no. 44.
83. Mapp, *Thomas Jefferson*, 294.
84. Ibid.
85. McDonald, *Alexander Hamilton*, 205 (emphasis supplied).
86. Ibid., 206.
87. Ibid., 207.
88. Smith, *Republic of Letters*, 442.
89. Ibid.

90. *McCulloch v. Maryland.*
91. Ibid., 403.
92. Ibid., 404.
93. Ibid., 407.

3. A Covenant with Death

 1. Bernard C. Steiner, *Life of Roger Brooke Taney* (Westport, Conn.: Greenwood Press, 1971), 87.
 2. Ibid.
 3. Ibid.
 4. Samuel Tyler, *Memoir of Roger Brooke Taney* (New York: Da Capo Press, 1970), 18.
 5. Ibid.
 6. Ibid., 124.
 7. Ibid.
 8. Steiner, *Life of Taney*, 376.
 9. Walker Lewis, *Without Fear or Favor* (Boston: Houghton Mifflin, 1965), 371.
10. Tyler, *Memoir of Taney*, 401.
11. Lewis, *Without Fear or Favor*, 378.
12. Ibid., 380.
13. Ibid., 269.
14. Charles W. Smith, *Roger B. Taney* (New York: Da Capo Press, 1973), 170.
15. *Scott v. Sandford*, 60 U.S. 393 (1857), 407. (Hereinafter *Dred Scott*)
16. Ibid., 409.
17. Ibid., 407.
18. Tyler, *Memoir of Taney*, 376–77.
19. Winthrop P. Jordan, *White Over Black* (Chapel Hill: University of North Carolina Press, 1968), 104.
20. Ibid., 248.
21. Walter Scheidt, "The Concept of Race in Anthropology and the Divisions into Human Races from Linneus to Demilier," in Earl W. Count, ed., *This Is Race* (New York: Shuman, 1950), 365.
22. Jordan, *White Over Black*, 248.
23. Ibid., 11.
24. Georges Cuvier, "The Animal Kingdom," in Count, *This Is Race*, 44.
25. Jordan, *White Over Black*, 498.
26. Ibid., 32.
27. Ibid., 501.
28. Ibid., 502.
29. Ibid., 276.
30. Ibid., 281.
31. Ibid., 442.
32. Ibid., 447.
33. Thomas Jefferson, *Notes on Virginia*. Ed. David Waldstreicher (New York: Palgrave, 2002), 139–40.
34. Ibid.

35. Ibid., 141–42.
36. Ibid., 142–43.
37. Jordan, *White Over Black*, 289.
38. Ibid., 276.
39. Ibid., 406.
40. *Dred Scott*, 407.
41. Lewis, *Without Fear or Favor*, 358.
42. Ibid.
43. *Dred Scott*, 409.
44. Ibid., 417.
45. Steiner, *Life of Taney*, 380.
46. *Dred Scott*, 451.
47. Ibid.
48. Ibid.
49. Ibid.
50. Ibid., 452.
51. Ibid., 432.
52. Ibid., 619.
53. Tyler, *Memoir of Taney*, 360.
54. Smith, *Roger B. Taney*, 173.
55. Lewis, *Without Fear or Favor*, 421.
56. Tyler, *Memoir of Taney*, 410.
57. Steiner, *Life of Taney*, 393.
58. Ibid., 394.
59. Lewis, *Without Fear or Favor*, 444–45.
60. Smith, *Roger B. Taney*, 173–34.
61. Ibid., 20.
62. Steiner, *Life of Taney*, 117.
63. Ibid., 343.
64. Lewis, *Without Fear or Favor*, 463.

4. The Roots of Modernity

1. Edward A. Purcell Jr., *Brandeis and the Progressive Constitution* (New Haven: Yale University Press, 2000), 137.
2. Sheldon M. Novick, *Honorable Justice* (New York: Little Brown, 1989), 27.
3. Ibid., 14.
4. Ibid., 27.
5. Ibid., 28.
6. Ibid., 17.
7. Ibid., 34.
8. Ibid., 53.
9. Ibid., 52.
10. Ibid., 66.
11. Ibid., 77.
12. G. Edward White, *Justice Oliver Wendell Holmes* (New York: Oxford University Press, 1993), 68–69.

13. Novick, *Honorable Justice*, 175.
14. White, *Justice Holmes*, 114.
15. Louis Menand, *The Metaphysical Club* (New York: Farrar, Straus & Giroux, 2001).
16. Richard Posner, ed., *The Essential Holmes* (Chicago: University of Chicago Press, 1996), xxii.
17. Samuel J. Konefsky, *The Legacy of Holmes and Brandeis* (New York: Plenum, 1956), 183.
18. *Buck v. Bell* 274 U.S. 200 (1927).
19. White, *Justice Holmes*, 126.
20. Paul A. Lombardo, "Three Generations, No Imbeciles: New Light on *Buck v. Bell*," *New York University Law Review*, vol. 60 (1985), 61.
21. White, *Justice Holmes*, 126.
22. Oliver Wendell Holmes Jr., "Book Notice," *American Law Review*, vol. 14 (1880), 233.
23. Oliver Wendell Holmes Jr., "Review of C. C. Langdell, *Summary of the Law of Contracts* and W. R. Anson, *Principles of the Law of Contracts*," *American Law Review*, vol. 14 (1880), 233.
24. White, *Justice Holmes*, 126.
25. Sheldon M. Novick, ed., *The Collected Works of Justice Holmes*, vol. 3 (Chicago: University of Chicago Press, 1995), 115.
26. Posner, *Essential Holmes*, 184
27. Oliver Wendell Holmes Jr., "The Path of the Law," *Harvard Law Review*, vol. 10 (1897), 457.
28. Oliver Wendell Holmes Jr., "Law in Science and Science in Law," *Harvard Law Review*, vol. 12 (1899), 443.
29. Novick, *Honorable Justice*, 169.
30. White, *Justice Holmes*, 292.
31. Novick, *Honorable Justice*, 196.
32. Ibid.
33. White, *Justice Holmes*, 16.
34. Ibid., 353.
35. Novick, *Honorable Justice*, 237.
36. Purcell, *Brandeis and the Progressive Constitution*, 11.
37. Konefsky, *Legacy of Holmes and Brandeis*, 1.
38. Ibid.
39. Purcell, *Brandeis and the Progressive Constitution*, 11.
40. *Lochner v. New York*, 198 U.S. 45 (1905).
41. Ibid., 70 (Harlan, dissenting).
42. Ibid., 64.
43. Ibid., 59.
44. Ibid., 62.
45. Ibid., 64.
46. Ibid., 61.
47. Herbert Spencer, *Social Statics, or, the Conditions Essential to Human Happiness Specified, and the First of Them Developed* (1851) 146–47.

48. *Lochner v. New York*, 61.
49. Ibid., 75 (Holmes, dissenting).
50. Konefsky, *Legacy of Holmes and Brandeis*, 82.
51. Neil Duxbury, "The Birth of Legal Realism and the Myth of Justice Holmes," *Anglo-American Law Review*, vol. 20 (1992), 84.
52. Konefsky, *Legacy of Holmes and Brandeis*, 82.
53. *Coppage v. Kansas*, 236 U.S. 1 (1915).
54. Ibid., 17.
55. Ibid.
56. Ibid., 26–27
57. Ibid., 26.
58. *Lochner v. New York*, 59.
59. *Muller v. Oregon*, 208 U.S. 412 (1908).
60. Philippa Strum, *Louis D. Brandeis* (New York: Schocken Books, 1989), 116.
61. Ibid., xi.
62. Ibid., 12.
63. Ibid., 20.
64. Ibid., 31.
65. Allon Gal, *Brandeis of Boston* (Cambridge: Harvard University Press, 1980), 81.
66. Strum, *Brandeis*, 27.
67. Ibid., 111.
68. Ibid., 95.
69. Gal, *Brandeis of Boston*, 56.
70. Strum, *Brandeis*, 52.
71. Ibid., 50.
72. Sir Arthur Conan Doyle, "A Scandal in Bohemia," in *The Adventures of Sherlock Holmes* (New York: Oxford University Press, 1998).
73. *Disanto v. Pennsylvania*, 273 U.S. 24 (1927), 43 (Brandeis, dissenting).
74. Konefsky, *Legacy of Holmes and Brandeis*, 68.
75. Strum, *Brandeis*, 120.
76. Ibid.
77. Konefsky, *Legacy of Holmes and Brandeis*, 87.
78. *Muller v. Oregon*, 420.
79. Ibid.
80. *Adkins v. Children's Hospital*, 261 U.S. 525 (1923).
81. Konefsky, *Legacy of Holmes and Brandeis*, 142.
82. *Adkins v. Children's Hospital*, 567.
83. Posner, *Essential Holmes*, 142.
84. Novick, *Honorable Justice*, 125.
85. Strum, *Brandeis*, 292–93.
86. Ibid., 299.
87. Purcell, *Brandeis and the Progressive Constitution*, 137.
88. Oliver Wendell Holmes Jr, "Book Notice," *American Law Review*, vol. 6 (1871), 141.
89. Konefsky, *Legacy of Holmes and Brandeis*, 184.

90. Ibid., 2.
91. *Meyer v. Nebraska*, 262 U.S. 390 (1923), 390.
92. Ibid., 399.
93. Strum, *Brandeis*, 311.
94. Ibid., 310.
95. White, *Justice Holmes*, 222–23.
96. Ibid., 319.
97. Ibid.
98. Ibid., 322.
99. Konefsky, *Legacy of Holmes and Brandeis*, 104.
100. *Schenck v. United States*, 249 U.S. 47 (1919).
101. Ibid., 51.
102. Ibid., 52.
103. *Abrams v. United States*, 250 U.S. 616 (1919).
104. Ibid., 628.
105. Ibid., 630.
106. *Whitney v. California*, 274 U.S. 357 (1927).
107. Ibid., 372.
108. Ibid., 377.
109. *Gitlow v. New York*, 268 U.S. 652 (1925), 673.
110. Strum, *Brandeis*, 237; see Pnin Lahav, "Holmes and Brandeis: Libertarian and Republican Justifications for Free Speech," *Journal of Law and Policy*, vol. 4 (1988), 451, 461–62.
111. Lahav, "Holmes and Brandeis," 464.
112. *Whitney v. California*, 375–76.
113. Novick, *Honorable Justice*, 355.
114. White, *Justice Holmes*, 471.
115. Novick, *Honorable Justice*, 323.

5. "Let Us Not Become Legal Monks"

1. Andrew L. Kaufman, *Cardozo* (Cambridge: Harvard University Press, 1998), 470–71
2. Ibid., 208.
3. Ibid.
4. Richard A. Posner, *Cardozo* (Chicago: University of Chicago Press, 1990), 90.
5. Ibid., 89.
6. *MacPherson v. Buick Motor Co.*, 217 N.T. 382 (1916).
7. *Palsgraf v. Long Island Railroad Company*, 162 N.E. 99 (1928).
8. Kaufman, *Cardozo*, 204.
9. Ibid., 205.
10. Ted Honderich, ed., *The Oxford Companion to Philosophy* (New York: Oxford University Press, 1995), 709.
11. Felix S. Cohen, "Transcendental Nonsense and the Functional Approach," *Columbia Law Review*, vol. 35 (1935), 809.
12. *United States v. Butler*, 297 U.S. 1 (1936).

13. Morton J. Horwitz, Thomas A. Reed, and William W. Fisher, eds., *American Legal Realism* (New York: Oxford University Press, 1993), xiv.

14. Karl N. Llewellyn, *The Bramble Bush* (New York: Oceana Publications, 1951).

15. Horwitz et al., *American Legal Realism*, 4.

16. Ibid., 44.

17. Ibid., 56.

18. Ibid., 61.

19. Ibid., 63.

20. Ibid., 205.

21. Kaufman, *Cardozo*, 456.

22. Ibid.

23. Ibid., 457.

24. Ibid.

25. Ibid., 460.

26. Anon Y. Mous., "The Speech of Judges: A Dissenting Opinion," *Virginia Law Review*, vol. 29 (1943), 625.

27. Ibid.

28. Posner, *Cardozo*, 136.

29. Ibid., 8.

30. John Henry Schlegel, *American Legal Realism and Empirical Social Science* (Chapel Hill: University of North Carolina Press, 1995), 83.

31. Ibid.

32. Clare Cushman, ed., *The Supreme Court Justices* (Washington, D.C.: Congressional Quarterly Books, 1995), 387.

33. Bruce Allen Murphy, *The Brandeis/Frankfurter Connection* (New York: Oxford University Press, 1982), 113.

34. William O. Douglas, *Go East, Young Man* (New York: Random House, 1974).

35. Horwitz et al., *American Legal Realism*, 235.

36. Howard Ball and Philip J. Cooper, *Of Power and Right* (New York: Oxford University Press, 1992), 77.

37. Barry Cushman, *Rethinking the New Deal Court* (New York: Oxford University Press, 1998).

38. Melvin I. Urofsky, "Conflict Among the Brethren," *Duke Law Journal*, vol. 1988 (1988), 71.

39. Ibid., 79–80.

40. Ball and Cooper, *Of Power and Right*, 92.

41. Urofsky, "Conflict," 80.

42. Ibid., 81–82.

43. Felix Frankfurter, diary entry dated January 11, 1943.

44. Melvin I. Urofsky, *Division and Discord* (New York: Oxford University Press, 1997), 34.

45. Ibid.

46. Cushman, *Rethinking the New Deal Court*, 390.

47. Ibid.

48. Ibid.

49. Urofsky, "Conflict," 105.
50. Ibid.
51. *West Virginia State Board of Education v. Barnette*, 319 U.S. 624 (1943).
52. Urofsky, "Conflict," 105.

6. "ATTAINDER OF BLOOD"

1. *Personal Justice Denied* (Washington, D.C.: The Commission on Wartime Relocation and Internment of Civilians, 1982).
2. U.S. Congress, *Hearings Before the Select Committee Investigating National Defense Migration*, 77th Congress, 2nd session, February 1942 (Washington, D.C.: Government Printing Office, 1942), 10973.
3. Ibid., 10974
4. Ibid.
5. Ibid.
6. Kenneth S. Davis, *FDR* (New York: Random House, 2000), 422.
7. Page Smith, *Democracy on Trial* (New York: Simon & Schuster, 1995), 120.
8. Ibid.
9. General DeWitt's *Final Report*, June 5, 1943, vii.
10. U.S. Congress, *Hearings*, 11014.
11. Roger Daniels, *The Politics of Prejudice* (New York: Holiday House, 1966), 47.
12. Ibid., 67.
13. Ibid.
14. Lothrop Stoddard, *Rising Tide of Color Against White World-Supremacy* (New York: Scribner, 1920).
15. *Skinner v. Oklahoma*, 316 U.S. 535 (1942).
16. Daniel J. Kevles, *In the Name of Eugenics* (New York: Knopf, 1985).
17. Michael Willrich, "Two Percent Solution: Eugenic Jurisprudence and the Socialization of American Law, 1900–1930," *Law and History Review*, vol. 16 (1998), 66.
18. Kevles, *In the Name of Eugenics*, 19.
19. Brief of the State of Oklahoma, *Skinner v. Oklahoma*, 20.
20. *Skinner v. Oklahoma*, 539.
21. Ibid., 541.
22. Ibid., 542.
23. Ibid., 545 (Stone, concurring).
24. Ibid.
25. Kevles, *In the Name of Eugenics*, 94.
26. Gabriel J. Chin, "Regulating Race," *Harvard Civil Rights–Civil Liberties Law Review*, vol. 37 (2002), 1.
27. Ibid., 20.
28. Ibid.
29. *Ozawa v. United States*, 260 U.S. 178 (1922).
30. *United States v. Thind*, 261 U.S. 204 (1923).
31. Ibid., 212.
32. Ibid., quoting *Encyclopedia Britannica* (11th ed.), 113.

33. *Ozawa v. United States*, 195.
34. Ibid., 207–8.
35. *United States v. Thind*, 215.
36. Ibid.
37. Smith, *Democracy on Trial*, 118
38. Daniels, *Politics of Prejudice*, 70.
39. Westbrook Pegler, "Fair Enough,"*Washington Post* (Feb. 14, 1942), 7.
40. Richard Orodenker, ed., *Twentieth-Century American Sportswriters*, 7th ed. (Detroit: Gale Group, 1996), 273.
41. Joseph McKerns, *Biographical Dictionary of American Journalism* (New York: Greenwood Publishing Group, 1989), 553.
42. Walter Lippmann, "The Fifth Column on the Coast," *Los Angeles Times*, Feb. 13, 1942.
43. U.S. Congress, *Hearings*, 11011.
44. Smith, *Democracy on Trial*, 103.
45. *Personal Justice Denied*, 88.
46. Dewitt's *Final Report*.
47. Francis Beverly Biddle, *In Brief Authority* (New York: Greenwood Publishing Group, 1976).
48. Smith, *Democracy on Trial*, 104.
49. *Personal Justice Denied*, 46.
50. Ibid., 135.
51. Ibid., 136.
52. Ibid., 161.
53. Smith, *Democracy on Trial*, 114.
54. Ibid.
55. Ibid., 28.
56. *Hirabayashi v. United States*, 320 U.S. 81 (1943).
57. *Korematsu v. United States*, 323 U.S. 214 (1944).
58. *United States v. Carolene Products Co.*, 304 U.S. 144 (1938).
59. Ibid., fn 4.
60. *Hirabayashi v. United States*, p. 101.
61. Ibid., 101–5.
62. Ibid., 106 (Douglas, concurring).
63. Ibid., 113 (Murphy, concurring).
64. *Korematsu v. United States*, 218.
65. Ibid., 219
66. Ibid., 233 (Murphy, dissenting).
67. Ibid.
68. Brief of Japanese American Citizens League, amicus curae, *Korematsu v. United States* (1944).
69. Ibid. In the case of Germany, the child's citizenship followed the father's.
70. Smith, *Democracy on Trial*, 106.
71. *Korematsu v. United States*, 239–40.
72. *Personal Justice Denied*, 66.
73. *Korematsu v. United States*, 22.

74. Ibid., 243 (Jackson, dissenting).
75. Ibid.
76. *Personal Justice Denied*, 181.
77. Kevles, *In the Name of Eugenics*, 166.

7. Autocracy of Caste

1. *The Slaughter-House Cases*, 83 U.S. 36 (1873).
2. Ibid., 60.
3. Fourteenth Amendment; *see* ibid., 43.
4. *Baron v. Baltimore*, 32 U.S. 243 (1833).
5. *Slaughter-House Cases*, 78.
6. Ibid., 96 (Field, dissenting).
7. *Plessy v. Ferguson*, 163 U.S. 597 (1896).
8. Mark Whitman, ed., *Removing a Badge of Slavery* (Princeton, N.J.: Markus Wiener Publishers, 1993).
9. Ibid., 12.
10. Ibid.
11. Ibid.
12. Charles L. Black Jr., "The Lawfulness of the Segregation Decisions," *Yale Law Journal*, vol. 69 (1960), 421, 422, n. 8.
13. *Plessy v. Ferguson*, 559.
14. George W. Stocking Jr., *Race, Culture, and Evolution* (Chicago: University of Chicago Press, 1982), 213.
15. Ibid., 215.
16. Ibid., 229.
17. Richard Kluger, *Simple Justice* (New York: Vintage, 1975), 91.
18. Ibid., 128.
19. Ibid.
20. Ibid., 280.
21. Ibid., 177.
22. Ibid., 180.
23. Ibid., 223–24.
24. *Murray v. Maryland*, 182 A. 590 (1936).
25. Kluger, *Simple Justice*, 192.
26. Whitman, *Removing a Badge of Slavery*, xxvii.
27. Ibid., 25.
28. Kluger, *Simple Justice*, 262.
29. Ibid., 264.
30. Ibid., 266.
31. *Sweatt v. Painter*, 339 U.S. 629 (1950).
32. *McLaurin v. Oklahoma*, 339 U.S. 637 (1950).
33. Whitman, *Removing a Badge of Slavery*, 29.
34. Kluger, *Simple Justice*, 293–94.
35. *Sweatt v. Painter*, 629.
36. Ibid.
37. *McLaurin v. Oklahoma*, 637.

38. Kluger, *Simple Justice*, 316.
39. Ibid.
40. Ibid., 315.
41. Ibid.
42. Juan Williams, *Thurgood Marshall* (New York: Times Books, 1998), 197.
43. Kluger, *Simple Justice*, 321.
44. *Briggs v. Elliott*, 349 U.S. 249 (1954).
45. Kluger, *Simple Justice*, 328.
46. Ibid., 340.
47. Ibid., 352.
48. Ibid.
49. Ibid., 353.
50. Ibid., 355.
51. Ibid., 336.
52. Ibid., 365.
53. Ibid., 366.
54. Ibid., 415.
55. Ibid., 421.
56. Ibid., 424.
57. Ibid., 482.
58. Ibid., 481.
59. Ibid.
60. Ibid., 487.
61. Ibid., 483.
62. Ibid.
63. Ibid., 503.
64. Ibid., 483–84.
65. Ibid.
66. Ibid., 440.
67. Ibid., 444.
68. Ibid., 447–48.
69. Ibid., 448.
70. Williams, *Thurgood Marshall*, 208.
71. Kluger, *Simple Justice*, 555.
72. Ibid., 554.
73. Ibid., 544–45.
74. Ibid., 545.
75. Ibid., 574.
76. Whitman, *Removing a Badge of Slavery*, 131–32.
77. Ibid.
78. Ibid., 146–47.
79. Ibid.
80. Kluger, *Simple Justice*, 615.
81. G. Edward White, *Earl Warren* (New York: Oxford University Press, 1987).
82. Ibid., 9.
83. Ibid., 223.

84. Ibid., 225.
85. *Brown v. Board of Education*, 347 U.S. 483 (1954).
86. White, *Earl Warren*, 280.
87. Kluger, *Simple Justice*, 684.
88. Ibid., 689.
89. Ibid., 690.
90. Whitman, *Removing a Badge of Slavery*, 285.
91. Kluger, *Simple Justice*, 402.
92. *Brown v. Board of Education*, 483.
93. Kluger, *Simple Justice*, 707.
94. Ibid., 711.
95. Ibid., 706.
96. Whitman, *Removing a Badge of Slavery*, 55.
97. Ibid., 52.
98. Ibid., 57.
99. James T. Patterson, *Brown v. Board of Education* (New York: Oxford University Press, 2001), xiv.
100. Ibid., xviii.
101. *Stell v. Savannah*, 220 F.Sup667 (S.D.Ga. 1963).
102. Ibid.
103. Ibid.
104. *Savannah v. Stell*, 333 F.2d 55 (1964).
105. Ibid.
106. *New York Times v. Sullivan*, 376 U.S. 254 (1964).

8. The Right to Be Let Alone

1. *McCulloch v. Maryland*, 17 U.S. 316 (1819).
2. *Tileston v. Ullman*, 318 U.S. 44 (1943).
3. *Poe v. Ullman*, 367 U.S. 497 (1961).
4. *Griswold v. Connecticut*, 381 U.S. 479 (1965).
5. Laurence H. Tribe, *Abortion* (New York: W. W. Norton, 1990), 94.
6. *Griswold v. Connecticut*, 510 (Black, dissenting).
7. Ibid.
8. *Eisenstadt v. Baird*, 405 U.S. 438 (1972).
9. Ibid.
10. Edward Lazarus, *Closed Chambers* (New York: Times Books, 1998), 364.
11. Tribe, *Abortion*, 28.
12. Ibid., 31.
13. Leslie J. Reagan, *When Abortion Was a Crime* (Berkeley: University of California Press, 1997), 11.
14. Ibid., 10.
15. J. L. Heilbron, ed., *The Oxford Companion to the History of Modern Medicine* (New York: Oxford University Press, 2003), 3.
16. Ibid.
17. *Roe v. Wade*, 410 U.S. 113 (1973).

18. Bernard Schwartz, *A History of the Supreme Court* (New York: Oxford University Press, 1993), 340.

19. Ibid., 348.

20. *Roe v. Wade*, 755 (Burger, concurring).

21. Paul Rosen, *The Supreme Court and Social Science* (Urbana: University of Illinois Press, 1972), 141.

22. *Roe v. Wade*, 735 (Stewart, concurring).

23. Ibid., 116.

24. Ibid., 153.

25. *Santa Clara County v. Southern Pacific Railroad*, 118 U.S. 394 (1886).

26. *Roe v. Wade*, 130.

27. Tribe, *Abortion*, 117.

28. Charles A. Gardner, "Is an Embryo a Person?" in J. Douglas Butler and David F. Walbert, eds., *Abortion, Medicine and the Law* (New York: Facts on File, 1992), 454–55.

29. Ibid., 456.

30. *Roe v. Wade*, 163.

31. Ibid., 174 (Rehnquist, dissenting).

32. Schwartz, *History of the Supreme Court*, 337.

33. John Hart Ely, "The Wages of Crying Wolf: A Comment on *Roe v. Wade*," *Yale Law Journal*, vol. 82 (1973) 920, 924.

34. Michael J. Flower, "Coming into Being: The Prenatal Development of Humans," in Butler and Walbert, *Abortion, Medicine and the Law*, 451.

35. *Akron v. Akron Center for Reproductive Health*, 462 U.S. 458 (O'Connor, dissenting).

36. Ibid., 458 (O'Connor, dissenting).

37. Lazarus, *Closed Chambers*, 357.

38. Schwartz, *History of the Supreme Court* 352–53.

39. Ibid., 353.

40. Lazarus, *Closed Chambers*, 357–58.

41. *Webster v. Reproductive Health Services*, 492 U.S. 490 (1989).

42. Ibid., 526.

43. Ibid.

44. *Planned Parenthood of Southeastern Pennsylvania v. Casey*, 505 U.S. 833 (1992).

45. Lazarus, *Closed Chambers*, 464.

46. *Thornburgh v. American College of Obstetricians and Gynecologists*, 476 U.S. 747 (1986).

47. Cushman, *The Supreme Court Justices*.

48. Ibid.

49. *Boddie v. Connecticut*, 401 U.S. 371 (1971).

50. *Poe v. Ullman*.

51. *United States v. Lopez*, 514 U.S. 549 (1995).

52. *Poe v. Ullaman*, 371.

53. *Mitchell v. W. T. Grant Co.*, 416 U.S. 600 (1974).

54. *Texas v. Johnson*, 491 U.S. 397 (1989).

55. *Planned Parenthood of Southeastern Pennsylvania v. Casey*, 833.
56. Ibid., 849.
57. Ibid., 860.
58. Ibid., 863.
59. Ibid., 860.
60. Ibid., 870.
61. Ibid.
62. Ibid., 856.
63. Ibid., 877.
64. Ibid., 885.
65. *Planned Parenthood of Southeastern Pennsylvania v. Casey*, 744 F. Sup1323, 1351 (E.D.Pa. 1990).
66. *Planned Parenthood of Southeastern Pennsylvania v. Casey*, 886.
67. *Planned Parenthood of Southeastern Pennsylvania v. Casey*, 744 F. Supp., 1357.
68. *Hodgson v. Minnesota*, 497 U.S. 417 (1990), 428.
69. Robert H. Mnookin, *In the Interest of Children* (New York: W. H. Freeman, 1985), 239.
70. Ibid., 240.
71. *Hodgson v. Minnesota*, 477–78.
72. *Planned Parenthood of Southeastern Pennsylvania v. Casey*, 892–93.
73. Ibid., 918 (Stevens, concurring in part and dissenting in part).
74. Ibid., 980 (Scalia, concurring in part and dissenting in part).
75. Ibid., 981.
76. Ibid., 984–85.
77. Ibid., 990.
78. Ibid., 991.
79. Ibid., 1001–2.
80. *Washington v. Glucksberg*, 521 U.S. 702 (1997).
81. *Loving v. Virginia*, 388 U.S. 1 (1967).
82. Ibid.
83. *Washington v. Glucksberg*, 705–6.
84. Ibid., 711.
85. Ibid., 735.
86. Ibid. (O'Connor, concurring).
87. Ibid.
88. Ibid., 754 (Souter, concurring).
89. Ibid., 785.
90. Ibid., 734.
91. Ibid., 786 (quoting John Keown, "Euthanasia in the Netherlands: Sliding Down the Slippery Slope?," in John Keown, ed., *Euthanasia Examined* (New York: Cambridge University Press, 1995), 261, 289.
92. Ibid., 786–87.
93. Ibid., 787.
94. Ibid.

9. LIFTER OR LEVELER?

1. *PGA Tour, Inc. v. Martin*, 532 U.S. 661 (2001).
2. Ibid.
3. Ibid.
4. *Strauder v. West Virginia*, 100 U.S. 303 (1879).
5. *Yick Wo v. Hopkins*, 118 U.S. 356 (1886).
6. *Plessy v. Ferguson*, 163 U.S. 537 (1896).
7. *United States v. Carolene Products Co.*
8. *Korematsu v. United States*, 323 U.S. 214 (1944).
9. Gerald Gunther, "In Search of Evolving Doctrine on a Changing Court: A Model for a Newer Equal Protection," *Harvard Law Review*, vol. 86 (1972).
10. *McClesky v. Kemp*, 481 U.S. 279 (1987).
11. Edward Lazarus, *Closed Chambers* (New York: Times Books, 1998), 189.
12. Ibid., 185.
13. John Calvin Jeffries, *Justice Lewis F. Powell, Jr.* (New York: Fordham University Press, 2001).
14. *Ballew v. Georgia*, 435 U.S. 223 (1978).
15. Lazarus, *Closed Chambers*, 202.
16. *McCleskey v. Kemp*, 292.
17. *Gregg v. Georgia*, 428 U.S. 153 (1976), 200.
18. *McCleskey v. Kemp*, 326 (Brennan, dissenting).
19. Ibid., 308.
20. Lazarus, *Closed Chambers*, 207.
21. *McCleskey v. Kemp*, 308.
22. Ibid., 309–10.
23. Philippa Strum, *Women in the Barracks* (Lawrence: Kansas University Press, 2002).
24. *United States v. Commonwealth of Virginia*, 766 F. Supp. (W.D.Va. 1991), 1407, 1421.
25. Ibid., 1415.
26. Ibid.
27. Strum, *Women in the Barracks*, 162–64.
28. *United States v. Commonwealth of Virginia*, 766 F. Supp., 1434.
29. Ibid.
30. *United States v. Commonwealth of Virginia*, 976 F.2d (4th Cir. 1992), 890.
31. Ibid., 892.
32. *Brown v. Board of Education*, 347 U.S. 483 (1954).
33. *Faulkner v. Jones*, 10 F.3d (4th Cir. 1993), 226, 232.
34. *United States v. Commonwealth of Virginia*, 852 F. Supp., 471, 476.
35. Strum, *Women in the Barracks*, 200.
36. Ibid., 211.
37. *United States v. Commonwealth of Virginia*, 852 F. Supp., 476.
38. Ibid.
39. Ibid.
40. *United States v. Commonwealth of Virginia*, 44 F.3d (4th Cir. 1995), 1229.
41. Ibid., 1234.

42. Ibid., 1238.
43. Ibid., 1235.
44. Ibid.
45. Ibid., 1239.
46. *United States v. Virginia*, 518 U.S. 515 (1996).
47. Cushman, *The Supreme Court Justices*.
48. Amy Leigh Campbell, "Raising the Bar: Ruth Bader Ginsburg and the ACLU Women's Rights Project," *Texas Journal of Women and the Law*, vol. 11 (2002), 157, 161.
49. Ibid.
50. *Reed v. Reed*, 404 U.S. 71 (1971).
51. *Craig v. Boren*, 429 U.S. 190 (1976).
52. Ibid.
53. Campbell, "Raising the Bar," 237.
54. *United States v. Virginia*, 518 U.S., 524.
55. Ibid.
56. Ibid., 533–34.
57. Ibid.
58. Strum, *Women in the Barracks*, 82.
59. *United States v. Virginia*, 518 U.S., 534.
60. Ibid., 534–35.
61. Ibid., 537–38.
62. Ibid., 566–67 (Scalia, dissenting).
63. Ibid., 539–40.
64. Ibid., 554.
65. Ibid., 540.
66. Ibid., 541.
67. Ibid., 542–43.
68. Ibid., 550.
69. Ibid., 585 (Scalia, dissenting).
70. Ibid., 585–86.
71. Ibid., 574.
72. Ibid., 550.
73. Ibid.
74. Strum, *Women in the Barracks*, 141.
75. *United States v. Virginia*, 518 U.S., 559 (Rehnquist, concurring).
76. Ibid., 550.
77. Strum, *Women in the Barracks*, 302.
78. *Regents of the University of California v. Bakke*, 438 U.S. 265 (1978).
79. *Hopwood v. Texas*, 78 F.3d 932, 944 (5th Cir. 1996).
80. *Gratz v. Bollinger*, 123 S.Ct. 2411 (2003).
81. Ibid., 2428.
82. *Gratz v. Bollinger*.
83. Ibid., 2332.
84. Ibid.
85. Ibid., 2340.

86. Ibid., 2339–41.
87. Ibid., 2333.
88. Ibid., 2338.
89. Ibid., 2339–40.
90. Ibid., 2358 (Thomas, dissenting).
91. Ibid., 2341.
92. Ibid., 2343.
93. Ibid., 2346.
94. Ibid., 2359 (Thomas, dissenting).

10. IN THE SUPREME COURT WE TRUST

1. Brief of Americans United for Separation of Church and State, *Church of the Lukumi Babalu Aye v. City of Hialeah.*
2. *Church of the Lukumi Babalu Aye v. City of Hialeah*, 723 F. Supp. 1467 (S.D.Fla. 1989).
3. Barry Klein, "Sect Cites Right to Sacrifices," *St. Petersburg Times* (March 27, 1989), B1.
4. George Volsky, "Religion from Cuba Stirs Row in Miami," *New York Times,* June 29, 1987.
5. *Church of the Lukumi Babalu Aye v. City of Hialeah*, 508 U.S. 520 (1993).
6. Ibid.
7. *Employment Division of Human Resources of Oregon v. Smith*, 494 U.S. 872 (1990).
8. Ibid., 877–78.
9. Ibid., 879.
10. *Reynolds v. United States*, 98 U.S. 145 (1879).
11. Ibid., 166.
12. *Braunfeld v. Brown*, 366 U.S. 599 (1961).
13. *Sherbert v. Verner*, 374 U.S. 398 (1963).
14. *Wisconsin v. Yoder*, 406 U.S. 205 (1972).
15. *Employment Division of Human Resources of Oregon v. Smith*, 887.
16. Ibid., 893–94 (O'Connor, concurring).
17. Ibid., 890.
18. Ibid.
19. Ibid., 902.
20. Ibid., 903.
21. Ibid., 905–6.
22. Ibid., 908–9 (Blackmun, dissenting).
23. Ibid.
24. Ibid., 912–15.
25. *Church of the Lukumi Babalu Aye v. City of Hialeah*, 557–58.
26. Ibid., 537.
27. *Church of the Lukumi Babalu Aye v. City of Hialeah* 723 F.Supp., 1472–76.
28. Ibid., 1475–76.
29. Ibid., 1476.
30. Ibid., 1485–86.

31. *Church of the Lukumi Babalu Aye v. City of Hialeah*, 564 (Souter, concurring).
32. Ibid.
33. Ibid., 575–76.
34. Ibid., 577.
35. *Lee v. Weisman*, 505 U.S. 577 (1992).
36. Ibid., 609, n. 11.
37. Ibid., 615 (Souter, concurring).
38. *Marsh v. Chambers*, 463 U.S. 783 (1983).
39. *Newdow v. U.S. Congress*, 313 F.3d 495 (9th Cir. 2002).
40. *Lemon v. Kurtzman*, 403 U.S. 602 (1971).
41. *Lamb's Chapel v. Center Moriches Union Free School District*, 508 U.S. 384, 397 (1993) (Scalia, concurring).
42. *Lynch v. Donnelly*, 465 U.S. 668, 687–88 (1984) (O'Connor, concurring).
43. Ibid.
44. *County of Allegheny v. ACLU*, 492 U.S. 573 (1989).
45. *Lee v. Weisman*, 587.
46. Ibid., 595.
47. *McCollum v. Board of Education, School District 71*, 333 U.S. 203 (1948).
48. *Lee v. Weisman*, 587.
49. Ibid., 593.
50. Ibid., 593–94.
51. Ibid.
52. The studies cited by Justice Kennedy were Brittain, "Adolescent Choices and Parent-Peer Cross-Pressures," *American Sociological Review*, vol. 28, no. 385 (June 1963); Clasen and Brown, "The Multidimensionality of Peer Pressure in Adolescence," *Journal of Youth and Adolescence*, vol. 14, no. 451 (December 1985); Brown, Clasen, and Eicher, "Perceptions of Peer Pressure, Peer Conformity Dispositions, and Self-Reported Behavior Among Adolescents," *Developmental Psychology*, vol. 22, no. 521 (July 1986).
53. *Lee v. Weisman*, 631–32 (Scalia, dissenting).
54. Ibid., 635.
55. Ibid.
56. Ibid., 642.
57. *Virginia Board of Education v. Barnette*, 319 U.S. 624 (1943).
58. *Lee v. Weisman*, 638–39.
59. Ibid., 637.
60. Ibid., 638–39.
61. *Edwards v. Aguillard*. 482 U.S. 578 (1987).
62. Ibid.
63. *McLean v. Arkansas Board of Education*, 529 F.Supp. 1255 (E.D.Ark. 1982).
64. Ibid., 1261–62.
65. *Edwards v. Aguillard*, 615 (Scalia, dissenting).
66. Ibid.
67. Brief of 72 Nobel Laureates et al., amicus curiae, in *Edwards v. Aguillard*.

68. *Edwards v. Aguillard*, 634 (Scalia, dissenting).
69. Ibid., 629.
70. *Aguillard v. Treen*, 634 F.Supp. 426 (E.D.La. 1985).
71. Ibid., 427.
72. Ibid., 428.
73. Brief of the National Academies of Science, amicus curiae, in *Edwards v. Aguillard*.
74. Ibid., 9.

11. Shouting Fire

1. Robert Andrews, ed., *Famous Lines: The Columbia Dictionary of Familiar Quotations* (New York: Columbia University Press, 1996), 441.
2. *U.S. News & World Report*, February 10, 1997, 44.
3. Brief of Deja Vu Consulting, Inc., and Deja Vu of Nashville, Inc., amicus curiae, in *City of Erie v. Pap's AM*, 529 U.S. 277 (2000), 3.
4. *City of Renton v. Playtime Theatres, Inc.*, 475 U.S. 41 (1986).
5. At the time of *Renton*, Rehnquist was an associate justice, but the text uses his current title of chief justice for simplicity's sake.
6. *Young v. American Mini Theatres, Inc.*, 427 U.S. 50 (1976).
7. *City of Renton v. Playtime Theatres, Inc.*, 50.
8. Ibid.
9. Ibid.
10. *Barnes v. Glen Theatre, Inc.*, 501 U.S. 560 (1991).
11. Ibid., 565.
12. Ibid., 566.
13. Ibid., 568.
14. *United States v. O'Brien*, 391 U.S. 367 (1968).
15. Ibid.
16. *Barnes v. Glen Theatre Inc.*, 572.
17. Ibid., 572.
18. Ibid., 589.
19. Ibid., 590.
20. Ibid.
21. Ibid., 574–75 (Scalia, concurring).
22. Ibid., 591 (White, dissenting).
23. Ibid., 584 (Souter, concurring).
24. Ibid., 584–85.
25. Ibid., 593.
26. Ibid., 594.
27. *City of Erie v. Pap's AM*.
28. Ibid., 311 (Souter, concurring in part and dissenting in part).
29. Ibid., 313 (Souter, concurring in part and dissenting in part).
30. Ibid., 316.
31. Ibid., 297.
32. Ibid.
33. Ibid., 344, n. 2 (Souter, concurring in part and dissenting in part).

34. *Daubert v. Merrell Dow Pharmaceuticals, Inc.*, 509 U.S. 579 (1993).

35. *Kumho Tire Co. v. Carmichael*, 526 U.S. 136 (1997).

36. Brief of First Amendment Lawyers Association, amicus curiae, in *Erie City of Erie v. Pap's AM*, 8–12.

37. Ibid.

38. Ibid., 14.

39. Ibid.

40. *City of Los Angeles v. Alameda Books, Inc.*, 535 U.S. 425 (2002).

41. Ibid.

42. Ibid., 440.

43. Ibid.

44. Ibid., 466 (Stevens, dissenting).

12. The House That the Court Built

1. http.//www.Monticello.org/Jefferson/dayinlife/entrance/design.html.

2. Alexis de Tocqueville, *Democracy in America*, trans. by Francis Bowen (Cambridge, Mass.: Sever and Francis, 1862), 357–58.

3. *Hall v. Baxter Healthcare Corp.*, 947 F.Supp. 1387 (D.Or. 1996).

4. See, e.g., Matt Ridley, *Nature via Nurture Genes, Experience, and What Makes Us Human* (New York: HarperCollins, 2003).

5. *Kansas v. Hendricks*, 521 U.S. 346 (1997).

6. *Kansas v. Crane*, 534 U.S. 407 (2002).

7. Kansas Statute Annotated § 59–29a02(b).

8. *Kansas v. Crane*, 407.

9. Ibid., 412 (Kennedy, concurring).

10. Ibid., 407.

11. Ibid.

12. Ibid., 419 (Scalia, dissenting).

13. Ibid., 407.

14. *Olmstead v. United States*, 277 U.S. 438 (1928).

15. *Katz v. United States*, 389 U.S. 347 (1967).

16. Ibid., 512.

17. Ibid., 516.

18. *California v. Ciraolo*, 476 U.S. 207 (1986).

19. *United States v. Drayton*, 536 U.S. 194 (1988).

20. *Kyllo v. United States*, 533 U.S. 27 (2001).

21. Ibid., 29.

22. Ibid., 38.

23. Ibid.

24. Ibid.

25. Ibid., 40.

26. Ibid., 35.

27. *United States v. Lopez*, 514 U.S. 549 (1995), 616–17.

28. Ibid., 620.

29. *Grutter v. Bollinger*, 123 S.Ct. 2325 (2003), 2339.

30. Ibid., 2347.

BIBLIOGRAPHY

BOOKS AND ARTICLES

Abraham, Henry J. *Justices, Presidents, and Senators: A History of the U.S. Supreme Court Appointments from Washington to Clinton* (Lanham: Rowman & Littlefield Publishers, 1999).

Adams, Henry. *History of the United States during the Administration of Thomas Jefferson* (New York: Scribner's, 1886).

American Concentration Camps, Volumes 1–9 (New York: Garland Press, 1989).

Andrews, Robert. *Famous Lines: The Columbia Dictionary of Familiar Quotations* (New York: Columbia University Press: 1996).

Aveni, Anthony. *Behind the Crystal Ball: Magic, Science, and the Occult from Antiquity through the New Age* (New York: Times Books, 1996).

Bailyn, Bernard, ed. *The Debate on the Constitution: Federalist and Antifederalist Speeches, Articles, and Letters During the Struggle over Ratification*, Volumes 1 and 2 (New York: Library of America, 1990).

Ball, Howard and Philip J. Cooper. *Of Power and Right: Hugo Black, William O. Douglas and America's Constitutional Revolution* (New York: Oxford University Press, 1992).

Bedini, Silvio A. *Thomas Jefferson: Statesman of Science* (New York: Macmillan Publishing Co., 1990).

Biddle, Francis Beverley. *In Brief Authority* (Westport, Conn.: Greenwood Publishing Group, 1976).

Black, Charles L., Jr. "The Lawfulness of the Segregation Decisions," *Yale Law Journal*, vol. 69 (1960), p. 421.

Boas, Franz. *Race, Language and Culture* (New York: Free Press, 1940).

Bowen, Catherine Drinker. *Miracle at Philadelphia: The Story of the Constitutional Convention May to September 1787* (New York: Little Brown & Co., 1986).

Boyer, Paul S., ed. *The Oxford Companion to United States History* (New York: Oxford University Press, 2001).

Braman, Donald. "Of Race and Immutability," *U.C.L.A. Law Review*, vol. 46 (1999), p. 1375.

Breyer, Stephen. "Genetics and Legal Institutions," speech given at the Whitehead Institute for Biomedical Research, Whitehead Policy Symposium, May 12, 2000.

———. "The Interdependence of Science and Law," an address given to the annual meeting of the American Association for the Advancement of Science, February 16, 1998.

Brittain, Clay V. "Adolescent Choices and Parent-Peer Cross-Pressures," *American Sociological Review*, vol. 28 (June 1963), p. 385.

Brookhiser, Richard. *Founding Father: Rediscovering George Washington* (New York: Free Press, 1996).

Brown, B. Bradford, Donna Rae Clasen, and Sue Ann Eicher. "Perceptions of Peer Pressure, Peer Conformity Dispositions, and Self-Reported Behavior Among Adolescents," *Developmental Psychology*, vol. 22 (July 1986), p. 521.

Callahan, Daniel. "Abortion: Some Ethical Issues," in J. Douglas Buter and David F. Walbert, eds., *Abortion, Medicine and the Law* (New York: Facts on File, Inc., 1992).

Campbell, Amy Leigh. "Raising the Bar: Ruth Bader Ginsburg and the ACLU Women's Rights Project," *Texas Journal of Women and the Law*, vol. 11 (2002), p. 157.

Cardozo, Benjamin N. *The Nature of the Judicial Process* (New Haven: Yale University Press, 1921).

Chin, Gabriel J. "Regulating Race: Asian Exclusion and the Administrative State," *Harvard Civil Rights–Civil Liberties Law Review*, vol. 37 (2002), p. 1.

Clasen, Donna Rae and B. Bradford Brown. "The Multidimensionality of Peer Pressure in Adolescence," *Journal of Youth and Adolescence*, vol. 14 (December 1985), p. 451.

Cohen, I. Bernard. *Science and the Founding Fathers: Science in the Political Thought of Jefferson, Franklin, Adams, and Madison* (New York: W. W. Norton & Co., 1997).

Commission on Wartime Relocation and Internment of Civilians. *Personal Justice Denied: Report of the Commission on Wartime Relocation and Internment of Civilians* (Seattle: University of Washington Press, 1997).

Cornell, Saul. *Anti-Federalism and the Dissenting Tradition in America, 1788–1828* (Chapel Hill: University of North Carolina Press, 1999).

Crombie, A. C. *The History of Science: From Augustine to Galileo* (New York: Dover Publications, 1995).

Cushman, Barry. *Rethinking the New Deal Court: The Structure of a Constitutional Revolution* (New York: Oxford University Press, 1998).

Cushman, Clare, ed. *The Supreme Court Justices: Illustrated Biographies, 1789–1995* (Washington, D.C.: Congressional Quarterly Books, 1995).

Cuvier, Georges. "The Animal Kingdom," in Earl W. Count, ed., *This Is Race* (New York: Shuman, 1950).

Daniels, Roger. *The Politics of Prejudice: The Anti-Japanese Movement in California and the Struggle for Japanese Exclusion* (Holiday House, 1966).

Davis, Kenneth S. *FDR: The War President, 1940–1943* (New York: Random House, 2000).

Dewey, John. *My Philosophy of Law* (Boston: Boston Law Book Co., 1941).

———. *The Quest for Certainty* (New York: Minton, Balch & Co., 1929).

Diggins, John Patrick. *The Promise of Pragmatism: Modernism and the Crisis of Knowledge and Authority* (Chicago: University of Chicago Press, 1991).

Douglas, William O. *The Court Years, 1939–1975* (New York: Random House, 1980).

———. *Go East, Young Man: The Early Years* (New York: Random House, 1974).

Doyle, Sir Arthur Conan. "A Scandal in Bohemia," in *The Adventures of Sherlock Holmes* (New York: Oxford University Press, 1998).

Duram, James C. *Justice William O. Douglas* (Boston: Twayne Publishers, 1981).

Duxbury, Neil. *Patterns of American Jurisprudence* (New York: Oxford University Press, 1995).

———. "The Birth of Legal Realism and the Myth of Justice Holmes," *Anglo-American Law Review*, vol. 20 (1992).

Elkins, Stanley and Eric McKitrick. *The Age of Federalism: The Early American Republic, 1788–1800* (New York: Oxford University Press, 1993).

Ellis, Joseph. *Founding Brothers: The Revolutionary Generation* (New York: Alfred A. Knopf, 2000).

———. *American Sphinx: The Character of Thomas Jefferson* (New York: Vintage, 1998).

Ely, John Hart. "The Wages of Crying Wolf: A Comment on *Roe v. Wade*," *Yale Law Journal*, vol. 82 (1973).

Erickson, Rosemary J. and Rita J. Simon. *The Use of Social Science Data in Supreme Court Decisions* (Urbana: University of Illinois Press, 1998).

Faigman, David L. *Legal Alchemy: The Use and Misuse of Science in the Law* (New York: W. H. Freeman, 1999).

Finkelman, Paul. *Dred Scott v. Sandford: A Brief History with Documents* (New York: Bedford/St. Martin's Press, 1997).

Finley, Moses I., ed. *The Legacy of Greece: A New Appraisal* (Oxford: Clarendon Press, 1981).

Fisher, William W., Morton J. Horwitz, and Thomas A. Reed, eds. *American Legal Realism* (New York: Oxford University Press, 1993).

Fleming, Thomas. *Duel: Alexander Hamilton, Aaron Burr and the Future of America* (New York: Basic Books, 1999).

Flexner, James Thomas, *George Washington: Anguish & Farewell, 1793–1799*, vol. IV (New York: Little Brown, 1992).

Flower, Michael J. "Coming into Being: The Prenatal Development of Humans, in Abortion, Medicine and the Law," in J. Douglas Butler and David F. Walbert, eds., *Abortion, Medicine and the Law* (New York: Facts on File, Inc., 1992).

Frank, Jerome. *Courts on Trial: Myth and Reality in American Justice* (Princeton: Princeton University Press, 1949).

―――. *Law and the Modern Mind* (New York: Brentano's, 1930).

Friedman, Leon and Fred L. Israel. *The Justices of the United States Supreme Court, 1789–1969: Their Lives and Major Opinions* (New York: Bowker, 1969).

Gal, Allon. *Brandeis of Boston* (Cambridge: Harvard University Press, 1980).

Gardner, Charles A. "Is an Embryo a Person?" in J. Douglas Butler and David F. Walbert, eds., *Abortion, Medicine and the Law* (New York: Facts on File, Inc., 1992).

Glennon, Robert. *The Iconoclast as Reformer: Jerome Frank's Impact on American Law* (Ithaca: Cornell University Press, 1985).

Grant, Michael. *The Founders of the Western World: A History of Greece and Rome* (New York: Charles Scribner's Sons, 1991).

Grey, Thomas C. "Holmes and Legal Pragmatism," *Stanford Law Review*, vol. 41 (1989), p. 787.

Hall, Kermit L., ed. *The Oxford Companion to the Supreme Court of the United States* (New York: Oxford University Press, 1992).

―――. *The Oxford Companion to American Law* (New York: Oxford University Press, 2002).

Hamilton, Alexander, John Jay, and James Madison. *The Federalist* (Norwalk, Conn.: Easton Press, 1979).

Heilbron, J. L., ed. *The Oxford Companion to the History of Modern Science* (New York: Oxford University Press, 2003).

Holmes, Oliver Wendell, Jr. "Law in Science and Science in Law," *Harvard Law Review*, vol. 12 (1899)

―――. "The Path of the Law," *Harvard Law Review*, vol. 10 (1897).

―――. *The Common Law* (Boston: Little, Brown, 1881).

―――. "Book Notice," *American Law Review*, vol. 14 (1880).

―――. "Review of C. C. Langdell, *Summary of the Law of Contracts* and W. R. Anson, *Principles of the Law of Contracts*," *American Law Review*, vol. 14 (1880).

―――. "Book Notice," *American Law Review*, vol. 6 (1871).

Honderich, Ted., ed. *The Oxford Companion to Philosophy* (New York: Oxford University Press, 1995).

Horwitz, Morton J., Thomas A. Reed, and William W. Fisher, eds. *American Legal Realism* (New York: Oxford University Press, 1993).

Huff, Toby E. *The Rise of Early Modern Science: Islam, China, and the West* (Oxford: Cambridge University Press, 1995).

Hull, N. E. H. *Roscoe Pound and Karl Llewellyn: Searching for an American Jurisprudence* (Chicago: University of Chicago Press, 1997).

Jefferson, Thomas. *Notes on Virginia.* Ed. by David Waldstreicher. (New York: Palgrave, 2002).

Jeffries, John Calvin. *Justice Lewis F. Powell, Jr.* (New York: Fordham University Press, 2001).

Jordan, Winthrop P. *White over Black: American Attitudes toward the Negro,* 1550–1812 (Chapel Hill: University of North Carolina Press, 1968).

Kagan, Donald. *Pericles of Athens and the Birth of Democracy* (New York: Free Press, 1998).

Kaufman, Andrew L. *Cardozo* (Cambridge: Harvard University Press, 1998).

Keown, John. "Euthanasia in the Netherlands: Sliding Down the Slippery Slope?" in John Keown, ed., *Euthanasia Examined* (New York: Cambridge University Press, 1995), pp. 261, 289.

Ketcham, Ralph. *James Madison: A Biography* (Charlottesville: University of Virginia, 1990).

Ketcham, Ralph, ed. *The Anti-Federalist Papers and the Constitutional Convention Debates* (Denver: Mentor Books, 1996).

Kevles, Daniel J. *In the Name of Eugenics* (New York: Alfred A. Knopf, 1985).

Kluger, Richard. *Simple Justice: The History of Brown v. Board of Education and Black America's Struggle for Equality* (New York: Vintage, 1975).

Koch, Adrienne and William Peden, eds. *The Life and Selected Writings of Thomas Jefferson* (New York: The Modern Library, 1993).

Konefsky, Samuel J. *The Legacy of Holmes and Brandeis* (New York: Plenum Publishing Co., 1956).

Lavah, Pnin. "Holmes and Brandeis: Libertarian and Republican Justifications for Free Speech," *Journal of Law and Policy,* vol. 4 (1988).

Laycock, Douglas. "Continuity and Change in the Threat to Religious Liberty: The Reformation Era and the Late Twentieth Century," *Minnesota Law Review,* vol. 80 (1996), p. 1047.

Lazarus, Edward. *Closed Chambers: The First Eyewitness Account of the Epic Struggles Inside the Supreme Court* (New York: Times Books, 1998).

Lewis, Walker. *Without Fear or Favor: A Biography of Chief Justice Roger Brooke Taney* (Boston: Houghton Mifflin, 1965).

Llewellyn, Karl N. *The Bramble Bush: On Our Law and Its Study* (New York: Oceana Publications, 1951).

———. "Some Realism about Realism: Responding to Dean Pound," *Harvard Law Review,* vol. 44 (1931), p. 1222.

———. "A Realistic Jurisprudence—the Next Step," *Columbia Law Review*, vol. 30 (1930), p. 431.

Lombardo, Paul A. "Medicine, Eugenics, and the Supreme Court: From Coercive Sterilization to Reproductive Freedom," *Journal of Contemporary Health Law and Policy*, vol. 13 (1996), p. 1.

———. "Three Generations, No Imbeciles: New Light on Buck v. Bell," *New York University Law Review*, vol. 60 (1985).

Madison, James. *Notes of Debates in the Federal Convention of 1787* (New York: W. W. Norton & Co., 1966).

Maier, Pauline. *American Scripture: Making the Declaration of Independence* (New York: Alfred A. Knopf, 1998).

Mapp, Alf J., Jr. *Thomas Jefferson: Passionate Pilgrim: The Presidency, the Founding of the University, and the Private Battle* (New York: Madison Books, 1991).

———. *Thomas Jefferson: A Strange Case of Mistaken Identity* (New York: Madison Books, 1989).

McClain, Charles, ed. *The Mass Internment of Japanese Americans and the Quest for Legal Redress* (New York: Garland Publishing, 1994).

McCullough, David. *John Adams* (New York: Simon & Schuster, 2001).

McDonald, Forrest. *Alexander Hamilton: A Biography* (New York: W.W. Norton & Co., 1982).

McKerns, Joseph P. *Biographical Dictionary of American Journalism* (New York: Greenwood Publishing Group, 1989).

Menand, Louis. *The Metaphysical Club: A Story of Ideas in America* (New York: Farrar, Straus & Giroux, 2001).

Miller, William Lee. *The Business of May Next: James Madison and the Founding* (Charlottesville: University Press of Virginia, 1992).

Mnookin, Robert H. *In the Interest of Children: Advocacy, Law Reform, and Public Policy* (New York: W.H. Freeman, 1985).

Murphy, Bruce Allen. *The Brandeis/Frankfurter Connection: The Secret Activities of Two Supreme Court Justices* (New York: Oxford University Press 1982).

Neely, Alfred S. "Mr. Justice Frankfurter's Iconography of Judging," *Kentucky Law Journal*, vol. 82 (1994), p. 535.

Novick, Sheldon M. *Honorable Justice: The Life of Oliver Wendell Holmes* (New York: Little, Brown, 1989).

Novick, Sheldon M., ed. *The Collected Works of Justice Holmes: Complete Public Writings and Selected Judicial Opinions of Oliver Wendell Holmes*, Volumes 1–3 (Chicago: University of Chicago Press, 1995).

Nuland, Sherwin B. *The Mysteries Within: A Surgeon Reflects on Medical Myths* (New York: Simon & Schuster, 2000).

Ober, Josiah. *Political Dissent in Democratic Athens: Intellectual Critics of Popular Rule* (Princeton: Princeton University Press, 1998).

————. *The Athenian Revolution: Essays on Ancient Greek Democracy and Political Theory* (Princeton: Princeton University Press, 1996).

Olson, Richard. *Science Deified and Science Defied: The Historical Significance of Science in Western Culture,* Volumes 1 and 2 (Berkeley: University of California Press, 1982).

Orodenker, Richard. *Twentieth-Century American Sportswriters,* 7th ed. (New York: Gale Group, 1996).

Patterson, James T. *Brown v. Board of Education: A Civil Rights Milestone and Its Troubled Legacy* (New York: Oxford University Press, 2001).

Pegler, Westbrook. *Commentary,* February 14, 1942.

Peters, William. *A More Perfect Union: The Making of the United States Constitution* (New York: Crown Publishers, 1987).

Porter, Roy, ed. *Cambridge Illustrated History of Medicine* (Oxford: Cambridge University Press, 1996).

Posner, Richard A. *Cardozo: A Study in Reputation* (Chicago: University of Chicago Press, 1990).

Posner, Richard A., ed. *The Essential Holmes: Selections from the Letters, Speeches, Judicial Opinions, and Other Writings of Oliver Wendell Holmes, Jr.* (Chicago: University of Chicago Press, 1996).

Pound, Roscoe. "The Scope and Purpose of Sociological Jurisprudence (Pt. 3)," *Harvard Law Review,* vol. 25 (1912), pp. 489, 510–6.

————. "Mechanical Jurisprudence," *Columbia Law Review,* vol. 8 (1908), pp. 605, 609.

Purcell, Edward A., Jr. *Brandeis and the Progressive Constitution: Erie, The Judicial Process, and the Politics of the Federal Courts in Twentieth-Century America* (New Haven: Yale University Press, 2000).

Rakove, Jack N. *Original Meanings: Politics and Ideas in the Making of the Constitution* (New York: Alfred A. Knopf, 1996).

Rakove, Jack N., ed. *James Madison: Writings* (New York: Library of America, 1999).

Reagan, Leslie J. *When Abortion Was a Crime: Women, Medicine, and Law in the United States, 1867–1973* (Berkeley: University of California Press, 1997).

Resnick, Rosalind. "To One City, It's Cruelty. To Cultists, It's Religion," *National Law Journal,* September 11, 1989.

Richard, Carl J. *The Founders and the Classics: Greece, Rome, and the American Enlightenment* (Cambridge: Harvard University Press, 1994).

Rosen, Paul. *The Supreme Court and Social Science* (Urbana: University of Illinois Press, 1972).

Scheidt, Walter. "The Concept of Race in Anthropology and the Divisions into Human Races from Linnaeus to Deniker," in Earl W. Count, ed., *This Is Race* (New York: Shuman, 1950).

Schlegel, John Henry. *American Legal Realism and Empirical Social Science* (Chapel Hill: University of North Carolina Press, 1995).

Schwartz, Bernard. *A History of the Supreme Court* (New York: Oxford University Press, 1993).

Smiler, Scott M. "Note, Justice Ruth Bader Ginsburg and the Virginia Military Institute: A Culmination of Strategic Success," *Cardozo Women's Law Journal*, vol. 4 (1998), p. 541.

Smith, Charles W., Jr. *Roger B. Taney: Jacksonian Jurist* (New York: Da Capo Press, 1973).

Smith, James Morton, ed. *The Republic of Letters: The Correspondence Between Jefferson and Madison, 1776–1826*, Volumes 1–3 (New York: W. W. Norton & Co., 1995).

Smith, Jean Edward. *John Marshall: Definer of a Nation* (New York: Henry Holt and Co., 1996).

Smith, Page. *Democracy on Trial: The Japanese-American Evacuation and Relocation in World War II* (New York: Simon & Schuster, 1995).

Steiner, Bernard C. *Life of Roger Brooke Taney: Chief Justice of the United States Supreme Court* (Westport, Conn.: Greenwood Press, 1971).

Stocking, George W., Jr. *Race, Culture, and Evolution: Essays in the History of Anthropology* (Chicago: University of Chicago Press, 1982).

Stoddard, Lothrop. *Rising Tide of Color Against White World-Supremacy* (New York: Scribner, 1920).

Strum, Philippa. *Women in the Barracks: The VMI Case and Equal Rights* (Lawrence: Kansas University Press, 2002).

———. *Louis D. Brandeis: Justice for the People* (New York: Schocken Books, 1989).

———. *Brandeis: Beyond Progressivism* (Lawrence: Kansas University Press, 1993).

Tribe, Laurence H. *Abortion: The Clash of Absolutes* (New York: W. W. Norton & Co., 1990).

Tyler, Samuel. *Memoir of Roger Brooke Taney* (New York: Da Capo Press, 1970).

Urofsky, Melvin I. *Division and Discord: The Supreme Court under Stone and Vinson, 1941–1953* (New York: Oxford University Press, 1997).

———. "Conflict Among the Brethren: Felix Frankfurter, William O. Douglas and the Clash of Personalities and Philosophies on the United States Supreme Court," *Duke Law Journal*, vol. 1988 (1988), p. 71.

Walling, Karl Friedrich. *Republican Empire: Alexander Hamilton on War and Free Government* (Lawrence: University Press of Kansas, 1999).

White, G. Edward. *Justice Oliver Wendell Holmes: Law and the Inner Self* (New York: Oxford University Press, 1993).

———. "The Anti-Judge: William O. Douglas and the Ambiguities of Individuality," *Virginia Law Review*, vol. 74 (1988), p. 17.

————. *Earl Warren: A Public Life* (New York: Oxford University Press, 1987).

Whitman, Mark, ed. *Removing a Badge of Slavery: The Record of Brown v. Board of Education* (Princeton, N.J.: Markus Wiener Pub., 1993).

Williams, Juan. *Thurgood Marshall: American Revolutionary* (New York: Times Books, 1998).

Willrich, Michael. "Two Percent Solution: Eugenic Jurisprudence and the Socialization of American Law, 1900–1930," *Law and History Review*, vol. 16 (1998).

Wood, Gordon S. *The Creation of the American Republic, 1776–1787* (Chapel Hill: University of North Carolina Press, 1998).

————. *The Radicalism of the American Revolution: How a Revolution Transformed a Monarchical Society into a Democratic One Unlike Any that Had Ever Existed* (New York: Alfred A. Knopf, 1992).

CASES, BRIEFS, AND GOVERNMENT REPORTS

Abrams v. United States, 250 U.S. 616 (1919).

Adkins v. Childrens Hospital, 261 U.S. 525 (1923).

Aguillard v. Treen, 634 F.Supp. 426 (E.D.La. 1985).

Ballew v. Georgia, 435 U.S. 223 (1978).

Barnes v. Glenn Theatre, Inc., 501 U.S. 560 (1991).

Bowers v. Hardwick, 478 U.S. 186 (1986).

Braunfeld v. Brown, 366 U.S. 599 (1961).

Brief of the American Civil Liberties Union in Support of Pap's AM, amicus curiae, in *City of Erie v. Pap's AM* (2000).

Brief for Appellants, in *Roe v. Wade* (1973).

Brief for Appellees, in *Roe v. Wade* (1973).

Brief of Deja Vu Consulting, Inc., and Deja Vu of Nashville, Inc. in Support of Pap's AM, amicus curiae, in *City of Erie v. Pap's AM* (2000).

Brief of First Amendment Lawyers Association in support of Pap's AM, amicus curiae, in *City of Erie v. Pap's AM* (2000).

Brief of the Japanese American Citizens League, amicus curiae, in *Korematsu v. United States* (1944).

Brief of Mary Baldwin College, amicus curiae, in *United States v. Virginia* (1996).

Brief of the National Academies of Science, amicus curiae, in *Edwards v. Aguillard* (1987).

Brief of the National Family Legal Foundation in Support of the City of Erie, amicus curiae, in *City of Erie v. Pap's AM* (2000).

Brief of the National Women's Law Center, American Civil Liberties Union in support of Petitioner, amicus curiae, in *United States v. Virginia*.

Brief of Seventy-two Nobel Laureates et al., amicus curiae, in *Edwards v. Aguillard* (1987).

Brief for the Petitioner, United States of America, in *United States v. Virginia* (1996).

Brief for the Respondents, Commonwealth of Virginia, in *United States v. Virginia* (1996).

Brief of the Rutherford Institute in Support of Petitioners, in *Church of the Lukumi Babalu Aye v. City of Hialeah* (1993).

Brief of the State of Oklahoma, in *Skinner v. Oklahoma* (1942).

Brief of the United States of America, in *Hirabayashi v. United States* (1942).

Brief of Women's Schools Together, Inc. et al., in Support of Respondents, amicus curiae, in *United States v. Virginia* (1996).

Brown v. Board of Education, 347 U.S. 483 (1954).

Buck v. Bell, 274 U.S. 200 (1927).

Chaplinsky v. New Hampshire, 315 U.S. 568 (1942).

Church of the Lukumi Babalu Aye v. City of Hialeah, 508 U.S. 520 (1993).

Church of the Lukumi Babalu Aye v. City of Hialeah, 723 F.Supp. 1467 (S.D.Fla. 1989).

City of Erie v. Pap's AM, 529 U.S. 277 (2000).

City of Los Angeles v. Alameda Books, Inc., 535 U.S. 425 (2002).

Coppage v. Kansas, 236 U.S. 1 (1915).

County of Allegheny v. ACLU, 492 U.S. 573 (1989).

Craig v. Boren, 429 U.S. 190 (1976).

Cruzan v. Director, Missouri Department of Health, 497 U.S. 261 (1990).

Daubert v. Merrell Dow Pharmaceuticals, Inc., 509 U.S. 579 (1993).

Disanto v. Pennsylvania, 273 U.S. 24, 43 (1927).

Dred Scott case, see *Scott v. Sandford.*

Edwards v. Aguillard, 482 U.S. 578 (1987).

Eisenstadt v. Baird, 405 U.S. 438 (1972).

Employment Division v. Smith, 494 U.S. 872 (1990).

Employment Division v. Smith, 721 P. 2d 445 (Or. 1986).

Epperson v. Arkansas, 393 U.S. 97 (1968).

Everson v. Board of Education of Ewing Township, 330 U.S. 1 (1947).

Ex Parte Mitsuiye Endo, 323 U.S. 283 (1944).

General John DeWitt's Final Report, June 5, 1943.

Gratz v. Bollinger, 123 S.Ct. 2411 (2003).

Griswold v. Connecticut, 381 U.S. 479 (1965).

Grutter v. Bollinger, 123 S.Ct. 2325 (2003).

Harris v. McRae, 448 U.S. 297 (1980).

Hearings before the Select Committee Investigating National Defense Migration, H.R., Feb., 1942.

Helvering v. Hallock, 309 U.S. 106 (1940).

Hirabayashi v. United States, 320 U.S. 81 (1943).

H. L. Matheson, 450 U.S. 398 (1981).

Hodgson v. Minnesota, 497 U.S. 417 (1990).

Hopwood v. Texas, 78 F.3d 932, 944 (5th Cir. 1996).

Korematsu v. United States, 323 U.S. 214 (1944).

Kumho Tire Co. v. Carmichael, 526 U.S. 136 (1997).

Lamb's Chapel v. Center Moriches Union Free School District, 508 U.S. 384 (1993).

Lawrence v. Texas, 123 S.Ct. 2472 (2003).

Lee v. Weisman, 505 U.S. 577 (1992).

Lee v. Weisman, 728 F.Supp. 68 (1990).

Lemon v. Kurtzman, 403 U.S. 602 (1971).

Lochner v. New York, 198 U.S. 45 (1905).

Loving v. Virginia, 388 U.S. 1 (1967).

Lynch v. Donnelly, 465 U.S. 668 (1984).

MacPherson v. Buick, 217 N.Y. 382 (1916).

Marbury v. Madison, 5 U.S. 137 (1803).

Marsh v. Chambers, 463 U.S. 783 (1983).

Maryland v. Craig, 110 S.Ct. 3157 (1990).

McCleskey v. Kemp, 481 U.S. 279 (1987).

McCulloch v. Maryland, 17 U.S. 316 (1819).

McLaurin v. Oklahoma State Regents for Higher Education, 339 U.S. 637 (1950).

McLean. v. Arkansas Board of Education, 529 F.Supp. 1255 (E.D.Ark. 1982).

Mississippi University for Women v. Hogan, 458 U.S. 718 (1982).

Muller v. Oregon, 208 U.S. 412 (1908).

New York Times Co. v. Sullivan, 376 U.S. 254 (1964).

Ozawa v. United States, 260 U.S. 178 (1922).

Palko v. Connecticut, 302 U.S.319 (1937).

Paris Adult Theatre v. Slaton, 413 U.S. 49 (1973).

Personal Justice Denied: Report of the Commission on Wartime Relocation and Internment of Civilians (1982).

Planned Parenthood of Southeastern Pennsylvania v. Casey, 505 U.S. 833 (1992).

Planned Parenthood of Southeastern Pennsylvania v. Casey, 744 F.Supp. 1323 (E.D.Pa. 1990).

Plessy v. Ferguson, 163 U.S. 537 (1896).

Poe v. Ullman, 367 U.S. 497 (1961).

Reed v. Reed, 404 U.S. 71 (1971).

Regents of the University of California v. Bakke, 438 U.S. 265 (1978).

Renton v. Playtime Theatres, 475 U.S. 41 (1986).

Reynolds v. United States, 98 U.S. 145 (1879).

Roe v. Wade, 410 U.S. 113 (1973).

Schenck v. United States, 249 U.S. 47 (1919).

Scott v. Sandford (Dred Scott case), 60 U.S. 393 (1857).

Sherbert v. Verner, 374 U.S. 398 (1963).

Skinner v. Oklahoma, 316 U.S. 535 (1942).

Slaughter-House Cases, 83 U.S. 36 (1873).

Strauder v. West Virginia, 100 U.S. 303 (1879).

Sweatt v. Painter, 339 U.S. 629 (1950).

Texas v. Johnson, 491 U.S. 397 (1989).

Thornburgh v. American College of Obstetricians and Gynecologists, 476 U.S.
    747 (1986).

United States v. Butler, 297 U.S. 1 (1936).

United States v. Carolene Products Co., 304 U.S. 144 (1938).

United States v. Commonwealth of Virginia, 44 F.3d 1229 (4th Cir. 1995).

United States v. Commonwealth of Virginia, 852 F.Supp. 471 (W.D.Va. 1994).

United States v. Commonwealth of Virginia, 976 F.2d 890 (4th Cir. 1992).

United States v. Commonwealth of Virginia, 766 F.Supp. 1407 (W.D.Va. 1991).

United States v. Eichman, 496 U.S. 310 (1990).

United States v. O'Brien, 391 U.S. 367 (1968).

United States v. Thind, 261 U.S. 204 (1923).

United States v. Virginia, 518 U.S. 515 (1996).

Vacco v. Quill, 521 U.S. 793 (1997).

Washington v. Glucksberg, 521 U.S. 702 (1997).

Webster v. Reproductive Health Services, 492 U.S. 490 (1989).

Whitney v. California, 274 U.S. 357 (1927).

Wisconsin v. Yoder, 406 U.S. 205 (1972).

Yick Wo v. Hopkins, 118 U.S. 356 (1886).

ACKNOWLEDGMENTS

When I first decided to write this book, I never imagined just how long the road would be to completion. Over the three years of writing, numerous people have contributed in a multitude of ways. I must thank, first of all, the many research assistants who had some hand in compiling the stacks of primary and secondary sources that went into the book. These include Sophia Cope, Michael Shipley, Regina Perry Siu, and Kirsten Zittlau. I have also had the benefit of colleagues and friends who read various chapters of the manuscript and provided valuable feedback in their efforts. I am sure that their efforts to keep me from going astray were not always successful. These include Ash Baghwat, Cheryl Hanna, Reuel Schiller, and Scott Sundby. I would also like to thank my colleagues at Hastings and elsewhere who, at various times, suffered my queries and arguments as I practiced different ideas or theses that might be included in this book. These include John Monahan, Evan Lee, Calvin Massey, Joel Paul, Radhika Rao, Ugo Mattei, John Diamond, and Bill Schwarzer. I also want to express special thanks to Rory Little, Ash Baghwat, Aaron Rappaport, and Bill Schwarzer, who wrote letters and made phone calls on my behalf to justices of the Supreme Court. I also want to express special thanks to Justices Breyer, O'Connor, and Stevens for giving me some of their precious time to discuss the general subject of fact-finding in constitutional cases. As an academic, I am sometimes critical of their constitutional analyses, but I have only the utmost respect for them, and their colleagues, and am well aware of just how difficult their jobs are. I am deeply grateful for their input.

These acknowledgments would not be complete without my expressing gratitude to my original editors at W. H. Freeman, Erika Goldman and John Michael, for their early encouragement and complete faith in the value of this book. I also want to thank Robin Dennis at Henry Holt, my editor, for her excellent work and invaluable efforts in bringing the whole thing to fruition.

Finally, I owe so much to my wife, Lisa, to whom this book is dedicated. This book would be a tiny fraction of what it is but for her contributions.

Her enthusiasm for the project, and for me, never wavered. She read every page, and her editing skills were masterful. Any mistakes remaining in the book, of course, are mine; but I sleep more soundly having had Lisa's keen eyes read the manuscript in full—twice. I sleep more soundly, too, for having Lisa there at my side.

INDEX

abolitionism, 48, 52, 58–59, 61, 90
  Dred Scott decision and, 67
abortion, 208–44
  Akron v. Akron Center for Reproductive Health, 220, 226, 227, 237, 238
  bans of use of Medicaid funds for, 223
  Eisenstadt v. Baird, language of, 208
  history of regulation of, in U.S., 208–11, 215
  informed consent, 223, 227
  parental consent requirements, 223, 227–28, 237, 239–40
  partial birth, 243
  Planned Parenthood of Southeastern Pennsylvania v. Casey, 227–43, 359, 361
  before quickening, 209
  Roe v. Wade, see Roe v. Wade
  spousal consent requirements, 223, 227–28, 229, 230, 238, 240–41
  twenty-four-hour waiting requirements, 223, 227–28, 230, 237–39, 241
  viability testing, 223, 224, 225–26
  Webster v. Reproductive Health Services, 223–26, 228
Abraham and Isaac, parable of, 295–96
Abrams v. United States, 103
Adams, Henry, 35
Adams, John, 13, 34–35, 37
Adams, John Quincy, 15
Adams, Samuel, 13
adjudicative facts, 202
Adkins v. Children's Hospital, 97

adult entertainment establishments, *see* nude dancing and sex shops, regulation of
affirmative action, 285–94
  "critical mass," 291–92
  Gratz v. Bollinger, 286, 290
  Grutter v. Bollinger, 286–94, 343, 344–45, 359, 362–63
  Hopwood v. Texas, 286, 288
  quotas, 285, 291, 292, 293
  Regents of the University of California v. Bakke, 285, 286, 289
African-Americans
  civil rights cases, *see* civil rights cases
  Constitutional amendments guaranteeing equal rights to, 6, 162, 254
  slavery and, *see* slaves and slavery
Agassiz, Louis, 62
Air Force Academy, 265
Akron v. Akron Center for Reproductive Health, 220, 226, 227, 229, 237, 238
Almond, James Lindsay, Jr., 182
Amalgamated Association of Iron and Steel Workers, 93–94
American Civil Liberties Union (ACLU), 228
  Women's Rights Project, 273–74
American College of Obstetricians and Gynecologists, 229
American Dilemma, An (Myrdal), 172
American Law Review, 74
American Medical Association, 210
Ames, Fisher, 32–33

amici curiae ("friends of the court")
    briefs, 338–39
    fact-finding role of, 286, 290, 322, 359–
        60
animal sacrifice, Santeria religion and,
    296–99, 307–10
Annapolis, 265, 283
Anti-Federalists, 11–12, 14, 44, 162
    core beliefs of, 13, 16, 19–20, 25–29,
        36, 65, 99
anti-Semitism, 92
apes, 56
Aristotle, 25
Arnold, Richard, 3
Articles of Confederation, 11, 44
Asians
    hatred of, 134–35, 136
    the Japanese, see Japanese, the
    naturalization law and, 140–42
assimilation, 344
assisted suicide, 244–50
Athenian democracy, 22, 23–24, 31, 32,
    99, 104–5
    slaves in, 54
Atlantic Monthly, 69

Bakke, Allan, 285
Baldus, David, study of race and the
    death penalty, 257–61
Ballew v. Georgia, 258
Bank of the United States, 38–42
Barnes v. Glen Theatre, Inc., 324, 329,
    336
Barron v. The Mayor and City Council
    of Baltimore, 163
Beecher, Henry Ward, 67
Beeton, Isabella, 3–4
Bell, Griffin, 201
Bendetsen, Karl R., 149
Bernier, François, 55
Bickel, Alexander, 84, 196–97, 198
Biddle, Francis, 146
Biden, Joseph, 230–31
Bill of Rights, 7, 163, 205
    minority factions and, 32
    right to privacy and, 206
    Scalia's view of, 300, 301
    technological innovation and, 7
    Warren's jurisprudence and, 193
    see also individual amendments
Biological Basis of Human Nature, The
    (Jennings), 137
birth control, see contraception

Black, Charles L., Jr., 166, 206
Black, Hugo, 108, 127, 129, 295
    appointment to Supreme Court, 125
    Brown v Board of Education and, 190,
        191, 192, 202
    Korematsu decision, 154–55
    right to privacy and, 207
Blackmun, Harry, 258, 338
    background of, 211
    Barnes v. Glen Theatre, Inc., 331
    Employment Division of Human
        Resources of Oregon v. Smith,
        306–7
    McClesky v. Kemp, 258
    Planned Parenthood of Southeastern
        Pennsylvania v. Casey, 229, 233,
        238, 241
    Regents v. Bakke, 285
    Roe v. Wade, 211, 212–13, 215–19,
        220–21, 227
    scientific curiosity and research for
        Roe, 213, 215
blacks, see African-Americans
Blackstone, William, 21, 112
bloodletting, 2–5, 9
Blow, Taylor, 49–50, 67
Blumenbach, Johann Friedrich, 55–56
Boas, Franz, 159, 167
Boddie v. Connecticut, 231
Boger, Jack, 257
Book of Household Management
    (Beeton), 3–4
Bork, Robert, 300–301
Bracton, Henry de, 246
Brandeis, Adolph, 91
Brandeis, Louis Dembitz, 81, 88, 112,
    126
    background of, 90–94
    Frankfurter and, 120, 121, 122
    Holmes and, 70–71, 83–84, 85, 99–
        106, 124
    judicial restraint and, 128
    Muller v. Oregon, 90, 94–98
    nomination to the Supreme Court, 97–
        98
    Olmstead v. United States, 354, 355
    philosophy underlying judicial
        decisions of, 99–101, 104–5
Brandeis Brief, 95–98, 113
Braunfeld v. Brown, 302
Brennan, William, 128, 129, 193, 227
    Braunfeld v. Brown, 302
    Craig v. Boren, 274–75
    Edwards v. Aguillard, 321, 323

Employment Division of Human Resources of Oregon v. Smith, 306
McClesky v. Kemp, 258, 259
Regents v. Bakke, 285
right to privacy cases prior to *Roe v. Wade* and, 206, 208
Roe v. Wade, 212–13
Sherbert v. Verner, 302–3
Brewer, David, 96
Breyer, Stephen, 311
  City of Erie v. Pap's AM, 337
  on fact-finding processes of the Supreme Court, 358–62
  Grutter v. Bollinger, 286
  Kansas v. Crane, 349, 350
  United States v. Lopez, 362
  United States v. The Commonwealth of Virginia, 283
Briggs v. Elliott, 177–81
Brown v. Board of Education of Topeka, 162, 181–82, 187–203, 222, 280, 294, 343, 344, 359, 361, 363
  controversy over Clark's doll studies, 196–98
  deliberations of the justices, 191–92, 194–95
  the opinion, 196
  oral argument in, 187–91, 202, 214
  science used to disguise policy choice in, 222–23
  as turning point for the Supreme Court, 198–99
Bryan, Samuel, 20
Buchanan, James, 68
Buck, Carrie, 77, 78
Buck v. Bell, 77–78, 136
Bunting, Josiah, 283
Burger, Warren E., 211, 300
  Lemon v. Kurtzman, 313
  Regents v. Bakke, 285
  Roe v. Wade, 212, 213
Burnside, Ambrose E., 145
Burton, Harold, 192
"burying bones," 208, 235–36
Bush, George H. W., 227, 228, 230, 232
Bush, George W., 231, 232
Business Failures Project, 122–23
Butler, Pierce, 124

Cahn, Edmund, 197–98
California's Proposition 209, 292
"Call for a Realist Jurisprudence, The" (Pound), 114
Camper, Peter, 57

capital of the United States, battle over siting of, 39, 41–42
capital punishment, 255–61, 359, 360
Cardozo, Albert, 108, 109
Cardozo, Benjamin N., 84, 107–11, 126, 342
  background of, 108–9
  described, 110
  "Jurisprudence" lecture, 116–18
  nomination to Supreme Court, 107, 109, 116
  philosophy of law, 109, 110–11, 113, 114, 116–17
Carlucci, Joseph, 319
Carnegie Steel Company, 93–94
Carswell, G. Harold, 211
Carter, Robert, 176–77, 178, 179, 184–85, 190, 191, 202
Case of Libel, A (Denker), 158
Catholic Church, abortion and, 208, 209
Chaffee, Calvin C., 50, 67
Chein, Isidor, 184–85, 191
Choate, Joseph H., 90
church and state, separation of, *see* religion, free exercise of
Church of the Lukumi Babalu Aye v. City of Hialeah, 296–99, 307–10
City of Erie v. Pap's AM, 335–41
City of Los Angeles v. Alameda Books, Inc., 340, 341
City of Renton v. Playtime Theatres, Inc., 325–28, 335, 340, 341
civil rights cases, 162–204
  Briggs v. Elliott, 177–81
  Brown v. Board of Education of Topeka, see Brown v. Board of Education of Topeka
  McLaurin v. Oklahoma, 173–74
  Murray v. Maryland, 171
  in northern Delaware, 185–87
  Plessy v. Ferguson, see Plessy v. Ferguson
  in Prince Edward County, Virginia, 182–85
  science and, 167, 171–74, 175–77, 179–80, 181–87, 188–91, 195, 196–98, 199–200, 201, 222, 280
  Slaughter-House Cases, 162–65
  Sweatt v. Painter, 172, 174, 175
Civil War
  Dred Scott decision and, 65
  Holmes's service in, 70, 72–73, 77
  states' rights and, 162, 164, 165

Clark, Charles, 119
Clark, Kenneth, doll studies of, 176, 177, 179–80, 181, 183, 184, 185–86, 188, 190, 196–98, 223, 280, 361
Clark, Tom, 188, 192, 196
Clark, William, 122–23
Clay, Henry, 90–91
Clinton, Bill, 228
cloning, 345
Coffee, Linda, 212
Cohen, Felix, 111
Coleman, William, 176–77
college athletics, Title IX, 263, 264
Columbia Law Review, 273
Columbia Law School, 114, 119, 122, 272
Commager, Henry Steele, 136–37
Commentaries on American Law (Kent), 78–79
Commission on Wartime Relocation and Internment of Civilians, 159
commitment of sexual offenders, civil, 347–54
Common Law (Holmes), 80–82
Commons, John Roger, 140
Comstock Law of 1873, 210
concentration camps, Nazi, 160
conservatism, political versus judicial, 231–32
Constitution, U.S.
   amendments to, *see* Bill of Rights; *individual amendments*
   Anti-Federalists, *see* Anti-Federalists
   as architectural blueprint for the good society, 5
   as aspirational document, xv, 5, 205
   Bill of Rights, *see* Bill of Rights
   Commerce Clause, 361–62
   Federalists, *see* Federalists
   flexibility of, xiv
   right to privacy, *see* privacy, right to
constitutional law
   science and, *see* science and constitutional law
   stare decisis and, *see* stare decisis
   as work in progress, 342–43
contraception
   Comstock Law of 1873, 210
   right to privacy and state laws regulating, 206–8
Cook, Walter Wheeler, 122, 123
Coppage v. Kansas, 88–89
Corbin, Arthur, 110
County of Allegheny v. ACLU, 314

Cox, Archibald, 251
Craig, Curtis, 274
Craig v. Boren, 274–75
Craik, James, 2
Crane, Michael, 348–49
creation science, teaching of, 318–23, 359–60
criminals and criminal behavior
   civil commitment of "sexually violent predators," 347–54
   DNA data banks for crime prevention, 345
   sterilization of, 130, 136, 137–39, 159–60
Curtis, Benjamin R., 52, 63, 66–67
Cushing, Caleb, 69
Cuvier, Georges, 56
Czolgosz, Leon, 84

Darwin, Charles, 75, 76, 77
Daubert v. Merrell Dow Pharmaceuticals, Inc., 338, 340
Davis, John, 188–90, 196
death and dying, 244–50
death penalty, 255–61, 359, 360
Declaration of Independence, 6, 15
Dembitz, Lewis Naphtali, 90–91
democracy, 22–24
   direct or pure, 13, 22, 30–32, 99, 104–5
   equality and, *see* equality
   proliferation of nonwhite races and, 140
   representative, *see* representative democracy
   underlying concepts, 22–24
Denker, Henry, 158
Dewey, John, 111
DeWitt, John, 144–45, 146, 149–50, 157–58
Dick, Elisha Cullen, 2
Dillwyn, William, 59
DiMaggio, Joe, father of, 149–50
direct or pure democracy, 13, 22, 30–32, 99, 104–5
discrimination, 23
   affirmative action, *see* affirmative action
   civil rights cases, *see* civil rights cases
   equal protection, *see* equal protection
"Diseases of the Workers" (Hirt), 86
Double Jeopardy Clause, 347, 348
Douglas, William O., 108, 119, 124, 128–29, 153

appointment to Supreme Court, 123
background of, 121–22
Brown v Board of Education and, 192
Frankfurter and, 121, 126, 127, 129
as iconoclast, 124
judicial restraint and, 129
Roe v. Wade, 212, 213
draft card burning, 329–31
Dred Scott, 44–69
  constitutionality of Missouri
    Compromise, 63–67
  contemporary reaction to, 67–69
  dissenting opinion, 66–67
  facts of the case, 48–50
  key questions addressed in, 53, 63
  science of race and, 54–62
DuBois, W. E. B., 168
due process, 231, 234, 347
  right to privacy and, 207, 215, 232,
    236, 241–42, 244–45
  see also Fifth Amendment, Due Process
    Clause; Fourteenth Amendment, Due
    Process Clause

education
  affirmative action in, *see* affirmative
    action
  creation science, teaching of, 318–23,
    359–60
  prayer at public school graduation
    ceremonies, 311, 312, 314–17
  segregation of, *see Brown v. Board of
    Education of Topeka;* civil rights
    cases; *Plessy v. Ferguson*
Edwards v. Aguillard, 318–23, 359–60
Eighth Amendment, 259, 260–61
Eisenhower, Dwight D., 193, 211
Eisenstadt v. Baird, 207–8
Eliot, Charles William, 83
Ellison, Ralph, 198
Ellsworth, Oliver, 34
Ellwanger, Paul, 319
Elman, Philip, 192
Ely, John Hart, 218
Emerson, Irene, 49, 50
Emerson, John, 48–49
Emerson, Ralph Waldo, 72, 92, 106
empiricism, xi–xii
  Cardozo, 111
  Holmes and Brandeis and, 86–90, 94–
    98, 99–101, 105
  legal realism, *see* legal realism
  Lochner v. New York, importance of,
    86–90

Muller v. Oregon, 94–98
  see also science and constitutional law
*Employment Division of Human
  Resources of Oregon v. Smith,* 299–
    302, 304–7, 308, 310
English, Horace B., 181
environmental regulations, statistics and
  constitutionality of, 7
equality, 6, 22–24, 343–44
  conflict between liberty and, 251–52
equal protection, 6, 251–94
  affirmative action, *see* affirmative
    action
  discrimination allegations and levels of
    judicial review, 151–53, 154–55,
    254–55, 274, 275, 276, 279, 285,
    286, 293
  equal outcomes contrasted with, 251,
    294
  Fourteenth Amendment guarantees, *see*
    Fourteenth Amendment, Equal
    Protection Clause
  gender, *see* gender, equal protection
    and
  Martin case, 252–54
  McCleskey v. Kemp, 255–61
  *United States v. The Commonwealth
    of Virginia, see United States v. The
    Commonwealth of Virginia*
eugenics, 77, 136–40, 345, 353
  basic tenets of, 136
  challenges to basis for eugenic
    sterilizations, 160
evolution, theory of, 75–77
  Holmes's view of the law and, 77, 80–
    82, 85, 104, 105
  social Darwinism, *see* social Darwinism
  teaching of, 318–23, 359–60
executive branch of government, 34, 345
  Scalia's view of, 301
Executive Order 9066, 146, 150, 159
Ex Post Facto Clause, 347, 348

fact-finding by the Supreme Court, 309,
  314, 322–23, 336–37, 338–41, 357–
  64
  changing facts, 361–63
  see also science and constitutional law
factions, 24–25, 31–32, 38
  solutions to, 31–32
Falwell, Jerry, 225
Federal Bureau of Investigation (FBI),
  144, 151, 355
federalism, 10

Federalist, The, 11, 17, 34, 36, 39
Federalists, 13–14, 39, 162
    core beliefs of, 13, 16–22, 26, 29–33,
        36, 53, 65
    transfer of power, 36–37
Federalist Society, 15
Federal Rules of Evidence, 338
Field, Stephen, 164
Fields, James, 72
Fifteenth Amendment, 6, 162
Fifth Amendment, 206
    Dred Scott decision and, 64, 66
    Due Process Clause, 205–6
Figg, Robert, 177–78, 179, 180, 188
First Amendment, 7, 124, 128, 206, 221
    free speech, *see* free speech
    Holmes and Brandeis dissent, 102–5
    religious freedom, *see* religion, free
        exercise of
First Amendment Lawyers Association,
    338–39
flag burning, 330–31
Ford, Leland, 132, 149
formalism, legal, *see* legal formalism
Forrester, Owen, 256–58
Fourteenth Amendment, 6, 87, 244–45
    Due Process Clause, 139, 162, 205–6,
        207, 215
    Equal Protection Clause, 138, 151,
        162, 165, 236, 251, 259, 271, 273
    free exercise of religion and, 298
    privileges and immunities of U.S.
        citizenship, 162, 163, 164
Fourth Amendment, 206, 345, 354–57
    see also equal protection
Frank, Jerome, 113, 114, 116, 117–18
Frankfurter, Felix, 70, 97, 100, 102,
    106, 108, 116, 119–21, 177, 192,
    315
    appointment to Supreme Court, 126
    background of, 119–20
    Braunfeld v. Brown, 302
    Brown v. Board of Education and,
        191, 192, 194, 195–96, 214
    described, 126–28
    Douglas and, 121, 126, 127, 129
    "Felix's Happy Dogs," 120–21
    judicial restraint and, 128, 129
Franklin, Benjamin
    as Federalist, 13–14
    influence of science on, xiii
    Pony Express and, 7
free speech, 102–5, 163, 322–41
    "actual malice," 221

clear-and-present-danger test, 102–3,
    105
draft card burning, 329–30
flag burning, 330–31
New York Times v. Sullivan, 202–3,
    221
nude dancing and sex shops, regulation
    of, *see* nude dancing and sex shops,
    regulation of
obscenity cases, 221, 243–44
United States v. O'Brien, 329–30
violent pornography, 249–50
free will, 350–51
Frick, Henry Clay, 93

Galton, Francis, 136, 160
Gardner, Charles, 216–17
Garrett, Henry, 183–85
Garrow, David, 198
gender, equal protection and, 6, 236–37,
    261–84
    Craig v. Boren, 274–75
    Reed v. Reed, 274, 275
    Sorenstam model, 262–64
    Title IX model, 263, 264
    Virginia Military Institute case, *see*
        *United States v. The Commonwealth
        of Virginia*
genetic evidence, future of, 345–54
Gerry, Elbridge, 14
Ginsburg, Ruth Bader, 311, 358
    background of, 272–73
    City of Erie v. Pap's AM, 337
    Gratz v. Bollinger, 286
    Grutter v. Bollinger, 286
    Reed v. Reed, 274
    sexual equality, devotion to, 273–75
    United States v. Lopez, 362
    *United States v. The Commonwealth
        of Virginia,* 272, 275–83, 294
Goebel, Julius, 122
Goldberg, Arthur, 206–207
Goldmark, Josephine, 90
Goldsmith, Oliver, 55
Gotcher, Emma, 90
government, 15
    Anti-Federalist view of, 13, 16, 19–20,
        25–28
    Federalist view of, 13, 16–22, 26
    liberty and strong national, 15, 17, 20,
        30, 33
    optimal size of, 25
Grant, Madison, 135
Gratz v. Bollinger, 286, 290

Gray, Horace, 84
Gray, John, 74
Gray, Nina, 101–102
Greek democracy, *see* Athenian
    democracy
Grier, Robert, 68
Griswold, Erwin, 273
Griswold v. Connecticut, 206–7, 215,
    232
Grutter v. Bollinger, 286–94, 343, 344–
    45, 359, 362–63
    comparison to *United States v. The
        Commonwealth of Virginia,* 293–94
    sunset provision, 292–93
Gunther, Gerald, 254, 272
Gutterman, Leslie, 314

Hamilton, Alexander, xiii, 12–13
    Bank of the United States and, 41–42
    as Federalist, 12, 14, 18, 26, 29, 30,
        31, 36
    on human nature, 20
    Jefferson and, 15, 16–17
    McCulloch v. Maryland and, 38
Hancock, John, 14
Hand, Learned, 85, 127
Harlan, John Marshall, 86, 233
    dedication to precedent, 231, 232, 234
    Plessy v. Ferguson, 166–67
    Poe v. Ullman, 231, 232, 234, 247
    right to privacy and, 205, 207, 215,
        355–56
    as Souter's judicial hero, 231, 232,
        247
Harvard College, 70, 71–72, 211, 230,
    277
Harvard Law Review, 114, 273
Harvard Law School, 168
    case method, 79, 80
    faculty of, 74, 79, 83, 120, 121
    future Supreme Court justices who
        attended, 74, 91, 211, 230, 273,
        300
Harvard Magazine, 72
Haselbrock, Joe, 90
Haycraft, John B., 9
Haynsworth, Clement, 211
Hearst newspapers, 142
Hemenway, Alfred, 84
Hendricks, Leroy, 347
Henry, Patrick, 12, 14, 25–26, 44
Hialeah (Florida), 296–99, 307–10
Hill, Oliver, 184
Hippocratic Corpus, 2–3

Hirabayashi, Gordon, 151
Hirabayashi v. United States, 150–53,
    155
hirudin, 9
Hitler, Adolf, 77
Hobbes, Thomas, 21
Holmes, Fanny, 80
Holmes, Oliver Wendell, Sr., 71, 72–73
Holmes, Oliver Wendell, Jr., 9, 70, 107,
    109, 112–13, 116, 117, 120, 121,
    127, 136, 218
    background of, 70, 71–74
    Brandeis and, 9–106, 70–71, 83–84,
        85, 124
    Civil War service, 70, 72–73, 77
    described, 71, 72
    evolutionary theory's influence on, 77,
        80–82, 85, 89, 104
    judicial restraint, 85–86, 99, 124
    legal formalism, break with, 79–82, 98
    on Massachusetts Count, 83
    public recognition, desire for, 83, 84
    science and law, views on, 75, 79–82,
        87, 89, 95, 100
Holmes, Sherlock, 95
Holt, Louisa, 181
Homestead, Pennsylvania, steelworkers
    strike of 1892, 93–94
Hoover, Herbert, 107
Hopkins, Samuel, 58–59
Hopkinson, Joseph, 43
Hopwood v. Texas, 286, 288
Houston, Charles, 168–69, 171
Howard Law School, 168–69, 170, 176
Huesmann, Raul, 309
Hughes, Charles Evans, 105–6
Hull, Cordell, 132
human nature, 12
    Anti-Federalists view of, 13, 19–20
    changes in conception of, 6
    Declaration of Independence and, 6
    eighteenth-century philosophers, views
        of, 21
    Federalist view of, 13, 18–22
    in groups or mobs, 18
    nature versus environmental influences,
        19
Hume, David, xiii, 18, 19
humours, four, 3
Hunter, John, 57
Hutchins, Robert, 119

immigration controls, 136, 139, 140
Independent, 67

Jacklin, Carol Nagy, 266–67
Jackson, Andrew, 45
Jackson, Robert, 125, 155, 159, 192, 195, 305–6, 336–37
Jackson, Thomas "Stonewall," 265
James, William, 75, 83, 111
Jane (abortion organization), 210–11
Japanese, the
    Hirabayashi v. United States, 150–53
    internment of, 131–34, 142–60, 195
    Korematsu v. United States, 150, 154–59, 255
    Ozawa v. United States, 140–41
Jay, John, 34
Jefferson, Thomas, xiii, 39, 277
    as ambassador to France, 17
    Anti-Federalist beliefs and, 14, 28, 99
    Bank of the United States and, 40, 41
    on constitution making, 18
    Declaration of Independence, 6
    Hamilton and, 15, 16–17
    Madison and, 14, 15–16, 17, 28, 29, 30
    Marbury v. Madison and, 37–38
    Marshall and, 35–36
    on Missouri Compromise, 49
    Monticello, 342
    patrician background of, 16
    on slavery and nature/nurture debate, 59–60
Jeffersonian Republicans, 14, 162
Jennings, Herbert, 137
Johns Hopkins University, 119, 123
Johnson, Grove, 134–35
Johnson, Hiram, 134, 193
Jones, Robert, 346, 352–53
Jones, Walter, 43
Journal of Psychology, 184
judicial activism, 129, 231–32, 304
    prior to the 1930s, 124
    of the Warren Court, 129
judicial conservatism, 231–32
judicial restraint, 99, 124, 231
    Douglas and, 129
    Frankfurter and, 128, 129
    Holmes and, 85–86, 99, 124, 128
judicial review, 15
    discrimination allegations and levels of, 151–53, 154–55, 254–55, 274, 275, 276, 279
    of free speech cases, level of, 327–28
    Marbury v. Madison and birth of, 38, 44
judiciary, 34
    countermajoritarian function of, 222

Federalist versus Anti-Federalist views of, 36
Supreme Court, see Supreme Court

Kagan, Donald, 23
Kansas v. Crane, 347, 348–50
Kansas v. Hendricks, 347, 348, 351
Katz v. United States, 355–56
Kelley, Florence, 90, 94
Kennedy, Anthony M., 227, 301
    Barnes v. Glen Theatre, Inc., 331
    City of Erie v. Pap's AM, 337
    Lee v. Weisman, 311, 314–17
    Lukumi, 308, 309
    Planned Parenthood of Southeastern Pennsylvania v. Casey, 228, 229, 233, 234–41, 243
Kent, James, 78
King, Rufus, 49
Kiser, Jackson L., 265, 270–71
Knights of Columbus, 317–18
Knox, Ellis O., 178
Knox, Philander, 131
Kolbert, Kathryn, 228–29
Korematsu, Fred, 151, 159
Korematsu v. United States, 150, 154–59, 255
Krech, David, 179
Krol, John, 218
Kumho Tire Co. v. Carmichael, 338
Kyollo v. United States, 356–57

labor legislation, 86–90, 128
    Lochner v. New York, 86–90
    Muller v. Oregon, 90, 94–98
    social Darwinism and, 86, 87–88
Lamarck, Jean-Baptiste de Monet de (Chevalier de), 75–76
Langdell, Christopher Columbus, 79, 80, 82, 119
Laski, Harold, 77, 78
Latrobe, John, 46
"Law in Science and Science in Law" (Holmes), 82
Law of Contracts (Langdell), 79
Lear, Tobias, 1, 4
Lee, Henry, 5
Lee, Henry "Light Horse Harry," 16
Lee, Robert E., 16, 314
leeches, 3, 9–10
Lee v. Weisman, 311, 312, 314–17
legal formalism, 109, 111–12, 119
    Holmes's break with, 79–82, 98, 112–13

legal realism, 81, 111–24
   divisions among proponents of, 113–18
   Holmes as bridge between formalism and, 82
legislative branch of government, 34, 345
   Scalia's view of, 300, 301
   state legislatures, *see* state legislatures
legislative facts, 202
Lemon v. Kurtzman, 313
Lenin, Vladimir, 144
libertarianism, 100, 104
liberty
   conflict between equality and, 251–52
   factions and, 24
   labor law interpreted as infringement on, 87
   right to privacy and, 207
   slavery and, 58, 61
   strong government and, 15, 17, 20, 30, 33
Life of George Washington, The (Marshall), 2, 38
Lincoln, Abraham, 74
   Dred Scott decision, reaction to, 68
Linnaeus, Carolus, 55
Linz, Daniel, 339–40
Lippmann, Walter, 144, 158
Llewellyn, Karl, 81, 107, 112, 113–17, 123
Lochner v. New York, 86–90, 89, 207, 218
   Roe v. Wade compared to, 235, 236
Logan, Mary, 69
logic, legal, 81
   precedence over experience, *see* legal formalism
Long, John D., 83
Longfellow, Henry Wadsworth, 72
Los Angeles Times, 142
Lott, James, 270
Lovett, Edward P., 169
Loving v. Virginia, 245
Lowell, James Russell, 72
Lowell, John, Jr., 79
Lowell Lectures, 79, 80
Lynch v. Donnelly, 313
Lynd, Robert, 172

MacArthur, Kenneth C., 139
McCarthy, Joseph, 143
McCleskey v. Kemp, 255–61, 359, 360
McClesky, Warren, 255–56

McCorvey, Norma, 211–12
   see also Roe v. Wade
McCulloch, James, 42
McCulloch v. Maryland, 36, 38–44, 205
McKinley, William, 84
McLaurin, George W., 173–74
McLaurin v. Oklahoma, 173–74
McLean, John, 52, 63
MacLeish, Archibald, 147
McLemore, Henry, 142–43
MacPherson v. Buick Motor Co., 110
McReynolds, James, 100, 124
Madison, James, 23, 39
   on factions, 24, 25, 31, 32
   as Federalist, 11, 14, 17, 29, 31–32, 33, 39
   on human nature, xii–xiii
   influence of science on, xiii
   Jefferson and, 14, 15–16, 17, 28, 29, 30
   Marbury v. Madison, 37–38
   as president, 42
   on slavery issue, 62
Mahoney, Maureen, 291
majority rule, 23
   countermajoritarian function of the judiciary, 222
   First Amendment and religious practices, 305
Malthus, Thomas, 75
Manual of Medical Jurisprudence, 74–75
Marbury, William, 37, 38
Marbury v. Madison, 36, 37–38, 44, 69
Margold, Nathan, 170
Marquardt, Fritz, 9
marry, right to, 245
Marsh, George P., 48
Marshall, John, 16, 53, 163, 194
   appointment as chief justice, 34–35, 37
   Jefferson and, 35–36
   Supreme Court under, 34–35, 36–44, 69, 205
   on Washington, 2, 4–5
Marshall, Thurgood, 129, 176–77, 227, 240
   background of, 169–70
   Barnes v. Glen Theatre, Inc., 331
   civil rights cases and, 170–71, 173–74, 176, 177, 178, 191, 214, 280
   Employment Division of Human Resources of Oregon v. Smith, 306
   McClesky v. Kemp, 258
   Regents v. Bakke, 285
   Roe v. Wade, 212, 213, 221

Marsh v. Chambers, 312, 314–15
Martin, Casey, 252–54, 262
Martin, Luther, 14, 25, 42–43
Martin case, 252–54, 263
Martinez, Julio, 297–98
Mary Baldwin College, 270, 271, 277,
    280, 358–59
Maryland Abolition Society, 61
Mason, George, 14, 27
Massachusetts Supreme Judicial Court,
    83
Mayo Clinic, 211, 213, 215
Megan's law, 347
Mencken, H. L., 171
mentally defective, sterilization of, 77–78,
    136, 137
Metaphysical Club, 75
Meyer v. Nebraska, 100
Miller, Samuel, 164
minority rights, 29, 33
Minton, Harold, 192
Missouri Compromise, 49
    Dred Scott and constitutionality of, 63–
    67
Mnookin, Robert, 240
Montesquieu, Charles-Louis de Secondat,
    xiii, 10, 28, 29–30, 33
Moore, Clement Clarke, 59
Moore, Underhill, 122, 123
Mormons, 302
Morris, Robert, 39
Morton, Samuel George, 62
Muller, Curt, 90
Muller v. Oregon, 90, 94–98
Murphy, Frank, 153, 155–57, 158
Murray v. Maryland, 171
Myrdal, Gunnar, 172, 174

NAACP (National Association for the
    Advancement of Colored People),
    168–69
    civil rights cases, *see* civil rights cases
    founding of, 168
    Legal Defense Fund (LDF), 256, 257
    Margold plan, 170–71, 172, 174
    transition to direct assault on
        segregation, 172–75
Nakamura, Grace, 148
Nathan, Gratz, 108
National Academy of Science (NAS),
    322
National Consumers' League, 90
National Council of Catholic Bishops,
    218

national government
    division of authority between state
        governments and, 34
    enumerated powers of, 26, 40, 41
    implied powers of, 40, 41, 43, 44
    see also government
National Right to Life Committee, 216
naturalization law, 140–42
natural philosophy, framers of the
    Constitution and, xii, xiii
nature/nurture debate, 160
    race and, 58–61, 159, 167
    social Darwinism, *see* social Darwinism
Nature of the Judicial Process, The
    (Cardozo), 110
Nazi Germany, 160, 195
Nelson, Samuel, 52
Netherlands, euthanasia in, 248
Newcombe, Richard S., 108
New Deal, Supreme Court and the, 124–
    26
Newton, Isaac, xiii, 54
New York Journal, 11
New York Times, 197
New York Times v. Sullivan, 202–3, 221
New York Tribune, 67
Nicklaus, Jack, 253
Nineteenth Amendment, 6, 97, 273
Ninth Amendment, right to privacy and,
    206, 207
Nixon, Richard M., 211
Nizer, Louis, 158
North Carolina AT&T, 294
Notes on Virginia (Jefferson), 59–60
nude dancing and sex shops, regulation
    of, 324–41
    Barnes v. Glen Theatre, Inc., 324, 329,
        336
    City of Erie v. Pap's AM, 335–41
    *City of Los Angeles v. Alameda Books,
        Inc.,* 340, 341
    *City of Renton v. Playtime Theatres,
        Inc.,* 325–28, 335, 340, 341
    indecency statutes, 325, 328–41
    science of effects of, 325, 326, 327,
        335–36, 338–41
    secondary effects, 326, 328, 333–34,
        335, 337–38, 339–40, 341
    *Young v. American Mini Theatres,
        Inc.,* 326
    zoning laws, 325–28, 341

O'Brien, David, 329–30
obscenity cases, 221, 243–44

O'Connor, Sandra Day, 227, 311
Akron v. Akron Center for
Reproductive Health, 220, 226, 237
appointment to Supreme Court, 224
background of, 224–25
Barnes v. Glen Theatre, Inc., 331
City of Erie v. Pap's AM, 337–38
City of Los Angeles v. Alameda Books,
Inc., 340, 341
confirmation hearings, 224–25
Employment Division of Human
Resources of Oregon v. Smith,
305–6, 307
on fact-finding processes of the
Supreme Court, 358, 359–60, 362–
63
Grutter v. Bollinger, 286–93, 362–63
Planned Parenthood of Southeastern
Pennsylvania v. Casey, 228, 229,
233, 234–41, 243
Washington v. Glucksberg, 246–47
Webster v. Reproductive Health
Services, 225–26
Oliphant, Herman, 122, 123
Olmstead v. United States, 354, 355
Olson, Culbert, 132–33
Olson, Theodore, 283
Origin of Species (Darwin), 75
Ozawa v. United States, 140–41

Palmer, Arnold, 253
Palmieri, Edmund L., 272
Palsgraf v. Long Island Railroad
Company, 110
Parker, Joel, 74
Parker, John, 178–79
Parsons, Theophilus, 74
"Path of the Law, The" (Holmes), 82
Pearl Harbor, 131, 136, 144
Peckham, Rufus, 86–87, 89
Peek, George, 120–21
Pegler, Westbrook, 143, 158
Pericles, 23, 104
Philippines, 144, 145
Phillips, Thomas, 56
physician-assisted suicide, 244–50
Pichardo, Ernesto, 296, 297, 298
Pierce, Charles Sanders, 75, 106, 111
Pinkerton Detective Agency, 93–94
Pinkney, William, 43, 46, 49, 59, 71
Pitney, Mahlon, 89
Planned Parenthood of Southeastern
Pennsylvania v. Casey, 227–43, 359,
361

dissenting opinions, 234, 241–43
equality of women as basis of abortion
right, 236–37
informed consent provisions, 227
joint primary opinion, 234–41
judicial conference, 229–30
oral argument, 228–29
parental consent provision, 227–28,
237, 239–40
Souter's role in alignment of justices,
230–33
spousal notification rule, 227–28, 229,
230, 237, 238, 240–41
twenty-four-hour waiting period, 227–
28, 230, 237–39, 241
undue burden test, 237–41, 242, 243
Plato, 23
Pledge of Allegiance, 312, 313, 317–18
Plessy, Homer Adolph, 165, 166, 195
Plessy v. Ferguson, 165–67, 170, 174,
175, 254, 344
Brown v. Board of Education and,
194, 196
Roe v. Wade compared to, 235, 236
Poe v. Ullman, 206, 231, 232, 234,
247
Pollock, Frederick, 101
polygamy, 302
Posner, Richard, 118
Pound, Roscoe, 81, 113, 114–17
Powell, Lewis F., Jr.
McClesky v. Kemp, 258, 259, 261
Regents v. Bakke, 285
Roe v. Wade, 212, 213, 221
Powell, Thomas Reed, 122
pragmatism, 111
prayer at school graduation ceremonies,
311, 312, 314–17
Preate, Ernest, Jr., 229
precedent, see stare decisis
pregnancy
end of the first trimester, 217, 221,
226
quickening, 209, 210, 219
science of, 213–22, 225–26, 235–36
termination of, see abortion
viability, 217–18, 225–26, 235–36,
242
prejudice, 59
racial, see race
Prescott, William, 72
privacy, right to, 205–50, 345, 354–57
death and dying, 244–50
Eisenstadt v. Baird, 207–8

privacy, right to (*con't*)
  finding basis for, in the Constitution,
    206–7, 215–16
  Griswold v. Connecticut, 206–7, 215,
    232
  *Planned Parenthood of Southeastern
    Pennsylvania v. Casey*, 227–43
  Roe v. Wade, see Roe v. Wade
  *Webster v. Reproductive Health
    Services*, 223–26, 228
Progressivism, 85, 89, 124, 128
  eugenics and, 136–37, 139–40
  Holmes and agenda of, 85–86
  legal realists and, 119
pro-life movement, 208, 223, 225
Protagoras, 23

race
  anti-miscegenation laws, 245
  Asians, hatred of, 134–35, 136
  civil rights cases, *see* civil rights cases;
    segregation
  Dred Scott decision and
    eighteenth-century science, 54–62
  environmental contributions to
    perceived racial differences, 159, 167
  equal protection, *see* equal protection
  Japanese internment, 131–35, 142–60,
    195
  naturalization law and, 140–42
  nature/nurture debate, 58–61, 159, 167
  Progressives and, 139–40
  racial purity, concerns about, 135, 209
Races and Immigrants in America
    (Commons), 140
Randolph, Edmund, 39, 40, 146
Randolph, Peyton, 16
Rawlins, George, 2
Reagan, Ronald, 224, 225, 232, 300
realism, legal, *see* legal realism
"Realistic Jurisprudence—The Next Step,
    A" (Llewellyn), 114
Redfield, Robert, 173
Reed, Stanley, 126, 192, 195, 196
Reed v. Reed, 274, 275
*Regents of the University of California v.
    Bakke*, 285, 286, 288, 290
Rehnquist, William, 47, 224, 300, 311, 340
  Barnes v. Glen Theatre, Inc., 329, 331
  City of Erie v. Pap's AM, 337
  *Planned Parenthood of Southeastern
    Pennsylvania v. Casey*, 229–30, 234
  Regents v. Bakke, 285
  Renton, 326, 327, 328

Roe v. Wade, 212, 213, 218
United States v. Lopez, 361–62
*United States v. The Commonwealth
    of Virginia*, 276, 282
Washington v. Glucksberg, 246, 247–
    48
*Webster v. Reproductive Health
    Services*, 225, 228
religion, free exercise of
  Braunfeld v. Brown, 302
  *Church of the Lukumi Babalu Aye v.
    City of Hialeah*, 296–99, 307–10
  compelling interest standard, 302–3,
    306, 307, 311
  County of Allegheny v. ACLU, 314
  Edwards v. Aguillard, 318–23,
    359–60
  *Employment Division of Human
    Resources of Oregon v. Smith*, 299–
    307, 310–11
  endorsement test, 313–14
  Establishment Clause, 303–4, 311–23
  Free Exercise Clause, 295–311
  Lee v. Weisman, 311, 312, 314–17
  Lemon v. Kurtzman, 313
  Lynch v. Donnelly, 313
  Marsh v. Chambers, 312, 314–15
  Reynolds v. United States, 302, 304–5
  Sherbert v. Verner, 302–3, 306
  Wisconsin v. Yoder, 303, 306
representative democracy, 13, 22, 31, 32–
    33
reproductive rights, *see* abortion; privacy,
    right to
Republican Party, 42
  Jefferson and, 35, 36
  pro-life stance of, 208, 223, 224
Reston, James, 197
Reynolds, Quentin, 158
Reynolds v. United States, 302, 304–5
Richardson, Richard C., 267–68
Riesman, David, 267
Rising Tide of Clor, The (Stoddard), 135
Roberts, Owen, 111–12, 124, 125, 154,
    155, 159
Robertson, Archibald Gerald, 182–83
Robinson, Elsa, 180
Robinson, Spott, 176
Roe v. Wade, 204, 208, 211–44, 213
  Blackmun's majority opinion, 215–19
  challenges to, *see specific cases, e.g.,
    Planned Parenthood of Southeastern
    Pennsylvania v. Casey; Webster v.
    Reproductive Health Services*

changes in composition of the Supreme Court after first arguments, 212
deliberations of the justices, 212
facts of the case, 211–12
science of pregnancy and, 213–22
viability standard in, 217–22, 223, 226, 235, 242, 361, 363
Roosevelt, Eleanor, 143, 146
Roosevelt, Franklin D., 143, 147
Court-packing plan, 124–25
Japanese internment and, 146, 158, 159
Supreme Court nominations, 123, 125–26
Roosevelt, Theodore, 84–85, 137, 139–40
Roper, John, 74
Rudman, Warren, 230
Rush, Benjamin, 19
Rutledge, John, 34

Sacco and Vanzetti case, 126
Sanford, John H., 50
Sanger, Margaret, 137
Santeria religion, 296–99, 307–10
Scalia, Antonin, 231–32, 340
appointment to Supreme Court, 224, 300
background of, 300
Barnes v. Glen Theatre, Inc., 331–32, 333
City of Erie v. Pap's AM, 337
Edwards v. Aguillard, 319–20, 321
Employment Division of Human Resources of Oregon v. Smith, 299, 301–2, 304–6, 308, 311
Grutter v. Bollinger, 291
Kansas v. Crane, 349–50
Kyollo v. United States, 356–57
Lee v. Weisman, 311, 316–17
Lemon test and, 313
Planned Parenthood of Southeastern Pennsylvania v. Casey, 229, 234, 241–43
Pledge of Allegiance case, comments of, 317–18
United States v. The Commonwealth of Virginia, 276, 277–78, 279, 280–81
Scarlett, Frank, 200, 202
Schenck v. United States, 102–3
science
conception of human nature and, see human nature

constitutional law and, see science and constitutional law
defining, xi
grounding of policy decisions in, xii–xiii
statistical measurement, see statistics
as study of factual or empirical evidence, see empiricism
technological changes, see technological innovation
science and constitutional law
abortion decisions and science of pregnancy, see pregnancy, science of; individual decisions
affirmative action cases, 290
on assisted suicide, 247–48
civil rights cases, 167, 171–74, 175–77, 179–80, 181–87, 188–91, 195, 196–98, 199–200, 201, 280
contemporary knowledge, role of, 5–7
death penalty and, 257–61
disputed or changeable facts, 203–4
Establishment Clause cases, 316–17, 318–23
fact-finding, see fact-finding by the Supreme Court
free exercise of religion and, 306
interplay of, xii–xiv, 7–8
Japanese internment cases and, 131, 153, 156–57, 159–60
nude dancing and sex shops, science on effects of, 325, 326, 327, 335–37, 338–41
racial divisions and naturalization, 140–42
sexual offenders, commitment of, 347–52
see also individual decisions
scientific method, 5
Scott v. Sandford, see Dred Scott
search and seizure, protection from unreasonable, 354–57
Second Amendment, 7
segregation, 166, 170
civil rights cases, see civil rights cases
Margold plan, 170–71, 172, 174
preventing intermarriage, 172
scientific study and evidence of effects of, 167, 171–74, 175–77, 179–81
transition to direct assault on segregation, 172–75
Seitz, Collins, 186–87
separation of powers, xiii, 33–34, 300
Sergeant, Elizabeth Shepley, 105

Seward, William, 53–54, 68
sexual offenders, commitment of, 347–52
sexual violence, genetics and, 346–54
Sherbert v. Verner, 302–3, 306
She Stoops to Conquer (Goldsmith), 55
Shintoism, 133–34, 156
silicone breast implant litigation, 346
Skinner v. Oklahoma, 130, 137–39, 159–
60
Slaughter-House Cases, The, 162–65
slaves and slavery, 162
   abolitionism, *see* abolitionism
   Dred Scott, 44–79
   institutionalization of, 58
   Missouri Compromise, 49
   notions of equality and, 22–23
   science of race and, 54–62
   Taney's views on, 47–48, 53
   three-fifths compromise, 61
small republics
   Anti-Federalist view of, 13, 28
   factions and, 31–32
   Montesquieu's view of, 10, 28, 29–30
Smith, Alfred, 299–300
social Darwinism, 86–89, 97, 104, 105,
   124, 236
Social Statics (Spencer), 75, 87
sociological jurisprudence, 81, 113
   Cardozo and, 109
   Muller v. Oregon and, 97
Sorenstam, Annika, 262–64
Souter, David, 311, 358
   appointment to Supreme Court, 227,
      230
   background of, 230
   Barnes v. Glen Theatre, Inc., 331, 333–
      34, 335, 336
   City of Erie v. Pap's AM, 335–37, 338
   confirmation hearings, 230–31
   Gratz v. Bollinger, 286
   Grutter v. Bollinger, 286
   Lukumi, 310
   *Planned Parenthood of Southeastern
      Pennsylvania v. Casey,* 229, 232–33,
      234–41, 243
   United States v. Lopez, 362
   Washington v. Glucksberg, 247, 248–
      49
speech, *see* free speech
Spencer, Herbert, 75–77
   influence of, 76–77, 87–89, 97, 104,
      105, 124, 236
sports and equal protection, 262–64
   Martin case, 252–54, 263

Sprock, Peter, 342
stare decisis, xiv, 7–8, 161–62
   Harlan's dedication to, 231, 232, 234
Starr, Kenneth, 229
state government, division of authority
   between national and, 34, 345
state legislatures
   fact-finding by, 340, 359, 360, 364
   Holmes's judicial restraint and view of,
      85–86, 99
   legislative intent, 319
   Souter's arguments in *Washington v.
      Glucksberg,* 248–50
states' rights:
   Civil War and, 162, 164–65
   contemporary conditions and, 10
   Dred Scott decision and, 63, 65, 66
   founding fathers' views of strong
      national government versus, 13, 16–
      22, 25–30
   historical grounding of arguments over,
      15
   McCulloch v. Maryland, 42–44
   Slaughter-House Cases, 162–65
   slavery and, *see* slaves and slavery,
      states' rights and
   Taney and, 53
   Tenth Amendment and, 40, 44
   at time of crafting the Constitution, 10
statistics, 6, 82, 274–75
   constitutional law and, 7
   legal realism and, 115, 118–19
   in *McKlesky v. Kemp,* 258–61
   see also science and constitutional law
Stell v. Savannah, 200–201, 202, 203
sterilization
   of criminals, 130, 136, 137–39, 159–60
   of mental defectives, 77–78, 136, 137
   Nazi practices, 160
Stevens, John, Jr., 20–21, 29, 30, 337
Stevens, John Paul, 227, 311
   Barnes v. Glen Theatre, Inc., 331
   City of Eric v. Pap's AM, 341
   on fact-finding processes of the
      Supreme Court, 358–62
   Gratz v. Bollinger, 286
   Grutter v. Bollinger, 286
   Martin case, 253
   McClesky v. Kemp, 258
   *Planned Parenthood of Southeastern
      Pennsylvania v. Casey,* 229–30, 233,
      238, 241
   Regents v. Bakke, 285
   United States v. Lopez, 362

Stewart, Potter, 127, 206, 224
  Katz v. United States, 355
  on obscenity, 243–44
  Regents v. Bakke, 285
  Roe v. Wade, 212, 214–15, 216
Stimson, Henry L., 121, 146–47, 150,
  158
Stoddard, Lothrop, 130, 135
Stone, Harlan Fiske, 122, 125, 139, 151–
  52
Stone, Monica, 149
Storer, Horatio R., 209
Story, Joseph, 35, 43
Strauder v. West Virginia, 254
strict constructionism, 40, 52, 53,
  300
Stroup, Robert, 256
Strum, Philip, 282
suicide, assisted, 244–50
Sullivan, Mark, 116
Sumner, Charles, 67–68, 161
Sununu, John, 230
Supreme Court
  appointment of justices to, 34–35, 37,
    84–85, 97–98, 107, 109, 123, 125–
    26, 192, 193, 211, 224, 227, 230,
    300–301
  Article III of the Constitution and,
    345
  balancing tests, 301, 304
  bright lines, 221, 301
  Brown v. Board of Education as
    turning point for, 198–99
  Dred Scott decision's effect on
    reputation of, 69
  fact-finding, *see* fact-finding by the
    Supreme Court; science and
    constitutional law
  location in 1856, 51
  under Marshall, 34–35, 36–44, 69,
    205
  perceived legitimacy of, 233
  Roosevelt's plan to pack the, 124–25
  social Darwinism and, 86
  unanimous decisions, pressures in
    controversial cases for, 153, 192,
    195–96
  Warren Court, hallmarks of the, 193–
    94, 198–99
  see also individual cases and justices
survival of the fittest, 75, 88, 105
Sutherland, George, 124, 125–26, 140–
  41
Sweatt, Herman Marion, 172–73

Sweatt v. Painter, 172, 174, 175
Swift, Jonathan, 161

Taft, William H., 97–98, 101, 102, 354
Taney, Alice, 50–51
Taney, Anne, 50–51
Taney, Roger Brooke, 242–43
  described, 46–47
  Dred Scott and, 45–69
  interpretation of the Constitution
    according to science of eighteenth
    century, 52, 54, 62, 64
  legal legacy of, 47
  personal tragedy, 50–51
  states' rights and, 53, 65, 66
  as strict constructionist, 52, 53
  views on slavery, 47–48, 53, 63–64
Taylor, Alfred Swain, 74
technological innovation, 6–7
  Fourth Amendment privacy rights and,
    354–57
  viability standard in *Roe v. Wade, see*
    Roe v. Wade, viability standard
Terry, David, 164
Thayer, James B., 78
Third Amendment, 206
Thirteenth Amendment, 6, 162
Thomas, Clarence, 231–32, 340
  appointment to Supreme Court, 227
  City of Erie v. Pap's AM, 337
  Grutter v. Bollinger, 290, 294
  Kansas v. Crane, 349
  *Planned Parenthood of Southeastern
    Pennsylvania v. Casey,* 229, 234
  *Thornburgh v. American College of
    Obstetricians and Gynecologists,* 238
Thucydides, 24
Thurmond, Strom, 178
Ticknor, William, 72
Tileston v. Ullman, 206
Title VI, 285
Title IX, 263, 264
Tocqueville, Alexis de, 345
Tourgée, Albion, 165
Treatise on Human Nature (Hume), xiii
Truman, Harry, 147
Turner, John, 256
Twain, Mark, 254
Tyler, Samuel, 67
tyranny, Federalist versus Anti-Federalist
  views on, 24, 29, 33

United States Court of Appeals for the
  Fifth Circuit, 286, 288

United States Court of Appeals for the
    Ninth Circuit, 313, 317
U.S. House of Representatives, 34
U.S. Justice Department, 265
    Office of Legal Counsel, 300
U.S. Senate, 34
    approval of Supreme Court justice
        nominations, 34
    state size and representation in the,
        61–62
United States v. Butler, 111–12
United States v. Carolene Products Co.,
    footnote four in, 151–52, 154, 254–
    55
United States v. Lopez, 232, 361–62
United States v. O'Brien, 329–30
United States v. The Commonwealth of
    Virginia, 264–84, 343, 344, 358–59
    adversative method of instruction,
        question of, 266–68, 270, 277, 278–
        79, 281–83
    analysis of the opinion, 280–84
    background of, 264–65
    changes required to admit women,
        question of, 279, 281, 283–84
    comparison to Grutter v. Bollinger,
        293–94
    dissenting opinion, 276, 277–78, 279,
        280
    Fourth Circuit Court of Appeals,
        decisions of, 268–69, 271–72
    group vs. individual, equal protection
        of, 280–81
    level of scrutiny of gender cases, 276,
        279
    oral arguments, 283
    original trial, 265–68
    segregated education's benefits,
        question of, 266, 267, 270, 277, 358–
        59
    Supreme Court opinion in, 272, 275–
        84
    trial court's ruling on task force
        conclusions, 269–71
United States v. Thind, 140–42
University of California, at Davis,
    Medical School at, 285
University of Maryland, law school of,
    171
University of Michigan, 286–94, 359
University of Oklahoma, 172, 174,
    175
University of Texas at Austin, law school
    at, 172, 174, 175
University of Texas School of Law, 286,
    288
University of Virginia, 277

Vallandingham, Clement, 145
van den Haag, Ernest, 200
Van Devanter, Willis, 124, 125
Veblen, Thorstein, 122
Velez-Diaz, Angel, 309
Vinson, Frederick, 174–75, 192, 196
Virginia Board of Education v. Barnette,
    317
Virginia Constitution, 18, 27
Virginia Declaration of Independence, 23,
    27
Virginia Military Institute
    adversative method of instruction at,
        265, 266–68, 278–79, 281–83
    changes required to admit women,
        279, 281, 283–84
    exclusion of women at, 265
    history of, 264
    see also United States v. The
        Commonwealth of Virginia
Virginia Women's Institute for
    Leadership (VMIL), 270–71, 277,
    278, 280, 358–59
Voorhis, Jerry, 133
voting rights, 168
    Fifteenth Amendment, 6, 162
    Nineteenth Amendment, 6, 97, 273

Wallace, Alfred Russel, 75
Wallace, Henry, 143
Waring, J. Waties, 180
War of 1812, 42
Warren, Earl, 129, 206
    appointment to Supreme Court, 192,
        193
    background of, 192–93
    Brown v. Board of Education and,
        192, 194, 195, 196–97, 198
    hallmarks of the Warren Court, 193–
        94, 198–99
    Japanese internment and, 132, 133,
        144, 158
    United States v. O'Brien, 330
Warren, Samuel, 91, 92
Washburne, Emory, 74
Washington, Booker T., 168, 174
Washington, George, xiii, 13
    Bank of the United States and, 38–40
    bloodletting and death of, 1–5
    nomination of chief justices, 34

Washington, Martha, 1, 4
Washington v. Glucksberg, 244–45
Webster, Daniel, 43
Webster, Noah, 13, 18–19, 31
Webster v. Reproductive Health Services,
 223–26, 228
Weddington, Sarah, 212
Weinstein, Jack B., 188
Weisman, Deborah, 312, 314–15
Wells, H. G., 137
Wertham, Frederic, 185–86
West Point, 265, 268, 282
White, Byron, 207
 Barnes v. Glen Theatre, Inc., 331, 332–
  35
 *Planned Parenthood of Southeastern
  Pennsylvania v. Casey,* 229, 234
 Regents v. Bakke, 285
 Roe v. Wade, 212, 218, 224
White, Charles, 57–58
White, G. Edward, 193
White, William, 168
White House Conference on Children
 and Youth, 176
Whitman, Walt, 83

Whitney, Anita, 103
Whitney v. California, 103–4
Wilkie, John, 216
William and Mary, The College of,
 277
Williams, Roger, 312
Wilmut, Ian, 345
Wilson, Heather Anne, 270, 272
Wilson, Woodrow, 97
Winthrop, James, 27–28
Wirt, William, 43
Wisconsin v. Yoder, 303, 306
Wise, Stephen, 109
women
 equal protection by gender, 6, 236–37,
  261–84
 labor law protecting, 90, 97
 Nineteenth Amendment, 6

Yale Law Journal, 197
Yale Law School, 110, 119, 122, 123
Yates, Robert, 11
Yick Wo v. Hopkins, 254
Young v. American Mini Theatres, Inc.,
 326, 340

ABOUT THE AUTHOR

A professor of law at the University of California, Hastings, David L. Faigman is the author of *Legal Alchemy* and a frequently cited expert on scientific evidence. He lives in Mill Valley, California.